DEVELOPING WOMAN'S POTENTIAL

✿✿✿✿✿✿✿✿✿✿✿ Developing

Iowa State University Press, Ames, Iowa

"WHAT A MISFORTUNE TO BE A WOMAN! AND YET THE
WORST MISFORTUNE IS NOT TO UNDERSTAND WHAT A
MISFORTUNE IT IS."

> ✣ *Kierkegaard*

"THERE ARE ONLY THREE THINGS TO BE DONE WITH A
WOMAN. YOU CAN LOVE HER, SUFFER FOR HER, OR TURN
HER INTO LITERATURE."

> ✣ *Lawrence Durrell* (JUSTINE)

Woman's Potential

EDWIN C. LEWIS

Edwin C. Lewis is professor of psychology, Iowa State University, and chairman, University Honors Program, Iowa State University. He holds an undergraduate degree from Wittenberg College and obtained the master and doctoral degrees from Ohio State University. Before holding his current position he was counseling psychologist, Student Counseling Service, Iowa State University. He has written several research articles in the professional journals of his field and is currently conducting research concerning attitudes toward women in their various societal roles.

© 1968 The Iowa State University Press
Ames, Iowa, U.S.A. All rights reserved

Composed and printed by
The Iowa State University Press

Stock #1704

First edition, 1968

Library of Congress Catalog Card Number: 68–20269

✿ ✿ ✿ ✿ **TO NANCY AND ELIZABETH,**
the females I know best—and understand least

Preface

A MAN who assumes the task of writing about women is at best presumptuous and very likely foolhardy. Throughout history the essence of woman has been mystery, and few have dared (or bothered) to plumb it far. I have written this book, therefore, with considerable trepidation, but also with the conviction that in the current debates concerning the role of women in our society there is a need for a close look at evidence on which to base a rational opinion. This book is designed to provide such an examination.

Let me stress that I am writing as a psychologist first and a man second. As a psychologist I have been interested for many years in the efficient use of our human resources, of which women represent the largest area of waste, and I have spent considerable time counseling with young women who were trying to plan their educational and vocational futures. As a counselor I am committed to the belief that every person—regardless of race, social class, or sex—should have the opportunity to develop goals in accordance with his abilities and to work toward those goals, unhampered by the restrictions of outmoded social traditions. Most young women, however, have not had this opportunity. They are hindered by the narrow vision of those around them, as well as by their own narrow view of themselves and their world. If young women are to have unlimited opportunity to develop as individuals, I believe that those persons responsible for their guidance—especially parents and teachers—should have a more realistic view of the present and potential status of women in our society.

I have tried in this book to be objective within the limits of my personal experience and beliefs. To this extent I believe I have an advantage, as a man, in writing about women. Most books and articles about women have been written by women, and many have been justifiably criticized for being too emotional and biased. It is difficult, and perhaps impossible, for a female writer to be objective in discussing women's roles. In many cases, their views and arguments are in support of their own role, and perhaps are an attempt to justify it. The result may be interesting but not objective. In any case, however, I emphasize again that my being a man should be of secondary concern. I am writing as a psychologist and I hope that my views will be judged on this basis.

The format of the book itself is designed to provide a balance between the basic ideas and the evidence on which they are based. I have attempted to stick as closely as possible to research data, synthesizing it within a framework to make it meaningful to persons responsible for helping young women make plans for the future. The main body of the book, therefore, presents a synthesis of the current available evidence regarding women in our society. The research studies on which this material is based are cited in the Appendix and keyed to the Bibliography. An appendix to each chapter is included separately, and the reader wishing more detailed information concerning the research pertaining to a given chapter will find it in that chapter's section of the Appendix. In this way, the main body of the book can be read without stumbling over research citations every few sentences, while the basis for its content should be evident in the Appendix.

It's not possible to acknowledge everyone who has contributed suggestions and encouragement for this book. Among the writers and publishers who have given permission for quotations from their works are the following: Aldine Publishing Company, for permission to quote from *Great Aspirations*, James A. Davis, © 1964 by the National Opinion Research Center; Appleton-Century-Crofts, for permission to quote from *The Achievement Motive*, David McClelland and associates; M. J. Arlen and the New York Times Co., for permission to quote from "The Girl With the Harvard Degree," © New York Times Co., 1962; Mary Bunting and the New York Times Co., for permission to quote from "A Huge Waste: Educated Womenpower," © New York Times Co., 1961; Columbia University Press, for permission to reprint a figure from *Womanpower*, National Manpower Council; Condé Nast Publications, Inc., for permission to quote from "Female-ism: New and Insidious," Diana Trilling, *Mademoiselle*, June, 1960; Educational Testing Service, Princeton, N. J., for permission to use a table from *The American High School Today*, James M. Conant, © McGraw-Hill Book Co.; *Fortune Magazine*, for permission to quote from "The Great Back-to-Work Movement," Daniel Bell, and "Women as Bosses," Katherine Hamill; Harper and Row, for permission to quote from *America's Resources of Specialized Talent*, Dael Wolfle, *Educating Our Daughters*, Lynn White, *Executive Careers for Women*, Frances

Maule, and *Occupational Planning for Women,* Marguerite Zapoleon; Holt, Rinehart, and Winston, Inc., for permission to quote
from the *Handbook of Applied Psychology,* Douglas Fryer and
Edwin Henry, eds.; Houghton Mifflin Co., for permission to quote
from *The Revision of the Stanford-Binet Scale,* Quinn McNemar;
Little, Brown, and Co., for permission to quote from *Women in the
Modern World,* Mirra Komarovsky, © 1953 by Mirra Heyman; The
Macmillan Co., for permission to quote from *Differential Psychology,* 3rd ed., Anne Anastasi, and *The Natural Superiority of
Women,* Ashley Montagu; Public Affairs Press, for permission to
quote from *New Horizons for College Women,* Leo and Ouida
Muller, eds.; Routledge and Kegan Paul, Ltd., for permission to
quote from *Women's Two Roles: Home and Work,* Alva Myrdal
and Viola Klein; *Saturday Review,* for permission to quote from
"How To Educate a Woman," Louis Norris; Society for Research
in Child Development, Inc., and Dr. Wilton Krogman, for permission to reprint a figure from "The Physical Growth of Children:
An Appraisal of Studies 1950–1955," Monograph No. 20, Society for
Research in Child Development; John Wiley and Sons, Inc., for
permission to quote from *Birth to Maturity: A Study in Psychological Development,* Jerome Kagan and Howard Moss; The Williams
and Wilkins Co., for permission to quote from *Sex and Internal
Secretions,* 2nd ed., William C. Young, ed.

I am also grateful to the administrators of the Iowa State University Library for their willingness to acquire relevant materials
for me and for providing me with space for research; and to my colleagues for tolerating, and even encouraging, my interest in the
problems of women. I thank Rose Summers, who carried the responsibilities of editor far above and beyond the normal call of
duty and who helped breathe life into a professor's musty verbiage;
and Kay Baker for her conscientious efforts in typing the manu-
script. And for her unflagging encouragement and help I thank my
wife, Nancy, who finds my claim to being an "expert" on women
quite amusing but who is more a part of this book than probably
even she knows.

EDWIN C. LEWIS

Contents

★ ★ ★ ★ ★ ★ ★ ★ ★ ★DEVELOPING WOMAN'S POTENTIAL

Introduction: Revolution in a Man's World

**THE SOULS OF WOMEN ARE SO SMALL
THAT SOME BELIEVE THEY'VE NONE AT ALL**

✘ Samuel Butler

THIS IS A BOOK ABOUT WOMEN. It is far from being the first word and most certainly will not be the last. Since time began, women have been a frequent concern of philosophers, writers, and other learned persons. More recently, science has entered the picture, and psychologists have considered sex to be a major variable in human development. So much has been written about women, in fact, that they should no longer be a mystery to anyone: Their physiology has been studied, their personalities have ben dissected, and their spiritual qualities have been analyzed. Yet an element of mystery remains. Despite thousands of years of concern, something important about women has eluded the grasp of the philosophers and scientists. Somehow in our eagerness to know and understand women as a group, we have overlooked women as individuals. We have forgotten that a woman is, above all else, a person. We have surrounded women with myriad restrictions and demands, assuming that what is good for some women is good for all. The individual woman, as a person, has been ignored.

Until recently, this has not been a matter of major concern.

Most women have accepted society's view of them, docile and content to limit their lives to being wives and mothers and to restrict their self-expressions as individuals to areas approved by society. Society has reciprocated by demanding little except that they be "good" wives and mothers. Difficulties arise only for the woman who is different, who wants to be treated as an individual. She is threatening the normal pattern of her society and must therefore be put in her place.

❧ ❧ ❧ THE FEMINIST MOVEMENT. Women have made sporadic attempts to assert themselves, notably in the feminist movement of the late nineteenth and early twentieth centuries which was the concern of only a minority of women. Most women then were reasonably content to maintain the traditional role, rather than risk a more emancipated status. Eventually, society compromised with the feminists, and the uproar died away.

❧ ❧ A NEW UPRISING. Now another uprising seems to be taking place, but of a different nature. Whereas the feminists demanded that women, as a group, should be treated with more respect and given rights equal to those of men, the modern revolutionaries are concerned, instead, with the woman as an individual. They recognize that women, as individuals, have abilities and needs which vary to the same extent as do those of men, and that they should be allowed—and, indeed, encouraged—to discover and respond to the unique aspects of themselves. For perhaps the first time, women are asking to be viewed as individuals. Reluctantly society is beginning to do so. It is a slow process; many thousands of years of inertia have to be overcome. But a tide seems to be moving in this direction, and the purpose of this book is to give this trend an additional nudge.

❧ ❧ ❧ A NEW CHANGE. The extent of this trend is evident in the popularity of recent publications concerning the role of women in our society. This has been a frequent subject of sociologists and psychologists for several decades, but until recently they seemed to be crying in a wilderness of apathy. The average woman limited her reading to magazine stories glorifying the housewife, and the average man couldn't imagine the existence of a problem. Professionals who were concerned about the lack of productive utilization of abilities among capable and well-educated women, as well as the possible injury to their self-concepts, were helpless.

Now, however, a change is noticeable. Where it began is difficult to determine, but 1963 must be recognized as the year in which the momentum reached discernible proportions. That year saw two events which have subsequently proved quite important in alerting the public to the needs and problems of women: the publication of Betty Friedan's *The Feminine Mystique,* and the establishment by the late President Kennedy of the Commission on the Status of Women. Mrs. Friedan's book, while hardly a model of an objective, well-reasoned treatise, succeeded at least in putting a burr under society's seat. Having been exposed to her emotional, overstated, but reasonably valid charges, society could not continue to be complacent about the way in which half of its population was being treated.

Perhaps if Mrs. Friedan had been alone in her concern the uproar would have died away, but at the same time others, with stronger professional qualifications, were mining the same lode. For example, in early 1963 a symposium on the topic, "The Potential of Women," was held at the San Francisco Medical Center of the University of California. Participants included men and women with outstanding professional reputations. That these persons saw fit to devote their time and energy to a consideration of the role of women in our society and that the points which they made were significant, further impressed both the professional and lay public with the importance of the problem.

President Kennedy's commission to study the role of women in our society and to recommend action which might be taken by the federal government to improve their status presented its findings to President Johnson in 1965. These are now available in the publication, *American Women,* edited by Margaret Mead and Frances Kaplan. Thus the people of the United States, through their elected representatives, have finally taken cognizance of the confused and ambiguous status which women have occupied for many years and have indicated a desire to take constructive action.

In the long run, however, the influence of governmental intervention is limited. The confused status of women is not, for the most part, the result of legal restrictions. The basic problem is one of attitudes—those of society in general and those of the women themselves. If significant changes in the role and status of women in our society are to take place, they must be initiated by the women concerned. Women must free themselves from the implicit restrictions which they have imposed on their self-concepts and their lives. They must be encouraged to view themselves as individuals and to make plans in accordance with their unique qualities. For most women this will not be an easy task. As Rose (1961) pointed out, most women are still timid about exploring possibilities open to them, reacting only superficially to the great economic, political, and social changes of the last fifty years. They have not purposefully directed their lives. Now they are being challenged to assume this responsibility. The traditional restrictions are gradually being removed. It remains for women to take advantage of their opportunities.

To do so, they will need the help of those persons in our society who have the responsibility of influencing educational and vocational development: teachers, counselors, businessmen, government leaders, and other professional persons. Beginning with the girl's early experiences, her development as an individual is influenced by those around her. She can be helped to acquire an image of herself as an individual and a desire to achieve her individual potential, or she can be stamped into a mold. Much depends on the attitudes and beliefs of those who shape her destiny. The true emancipation of women must begin with enlightened professionals within the educational and occupational world, who understand the complexity of individual differences subsumed under the label "female," and who provide girls and women with opportunities to discover and utilize their individual talents.

It is toward these persons that this book is aimed. Its major purpose is to help professional persons working with girls and women better to understand the female sex. To this end, the following pages will attempt to present a picture of the female in our society, as viewed from a psychological perspective, which may be used as a basis for realistic educational and vocational planning with individual girls and women. A first consideration will be the current status of women in modern society followed by information concerning the developmental, occupational, and educational characteristics of females in greater detail.

THE STATUS OF THE MODERN WOMAN. The major dilemma of the modern woman is that she is striving to become a person without knowing what kind of person she wants to become—groping toward a sense of personal identity, but with only a vague notion as to how this identity may be achieved. As long as her role was limited to that of wife and mother she had few problems; this was the source of her identity and, like it or not, she knew where she stood. Now she may sense that being a wife and mother are not enough, but she is thwarted from becoming something more. Society seldom gives up its traditions without a struggle, and the modern woman is finding the struggle a difficult one.

A PERSISTENT STEREOTYPE. Despite the mounting cry that women are psychologically and socially the equal of men, a large proportion of our society, both male and female, seems to believe that women in some respects are inferior. This and similar opinions apparently have an emotional basis and are thus resistant to change by rational appeals. This means that girls who want to plan their lives as individuals will probably meet with negative, stereotyped reactions not only from men but from other women as well.

This is not to say that such stereotypes cannot be overcome. With increased awareness of the need for women to be treated as individuals, the time may not be too far distant when women will no longer be considered inferior to men. In the meantime, however, the modern woman must expect to encounter obstacles in her search for identity as a person.

≉ ≉ WOMEN AS A MINORITY GROUP. It may seem strange to classify women, who hold a numerical majority over men in this country, as a minority group, but their psychological and sociological status in our society can be explained by the use of minority-group principles. By focusing attention on women as a group, society has blinded itself to women as individuals, in the same way that a Negro is reacted to first as a Negro and secondly as a person.[1] Hacker (1951), for example, points out that women have the social status of a minority group in several respects: they are subject to discrimination (e.g., in jobs), there is a significant degree of "social distance" between them and the superior group (men), and women who are attempting to enter the traditional domain of the superior group—who might be termed "marginal women"—encounter the problems and resistance typical of those designed to thwart a minority-group member who is threatening the traditions of his society. This may explain why federal civil rights legislation prohibits job discrimination based on sex as well as on racial and religious criteria, a stipulation which is creating considerable confusion in the occupational world.[2]

---

[1] In this respect, Montagu (1953) has pointed out that women in the nineteenth century were treated in much the same manner as Negroes are today. They were thought to be less intelligent than men, more emotional and unstable, helpless in a crisis, weak and sickly, having little judgment and sense, and employable only in routine and menial tasks. In short, they were considered to be second-class citizens.

[2] The Equal Employment Opportunity Commission, created to enforce the civil rights laws, has ruled that it shall be unlawful to: (a) treat jobs as men's or women's work unless the employee's sex is a bona fide occupational qualification; (b) refuse to hire or promote either men or women because of the preferences of co-workers, the employer, clients, or customers, unless the need is obvious; (c) forbid the hiring of married women unless the same rule applies to married men; (d) use seniority lists separated according to sex; and (e) publish separate "male" and "female" help-wanted ads. In view of the many traditions which these regulations threaten to overturn, considerable turmoil is expected in their enforcement.

If women are to be viewed as individuals by themselves as well as by others, these minority-group attitudes must be overcome. Sex differences exist, of course, and will continue to exist, but differences do not imply that one group is superior to another. Both men and women have something worthwhile to contribute to society, and both should be given equal opportunity to make their contributions.

꙳ ꙳ THE CONFLICT OF ROLES. Theoretically, the modern woman has a choice of roles. Within limits, she can decide to be a homemaker, a career woman, a community leader, or some combination of these. Presumably she is free to make her choice in terms of what best fits herself as a person. In practice, however, she is not so free, nor is her choice so rational. The twentieth-century woman is still handicapped by the shadow cast by her nineteenth-century ancestor.

In the nineteenth century, according to Kluckhohn (1953), women could be placed neatly into one of several classes: the working girl (limited to those of lower class, and then only until they had acquired a suitable husband); the suffragette (tolerated, perhaps, but not envied); the pioneer woman (gradually less in demand, as new frontiers diminished); and the genteel lady. The latter was the pinnacle of success as a woman, living a life of leisure and considered the ultimate in femininity: an ornament for her husband, a testimonial to his wealth. For her to have sought employment would have been an outright admission that her husband was unable to provide for her. Small wonder that, even now, many men feel that an employed wife signifies a husband who is an inadequate provider for his family.

This extremely shallow image offered little in the way of intrinsic rewards to the women themselves. A large part of modern society professes to recognize these drawbacks, at least verbally, and gives lip service to the importance of a fuller realization of the individual woman's needs and abilities. Yet when the woman tries to implement these needs, she runs up against an old-fashioned attitude barrier, which inculcates in both boys and girls the notion that in some way women ought to be able to find complete satisfaction within their families and that any woman who does not find this is somehow less adequate as a woman. This notion is expressed in many ways: in our mass media, in which the well-adjusted, normal woman is invariably a housewife; in our children's literature, in which the normal family has a father who goes off to work and a mother who stays home with the children; in the restrictions placed on working women, to be described later; and in the feeling which most of us, men and women alike, get when we hear the phrase, "working woman."

This does not mean that the choice lies between only two

roles: homemaker or career. For most women, on the contrary, the logical outcome is probably some combination of these. And there are other roles, to be discussed later, to which women may turn for certain kinds of satisfactions. These two roles, however, are most often compared and contrasted in the literature, with the implication that a woman must choose one or the other.

As a result of society's emphasis on the intrinsic value of the homemaking role for women, a girl grows up assuming that this will be her lot in life. If, for some reason, she later decides to move in a different direction, she is likely to do so with some feeling of rebellion against the traditional standards and concomitant feelings of guilt. Psychoanalysts have suggested that this may be an explanation of women's anxieties in the modern age. Whether this is at the root of the problem is debatable, but certainly it is not easy for a woman in our society *not* to become a housewife.

Another complicating factor is that at the moment women have no clear-cut role in our society, whereas men do. A man's role centers on his job, which strongly influences his social status and his relations with other people. One of the first things that the typical person wants to know when being introduced to a man for the first time is, "What does he do?" while the typical questions concerning a woman are likely to be: "Who is her husband?" "What does he do?" "How many children does she have?" In other words, one perceives a woman in terms of the "significant others" in her life rather than as an individual. This means that a woman's status and, to some extent, her personality are determined by her husband and family. Parsons (1953) has pointed out that in our society a man's job influences not only his social status but also that of his wife and children. A married woman's job, on the other hand, has little influence on her own social status, as evidenced by the fact that the majority of working wives is likely to be employed in some form of secretarial or clerical work, which would be considered lower-middle-class occupations. In relatively few situations is a woman's occupational status on the same level or above that of the men of her social class, including her husband.[3]

Women face another handicap in determining their future roles: some of the essential factors are not directly under their control. A woman may hope to marry and raise a family, but she will probably be reluctant to plan too heavily on it. Approximately 95 per cent of all women do marry eventually, and there is good reason to think that most of those who don't, fail to do so out of

---

[3] Parsons (1953) believes that when a woman's job is of a status equal to or above that of her husband, a profound alteration in family structure results. The evidence for this contention, however, is not impressive and it must be assumed at the present time to be only a conjecture.

choice, either consciously or unconsciously. But the fact remains that few women want to "push their luck" by preparing too completely or too openly for the right man to come along and sweep them into the kitchen. The hope chest is just that, a symbol of a hoped-for future but not a guarantee. Thus the girl who hopes to marry and become a homemaker believes that she must plan for the eventuality of not marrying, while the girl who would prefer a career must prepare herself for the probability that she will marry and have children, which she will then feel obligated to stay home and take care of. In both cases, therefore, plans and preparations for the preferred goal must be diluted with plans and preparations for a quite different one.

Many problems which women experience with regard to themselves and their roles in society come from within their own emotional make-up. It is true that these feelings are reinforced by attitudes and behaviors of others, but most women who are prevented from becoming what they want to become are prevented more by forces from within themselves than from without. An additional example of this is the feeling that many women seem to have that in most areas of behavior they are less free than men to follow their own inclinations. Certainly they have some good reasons for believing this: girls are reared with greater restrictions on them than are boys; their own mothers very likely gave in to the men in the family, perhaps willingly, perhaps with a martyred attitude; and most of the major decisions in the country are made by men. From all angles, the girl is taught that her own desires and wishes must be subjugated to those of men, and that submitting to a man somehow makes her a better woman.

There is no evidence that such an attitude is justified or necessary. In many families it may contribute to marital harmony, of a sort, by obviating a decision as to whose wishes shall prevail. But this is accomplished at the expense of individual initiative and development on the part of the woman. Any dramatic or profound change in society's attitudes toward women will have to be instigated by the women themselves, and it will have to start with the belief by women that they are just as good as men and that their rights and needs are just as important.

The present situation has several unfortunate results. It produces a "self-fulfilling prophecy": women think they ought to be subservient to men so they act that way, thereby encouraging their husbands to treat them in accordance with this behavior and promoting the same belief in their daughters. Understandably, many women who hold this attitude also resent it. Some react to their frustration by trying to prove that their needs are really *more* important than those of their husbands or children. The result is guilt feelings on the part of the woman for behaving in a way she believes to be wrong, anxiety among other members of her family who don't understand the reasons behind her demands, and an inability of both the husband and wife to look upon their needs as of *equal* validity and importance rather than more or less important than those of the other person.

These problems, arising from the need to adjust to the demands of various roles, are encountered by most girls during their development, but they are perhaps most evident among college girls who are exposed to a greater variety of role possibilities. According to Mueller (1949, p. 362):

The central problem for the young college woman of today is the difficulty of choosing and preparing for [an] ambiguous life pattern . . . especially of fitting the role of homemaker into all the other roles she wants to play in her life.

The problem is really not that of choosing a single role and discarding all others, but rather one of finding ways of integrating several diverse roles. Men do this with much less difficulty. A man may be a husband, a father, and a successful businessman all at the same time, but he can keep his roles relatively well separated without too much trouble. This is more difficult for a woman, not only because her roles are more likely to conflict with each other, but also because she may feel that any attempt she makes to separate them is somehow wrong.

Perhaps this is overstating the role problems of women. No one knows just how confused or dissatisfied women really are. Many writers, especially women, seem to think that these kinds of problems put a tremendous burden on the modern woman to make choices which are unfair and unrealistic, while others conclude that despite the difficulties most women seem to be satisfied with their roles. The truth is probably that none of what has been said here applies to all women; but enough of it applies to enough women to make the problem one of serious proportions.

❧ ❧ THE WOMAN IN A MAN'S WORLD. In one sense, the modern woman, despite her increasing freedom, may still be justified in feeling that she is trapped in a man's world. The activities to which our society assigns the highest status are primarily those in which men have traditionally predominated. Despite the lip service usually paid to the importance of the wife and mother, the woman's role is generally viewed as supplementary, secondary, and sometimes inferior. Most research concerning psychological characteristics and employment, for example, is based on men, and if women are studied at all—which they often aren't—the emphasis is on the extent to which they differ from men. Wives tend to be seen as extensions of their husbands rather than as individuals in their own right. This may lead the man to consider his wife as one of his possessions, an object which contributes to his self-concept in the same way as does his car or his house.

Montagu (1953) has argued that the motivation for this attitude is based on men's jealousy of women because of their ability to bear children. Whatever the cause, throughout history men have repeatedly, and for the most part successfully, relegated women to a position of secondary importance in society.

The result is that women learn to think of themselves as inferior because they are different from men. Freud invented the concept of "penis envy" to describe and explain the girl's dissatisfaction with her sex. This may be needlessly extreme as an explanation, but regardless of the reason many women grow up with a strong antipathy toward being female. Since with the exception of a few extreme but well-publicized cases one's sex is irreversible, the woman can only bear her frustration more or less gracefully.

This problem is complicated by the usual attitude of men toward the working wife. This will be discussed in more detail later, but it is sufficient to note at this point that in few instances is a woman's employment accepted by her husband as a substitute for her household responsibilities. Most husbands seem to feel that the managing and care of the household and family members is the wife's responsibility no matter what else happens. She can do other things if she likes, as long as this responsibility is fulfilled. Thus any outside activity which the wife takes on must be in addition to her "primary" responsibility. The wonder is not that more women don't seek outlets outside the home, but that so many find the time and energy to do so.

Is there a way out of this dilemma? Yes, if both husbands and wives are willing to consider each other as individuals rather than as extensions of stereotypes. The woman must develop the belief that being a woman does not *ipso facto* make her inferior to men, but it does make her different in some important ways. She must learn that difference does not imply inferiority. By the same token, the husband must be willing to view his wife as an individual with needs as strong and as varied as his own. These needs will be different from his in some ways, but just as important.

❧ ❧ ❧ THE LIFE PATTERN OF WOMEN. Women are also handicapped in their search for identity by the discontinuity of their lives, which gives them little chance to develop a consistent, integrated concept of themselves as individuals. The numerous shifts which occur in their lives, and the uncertainties of their futures, probably tend to make them more susceptible than men to the pressures of society. They welcome predetermined roles which do not require them to chart their own course in life.

Until high school graduation, there is little basic difference in the life patterns of boys and girls. They share the same experiences and spend a good deal of time together. Their worlds are not greatly different. After high school, the girl will most likely go to college or take a job. In either case, her experiences are still more similar to those of the men her age than they are different. She has constant association with other people, both male and female, and is still living in a "man's world."

Then comes marriage, and her life changes dramatically. She assumes the role of housewife and, in due course, of mother. She now lives in a world quite different from that of men, a world peopled primarily by small children and other mothers. If she was trained for a vocational field, she is probably no longer using her training. She has slipped, more or less easily, into the approved cultural role for women, but one for which her previous experiences have probably not well prepared her.

This remains the situation for an indeterminate number of years, depending in part on the number of children she has and the spacing between them. The time may eventually come, however, when she feels a desire to move back into her original role of being an equal partner in society rather than an inferior homebody. Most women do not reach this point until their children are of school age, many not until their children have left home, and some not at all. But most women do reach it eventually, for reasons which will be explored later.

Being a full-time homemaker occupies approximately one-third to one-fourth of a woman's adult life. Beyond that, she must either find ways to continue to make her homemaking a full-time job or else locate outlets for her leftover time and energy. If she doesn't, her family may suffer. As Mary Bunting (1961a, p. 112) has put it:

The woman who, in her early thirties, sees her last child enter school and then faces blankly the next forty years left to her by the actuaries with no notion of how to realize herself as an individual, is likely to begin to blame the marriage for her plight. A dissatisfied woman is seldom either a good wife or a good mother.

Many women come to find that they need more than their role as wife and mother to feel worthwhile as persons. But by the time they discover this, there may be time for only a half-hearted effort at something else. To be met effectively the problem must be anticipated, rather than allowed to drift to the surface when it's too late for a remedy.

❧ ❧ ❧ THE WOMANPOWER GAP. Society is crippled when the talents of a substantial portion of its members are not effectively utilized. It is generally agreed that women account for the largest pool of untapped resources in our country. This is especially important in occupations requiring above-average ability, in which manpower is severely limited, but the "womanpower gap" permeates all occupational levels. Estimates of future population growth and economic expansion needed to meet it indicate that the labor force will need 94 million workers by 1975 and 101 million by 1980. Much of this increase must come from women. As the need for well-educated and highly skilled workers increases, society will be less able to allow a significant proportion of its population to leave the labor market or settle for low-level jobs. An effort must be made to encourage women to utilize their skills more productively.

In a free society, of course, each person chooses his own way of life. Women cannot be coerced into advanced education and employment. They must seek it willingly, with the knowledge that such a step need not create friction with their desire to be married and have children. Some women will choose the traditional role anyway, but the choice should be free from the social restrictions which have impeded women up to now.

❧ ❧ ❧ A CHALLENGE FOR THE FUTURE. We have seen that two lines of social development are rapidly drawing together. Women, long relegated to a secondary position in our society, are asserting themselves, not just as a group but as individuals too. At the same time, society is recognizing a greater need for the effective utilization of the abilities and skills of all of its members, women included. The time is ripe for women to take a position of true equality in our society.

To do so, however, they will need the help of enlightened persons in many areas: from teachers, from counselors, and from employers. The individual girl planning her future and the individual woman wondering what to do with the rest of her life are scarcely in a position to see themselves in the context of modern society. It is the professional educator and the employer who must have the vision to help girls plan realistically for the future and to help women take advantage of opportunities in the present.

This means that persons working with girls and women in their educational and vocational planning must be thoroughly familiar with the variables which should be considered in this planning. They must know something about the way in which girls grow up in our society, and how they are influenced by this process. They should understand the differences between males and females and know how these can best be interpreted. They should be familiar with the current employment status of women as well as the projected trends. Finally, they should know the ways in which girls are educated and how these might be improved. Above all, they should understand the current status of women in our society without being blinded to changes that are taking place. We must live in the present, but we must prepare for the future.

The Girl Grows Up

A four-year-old who had visited a family in which there was a new baby was later asked at home whether the baby was a boy or a girl. "I don't know," she replied. "It's so hard to tell at that age, especially with their clothes off."

To UNDERSTAND WOMEN, we must begin at the beginning. It has been said that a person is born male or female but must learn how to be a man or a woman. This is a major part of the developmental process, and persons responsible for guiding girls in their development must understand its nature. People, like nations, are a product of their history. In order to understand the present status of women in our society, and to predict the future, we must examine the process by which the girl in our society grows up.

The developmental process can be viewed as consisting of two major components: physical and psychological characteristics. These of course interact, but since psychological traits are more subject to change it seems reasonable to deal with each separately.

❧ ❧ ❧ PHYSICAL DEVELOPMENT. The concept of sex differences in development signifies, above all else, the very obvious physical and physiological differences between boys and girls. The fact of being either male or female is incontrovertible, except in a few exceptional cases, and its importance cannot be denied. Details of the physical development of girls are unimportant here. Instead, attention will be paid to those aspects of physical development which have particular relevance for the role of women in our society.

✤ ✤ DEVELOPMENTAL ACCELERATION. Other than the specific physiological differences associated with being male or female, the most outstanding sex difference in physical development is that girls, on the average, reach the successive stages of development earlier than do boys. At any age, girls have achieved a greater percentage of their adult height and weight than have boys and are advanced over boys in skeletal development. Thus at almost any stage of development a girl is likely to be more physically mature than most boys her own age. It is probable that a corresponding acceleration also takes place in nonphysical areas of development, but evidence is less convincing.

This difference in rate of physical growth has important implications for other areas of development. For one thing, it may cause adolescent girls to associate socially with older boys, which in turn probably contributes to the attitude held by both sexes that males are the superior sex.

Another problem is the extent to which this acceleration may affect school learning. It has been suggested that girls have an advantage over boys during the early phases in subjects involving physical as well as mental skills, such as reading, and that this in turn causes discouragement and resentment on the part of boys. On this basis, the suggestion has been made that girls be admitted to school at an earlier chronological age than boys. As a general rule this seems an extreme step and would probably create more problems than it would solve. But as elementary school programs are taking greater cognizance of individual differences, the developmental acceleration of girls should be considered to be an important variable. For example, in schools in which educational acceleration is permitted by methods such as early admission to kindergarten or to first grade, girls would be more likely candidates for such special provisions than would boys of equal intellectual ability.

✤ Puberty. The point at which the physical development of girls becomes significantly different from that of boys is the onset of puberty. The girl is no longer a child but is instead becoming a woman, acquiring the physical characteristics of her sex plus the social and cultural attributes associated with it. This phase may have a strong influence, both physically and psychologically, on her total developmental pattern and may thus underlie problems which arise later in life.

For girls, the beginning of adolescence is marked by a specific physiological criterion—the onset of menstruation, called the *men-*

arche. The shift to adolescence is thus rather abrupt for most girls, in contrast to the more gradual transition for boys. It might therefore be expected that the emergence into adolescence is a greater emotional jolt for girls than for boys and creates more adjustment problems for them. There is little evidence for such a conclusion, however, although it is undoubtedly true that in individual cases in which parents have badly handled the first menstruation the girl may suffer an emotional trauma which may affect her attitude toward herself.

Facial blemishes or the wearing of glasses or teeth braces may cause considerable anxiety for a girl, and in her frustration she may make rather extreme attempts to overcome the problems. The amount of anxiety generated by what may seem to adults to be relatively minor and temporary defects and the time and money which girls spend to correct them lead Stolz and Stolz (1944) to conclude, ". . . even temporary deviations from sex-appropriate development are likely to produce definite problems of adjustment for adolescent girls."

The first menstruation does not transform a girl into a woman overnight. Time is required for the establishment of a regular monthly menstrual cycle, often as long as two years or more. This may result in considerable embarrassment and anxiety for the young girl, who not only is trying to adjust to having menstrual periods but is not even sure when they will occur.

The developmental acceleration of females is especially evident when puberty is reached, since girls reach this stage approximately 2 years earlier than do boys. The average age at which girls have their first menstruation is approximately 12.5 years, and most girls reach this stage sometime between the ages of 10 and 16. (Figure 2.1 shows the distribution of ages at which the menarche occurs.) By contrast, the average age at which boys reach puberty—as estimated from less specific criteria—is approximately 14.5 years, with a range from 11 to 18 years. These figures are compromises from data presented by various researchers who have not completely agreed on the averages. The important implication is that there is a period approximating the junior high years when most girls have reached puberty and most boys their age haven't. This difference in level of maturity often results in important sex differences in interests and attitudes during this period and causes girls to seek companionship with older boys, closer to their developmental stage. Attempts to originate social activities among boys and girls of the same age during this period can be frustrating to all concerned.

To those observing the young adolescent girl, the most obvious indications of her new maturity are a growth spurt and the development of physical features associated with womanhood, a spurt be-

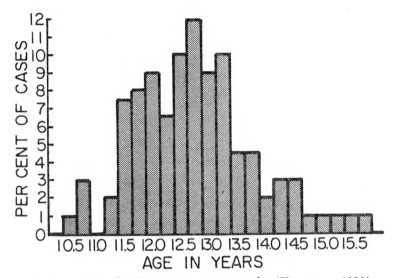

Fig. 2.1. Distribution of age at menarche (Krogman, 1955).

ginning to take place approximately one year before the menarche, reaching its peak at about the time of first menstruation. According to Shuttleworth (1937), the three major phases of female growth in early adolescence are: a slight decelerating phase, lasting about 2 years; a sharply accelerating phase, also lasting about 2 years; and a very sharply decelerating phase, lasting 4 to 5 years. In another report, Shuttleworth (1949b) has pointed out that girls at 11 years show the greatest variability in stature and stage of sexual maturation, physical size being closely associated with degree of sexual maturity.

Accompanying the menarche are other equally important physiological changes, including a leveling off of systolic blood pressure, a decline in pulse rate, and a sudden drop in basal metabolic rate. Such changes may have important effects on the girl's temperament and energy level, until her body has adapted to them.

❧ *Early vs. Late Maturers.* Since puberty is an important transitional stage in development, it seems logical to inquire as to the effects on a girl of being at one extreme or the other in rate of development.

One obvious fact is that early-maturing girls are, for a time, not only larger than other girls but are also larger than most boys their age. Evidence is incomplete as to the effect that this period of "hugeness" may have on the girl. It seems reasonable to assume that it affects her self-concept and may for a time cause her to be self-conscious and embarrassed both by her size and by the development of her physical sex characteristics. But there is little substantial evidence to show that the early-maturing girl is affected by her rapid development in any long-term, consistent manner. It is likely that the way in which the early-maturing girl reacts to these changes is a product of many factors in addition to the age at which the changes occur.

Following the growth spurt, the girl's growth rate decelerates and she soon reaches her mature size. Unlike early-maturing boys, who generally end up larger and better developed than their peers as adults, girls who reach puberty early also stop growing at an early age. The early-maturing girl tends to become a short, petite adult, whereas the girl who matures slowly eventually becomes a large adolescent and adult. These differences are not great and there is considerable variation among individual girls, but such information might take some of the worry out of being tall for the girl who has begun her growth spurt early.

Several attempts have been made to locate differences in interests and personality characteristics between early and late maturers. To some extent this search has been successful among boys: there seems to be conclusive evidence that early-maturing boys turn out to be more psychologically and emotionally mature and more masculine than do late maturers. Among girls, however, the differences are less striking. Early-maturing girls seem to have more mature interests than girls of the same age who develop less rapidly, and the former are probably seen in a more favorable light by their peers. But since physical characteristics play a less important role in determining status among adolescent girls than among boys, it is unlikely that personality differences between early and late maturers are as great for girls.

❧ ❧ HEALTH AND PHYSICAL DEFECTS. Physically, men are inferior to women. To be sure, men are larger and stronger, but women live longer, have a lower death rate at all ages, and have fewer physical defects. In truth, women are far from being the weaker sex.

From conception on, females are more likely to survive. About 20 to 25 per cent more boys than girls are conceived, but only about 5 to 6 per cent more boys are born, and the sex ratio becomes equal shortly after birth as boy babies are less likely to survive. Anastasi (1958), in summarizing these data, notes that a similar situation exists among lower animals, lending support to the belief that it reflects a basic difference between the sexes. On the other hand, as Conrad (1962) has suggested, sex-role differences may also contribute to the greater longevity of women. Males, for example, are more likely to die in accidents because their role requires them to take greater risks and to deal with lethal objects. They also are more likely to be employed in jobs which involve greater risk. In addition, the fact that women are more emotional may allow them to tolerate emotional stress with less physical damage than is suffered by men under tension. It seems that both biological and social influences have conspired to enable women to outlive men in our society.

Men not only have a shorter life span than women, but they are more apt to suffer from physical defects while they are alive. Among those defects more prevalent among men are high-frequency auditory defects, stuttering, alexia, and epilepsy, not to mention left-handedness, an inconvenience in our society if not necessarily a defect, unless one happens to be a first-baseman.

Many minor physical defects are genetically "sex linked," meaning that they occur much more frequently among males than among females[1] and are transmitted by genes on the sex-determining chromosomes. Such defects are usually produced by a defective gene carried by the X chromosome of the pair, since the Y chromosome contributes little to the formation of characteristics. Since an XX combination results in a female, it is likely that the other X chromosome will carry a normal gene for that characteristic, which will counteract the influence of the defective gene. Therefore a girl may well "carry" a gene for a defective sex-linked characteristic, but she is unlikely to display the characteristic herself. A male, on the other hand, is produced by an XY combination; if the X chromosome carries a defective gene, it is unlikely that the Y chromosome, being small and ineffective, will carry a normal gene for the corresponding characteristic. The result of these genetic manipulations is that sex-linked defects are generally found in males but are usually transmitted by females. Genetically, the female holds most of the trump cards.

Sensory defects in particular have been the subject of considerable investigation. In the auditory area the differences generally favor girls; boys are likely to have greater difficulty in hearing high-frequency sounds and to have more tonal dips. Perhaps such differences are sex linked in the manner described above.

The situation with regard to vision is more complicated. It has generally been taken for granted that color blindness is sex linked and that boys are much more likely to be afflicted with it. The evidence, however, is not entirely consistent, suggesting that the complex nature of color perception may not have been sufficiently appreciated. Perhaps sample inadequacies are partly responsible

---

[1] Montagu (1953, pp. 79–80) lists 27 such characteristics, all of which are found more frequently among men.

for the confusion, but such results make one suspicious of sweeping generalizations about color blindness.

Nor is there any consistent sex difference in other forms of eye defects. Studies involving reading ability and physical effectiveness of the eyes in reading have uncovered more eye defects among girls who have reading problems than among boys with similar difficulties; likewise, boys tend to do better on vision tests. Such studies, however, do not take into account other factors which may be contributing to the results, such as differences in motivation, attitude, and experience. We can thus conclude only that there is no firm evidence that eye defects are significantly more prevalent among either sex.

✄ ✄ ✄ PSYCHOLOGICAL DEVELOPMENT. Being a girl has tremendous psychological implications over and above the physical differences between males and females. Girls are treated differently from boys and different kinds of behaviors are expected of them, which in turn has an important bearing on women's attitudes toward themselves and their role in society.

✄ ✄ THE GIRL AND HER FAMILY

✄ *The Parent-Child Relationship.* Even before birth, the sex of the child is a matter of great interest—and frequently of concern—to the expectant parents. If it is their first child, they probably hope it will be a boy and refer to the fetus as "he" rather than "she." Many girls, therefore, come into the world at a bit of a disadvantage.

In most families it is the mother who has by far the greatest day-to-day influence on the development of the child. Sears and his co-workers (1957) have uncovered some interesting data concerning the child-raising practices of mothers, based on intensive interviews of 379 mothers, which have important implications for the understanding of how some of the typical psychological differences between the sexes come about.

The Sears group found that most mothers tend to be less strict and more permissive with their sons and to demand more conformity of their daughters. Boys are allowed more freedom and are encouraged to engage in more active, aggressive behavior. Girls are expected to act like "little ladies" and are praised for doing so, whereas the boy who is overly quiet is the object of concern—he is supposed to be a "real boy."

These differences in child-raising attitudes and behaviors toward sons and daughters are expressed in several ways within the family. For example, the Sears group noted that distinctions usually made in the kinds of household tasks in which it is expected that the boy or girl will engage are generally consistent with the child's sex role, as projected into the future. Boys are given more training and experience in independence and self-assertion while they are growing up, which may explain why these characteristics are exhibited more strongly by men than by women. In contrast the girl, as early as the preschool years, is likely to be more dependent. At first this dependency is centered on her mother, but it may later be transferred to other persons, such as teachers, and may be partially responsible for the greater ease with which girls adapt to the demands and requirements of school.

Interactions among parents and their children are highly complex and will, of course, vary from one family to another. However, two patterns are reasonably consistent: (a) in the majority of families the mother has a more nurturant relationship with the children than does the father; and (b) girls generally receive more love and affection from *both* parents than do boys. Girls are more likely to be disciplined by their mothers and boys by their fathers. Thus boys are more apt to be punished physically whereas girls are more often disciplined by love-oriented techniques, which in the long run have more lasting effects. Sears *et al.* (1957) suggest that this may explain why girls develop self-control and a sense of conscience more readily than do boys.

Sears *et al.* (1957) also report that the parent by whom the child is "controlled" depends to some extent on the size of the family. ("Control" refers to the parent to whom the child is more likely to respond or relate.) If a girl is an only child she is probably controlled by her mother, but in larger families the father participates more in the control of the first child than of later ones, regardless of their sex. Thus a girl who is an only child is likely to have been controlled primarily by her mother, whereas a first-born girl has probably been controlled to some extent, and perhaps largely, by her father. Girls who come later in the family are generally controlled more by their mother than is the oldest girl.

The Adolescent Years. In adolescence as in childhood, the girl is rewarded by her parents for conforming and for being a "lady." Parents expect their daughters to have good manners, to have social skills, to respect authority, and to be moral. Although there may be some conflict concerning the rules and regulations which the girl is expected to follow, most teen-age girls nevertheless expect and want some limits set by their parents. In most cases their verbal complaints are primarily designed to satisfy their developing need to feel less dependent on their families or to meet the expectations of their peer group, rather than because they actually want all restrictions removed.

Conflicts are likely to occur more frequently between the adolescent girl and her parents than between a boy and his parents. This is partly because of the greater restrictions put upon girls by their parents, but also because girls generally have a more emotional relationship with their parents than do boys. The amount of parent-daughter conflict increases during adolescence, at least until the age of 17, and is more likely to occur with the mother, if only because there are more total interactions between the girl and her mother.

One of the major tasks of adolescence is the achievement of emancipation from the family. That emancipation comes earlier and more easily for boys than for girls is hardly surprising in view of the evidence that, during childhood, boys are treated so as to promote the development of characteristics which will aid later emancipation, whereas girls are encouraged to be dependent on their families. At all ages, girls are subject to considerably more protection and supervision by adults than are boys, who are chaperoned only in their relations with girls of their own social class.

Since girls have fewer opportunities in which to learn to meet new situations and to develop self-confidence, many come to believe that they are incapable of becoming autonomous individuals. The result is that many young women never really become independent persons; at the proper time they simply shift their dependence from their parents to their husbands. Perhaps, therefore, many married women do not really want to be more on their own, to develop their abilities, to be less tied down by their families. They may appear, to an outsider, to live a narrow and unstimulating existence, but to them it represents security. They are afraid to attempt to be anything other than dependent housewives.

❧ ❧ DEVELOPMENT OF THE APPROPRIATE SEX ROLE.[2] Being a woman is a product not only of physical structure and physiological functioning but also—more importantly—of attitudes and behavior. Thus, to achieve full development as a woman, a female must learn how to think and behave as women are expected to think and behave in her society. This is one of the most important and long-lasting concepts she will ever learn and it will permeate her entire personality.

A tracing of the course by which the concept of sex-appropriate behavior develops would be simplified considerably if it could be established that physical and physiological forces play a major role. Research, however, continues to show that such influences are relatively unimportant as compared with cultural and psychological factors. This is evident in the survey by Hampson and Hampson

---

[2] The view of sex-role development presented here has been most strongly influenced by the writings of Brown (1958b) and Lynn (1966).

(1961) of studies involving hermaphrodites—individuals born with physical abnormalities such that they are not easily classified as either male or female, but instead have physical attributes of both sexes. The authors were particularly concerned in their survey with children who were later determined—on the basis of further development of the sex organs, arrangements of the chromosomes, or other physiological evidence—to be of the sex opposite to that for which they had been raised. They found that, in such cases, the child's "gender sex"—i.e., his sex orientation and behavior—were more frequently in accord with the expectations of his parents than with his physical structure. Their conclusion is significant (p. 1413):

One can conclude that an individual's gender role and orientation as boy or girl, man or woman, does not have an innate, preformed, instinctive basis as some have maintained. Instead, the evidence supports the view that psychologic sex is undifferentiated at birth, a sexual neutrality in place of the Freudian bisexuality, and that the individual becomes differentiated as masculine or feminine, psychologically, in the course of the many experiences of growing up.

Therefore we must turn to an examination of the psychological influences which play the major part in the development of the appropriate sex role in order to understand the process by which girls become women.

It is generally agreed that the concept of "sex role" includes at least three aspects: (a) sex-role adoption—the person's overt behavior: whether he acts like a man or a woman; (b) sex-role preference—the sex which he would prefer to be; and (c) sex-role identification—the role which the individual internalizes. Obviously there can be various combinations of each of these, and alternations are more common in some than in others.

Inappropriate *sex-role adoption* is least common and most strongly condemned by society. At its most extreme it can become sexual inversion—the adoption of the psychological identity of the opposite sex—with homosexuality a less severe form. More commonly it may involve the selection of an occupation usually associated with the opposite sex or the acquisition of mannerisms characteristic of the opposite sex.[3]

Linton (1956) cites considerable evidence to show that males are more likely to adopt the inappropriate sex role than are females. He sees two major reasons for a greater tendency on the part of males to assume the female role: (a) the male role has greater pres-

---

[3] This is not meant to imply that there is any necessary connection between aberrant forms of sexual behavior and the adoption of a vocation typical of the opposite sex.

tige and is thus more strongly defended and harder to assume by women; and (b) some male roles are dependent on strength which women lack.

Sex-role preference is more frequently inappropriate than is sex-role adoption, especially among women. In his extensive survey of the literature concerning sex-role development, Brown (1958b) concludes that there is consistent evidence among both children and adults for masculine preference by both males and females. At all ages, males more strongly prefer the masculine role than do females the feminine role.

There are probably two major reasons for this. For one thing, in our society the male role is made to appear more desirable—males receive more privileges, attain greater achievements, and have greater prestige. It may have been Eve who first lamented, "It's a man's world," and to a large extent this is still the case.

Secondly, girls are *allowed* to envy boys and to prefer their role, but boys are strongly *discouraged* from reciprocating. Contrast, for example, the reactions of the typical parent, especially the father, whose son is a "sissy"—i.e., he prefers girls' activities—and whose daughter is a "tomboy"—i.e., she prefers boys' activities. Even the two terms themselves carry different connotations. Girls are more likely to have boys' names than vice versa; it is not uncommon to find a girl named or nicknamed Billie, Jamie, or Bobbie. Girls are also allowed to wear boys' clothing—jeans, slacks, father's old shirts—while the reverse is strongly forbidden for boys.

From the point of view of the psychologist, the most important aspect of sex-role development is *sex-role identification.* This refers to one's real feelings about oneself in relation to one's sex—in this case, the attitudes, beliefs, and concepts of what it means to the girl to be female. The importance of sex-role identification in the total process of development can hardly be overestimated. According to Kagan and Moss (1962, p. 271):

It would appear that the desire to be an *ideal male* or *ideal female,* as defined by the individual, comprises an essential component of everyman's model. Thus the position of a response on a cognitive dimension ranging from *highly masculine* to *highly feminine* is a primary determinant of its acceptability and, therefore, of its probability of occurrence [original italics].

Not surprisingly, we find that parents have an important influence on the sex-role development of their children. Even preschool children are very much aware of the kinds of activities which their parents consider appropriate for boys and girls, and the effect becomes stronger with increasing age. The parents, therefore, provide the primary means by which the child becomes indoctrinated into the appropriate sex role. As boys and girls grow older they expand their horizons, and it is at this point that the girl whose parents have given her an atypical indoctrination, perhaps by encouraging her to engage in boys' activities, may experience conflicts.

On the basis of their extensive investigation of child-rearing practices, Sears and his co-workers (1957) concluded that a child learns appropriate behaviors, including sex-role behavior, by means of three processes: (a) trial and error, by which some behaviors are rewarded and others are ignored and punished; (b) direct teaching; and (c) role practice. The latter involves identification with "significant others" who provide role models; in most cases, at least during the early years, the parents are the major sources for such identification.

There is substantial evidence that children begin to develop their concept of sex role at an early age and that even the concepts of preschool children are reasonably accurate. Children can make distinctions between males and females by about the age of 2, and shortly after, they learn which they are. At this point, however, the fact of being a boy or girl has little meaning. This meaning must be acquired gradually, through a variety of experiences, and it is usually attained by the time the child enters the first grade. From his survey of the literature, Brown (1958b, p. 233) concludes:

Preschool children as a group become fully aware of the fact that the world is divided into two groups of people and that, depending on whether one belongs to one group or the other, different behavior patterns are expected accordingly.

And Hartley (1964) points out that accurate sex status, self-identity, early evidence of sex-appropriate toy preferences, preoccupation with imitative houseplay, and the beginnings of concept formation all occur at about the age of 4, suggesting that a common element is operating to influence such development.

ᴥ *Influential Variables.* The rate and manner in which sex-role concepts develop is subject to the influence of several variables, among which are those of intelligence and social class. Bright children develop sex-role attitudes more rapidly than do those of average intelligence. Lower-class children develop an awareness of sex-appropriate behavior at an earlier age than do those of the middle class, with the differences especially pronounced among girls. Middle-class girls are more traditionally feminine in their perception of the female role, despite their aversion to domestic activities.

This may in turn explain why women with middle- and upper-class backgrounds tend to seek activities outside the home to supplement their housewife role, while at the same time maintaining a concern about their femininity.

Broader cultural influences also play a part in sex-role development. Anthropologists have established that the behaviors which are characteristic of males and females in our culture are not necessarily characteristic of males and females in all cultures and may in some instances be reversed. However, the importance of differences in sex role among various cultures should not be overemphasized. In reality there seem to be more similarities than differences, especially at the early ages.

One explanation for this consistency is that the degree of cleavage between sex roles within a society tends to be related to the extent to which the group is dependent on physical strength and cooperative family interaction for its survival. Since men are usually stronger than women, and since the women have to be available to nurse the babies, sex roles tend to be differentiated accordingly. The greatest differentiation occurs in primitive societies, whereas in societies such as our own, in which strength and a high degree of cooperative interaction among family members are relatively unimportant, less emphasis on sex differences in roles is evident.

How Sex Roles Are Learned. A major process by which behaviors are learned and attitudes are internalized is the process of identification, and its importance is especially evident in the learning of sex-role concepts. Since the mother has the greatest amount of contact with the children, it is natural that both boys and girls identify with her to some extent at an early age. Nevertheless, even among preschool children, girls will identify more strongly with their mothers than will boys.

In developing their sex-role concepts, girls begin with several advantages over boys. Among these, as Parsons (1953) has noted, are the continual presence of the mother in the home, opportunities for the girl to be involved from an early age in feminine activities, and the relative ease with which feminine activities may be comprehended by a child. Thus the girl gets an early start in learning what a woman does and is able to internalize this concept by identifying with her mother, while the boy must shift his source of identification to a more socially acceptable (male) figure.

Woodworth and Schlosberg have proposed that learning can be dichotomized into two kinds: learning what one is taught, and solving problems. Lynn (1962) has applied this concept to sex-role development, suggesting that the girl learns a lesson—i.e., how to be like her mother—while the boy must solve problems. These problems are twofold: (a) he must learn not to identify with his mother, which at first is the simplest thing for him to do, and (b) he must find out what it is that men do. The latter problem is especially difficult for boys whose fathers are engaged in jobs which are abstract and complex. The young son of a bricklayer undoubtedly has a more accurate conception of his father's occupation than does the son of a research chemist.

The outcome is that the girl, by identifying almost exclusively with her mother, tends to internalize as part of her sex role those activities in which her mother normally engages and those characteristics which are unique about her mother. One result may be that the girl becomes more dependent on her mother and has greater difficulty in developing emotional independence from her family than does her brother.

With whom, then, does the boy identify? Since he does not have his father as a continual source of identification, he tends to identify with what might be termed a "male stereotype," a sort of combination of his father and other men whom he knows or has read about.

Thus boys and girls typically acquire their sex-role concepts in different ways. These differences have important implications for other aspects of their development, some of which have been discussed by Lynn (1962). He suggests that this difference may explain in part why girls develop stronger affiliation needs than boys and are more interested in social relations, why girls are more field dependent in tests of perceptual development, why boys are superior in problem solving, and why girls are more conforming. This difference also allows the boy a wider choice of occupations, since by not identifying strongly with his father he comes to see no single occupation as *the* exemplification of his sex role in the sense that the housewife occupation is likely to be viewed by the girl.

The last statement, however, is subject to the qualification that many mothers are not full-time housewives. Do their daughters therefore develop nontraditional sex-role concepts? The answer is uncertain. Girls who come from less traditional backgrounds or whose mothers are working outside the home are a little more likely to have an egalitarian view of the woman's role than are the daughters of full-time housewives, but the difference isn't as great as one might expect. One suggestion has been offered by Hartley and Klein (1959), who note that many working mothers attribute their working to financial need rather than to a real desire on their part to work. Their daughters, therefore, apparently get the impression that the "traditional" housewife role is the expected and desirable one, even though their mothers are temporarily unable to follow it. Women who are happy about their work, however, and who communicate this to their daughters are more apt to influence them in the direction of a less traditional concept of the woman's role.

All of this seems to mean that the girl who grows up to become a housewife has learned this role from a very early age and has been prepared for it. But what of the girl who doesn't become a housewife, either by choice or by chance? Is it possible for a girl to develop a concept of herself as a female in terms other than those of being a housewife? The answer apparently is "yes, but it's difficult." When a girl's sex-role concept moves outside of the traditional areas, she is in a "no-woman's land" as far as society is concerned. Other than the traditional female professions, such as teaching and nursing, she has little to draw on for help in establishing herself as a nonhousewife female.

A boy has the advantage of being able to feel that being a man and engaging in masculine activities is important in its own right. The girl, on the other hand, must in a way *resign* herself to being a woman. Time after time she will hear, "You can't do that," or "You can't have that," because it's the prerogative of boys. Boys, of course, have similar limitations, but it is implied to them that girls' activities are not really of much value, whereas those things which girls want but can't have are considered to be important. The result is that the sex-role behavior of girls is more variable than is that of boys, and girls become increasingly confused and dissatisfied with the feminine role at the same time that boys are attaining a stronger masculine identification.

It has been said that in growing up, girls learn how not to be babies, while boys learn how not to be girls. Or, to put it another way, boys are rewarded by society for being male while girls are punished for being female. Thus it is understandable that boys, once they have located their role, accept it with more ease than do girls.

As a result, many girls reach late adolescence with considerable confusion as to what they want out of life and what kind of persons they want to, and can, be. Role conflict is frequent and often demonstrated by a wavering indecision between tomboyish and feminine behavior. Both roles gain the girl some measure of social acceptance by some persons under some circumstances, but they are difficult to combine in one person. Most girls eventually resolve the problem by rejecting the tomboy role, but in doing so they also may reject the possibility of competing with men on an equal basis and developing those personality characteristics which men use to good advantage in their jobs and their everyday lives.

The emphasis on a narrow concept of the feminine role forces many girls to deny important aspects of themselves and to adopt beliefs which may have no real basis. For example, the adolescent girl is encouraged to believe that men are superior to women, despite everyday evidence to the contrary. She can dispute this, probably without much success and certainly at the risk of social criticism, or she can accept it although she may feel it to be untrue. The easiest alternative, and the commonest, is to accept it by believing it. Thus most men and women come to believe that women are emotionally and intellectually inferior to men and most bright girls go out of their way not to appear bright; they learn to fake inferiority, even though they may not feel it. They believe they must do this in order to gain what to them is their main goal in life: a husband and family. The result is likely to be frustration and envy of men, which in turn may have detrimental effects on both sexes.

Is there a trend toward a resolution of this conflict? Some authorities believe that society is moving toward some sort of resolution, but there are dissenters. On the negative side is Parsons (1955), who believes that current changes in the American family are combining to heighten sex-role differences rather than reduce them. Among these are the separation of the family and the occupational system, which focuses attention on the husband's occupational role, and the isolation of the nuclear family, which gives the wife sole responsibility for the mother role. Brown (1958b), on the other hand, sees numerous signs that sex roles are converging. Among these are the increasing equality of educational experiences, the greater involvement of husbands in domestic tasks, a lessening of the traditional distinctions in men's and women's clothing, and an increase in the number of women entering masculine occupations. Time will tell who has the clearer crystal ball.

✄ ✄ SOCIAL DEVELOPMENT. Boys and girls do not become popular for the same reasons. Sex-appropriate behavior seems to be a major determiner of popularity, such that girls who are docile and ladylike, and boys who are active and aggressive, are more likely to be esteemed by their peers. In early adolescence, being developmentally "in phase" is important, but by late adolescence the girl who is developmentally accelerated tends to have higher prestige. Finally, to be acceptable a girl must be sociable and get along well with the opposite sex, a trait that is more important among girls than among boys as a determiner of popularity.

An important characteristic of social development during adolescence is the emergence of a close, "best-friend" relationship. This is a strong emotional attachment between two girls, each of whom seems to act as the other's alter ego. It seems to serve as a device by which the girl can begin to emancipate herself from her family and yet fulfill her needs for dependence and sharing. The girl who fails to develop such relationships may therefore miss an important phase of development and may later find it difficult to relate to other girls on a close, personal basis.

Although girls appear to develop an interest in social activities in general, and in dating in particular, at an earlier age than do boys, there is nevertheless no consistent evidence that they begin dating at a significantly earlier age than boys. This suggests that the physiological changes associated with reaching puberty are not the primary determiners of the onset of dating, since the expected 2-year sex difference has not been consistently established. Cultural expectation seems to be the overriding influence.

*⁣ *⁣ * PLANNING FOR THE FUTURE. Although high school girls are generally more advanced in their vocational planning than are boys of the same age, few girls are concerned with vocational "plans" in the same sense as are boys. The major long-range goals of most girls, both in high school and college, are marriage and children. These girls are interested in vocational and educational planning only to the extent that such activities provide them with an acceptable way of using their time until marriage and an additional vague "insurance policy" for some improbable future emergency.

As a result, the vocational plans of girls are generally uninspired, unimaginative, and often unrealistic. The typical girl tends to aim at jobs below her capabilities and to restrict her choices to a limited range of possibilities; once her mind is made up, she's unlikely to change it.

This occurs because the main function of a vocational goal among college girls, according to Sanford (1962, p. 264), ". . . often seems to be to facilitate satisfactory self-definitions and thus bolster self-respect during the early years of college." On the basis of an extensive survey of college women, Berry (1955, pp. 78–79) concluded that the typical college girl:

> . . . intends to make her major contribution through her role as marriage partner and mother. The raising of a happy, healthy family was mentioned by the majority as constituting the paramount life achievement. Very few of the young women evidence concern for making contributions to scientific knowledge or for professional achievement. The college women participating in the survey were not concerned to any perceptible degree with making a contribution to society other than through adequate performance in their roles as wife and mother.

This dream appears to have a major flaw inasmuch as a great many women seek employment outside the home after their children are of school age although they are often poorly prepared for such an undertaking. Counselors who work with high school and college girls often are frustrated to find that the typical girl has little interest in information concerning her probable future needs and problems. She hopes to marry and have children, and she refuses to plan beyond that. To her, the idea that she might eventually find that her home and family do not entirely satisfy her needs is hardly comprehensible.

Despite its lack of realism, this belief makes sense when viewed in the light of the previous discussion of sex-role development. These girls are simply following the path which has been laid out for them by society and which they have long since ceased to question. They have been imbued with the idea that marriage and children are the fulfillment of a woman's destiny, the ultimate in femininity, and that has become their only goal. Thus persons dealing with high school and college girls encounter them at a stage in their development when their attention is focused on this goal almost exclusively. At this stage a girl may need help in coping with anxieties concerning her future role as wife and mother as well as encouragement to make educational and vocational plans consistent with this role.

❧ ❧ THE CAREER GIRL. A minority of girls do not fit this picture, but instead intend to subordinate marriage to a career. Such girls are atypical, as career women themselves recognize. They are characterized by a greater desire for personal achievement than the typical girl and are more like men in their interests to the extent that within some male fields, such as medicine and law, women students have more "masculine" interests and values than have the men themselves.

In a sense, girls who plan for a career are less well adjusted than those who are content to become housewives. Not only is the career-oriented girl likely to have a rather poor self-concept, but she also probably lacks a close relationship with her family. As a result, she has tended to model herself after professional persons rather than after her family and friends, so that the future role which she has mapped out for herself probably has little similarity to that which her mother has played in her own family.

Although a direct relationship between career orientation and personal maladjustment among girls has not been established, it seems evident that the girl who aims for a career is likely to be frustrated and dissatisfied with herself as a person. There are several possible explanations for this, all of which may be interacting. On the one hand, the girl who wants to avoid the traditional role has to overcome many cultural roadblocks, and such efforts may take their toll in her personal adjustment. There is little question but that our society makes things smoother for the girl who follows the traditional pattern.

But there is still a large possibility that a career orientation among girls grows out of personal dissatisfactions, so that the career becomes a frustration outlet. For example, in the Vassar studies (Sanford *et al.*, 1956) the best adjusted women, both as students and later as alumnae, were the underachievers who did not prepare themselves for an unrealistic future by overemphasizing academic performance but instead maintained a "healthy integration" of the feminine role and their own intellectual aspirations. One must conclude that the road to good adjustment, for women, is that which stays within the traditional feminine role authorized by society.

✾ *Marriage vs. Career.* One problem in research concerning characteristics of "career women" is that a marriage-career dichotomy is not realistic. Many women manage to combine both successfully; they may emphasize one aspect of their lives over the other, but neither is excluded. More information is needed as to the kinds of combinations which are most satisfactory and the characteristics of women who are able to develop and successfully maintain a manyfaceted life. Perhaps not all women are capable of simultaneously handling several divergent responsibilities, just as not all men are capable of being both successful businessmen and successful husbands and fathers, but those girls who have the potential for such diversity need to be discovered early and encouraged to develop broad and flexible life plans.

✾ *✾* VOCATIONAL DEVELOPMENT OF GIRLS. The study of the process by which young people make vocational choices is an active field within occupational psychology. Much is currently being learned about the process of vocational development, but unfortunately for our purposes the research is limited almost entirely to boys. Little information is yet available concerning the process by which girls make vocational choices, and this gap will not be filled until girls are considered worthy of study in their own right.

On the basis of the little research that has involved girls, it seems that girls begin to make vocational choices earlier than boys, which is consistent with their developmental acceleration in other areas. Career commitment also varies during development: it is highest in early adolescence and then drops throughout high school as girls come to believe that their chances for marriage and a family will be handicapped by a strong commitment to a career. Finally, there is some evidence that the best adjusted women are those who have managed to devise a satisfactory marriage-career combination, with their job being on a relatively high level and consistent with their needs and abilities.

These data are obviously fragmentary. No one has yet undertaken to study the development of vocational choice among girls in any systematic way. Perhaps this is not considered to be important enough to study intensively, but in view of the growing importance of work in the lives of women in our society, the need for research seems obvious.

We must turn, therefore, to more fragmentary data concerning the process by which girls come to make vocational choices. It is generally agreed that interests play an important part in the vocational goals of boys, but most attempts to isolate vocational interests among women have ended in frustration. As noted earlier, girls tend to develop their vocational interests earlier, to have more homogeneous interests, and to have these interest patterns fairly well stabilized by the time they are graduated from high school. But the narrowness of the traditional range of female occupations and the difficulties which have been encountered in the development of interest inventories for women suggest that vocational interest does not play the kind of role in the vocational or curriculum selection of girls that it does among boys.

Nevertheless, boys and girls do differ in their job preferences and attitudes in some important ways: (a) girls prefer jobs involving working with people rather than with things; (b) girls prefer service rather than professional or career fields; (c) girls have more stable job attitudes; (d) girls are more likely to consider characteristics of the job itself in job selection; and (e) girls are less likely to consider pay and opportunities for advancement in job selection.

Personal values also play an important role in occupational choice, although they operate in different ways for boys and girls. In general, values are a less important determiner of job choice among girls, presumably because girls do not usually see a job as a major way of satisfying their personal needs and values, as do boys. To the extent that personal values are involved, girls tend to stress personal comfort and social service motivation, especially as they become older, and they are less concerned with power and esteem than are boys.

A summation of the evidence leads to the conclusion that girls do not consider an occupation to be an important part of their future and, consequently, their choice of a field is often based on short-term and perhaps trivial factors. Only later do many women find that the wife and mother roles are not enough, and their earlier careless choice of an occupation catches up with them. Their earlier job preparation may then be of little use to them, either because they are no longer interested in that kind of work—and perhaps never really were—or because it is incompatible with their other responsibilities. In any case, for many women the process of serious career planning begins, not in high school or college as it does for boys, but after they have reached their thirties and forties, when their children are no longer full-time responsibilities. In the meantime, important opportunities may have been missed.

⁂ ⁂ ⁂ ⁂ ⁂ ⁂ ⁂ ⁂ ⁂ ⁂ ⁂ ⁂ ⁂ CHAPTER THREE

Sex
and Abilities

SAMUEL JOHNSON, WHEN ASKED, "WHICH IS
MORE INTELLIGENT, MAN OR WOMAN?" RE-
PLIED, "WHICH MAN AND WHICH WOMAN?"

THE INDIVIDUAL IN OUR SOCIETY, given freedom to plan the course of his life, bases these plans primarily on what he knows about himself: his abilities, his interests, and his personality traits. If the educational and vocational paths of men and women are to be directed toward different goals, we then imply that there are fundamental differences between the sexes in these areas. Conversely, to the extent that assumed differences can be shown to be mythical, the traditional separation of goals and paths must be questioned. The purpose of this chapter and the one which follows is to explore the ways in which men and women differ in abilities, interests, and personal traits in a search for the true nature of being female.

⁂ ⁂ ⁂ THE BASES FOR SEX DIFFERENCES. The reasons for the existence of behavioral differences between males and females is a question which has long fascinated psychologists. The two extreme points of view are, first, that the cause is primarily biological, related to the obvious physical and physiological differences between the sexes; or second, that the majority of such differences are learned in a social setting. Most experts would probably hesitate to espouse one or the other of these approaches exclusively, but they nevertheless tend to favor one or the other in their thinking and writing.

For many years biological factors were thought to be the major determiners of sex differences in psychological characteristics, in the same way that such influences were thought to be responsible for racial and other group differences. In recent years, the trend has been reversed and scientists, with the encouragement of the cultural anthropologists, have tended to stress social or cultural influences, sometimes to the neglect of constitutional factors. The problem appears to be one of bringing both sides of the picture back into focus, in an attempt to learn how things really are rather than how one might like them to be.

❧ ❧ THE BIOLOGICAL VIEW. The biological view of the basis of sex differences in psychological characteristics rests on the assumption that the obvious biological differences which exist between the sexes must exert important influences in addition to those of a physical nature. It would be foolhardy to deny that such differences would not have some influence on psychological characteristics. The question is the extent to which such characteristics are thus affected and to what extent social and cultural factors may override this influence.

❧ ❧ THE SOCIAL OR CULTURAL VIEW. Most psychologists, however, while not denying the influence of biological factors, would argue that many important psychological sex differences are primarily the result of social or cultural influences. Proponents of this view tend to draw heavily on the work of the cultural anthropologists, such as Margaret Mead (1939), who have demonstrated that the "typical" sex-role differences do not exist in all societies. In addition, research concerning the development of sex roles in our society, discussed in the preceding chapter, provides further support for the argument that a large part of the sex differences that are assumed to be basic and inherent are in fact the product of differential influences during development.

There is no evidence which points conclusively to either biological or cultural influences as of overriding importance. Perhaps this means that the situation varies depending on which characteristics are under consideration. There appear to be two arguments supporting the present trend to stress social factors and to underplay the importance of biological influences, and the writer is in sympathy with both.

A cultural point of view makes greater allowance for the dynamic quality of psychological characteristics. It admits with greater ease the possibility that sex differences are not fixed, but instead may be altered by cultural and social pressures. It thus provides a much-needed rebuttal against those who attempt to use biological sex differences to support the view that one sex is innately superior to the other.

The biological view is more likely to cause an individual to be "typed" according to his sex. We know that many of the so-called "sex differences" do not apply to all members of that sex. But a person who holds that such differences are primarily due to biological factors is likely to feel that the characteristics of the individual are therefore fixed at conception and can be accurately estimated on the basis of whether the person is male or female. This is a dangerous and misleading view, and one which a cultural emphasis can help to dispel.

Is there any way in which the two views can be reconciled, or are they mutually exclusive? Some sort of compromise or integration of the viewpoints is necessary and not impossible. To begin with, it seems evident that sex differences in abilities are primarily the result of cultural influences that determine which abilities will be stressed for each sex, although there seems to be widespread agreement, throughout Western society at least, as to those abilities which men and women are expected to emphasize. In the case of motivation and personality, the situation is more obscure. Physical and hormonal influences are probably operating to some extent, as evidenced by the establishment of such differences as early as 3 years of age, but social influences also certainly play an important role.

The temptation is strong to oversimplify the ways in which biological and cultural factors influence the development of an organism. In reality, the situation is extremely complex, and scientists are currently learning a great deal more about the process than has heretofore been known. The two kinds of forces are not antagonistic, but in fact each depends on the other for the opportunity for its influence to be manifested. It is extremely difficult to conceive an inherited characteristic (other than perhaps a strictly physical condition) being displayed in the absence of some sort of environmental circumstance. Likewise, cultural influences must have an organism with certain inherited potentialities—not a blank slate— on which to operate. The key word is *interaction*. As the song about love and marriage says, "You can't have one without the other."

✄ ✄ ✄ SEX DIFFERENCES IN INTELLIGENCE

✄ ✄ "BUILT-IN" BIAS OF TESTS. The question of the comparative intellectual abilities of males and females leads the naive investigator down a beckoning rosy path, around a corner, and up to a solid brick wall: the method by which the measuring instrument is constructed. Anyone who looks for sex differences in intelligence must recognize that intelligence is measured by "intelligence tests" and that these tests are designed so as to include only those tasks which reflect what the authors of the tests consider to be "true" mental ability.

Designers of an intelligence test are faced with the task of protecting their instrument as much as possible from contamination by nonintellectual influences. If a person performs well on the test, not because he is actually more intelligent than others but because he has had certain advantages of a nonintellectual nature which have influenced his performance, his score tells very little about his actual ability and the test is of little value as a measure of intelligence.

Sex is of course not the only variable which complicates the measurement of intelligence. For example, middle-class children generally score higher on intelligence tests than do lower-class children, which some authorities attribute in part to a cultural bias in the test items. The same may be true in the case of other group differences. But persons who design intelligence tests have been especially sensitive to the possible influence of sex differences on test performance.

Elimination of Sex Differences by Design. The many ways—both obvious and subtle—that our culture exerts different influences on males and females as they grow up might, in turn, cause boys to learn certain kinds of behaviors more readily than girls, and vice versa. If these behaviors were included as items on an intelligence test, one sex or the other might then have an advantage. Thus the resulting sex difference in intelligence, as measured by such a test, would be due primarily—and perhaps entirely—to a greater familiarity with these kinds of behaviors by one sex or the other rather than to a true difference in ability.

This is the dilemma that persons who are brave enough to design intelligence tests must face sooner or later. One man who encountered it many years ago was Lewis Terman, in his construction of the Stanford-Binet Intelligence Scale. His solution was to limit the test to items on which the difference in performance between the sexes was negligible, or at least not to include a preponderance of items which favored one sex over the other. In effect he was assuming that, for the purposes of designing the Stanford-Binet, males and females did not differ significantly in general intellectual ability. Since the Stanford-Binet has long served as a model for subsequent measures of intelligence, both as an influence on the theory of intelligence and as a validation criterion, it is not surprising to find that most current tests, including the most recent revision of the Binet, follow the same procedure.

Many psychologists, however, have questioned this approach, raising two major arguments against the elimination of sex-biased intelligence-test items: Other group differences are left in; why make sex differences a special case? And, such a procedure does not reflect the realities of our society, in which men and women generally concentrate their activities in different areas requiring somewhat different abilities and in which other sex differences, such as in interests and aptitudes, are emphasized in planning for the future.

What, then, would be the best procedure? The value of an intelligence test is determined primarily by its predictive validity. The more accurately an intelligence test predicts performance on some external criterion, the greater its value to those who use it. If predictions can be improved by including sex-biased items, then by all means they should be included. As the traditional sex differences in occupations continue to become blurred, we will need increasingly more accurate measures of the abilities required to perform successfully in various fields. To some extent this will include "general intelligence." If our concept of general intelligence, or of the subabilities which compose it, is unduly restricted by a refusal to recognize the possibility of sex differences in certain areas, the accuracy of our predictions of performance in such areas will likewise be restricted.

It is generally acknowledged that many group differences, while perhaps giving an unfair picture of some persons on the basis of their restricted experiences, nevertheless have relevance for academic and vocational predictions, in that the same cultural handicaps which contribute to poor performance on the intelligence test will likewise handicap performance in school or on the job. In this respect, therefore, the test has some predictive value. The major difficulty arises when conclusions concerning inherent intellectual differences between groups are drawn from such measures.

This approach could logically be applied to differences between the sexes. Suppose we were to concentrate on designing tests which would have maximum predictive value for academic and vocational situations. Any differences then found would presumably be related to differential performance on the criterion. The explanation of the differences might lie in the disparity of opportunities and experiences encountered by men and women within our society. If this is true, the measured sex differences should decrease as differences in cultural experiences decrease. But there would be no need, and indeed no justification, for using such differences as a basis for drawing conclusions concerning the inherent intellectual capacities of men vs. women. In a sense, the bias is not really in the test itself but rather in performance on the criterion which the test is designed to predict. If the basis for the criterion bias is not innate, presumably it will change in the future, and this change would be reflected in the content of the tests which are designed to predict it.

✄ ✄ RESEARCH ON "GENERAL INTELLIGENCE." Despite the complications just discussed, the fact remains that there has been a tidal wave of research concerning sex differences in mental abilities. In order to understand this, we must shift our attention from the question of general differences in intelligence between males and females to a consideration of meaningful and worthwhile investigations of more specific problems within this area.

It is useful to know, for example, how the sexes compare in performance on the various kinds of items typically included in intelligence tests. (Terman was concerned that the total test did not unduly favor one sex over the other; but in order to get enough valid items he had to include specific items on which there were sex differences—he simply balanced them with other items which exhibited sex differences in the opposite direction.) It is also useful to know under what conditions reliable sex differences are located and what variables seem to influence the superior performance of one sex over the other.

The most extensive series of studies of intelligence are those reported by the Scottish Council for Research in Education in a 1949 monograph entitled, *The Trend of Scottish Intelligence*. This presents a comparison of two surveys of intelligence conducted in Scotland in 1932 and 1947. In 1932, a group intelligence test was administered to 90,000 children; in addition, about a thousand were given the Stanford-Binet (1916 form). In 1947, an attempt was made to administer a verbal group test to all Scottish school children born in 1936, the total number tested being more than 70,000. In addition, all Scottish children born on the first day of February, April, June, August, October, and December of 1936 (a total of 595 boys and 620 girls) were given the 1937 revision of the Stanford-Binet. In the 1947 individual testing, the boys obtained a mean IQ of 104.39 and the girls a mean IQ of 100.73; the boys were significantly superior, as had also been the case in 1932. On the group test, the girls, who had been slightly inferior in 1932, were significantly superior in 1947. The Council concluded (1949, p. 123), "It would seem that at least for present Scottish eleven-year-old children this verbal group test is biased in favour of girls and the Terman-Merrill Revision [Stanford-Binet] in favour of boys."

In general, the attempt to design the Stanford-Binet so as to eliminate sex differences in performance appears to have been reasonably successful. Although slight sex differences are reported in the standardization data for the 1937 revision, the authors attribute these to sampling biases. Subsequent research with the Binet has generally failed to locate any consistent sex differences.

The same is true with regard to the total scores on the Wechsler tests. Analysis of the standardization data for both the Wechsler Intelligence Scale for Children and the Wechsler Adult Intelligence Scale has failed to locate consistent differences in IQ scores between males and females. On the other hand, Wechsler does not seem to have tried to eliminate sex differences on the subtests inasmuch as sex differences are consistently found on several. In general, males do better on the subtests involving memory, numbers, and spatial relations, while females are superior on the subtests involving verbal and perceptual-motor skills. The fact that these differences are greater on the adult form than on the children's form suggests that cultural influences are a major basis.

Several conclusions may be drawn from the research to date. First, there is no consistent evidence of sex differences in intelligence, as measured by a variety of tests under a variety of conditions. In some ways it is rather surprising that sex differences aren't found more frequently in view of the sizes of some of the samples.

Second, due to the size of the sample, sex differences in average scores are sometimes significant. However, there seems to be no consistent pattern to the nature or direction of these differences, and one suspects that some are probably due to sample bias.

Third, studies involving group tests tend to show girls scoring higher than boys, but such results are questionable due to the highly verbal nature of such tests.

All in all, the studies surveyed here seem to lend further support to the conclusion drawn by Kuznets and McNemar (1940, p. 217) a number of years ago, based on a survey of studies involving sex differences in intelligence:

When large unselected groups are used, when age is taken into account, when possibilities of bias in test content are allowed for, startling differences between the sexes either in average tendency or in variations fail to emerge.

The question of sex differences in degree of intelligence seems to be essentially a false issue. Perhaps in the future some way will be found to show that the distributions of intelligence among boys and girls are not identical, but the overlap would nonetheless be so great that such a finding would not have any real implications for teaching or counseling. In the final analysis, the mental ability of a girl must be ascertained on the basis of her actual performance in comparison with others her own age, both male and female, with the same experiences. Simply knowing that she is a girl tells nothing about her level of intelligence.

✣ *Studies of Special Groups.* Most of the research summarized up to this point has dealt with comparisons of large, representative groups of males and females. Another approach is to focus on the extremes—those who are judged to be mentally gifted or retarded on the basis of test performance as well as other criteria.

One complication in studying sex differences among the mentally retarded or slow learners is the fact that boys who are of low intelligence are more likely to be placed in special classes than are girls of equally low ability. This may be the reason why boys in retarded groups are often found to score higher on intelligence tests than girls of the same classification. It may also explain why, in a "normal" classroom, the boys may have a higher average intelligence than the girls: the boys who would be at the low end of the distribution are more likely to have been segregated into special classes.

The most extensive study of gifted persons in this country is that begun by Lewis Terman in the 1920's and followed up to the present time. His original group of gifted children included 857 boys and 671 girls, whose mean Stanford-Binet IQ's were 151.4 and 150.4 respectively. As adults, 20 years after the study began, the same group was given the Concept Mastery Test, a specially designed test of mental ability with an unusually high ceiling. Their husbands and wives also took the test.[1] All were tested again approximately 10 years later. Comparisons of the results of the two adult testings are presented in Figure 3.1. The most striking result is that all groups improved their performance in the 10-year interval. The men significantly out-performed the women, and the gifted men and women scored substantially higher than their spouses in both testings.[2]

The increased sex difference in favor of the men in the later testings seems to be an important phenomenon and is supported by research with other groups. One explanation is that highly intel-

---

[1] The Stanford-Binet was also administered at this time to the children of the original group; the boys averaged 127.2 and the girls 128.2.

[2] Interpretation of the results of Terman's studies is subject to some limitations in view of the original selection procedure, which began with teachers' nominations of pupils whom they judged to be intellectually gifted. Those nominated were subsequently tested to determine their suitability for inclusion in the study, making it unlikely that a child would be selected if he were not first nominated by a teacher.

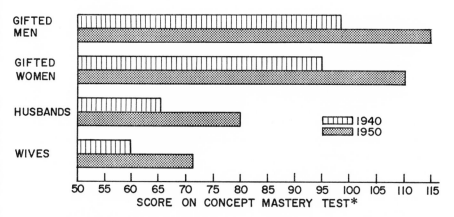

*THE CONCEPT MASTERY TEST HAS A CEILING OF 200; A SCORE OF 96
IS EQUIVALENT TO A STANFORD— BINET IQ OF 140.

*Fig. 3.1. Changes in intellectual performance of members of
Terman's gifted group, plus their husbands and wives, between 1940
and 1950 (Terman and Oden, 1959).*

ligent women have not, for the most part, had as much education
as men of originally equal ability. One wonders whether the failure
to obtain education commensurate with their abilities may not in
the long run result in the intellectual stagnation of many able
women.

⅋ *Conclusion.* At this point, it must be reiterated that there is no
evidence of consistent, substantial, or meaningful sex differences in
general intelligence. Certain specific subtest areas show differences
in performance, but even these are not entirely reliable and probably depend on both differential experiences and the composition
of the specific test under consideration.

⅋ ⅋ ACADEMIC ACHIEVEMENT. Although differences in intellectual
capacity between men and women are not outstanding, there are
notable differences in academic achievement of which intelligence
is assumed to be a major component. Scholastic comparisons between boys and girls reveal that girls are superior in almost all aspects of academic achievement: they get higher grades, more of
them graduate from high school with honors, they are more likely
to be accelerated and are less likely to be held back a grade. They
enter college with superior high school grades and continue to do
comparatively well in college.

The peculiar thing, however, is that girls are able to obtain higher grades than boys without demonstrating any consistent superiority on standardized tests of ability or of academic achievement. Although girls enter college with better high school grades, they do not exceed boys on entrance tests of scholastic ability. Even more remarkable, they receive grades equal or superior to those of boys in areas in which boys score higher on standardized achievement tests. This is especially evident in science courses, in which girls receive grades equal to those of boys despite evidence that boys are more interested in science, score higher than girls on standardized tests of science knowledge, and win more science scholarships. Clearly the discrepancies in grades are not based entirely on differences in mastery of the material. Other factors are conspiring to tilt the scales of evaluation in favor of girls, as will be shown later.

Science and mathematics show the greatest sex differences in interest and test performance, a difference which increases markedly with age. Among high school students, boys do considerably better than girls on tests of science ability and achievement regardless of the method by which the courses are taught. Here again, cultural factors are undoubtedly playing an important role in influencing both interest and achievement. Girls are not expected to like mathematics and science, or even for that matter to understand them, and the girl who pursues these subjects too vigorously runs the risk of attracting strange glances from her classmates.

Girls are also less likely than boys to take science courses in high school, which may explain in part why those who enroll in these courses perform as well as the boys. Girls in general avoid learning about science during high school; twelfth grade girls know little more about science and mathematics than do girls in the ninth grade. The few girls who do take science courses are likely to be both interested in and adept at such subjects, whereas many of the boys are in the class primarily because this is what boys are supposed to take, whether they have any real interest or ability in it.

It would seem, therefore, that girls may be a future source of largely untapped abilities in science and mathematics, if only their interest can be aroused. But this is not an easy task. One difficulty is that research concerning motivation has shown that girls do not respond to the same kind of incentives as do boys. Not surprisingly, the increased pressure for achievement in science and mathematics which has swelled during the past decade has had a greater influence on boys than on girls. This suggests that we can expect no dramatic upsurge of interest in science and math among girls, despite the pressures from society for achievement in these areas.

❧ Reasons for Girls' Higher Grades. An obvious question arises at this point: If there are no consistent sex differences in knowledge in most subjects, as measured by objective, standardized tests, why do girls consistently get higher grades in their academic courses? A number of suggestions have been offered as explanations, several of which seem to have some validity.

To begin with, girls have superior verbal ability, which enables them to express themselves more fluently and may give their teachers the impression that they know more about the material than do the boys. Their handwriting is also likely to be easier to read, which gives them an advantage on essay exams and on themes and papers.

A third factor is that the personality and behavior of girls are more apt to make a favorable impression on teachers and to produce higher achievement. It is generally accepted that boys are more often behavior problems in the classroom, especially in junior high when there is less personal contact with the teacher than in elementary school. Girls also benefit by a more cautious attitude in risk-taking situations so that they are less likely than boys to take large risks and are willing to settle instead for a medium level of reward. As a result, they are likely to achieve better than boys, although they are less likely to be outstanding. Finally, at least at the college level, there is some evidence that conformity is related to the grades that girls receive, although this isn't true among boys. Apparently, the girl who is a conformer has a good chance for academic success.

Girls also benefit from the unwritten assumption that girls are *supposed* to get better grades. Call it a "halo effect," a stereotype, or whatever you like, the fact remains that a girl is likely to get a higher grade just because she's a girl. Part of the explanation may lie in a suggestion by Drews (1961, p. 15):

Achievement in terms of grades may be partially due to the fact that most girls accept the values of the school and, at least to an extent, identify with teachers whereas many able boys do not.

The interaction between the sex of the teacher and that of the student also seems to play an important role in determining the grade which a student will receive. At the elementary level most teachers are women, which gives girls an advantage—women teachers are likely to favor girls in their classes and to reward them more. They are also more likely to be sympathetic to the problems of girls and to give them extra attention if they are having difficulty.

Although the sex ratio among high school teachers is about equal, girls continue to enjoy certain advantages there as well. Men

teachers generally tend to give lower grades than do women teachers, so that having a male teacher is a lesser advantage for a boy
than having a female teacher is for a girl. Thus in high school the
combination of female teacher and female student produces the
highest grades while the combination of male teacher and male student results in lower grades.

These observations should not obscure the fact that girls generally work harder in school than do boys. Because they tend to be
more conforming and more conscientious, they are more likely to
do what is expected of them academically. Perhaps one reason they
don't exceed boys on achievement tests is that their ability, as a
group, is lower. Students begin to drop out of school after they
have reached the legal age limit for compulsory attendance, and
those who leave are more likely to be (a) of low ability, and (b)
boys. Thus the group of girls that is left by the time high school
graduation is reached probably includes some whose intelligence is
as low as that of boys who have dropped out. The average intelligence of the remaining girls is therefore lower than that of the remaining boys. The surprising result is that the girls manage to
equal the boys on standardized achievement tests, and get better
grades as well.

✤ *Underachievement.* When a student performs at a level considerably below his potential, he is called an "underachiever." According to Shaw (1961, p. 22), "One of the most striking and most
universally agreed upon characteristics of underachievement is the
fact that it is predominantly a male problem." About twice as many
boys as girls qualify for the title, and boys tend also to show an
underachievement pattern at an earlier age. Underachievement in
boys can be spotted as early as the first grade, but generally not
among girls until near the end of elementary school.

Not only is the frequency of underachievement different between boys and girls, but the causes appear to differ, too. Among
girls, achievement seems to be related to a need to impress others,
while boys are more apt to achieve well because of a personal interest in the activity, regardless of what others may think. Conversely, girls who are underachievers are likely to be rebellious and
antisocial, perhaps using their low performance as a means of fighting the control of parents and teachers, whereas the underachieving
boy has failed to become personally involved in academic tasks.
Thus girls who are high achievers are more apt to be socially active
and conventional and to want credit for their achievement. The
high-achieving boy, on the other hand, probably has a high internal
achievement drive as well as a personal interest in the areas in

which he is working. More will be said about this difference in the discussion concerning achievement motivation in the next chapter.

It seems probable that underachievement is somehow related to the attitudes and behaviors of the parents, but the nature of the relationship is not well understood. The research to date suggests that underachievement among girls is related more to the mother's behavior than to the father's; despite some conflicting evidence, it can be tentatively concluded that girls who display a pattern of underachievement are likely to have mothers who attempt to "overcontrol" them. This relationship becomes more evident in college, although it must be kept in mind that underachievement in college may not necessarily have the same basis as underachievement in high school. In general, it seems that children with dominating parents tend to do well in high school but not so well in college. Since girls tend to be more responsive to the demands of their parents than are boys, it is more likely that girls will wait until college to act out their rebellion through underachievement.

❃ ❃ VARIABILITY. Differences between males and females in "average" scores or performances on tests of intellectual abilities have not been the only concern of psychologists. Closely associated is another statistical artifact of human behavior: dispersion around the average.

Historically, men have been assumed to be more intellectually variable than women. This conclusion has been based primarily on two kinds of evidence: (a) the much greater proportion of eminent men than women, and (b) the preponderance of males in institutions for the mentally retarded. Although both are not disputable as facts, their implications may be challenged.

Several factors have contributed to the scarcity of eminent women throughout history. Among these are the barriers which women have encountered when they have attempted to enter occupations in which prestige is usually attained, plus disparities in educational opportunities. Only recently have women been accorded the same kind of education as men, and this equality does not yet extend into many professional and graduate programs. The major handicap, however, is the sex-role stereotype which makes an oddity of the woman who strives to get ahead professionally. A girl needs considerably more drive and motivation, and perhaps ability, than a boy in order to break through the bars by which society attempts to circumscribe the behavior of women. It's little wonder, therefore, that few women have attained prominence.

Sex differences in institutionalized populations are also, for the most part, culturally determined. A mentally retarded boy will probably be noticed in a classroom, whereas a girl of equal ability is likely to be docile and thus perhaps be allowed to "get by." In addition, a mentally retarded girl is easier to keep at home. She can help with simple household tasks and she is less difficult to control physically than is a boy, especially when adolescence is reached.

Although this sort of evidence is not sufficient to allow us to ascribe greater variance in ability to boys, there is still a strong belief among many psychologists that intellectual variability is greater among males, and the evidence which they present cannot all be easily refuted. One kind of support for such an argument comes from Terman's study of gifted children, which included 857 boys and 671 girls. Terman and Oden (1947) suggest that this unequal sex ratio might reflect a true sex difference in variability, but they are reluctant to advance this conclusion strongly. It is possible that, considering the method by which the subjects were originally chosen (beginning with teachers' nominations), a nonintellectual sex bias could have been operating. Other studies of gifted children have not always found boys to predominate.

Studies involving large numbers of children have also provided some evidence that a disproportionate number of boys score at the upper and lower extremes on intelligence tests. These results have been interpreted as proof that males are more variable than females in intelligence. Although the evidence itself cannot be denied, the interpretation can be questioned. It is known that females are more predictable in test performance, meaning that their performance is more likely to be consistent with what would be expected. Perhaps the greater variability in male performance on intelligence tests is due to greater variation in attitude. Most girls probably do about as well as they can without great effort, while boys either work quite hard to perform well, or are disinterested and do poorly. The result is greater male variability in performance, but this does not necessarily mean that males are innately more variable in ability.

✼ ✼ PREDICTABILITY. Men complain that women are unpredictable, but science says otherwise. Most studies of predictability have been concerned with the prediction of academic grades and, in this area at least, girls are more predictable than boys. The major reason seems to be that girls are more conforming than boys and thus are less apt to perform erratically. If a boy is enthusiastic about a course, he works hard at it and may do exceptionally well; if he's disinterested he's likely to goof off. Girls, on the other hand, tend to do what's expected, usually without a great deal of enthusiasm. (Please bear in mind that this refers to the *average* boy and girl; there are many exceptions within both sexes who don't fit this pattern.)

❉ ❉ ❉ SEX DIFFERENCES IN SPECIFIC ABILITIES

❉ ❉ VERBAL ABILITY. It will probably come as no surprise to most men to learn that women are superior in verbal ability. Girls are consistently superior in linguistic functions at all ages: they talk earlier, have fewer reading disabilities and speech defects, and excel in verbal skills such as reading speed, opposites, analogies, sentence completion, story completion, and dissected sentences. Some of these areas deserve closer examination.

❉ *Speech.* Girls learn to speak earlier and increase their vocabulary faster than boys, although the difference is not large. Measurements of early infant vocalizations have been found to predict later intelligence among girls but not among boys, and language skills in general are more highly related to the development of girls' intellectual abilities.

Speech defects occur more rarely among girls than among boys, the difference being most evident in frequency of stuttering and stammering. Various investigators have reported sex ratios among stutterers from as low as 2:1 up to 10:1, and up to 20:1 among stammerers. Whatever the true ratio, the studies are consistent in showing such defects to be much more prevalent among boys.

The reasons for this discrepancy are unknown, although some guesses can be made. Schuell (1946) has noted that the sex ratio among stutterers is similar to that found for school behavior problems and believes there is some connection. She suggests that boys encounter unequal verbal competition with girls during the early school years due to slower maturation and that this in turn results in frustration, insecurity, and inhibitions in speech. Certainly it is evident that speech defects and anxiety are closely related, although the cause-and-effect relationship is not always clear.

❉ *Reading and Vocabulary.* Girls have an initial advantage over boys in reading ability. They generally begin to read earlier and are superior during the early elementary grades. The duration of this superiority, however, is open to question. Some studies have found that sex differences in reading skill disappear by the fourth grade, while others have located sex differences in reading ability into high school. One would expect some decline in sex differences in the higher grades, however, if only because the poorest readers are gradually being left behind to repeat the earlier grades.

The cause of girls' superiority in reading has not been isolated, although several promising suggestions have been offered. One possibility is that it is due primarily to greater word fluency rather than to superior word comprehension, a contention supported by lack of sex differences on vocabulary tests and the fact that most reading tests stress speed. An additional factor, however, is that most early instruction in reading is provided by female teachers, which may give girls an advantage. In Germany, by contrast, the majority of elementary school teachers are men, and boys are superior to girls in reading. Although there is no evidence that female teachers do in fact behave differently toward boys and girls in reading instruction, it is possible that a woman teacher serves as a better learning model for girls than for boys.

✄ *Conclusion.* We may thus conclude that girls are likely to be generally superior in verbal ability and thus more interested in verbally oriented courses and occupations. Their superiority, however, appears to be primarily a function of greater verbal fluency rather than of exceptional mastery of word meanings and concepts.

Although Anastasi (1958) has suggested that the superior verbal ability of girls may be related to sex differences in rate of maturation, it is more likely that the cause lies in social and cultural influences. McCarthy (1953) has suggested two such possibilities: (a) boys engage in more active manipulative games whereas girls' games are likely to be quieter and to involve more conversation; (b) girls have a greater amount of verbal interaction with their mothers than do boys which could be due to stronger identification with the mother on the part of the girl as well as to the mother's own preferences. McCarthy notes that, in her experience, girls with speech defects generally have had or are having problems in their relationships with their mothers. One wishes for more explicit evidence on this point.

✄ ✄ MECHANICAL ABILITY. Men outperform women on most tests of mechanical ability or mechanical comprehension, although such differences do not appear to be innate but instead are due to differential cultural experiences. Sex differences in motor and mechanical behaviors are not evident among preschool children, but as they grow older boys are given more encouragement to develop mechanical interests and, as a result, they come to perform better on tests of mechanical knowledge. Among adults, women can learn mechanical tasks about as well as men, given equal motivation and a slightly longer learning period.

It seems, therefore, that male superiority in mechanical performance is primarily a function of experience and previous learning opportunities rather than of innate superiority in mechanical ability. Studies made during World War II, when many women were pressed into service in traditionally male technical jobs, frequently showed little difference in the performance of male and female workers operating the same machines. On the other hand, there is some doubt that mechanical ability is actually a special ability among women, since it has been found to have a fairly high relationship to intelligence among women.

Most mechanical ability tests, which generally emphasize the comprehension of mechanical principles and familiarity with mechanical devices, have been designed primarily for use with men. When used with women, their reliability and validity are lower and the results are therefore questionable, generally because they are too difficult for most women, whose scores tend to bunch near the bottom. A few attempts have been made to devise mechanical aptitude tests especially for use with women, generally by adapting men's tests using the easier items. Examples include the women's form of the Bennett Test of Mechanical Comprehension and a Women's Mechanical Test for use with Navy women. Neither has achieved popularity in general use.

&& NUMERICAL ABILITY. We are accustomed to thinking of mathematics in its various forms as a male province. Girls are not supposed to like math or to do well in it. We are surprised when we find a girl who violates this assumption, but we allow for individual peculiarities and continue to think of boys as being superior in numerical ability. Is this justified by the evidence?

The answer depends on what age we are talking about. Research with preschool children has shown little sex difference in the development of numerical concepts; boys do not exhibit their expected numerical superiority until some time during elementary school. There is some evidence, in fact, that during the preschool years girls are superior to boys in the development of number concepts, perhaps related in some way to their superiority in verbal ability, although boys are more likely to pay attention to quantitative aspects of a situation. It also appears that, at least during grade school, boys' superiority is primarily evident in numerical reasoning, whereas in computation girls have a slight edge due to their quickness. But as the students progress through the grades the reasoning aspect becomes progressively more important in number skills, giving the boys an increased advantage.

How can sex differences in numerical ability be best explained? Any explanation must take into account the fact that such differences do not become evident until middle childhood. A contributing factor is the increased emphasis with age placed on numerical reasoning, at which boys excel, but it is doubtful if this is the whole story. Attitudes toward math also play an important part in performance in math courses and on math ability tests, and boys are typically given considerably more encouragement than are girls, especially as they move into adolescence and distinctions between masculine and feminine activities become more significant. It is frequently implied to girls, by their parents and even by their teachers, that less is expected of them in mathematics because girls don't understand such things very well. Small wonder that most girls are content to get by with a minimum of effort in math.

It would seem, then, that the key factor in the development of mathematical ability among girls is that of interest. If a girl can be encouraged to become interested in mathematics, she should be able to compete with boys with equal interest. To be sure, individual differences in numerical ability do exist, but they do not seem to be directly related to sex.

❧ ❧ PERCEPTUAL SPEED. Perceptual speed refers to the ability to perceive and respond quickly to small differences in stimuli. It is the ability most highly measured by the so-called "clerical aptitude" tests, which generally test one's speed in recognizing similarities or differences between pairs of names or numbers.

Females show consistent superiority on tests of perceptual speed at all ages. For example, the normative data for the Minnesota Clerical Test show that only about 16 per cent of the male workers in the general population reach or exceed the median of the females, and similar results are evident on other tests of this nature.

❧ ❧ SPATIAL RELATIONS. Sex differences in spatial relations follow the pattern for mechanical ability in several respects. Among preschool children there is no evidence of a sex difference, but by adolescence boys are clearly superior. Spatial relations also seems to be less well defined as a special ability among girls, as is true with mechanical ability. Finally, high spatial relations ability among girls is often associated with inappropriate sex-typed behavior.

❧ ❧ MEMORY. Sex differences in memory seem to depend on what is memorized. For example, girls generally do better than boys in memory tasks involving verbal concepts, while memory tasks involving numerical concepts more often show differences in favor of boys. The explanation would seem to be that sex differences in memory ability are related to abilities and interests in the area being tested.

❧ ❧ ARTISTIC ABILITY. The existence of sex differences in artistic ability is difficult to prove since, with age, differential experience and training in art plays an important role in artistic performance.

In addition, there is some disagreement as to what constitutes artistic ability in the first place; the tests now in use have rather low validity as a result of this confusion.

On most art tests, whether of art ability or simply of art judgment, girls excel consistently once adolescence is reached. This, however, would seem to be primarily a cultural phenomenon rather than an innate sex difference, inasmuch as girls improve during adolescence while boys remain at the same level, and may even decline. In our society, an interest in art during adolescence is considered to be a feminine characteristic and is therefore avoided by most boys.

✄ ✄ MUSICAL ABILITY. The situation concerning musical ability is similar to that for art: there is no agreed-upon performance criterion, which leaves the validity of musical ability tests in doubt. The best known of these are the Seashore tests of musical ability, on which no consistent sex differences have been discovered. With increased age there is a tendency for women to score higher than men, but no difference is found when comparisons are made among men and women who have had comparable amounts of musical training.

✄ ✄ SPATIAL ORIENTATION. Men frequently complain that women have no sense of direction, and research concerning spatial orientation indicates that this contention may be justified. Women perform less well than men when required to determine the position of themselves or of objects in unfamiliar or distorted situations. Witkin and his co-workers (1954, 1962) have found consistent evidence that females are more dependent on the visual field than are males, a sex difference noticeable as early as 8 years of age. Witkin believes that this in turn reflects a tendency for women to be less "psychologically differentiated" than men, which he suggests may be related to the tendency of women to be more dependent in interpersonal situations and to utilize a global field approach in dealing with problems.

✄ ✄ SCIENCE APTITUDE. Whether there is such an entity as "science aptitude" may be open to question. Tests with this label have, however, been devised and thus far have shown no great difference between boys and girls at the elementary level. This suggests that the fact that science courses and science occupations are overwhelmingly populated by males is primarily a function of differential interest and encouragement rather than of superior ability.

❧ ❧ ❧ PROBLEM SOLVING AND CREATIVE THINKING

❧ ❧ PROBLEM SOLVING. In some aspects of problem solving men are definitely superior to women, in others there is little sex difference, but in few if any problem-solving situations do women outperform men. Women do relatively well in situations in which a prescribed pattern of thinking is required, but they fall behind men in problems requiring the applications of new principles or a restructuring of their thinking. Women seem to have greater difficulty in overcoming a "mental set" than do men, which may be related to the finding, described above, that in perceptual situations women are more dependent on the "field" and find it more difficult to "break away" from it.

Poorer performance by women in many problem situations seems to be partly a function of their attitude: they seem to feel that proficiency in problem solving is not "feminine," especially when competing with men. It has been found that the problem-solving ability of women can be improved by restricting the group being studied entirely to women, by using female experimenters, and by reducing the masculine content of the problems. The failure of women to compete successfully with men in problem situations seems to be due primarily to conflicting motives rather than to lack of ability.

❧ ❧ CREATIVITY. Creativity has only recently become the subject of intensive research by psychologists, and this research is still in its early stages. As a result, the relationship of many variables—including sex—to creativity is not yet clear. Some studies have found little sex difference in tests of creative thinking among grade school children, while others show boys to have the advantage.

Among adolescents, boys consistently do better on tests of creativity. It is likely that peer group pressure operates at this level to discourage the person who is "different" and that such pressure is put more effectively on girls. Since most creativity tests are designed to measure unusual responses to standardized situations, girls who have been persuaded to conform would be penalized in their performance on such a test.

As to the development of creativity, girls who show creative interests and behaviors as adults demonstrate these kinds of interests as children. There is apparently some continuity in the development of creativity among girls so that it is possible to predict those who will become creative adults by their interest in imaginary play and artistic expression when young. There is no evidence that creativity among girls is related to masculine behaviors and interests, although creative production among college girls is related more to the intellectual interests and expectations of the girls' fathers than of their mothers.

✄ ✄ ✄ MOTOR ABILITIES. Boys are superior to girls in most kinds of motor behaviors, and this difference is evident even during the preschool years. Sex differences in motor skills are, however, most noticeable during adolescence, when girls definitely fall behind boys in motor development. Boys continue to improve with age in motor skills, but among girls there is little relationship between age and performance once adolescence is reached.

Most of the research with adults has involved college students as subjects, which may not be a representative group. Such studies have shown women to be superior at learning simple motor tasks, perhaps because of their advantage in manual dexterity. There is some evidence that women reach their peak performance in skills such as reaction time and speed of movement at an earlier age than do men, which would be consistent with sex differences in rate of development. The ability of women to learn motor tasks as well as men—or better—suggests that some of the discrepancy found in adolescence is due to differences in motivation and interest rather than to differences in actual ability.

Manual dexterity is one area in which females excel at all stages of development and is first evidenced in the earlier age at which girls learn to dress themselves. Among adolescents and adults, this difference is evident in the norms for various tests of manual dexterity, which show that women consistently outperform men. For this reason, women are preferred for industrial jobs which require fine motor control, such as in the assembling of delicate components of electronic equipment. With the growth of the electronics industry and related areas, it is likely that the demand for women employees will grow apace.

A more varied and confusing picture is presented for sex differences in *reaction time* and *eye-hand coordination*. It is generally agreed that during childhood boys are superior in reaction time. Beyond that point, however, the evidence is inconsistent.

No reliable sex differences have been located for spatial eye-hand coordination and bimanual coordination. Boys, on the other hand, are significantly superior in temporal eye-hand coordination during adolescence. Jones and Seashore (1944) have noted, however, that there is considerable overlap between boys and girls in all of these areas, even those in which there are significant differences, to the extent that there is no justification for discriminating against one sex or the other in a job situation involving any of these abilities.

✷ ✷ ✷ STRENGTH AND VITAL CAPACITY. Also pertinent to job planning are sex differences in strength and vital capacity. The latter is an index of energy output and shows male superiority to grow from an average of about 7 per cent in early childhood to about 35 per cent among adults. It is likely that concomitant differences in energy output are related to the development of sex differences in areas such as play interests, achievement drive, and preferences for active and adventurous pursuits.

Sex differences in strength are not significant until about the age of 14, although boys tend to have the advantage prior to this. From 14 on, however, boys become considerably stronger than girls, until by about the age of 16 there is little overlap between the sexes on tests of strength.

Jones (1947a) argues that such differences are due primarily to biological influences, as evidenced by the close relationship between the amount of gain and onset of menarche among girls. However, motivational differences may also be important. During adolescence boys gain status from physical prowess while such skills do not enhance a girl's feminine image. This is reflected in the greater variability in strength among women as compared with men. Nevertheless, there are important differences in physiological potential between the sexes, and it is therefore unlikely that any amount of physical education and practice would make most women as strong as most men.

Another notable feature is that males show greater stability in bodily functions such as body temperature, basal metabolic rate, acid-base balance of the blood, and blood sugar level. One result is that girls are ten times as likely as boys to suffer from glandular obesity. The fact that these homeostatic mechanisms operate within narrower limits in males could have important implications for personality differences between men and women.

✷ ✷ ✷ CONCLUSION. The most consistent thread running through this chapter is the lack of proof that sex differences in abilities have an innate, sex-linked basis, except for those which are directly tied to physical characteristics. In nearly all other cases, those differences which do exist can be related to differential cultural influences. This corresponds to the conclusions drawn by Flanagan and his co-workers (1964, p. 3-3) from the Project Talent study of students in nearly one thousand high schools: "When very large differences occur between scores of boys and girls, they almost always reflect great differences between the sexes in amount of interest." This means that persons analyzing girls' abilities or working with girls in any situation must be very cautious about drawing simplistic conclusions based on sex alone.

The Female Personality

"THE TROUBLE WITH MOST WOMEN," SAID THE MAN, "IS THAT THEY TAKE THINGS TOO PERSONALLY."
"THAT'S NOT TRUE," REPLIED THE WOMAN. "*I* DON'T."

WOMEN ARE THE EQUAL OF MEN, but this doesn't mean that they are the same. As we saw in the previous chapter, men and women don't differ greatly in abilities, other than in physical abilities. The key, then, to understanding women lies in their interests and personality traits. To be sure, women differ among themselves a great deal in personality, but some differences exist between men and women which are typical and which have important implications for the educational and vocational planning of girls.

✄ ✄ ✄ INTERESTS. In our society males and females tend to develop divergent interests, although the degree of difference seems to be diminishing with succeeding generations. No attempt will be made here to list all of the areas in which the interests of boys and girls differ. Instead, consideration will be given to a few areas which are especially significant in the understanding of true differences between men and women and which have important implications for the educational and vocational planning of girls.

The evidence is consistent that men tend to be more interested in scientific, mechanical, political, computational, and vigorous activities, while women prefer literary, musical, artistic, social service, and sedentary activities. Differences in physical activity are especially notable in adolescence, when girls' interest drops sharply while boys' interest remains high. Apparently physical activity is negatively related to femininity in our society.

❧ ❧ INTEREST AREAS

❧ *Reading.* A decided sex difference in reading preferences begins to be evident in the early stages of reading development. Girls typically read more books, especially more fiction and more "good" literature. Boys read more comic books in junior high and early high school, and there are consistent differences in the kinds of comic books preferred. In selecting books, girls generally prefer fiction, biographies, and stories about real people; boys prefer adventure stories, mysteries, and sports stories. During adolescence, special magazines are available for boys and girls, and their contents reflect the typical sex differences in interests at that stage. Boys' magazines emphasize adventure and sports stories, along with articles concerning outdoor and sporting activities as well as mechanical features. Girls' magazines focus on glamour, stories about people, clothes and make-up, and social activities. Since reading is a solitary activity and therefore subject to less social pressure than are most other kinds of interests, the presence of marked reading preferences seems more likely to reflect "true" interests than do preferences in other areas.

❧ *Academic Preferences.* At least by junior high, if not before, sex differences in preferences for academic subjects become evident: boys prefer science, mathematics, history, and social studies, while girls prefer English, commercial subjects, and languages. Such differences are congruent with sex differences in abilities, as described in the previous chapter. But the question still remains: Are these preferences due to innate differences in abilities, or are the ability differences due in part to differential academic experiences produced by culturally conditioned subject-matter preferences? At the moment no final answer is available, although cultural influences can account for some, if not all, of these findings.

❧ ❧ DEVELOPMENT OF INTERESTS. Sex differences in interests become evident between the ages of 6 and 12, so that by the end of elementary school, sex differences are quite noticeable and are taken for granted. These persist through adolescence, although the tendency of psychologists to emphasize the amount of difference between the sexes during this period may have obscured the considerable similarity which also exists. Even during adolescence, the period during which sex differences in interests are greatest, boys and girls

have many interests in common; and the differences which do exist
are generally a matter of degree rather than of an all-or-none
nature.

As adults, men and women gradually develop interests which
are more alike, so that by the later years it is rather difficult to
locate consistent sex differences. This does not mean, however,
that men and women move at an equal rate toward some central
communality. Rather, what seems to happen is that men's interests
become more feminine. It is not unusual, for example, to read of
a middle-aged man taking first prize in a cooking contest, or to find
older men taking up knitting or crocheting.

Several possible explanations for this trend suggest themselves.
Perhaps older men feel less need to promote a highly "masculine"
image and can allow themselves to develop interests in nonmascu-
line activities. But the most important factor in this change would
appear to be the declining physical abilities and energies of men as
they grow older and find themselves less able to engage in active
pursuits and consequently less able to draw satisfactions from them.
They often, therefore, turn to less strenuous pastimes, which may be
suggested by the interests of their wives.

The development of interests appears to be highly related to
sex-role development, as described in a previous chapter. Boys and
girls develop different interest patterns from an early age, often
reflecting perceptions which boys and girls have of their appropriate roles in our society.

The development of appropriate sex-typed interests is apparently more crucial for boys than for girls, in terms of their influence
on later development. The sexual adjustment of adult males, for
example, is related to the development of appropriate sex-role
interests in childhood, but this seems less significant for women.

Among girls, on the other hand, the development of certain
interest patterns is related to the eventual decision to concentrate
on a career or on a family role as an adult, although these patterns
do not differentiate until high school.

Girls tend to develop a stable and mature interest pattern
sooner than do boys. Many girls have established an interest pattern by the time they enter high school, the most likely shift from
then on being toward greater social service interests.

Most of the research on interests has dealt with convenient
categories of interests. This approach, however, may be insufficient
in that it does not indicate the operation of more basic interest
clusters which underlie the typical interest patterns. The technique
of factor analysis has been applied by a few investigators in attempts to locate these "basic" clusters. In general, the results suggest that women have the same basic interest clusters as do men,

with the addition of a cluster which might be called "antimascu-
line" or "noncareer" interest. The influence of the latter category
becomes a problem when interests are used as a basis for vocational
planning, as will be discussed in some detail later.

❧ ❧ RELATED VARIABLES

❧ *Abilities.* The development of interests is related to strengths
and weaknesses in abilities among boys but not among girls, who
seem more inclined to base their interests on role expectations.
This may in turn explain why sex differences in interests are
typically greater than are sex differences in abilities.

The influence of role expectations is less strong among persons
of high intelligence. The scholastic interests of boys are fairly similar, regardless of intellectual level, but the academic interests of
girls vary considerably from one level to another. Activity interests,
on the other hand, are strongly differentiated by sex, regardless of
ability level, until well into adulthood.

❧ *Social Class.* Interests vary to some extent according to social
class, although such differences are generally not striking. The
variation which occurs can be attributed primarily to limitations in
finances and environmental opportunities on the part of lower-class
girls.

❧ *Family Composition.* The size and composition of the family
may have important effects on the development of interests of the
individual members. Much of this influence operates through the
transmission of interests from parent to child and from older to
younger children. But more subtle influences are also in operation,
such as the sex of the child's siblings. For example, girls with older
brothers have been found to show higher interest in economic activities than do other girls, and other influences of a similar nature
will doubtless be located by further research.

❧ ❧ ❧ PERSONALITY AND ADJUSTMENT.

In our society,
the most consistent differences between males and females occur in
personality characteristics and emotional adjustment. Girls are
more emotional than boys at all ages—i.e., they report more worries,
more fears, and have more nervous habits—whereas boys are more
likely to be behavior problems. Even as early as the preschool
years, girls show more affection, while boys are more hostile and
aggressive, and these patterns persist into adulthood.

The extent to which personality characteristics remain stable
during development has been investigated by Kagan and Moss

(1960), utilizing longitudinal records. Passive and dependent behaviors, which were the focus of the study, were found to be stable for females between childhood and adulthood but were not stable for males. The authors (Kagan and Moss, 1960, p. 581) concluded that ". . . females who were passive as children were apt to accept their dependent behavior in adulthood and show minimal anxiety over their dependent motives," which seems reasonable in light of the fact that in our society passivity and dependency are much more acceptable characteristics for females than for males.

❧ ❧ EMOTIONAL STABILITY. Although women seem consistently to display more overt emotional instability than do men, there is other evidence which suggests that men may simply find other outlets for their tensions. For example, alcoholism is much more prevalent among men. Keller (1958) has estimated that, of 5 million established alcoholics in the United States, 5 out of 6 are men. However, in recent years the frequency of alcoholism among women has been increasing and they may eventually equal males in this dubious achievement.

Women alcoholics may differ from males in quality as well as quantity. Alcoholism among women seems to be more closely related to other personality difficulties or to strong emotional stress, and the onset of the problem can be more readily traced to a highly emotional event than is the case among men.

Another kind of evidence of instability is suicide attempts, both successful and unsuccessful. According to Hirsh (1959), women are more likely than men to attempt suicide but are less likely to succeed. His data show that males are four times as likely as females to commit suicide in the United States; this ratio varies from 5:1 in Norway to slightly more than even in Japan. Women typically use less lethal suicide methods and are therefore less likely to be successful. Female suicide rates are higher in countries in which the status of women is inferior to that of men, such as in the Far East.

Many suicide attempts are, of course, not meant to succeed but are designed primarily to call the attention of others to the individual's problems or to manipulate another person. This is especially true among adolescents and probably explains why the sex ratio of suicide attempts is 6:1 in favor of girls during this period.

A further source of evidence concerning emotional instability is frequency of psychosomatic illnesses. Such illnesses—e.g., hypertension and ulcers—are more commonly found among men, although the historical trend is peculiar. Prior to about 1900, ulcers occurred more frequently among women, but 10 years later the incidence of ulcers in both sexes was about equal. Since then ulcers have become increasingly a male disorder, to the point that in 1940 approximately four times as many men as women were afflicted with this ailment. One conclusion that might be drawn is that women have developed better reactions to stress than have men during the past half-century. Even if this is not the explanation, the dramatic shift in the incidence of this disorder strongly argues that the current tendency of men to suffer from ulcers with considerably greater frequency than women is not due to a sex-linked physiological weakness. It is possible, however, that a greater amount of emotional stress and anxiety is necessary to produce ulcers among females.

It can therefore be concluded that the greater degree of emotional instability displayed by girls and women is probably not indicative of any basic sex difference but is instead due to a greater acceptability of this behavior on the part of women. Men can be emotionally aroused, too, but they suppress it and it comes out in other ways. As Montagu (1953) has suggested, women's ability to express their feelings is probably a favorable characteristic since it makes them better able to withstand emotional pressure; in his words, women are better "shock absorbers" than men.

❧ ❧ PERSONALITY CHARACTERISTICS

❧ *Anxiety and Stress Reactions.* At all ages, girls exhibit more anxiety than boys, both on personality inventories and in real-life situations. Under stress, their performance is more apt to deteriorate, especially in achievement-oriented situations. On the other hand, they sometimes withstand prolonged stress better than do men. Montagu (1953), for example, has noted that in Britain during the World War II bombings women were less subject to shock, hysteria, and neurotic reactions than were men.

Any attempt to explain these contradictions must take several factors into consideration. For one thing, it is more acceptable for women to lose emotional control under stress; the "helpless female" is still a rewarding role for many women to play. Men, on the other hand, are expected to "rise to the occasion" and respond adequately to emergencies. In addition, it is likely that in most stress situations the man will feel more responsible and therefore feel it more necessary to remain calm. Finally, the specific situation may have a great deal to do with the reaction; it may be fallacious to try to consider stress reactions as a unitary concept. We must therefore conclude that no outstanding sex differences are observed in reactions to stress and that those which do occur may be influenced to a large extent by social expectations.

❧ *Dependency.* A number of important observations concerning dependency needs and behavior can be made from the Fels longitudinal research reported by Kagan and Moss (1962). Girls are consistently rewarded for dependency behavior while independence is stressed more for boys, but the degree of importance placed on it varies from one developmental stage to another. Girls who as children are dependent on female adults tend to transfer their dependence to their husbands when they grow up, perhaps as a means of gaining a relationship with a father-figure which was missing during their childhood. On the other hand, girls who as children and adolescents are independent of their families tend to maintain this independence into adulthood; their dependency needs are satisfied by relationships with their friends. The authors also note that girls with well-educated fathers tend to avoid dependency relationships with men, perhaps because they are rejecting the traditional female role.

In any case, dependency and passivity are much more stable among women than among men. A deviation from this pattern is likely to be characteristic only of women who are trying to avoid the typical female role in this as well as in other ways.

❧ *Aggression and Dominance.* It is well established that boys exhibit more aggressive behaviors at all stages of development than do girls, although this distinction seems to be due primarily to social expectations. More pressures are put on boys, but they are also allowed more freedom to express their aggressions openly, resulting in aggressive behavior becoming an important part of the masculine role in our society. Sears (1965), however, has noted that there is also a considerable overlap between boys and girls in aggressive behaviors, such that aggression is not a reliable criterion of an individual's achievement of the appropriate sex role.

The antecedents of sex differences in aggressive behavior are not yet fully understood. The bulk of the evidence points to a differential treatment of sons and daughters by parents as a precipitating factor, although the extensive study of child-raising practices by Sears and his co-workers (1957) failed to confirm this. However, the latter group concede that their analysis of the children's behavior was based primarily on reports of the mothers, who may have unconsciously made allowances for sex differences in their reporting.

On the basis of the Fels studies, Kagan and Moss (1962, p. 100) suggest that sex differences in aggression may be due to greater punishment and disapproval by adults of the preschool aggression of girls:

The resulting conflict is likely to produce inhibition of aggressive behavior in order to attenuate the anxiety over alienation from the

social environment as well as a discrepancy between a girl's behavior
and her schema of the ideal female personality.

We must bear in mind that, as in the case of anxiety, we are
speaking here of sex differences in aggressive *behaviors*. The fact
that boys express such behavior more frequently does not necessarily mean that they have more aggressive and hostile feelings. Sears
(1961) has reported that when aggression is subdivided into various
kinds, the pattern of sex differences becomes more complicated.
Although boys continue to score higher than girls on *antisocial aggression*—which is the concept most people have of aggression
in general—girls score higher on *prosocial aggression,* as measured by insistence on strong limits and severe punishments, and on
aggression anxiety (fear of aggression). Sears also found that children of both sexes who are punished when young for being aggressive tend to show low antisocial aggression when older, but that
girls differ from boys in that (a) girls who are punished when young
for being aggressive show high prosocial aggression when older, and
(b) girls who show a high degree of aggression when young exhibit
high aggression anxiety when older. Apparently the aggression of
boys and girls becomes channeled into different outlets, with that of
the girls becoming expressed either as fear of aggression from
others—girls are generally more fearful—or as insistence on strong
penalties for misbehavior or misconduct, a socially acceptable
outlet.

Similar patterns are evident in dominance behavior. Boys tend
to be more domineering and authoritarian, while girls are more
docile and are more easily persuaded to change their opinions and
their goals. In many cases, of course, women do dominate others,
even men, but this is usually accomplished in an indirect way. The
chances are that most women would feel uncomfortable displaying
openly aggressive or dominant behavior, since this is in direct
contradiction to the accepted feminine role.

Introversion-Extraversion. This personality dimension, originally proposed by Jung, has become an important staple of popular
discussions of personality characteristics. Typing people is a common pastime and the dimension of introversion-extraversion, con-
verted to a dichotomy, has proved popular. It has also occasionally
been the subject of serious investigation. Although the tendency
has been to find women more introverted than men, there appears
to be a considerable amount of variation within each sex, so that it
is misleading to think of either of these characteristics as descriptive
primarily of one sex or the other.

❧ *Affection.* Just as women seem to express themselves more openly in most areas of emotion, with the exception of aggression and hostility, they are apparently freer to express positive feelings toward other persons. Girls are more affectionate than boys, both with members of the same and of the opposite sex. This is encouraged by our society, which allows a girl to display more openly her affection, especially physical affection, for her parents than it allows her brother. Similarly, a certain amount of physical display of affection is permissible between grown women, while adult men are allowed very little.

One result seems to be that a need for affection is more acceptable for girls than for boys, since it is evident that it is approved by society. Therefore a girl who is "starved for affection" can freely acknowledge this need and her frustration at not having it satisfied, while a boy in the same circumstance would probably sublimate it in some way.

❧ *Self-confidence.* In one sense, women are less self-confident than men. They tend to see themselves as less adequate and less capable than men, although there is no evidence that they feel badly as a result. Since in our society much more is expected of males than of females in the way of achievements, it may be perfectly acceptable for women to have less confidence in themselves. And, in fact, despite their lower degree of self-confidence, women are generally more self-accepting than men.

Since women are not expected to set high goals and to perform outstanding achievements, it is not surprising to find that women generally set lower goals than men and are thus less apt to fall frustratingly short of them. Sumner and Johnson (1949, pp. 489–90), in a study involving goal-setting behavior by college students, reported the following sex difference:

The women, tending conspicuously to lower discrepancies and frequently to underevaluations, appear more restrained, timorous, and reality-oriented than the men who with higher discrepancies and conspicuous overevaluation exhibit throughout a greater tendency to expansiveness, daringness, and irreality.

This doesn't entirely settle the question of sex differences in self-confidence, since one's self-confidence depends on how he perceives himself in relation to his goals. In individual cases a girl may see herself as being inadequate to achieve her goals and her self-confidence may be undermined. But for the most part the goals which girls set are not as high as those of boys and are thus not as apt to cause the girls to seriously question their adequacy as persons.

✤ *Masculinity-Femininity.* The concept of "masculinity-femininity," as applied to individuals, has long been of interest to the general public. A common way of describing persons is to say that certain attributes are "characteristic" of one sex or the other. Thus we may say of an aggressive, dominant female that she is "masculine" in her behavior, and a man who designs women's clothes might be said to have "feminine" interests. These labels are typically derived from interests and personality characteristics.

Psychologists have also studied the dimension of masculinity-femininity as a promising variable in the constant search for better ways to describe and understand human behavior. Many personality and interest inventories include an "M-F" scale as one of the relevant dimensions along which individuals can be compared, and research utilizing such instruments has been influential in shaping current concepts of differences between the sexes. It is therefore important to consider what these scales are actually measuring.

A pioneering study of masculinity-femininity, which strongly influenced subsequent work, was conducted by Terman and Miles and reported in 1936 in their book, *Sex and Personality.* It describes the construction of an instrument called the Attitude-Interest Analysis, which was so named to disguise its real purpose from the persons to whom it was administered. It was composed of items to which men and women typically gave different responses and included several parts: word association, inkblot association, information, emotional and ethical attitudes, interests, opinions, and "introvertive responses." The items were presented in a multiple-choice form, each response being scored "plus" or "minus" according to whether it had been found to be a response typical of men or of women. Significant sex differences were found between the scores of men and women at all ages beginning with adolescence, from which Terman and Miles concluded that males and females could be differentiated distinctly on the basis of a wide variety of interest and personality characteristics.

The Terman-Miles M-F Test, as it has come to be known, is no longer used extensively, either for diagnosis or for research. It is of interest primarily because of the attention which it focused on the dimension of masculinity-femininity as a variable to be included in the study of human behavior. Subsequent measures of masculinity-femininity owe their construction in large part to the work of Terman and Miles. The basis and philosophy of later tests are similar to theirs, and in some cases many of the items themselves are the same. Masculinity-femininity scales are frequently included on personality and interest inventories, and special M-F scales have been developed for research purposes.

Scores on M-F tests seem to be highly related to certain aspects of behavior and unrelated to others. Subsequent investigations have confirmed Terman and Miles' (1936) conclusion that there is little relationship between M-F scores and physical characteristics within either sex. On the other hand, education and occupation do have some influence, especially among women, the more intelligent and better educated appearing more "masculine" on such measures. In the research with Terman's gifted group, little difference was found between the gifted boys and the boys in the control group on the Terman-Miles test during adolescence and early adulthood, but the gifted girls were more "masculine" than the girls in the control group.

The only special ability which has been found to be related to masculinity-femininity is mechanical ability. The relationship is close enough that tests of mechanical ability may be useful as disguised measures of masculinity (as defined by interests), at least among men.

Despite the widespread use of M-F tests, as incorporated in personality and interest measures, many psychologists question their validity and usefulness. One problem concerns the dichotomization of characteristics into either "masculine" or "feminine" categories. It is true that the scales are presented as a continuum rather than as dichotomies, and the authors are quick to stress that no individual can necessarily be classified on one side or the other of some arbitrary line dividing masculine and feminine persons. Yet the term "masculinity-femininity" implies a dichotomy, and the scoring is generally based on whether men or women typically give a certain response to a certain item. In this regard, most psychologists would probably support the point of view expressed by Super and Dunlap (1950, p. 102):

Masculinity and femininity are scaled traits rather than dichotomies; some men are rather feminine, and some women are rather masculine, in their interests. Since interests are at least to some extent culturally developed, this may be a reflection of the fact that women are the carriers of culture rather than a proof that men who like art, literature, or people are effeminate; they may have been more exposed to culture and to human values than most men. In other words, for a man to obtain a "feminine" score on an M-F scale indicates very little about his essential "masculinity."

Is masculinity-femininity a true dimension along which human characteristics can be ordered? The evidence suggests otherwise.

There are probably at least two dimensions involved, and perhaps several. Anastasi (1958) points out that differences on the Terman-Miles M-F test are quite specific, so that a total M-F score may be obtained in many different ways. For example, engineers and high school boys both obtain high masculine scores, but their responses to individual items follow different patterns.

Klein (1950) has argued against the validity of tests of masculinity-femininity on the grounds that concepts of masculine and feminine behavior are tied closely to sex stereotypes in our society. As she notes, the terms "masculine" and "feminine" do not mean "of male or female sex" but instead are used to describe tone qualities. Everyone has both kinds of characteristics, and it is thus misleading to classify personality traits according to sex. There may be no relevance to the fact that one kind of characteristic is more likely to be displayed by men than by women, or vice versa. The labels "masculine" and "feminine" are thus of little value and perhaps should therefore be discarded in psychological measurement in favor of less value-loaded terms. On the other hand, evidence that M-F scales differentiate men from women about equally well in a variety of different cultures suggests that a rather basic distinction is being measured, although this does not necessarily invalidate the cultural stereotype argument.

The other major criticism of M-F scales is that the lack of consistency among the items makes the interpretation of results very difficult. Several kinds of evidence attest to the complexity of such measures. One approach has been to analyze the kinds of items which make up M-F tests. From such an analysis, Nichols (1962) concluded that they could be categorized into three types: (a) subtle items—those which actually differentiate between men and women but which most people would not expect to do so; (b) stereotype items—those which most people think would differentiate but which actually don't; and (c) obvious items—those which are thought to differentiate and actually do. Most M-F scales contain all three kinds of items, calling into question the meaning of their scores.

A second approach has been the intercorrelation of scores among various M-F scales. In general these correlations are far from impressive, suggesting that the scales are not tapping entirely the same characteristics. Webster (1956) carried this approach one step further in the Vassar studies, factor analyzing the results from several M-F scales. He located three "femininity" factors: (a) "conventionality"—a preference for conventionally feminine roles and interests; (b) "passivity"—a lack of aggressiveness, dominance, and manipulativeness; and (c) "feminine sensitivity"—including emotionality, fantasy, introspection, neurotic trends, and aesthetic interests.

Perhaps further research using factor analysis will provide more information as to just what M-F scales are actually measuring. In the meantime, we must conclude that the concept of masculinity-femininity has not proven to be a valid or useful addition to the measurement of personality or interests. M-F scales are inconsistent; there is little agreement as to what a specific score means; and there is some question as to whether only one dimension is involved. In addition, the dichotomous nature of the term "masculinity-femininity" serves to perpetuate a stereotype concerning differences between men and women which has long since been proven psychologically unsound.

❧ ❧ BEHAVIOR PROBLEMS. The child who is a disciplinary problem in school is often considered to be maladjusted. Teachers have been encouraged to view behavior problems among their students as symptoms of emotional difficulty; the tendency therefore is to equate the frequency with which a child creates a disturbance in the classroom with his degree of emotional instability. On this basis, teachers are inclined to conclude that boys are less stable, since by far the majority of those pupils referred by teachers as learning and/or behavior problems are boys.

A number of factors contribute to this. One is the difference between boys and girls in rate of development, which causes boys to fall behind girls and to meet with more frustration in school. A second influence is the greater degree of open aggression which is permitted and expected from boys. Boys are given more freedom and encouragement to act out their feelings in many situations, and it should not be surprising that they have greater difficulty than girls in curbing these impulses in the classroom.

In addition, the biases of the teacher may play an important part in determining which students are singled out as "problems." During the early grades most teachers are women who expect girls to be nice and ladylike and boys to be ruffians. Since people tend to perceive what goes on around them in such a way as to reinforce their expectations, it is not surprising that these teachers tend to observe the boys in their classes as being greater sources of difficulty. Girls' misbehavior is passed off as less serious or, if it persists, the girl is assumed to be a special case worthy of concentrated study. Eventually the children get the idea. Boys are expected to misbehave, so they do. Girls are rewarded for good deportment, so they conform. This pattern becomes accentuated as they progress through school.

Not only are boys, in subtle ways, almost encouraged to misbehave in school, but they are concomitantly encouraged to dislike school. Misbehavior represents some sort of rebellion, even though relatively minor and brief at first, but as it continues to be expected, and in some ways encouraged, it can develop into a real antagonism toward school. But, after all, aren't boys supposed to dislike school? This is part of our concept of the "real boy," at least among adolescents. Perhaps this conception is changing, as society provides greater rewards for intellectual accomplishments. Yet the inertia of tradition is still to be overcome if both boys and girls are to learn to respect and desire an education.

❧ *Juvenile Delinquency.* The most discussed area of behavior problems is undoubtedly that which is termed "juvenile delinquency." In brief, "juvenile delinquents" are adolescents who have been in difficulty with the law and who are too young to be classified as adult criminals. The upper age limit varies, but in most states it falls somewhere between sixteen and eighteen. Delinquents are usually dealt with by juvenile courts, in which a greater emphasis is put on rehabilitation as opposed to punishment than would normally be the case with adult criminals.

Data concerning juvenile delinquency are difficult to interpret since official information is based on police and court records, which requires that a charge be filed against the youngster, either on the complaint of the police or a private citizen. In either case, the probability is high that a young person who commits an offense may not actually be charged with it; he will be "let off" on the promise that he will behave in the future. The likelihood that a person who commits such an offense will actually be formally charged thus depends on several variables, among these being his or her socioeconomic status in the community, father's occupation and influence, and sex.

One of the most consistent findings concerning juvenile delinquents is that about three-fourths are boys. To some extent, this reflects a real sex difference in frequency of committing antisocial acts. Boys tend to display more open aggression and to be less well supervised. On the other hand, most experts would agree that the typical data tend to overestimate the sex difference, since girls are less likely to be charged with an offense than are boys. The mores of our society are such that we tend to deal more leniently with girls who have committed antisocial acts than we do with boys. Boys are supposed to be able to take care of themselves and to take their punishment "like a man," while girls need protection and guidance.

The same kind of sex difference is also evident among adult criminals, with an even greater proportion of men than women being sent to prison; the ratios are reported to be as high as 25:1.

Not only does the frequency of reported delinquent acts vary considerably for boys and girls, but the characteristics of the delinquent behavior itself show decided sex differences which tend to increase with age. Boys are generally charged with offenses against property or persons, such as assault or stealing, while girls are more likely to be charged with sex offenses or incorrigibility. By the same token, boys are more likely to be charged by the police and girls by their parents.

Sex differences are also evident in background factors related to delinquency, which show that delinquency is not the same phenomenon for girls as it is for boys. Female delinquents are more likely to come from broken homes and to have poorer peer relationships and school attendance. The boys are likely to be of average intelligence and socioeconomic status, while the girls are more variable in these respects. These findings support Nye's (1958) contention that delinquent behavior is more closely related to family variables among girls than among boys, which he believes is to be expected since girls are generally more involved with their families.

❧ ❧ ❧ ATTITUDES AND VALUES

❧ ❧ ATTITUDES. Attitudes may be considered as an aspect of personality, but they also represent an important area of human development in their own right and have been the subject of a considerable amount of research concerning sex differences. Studies of high school and college students agree that women are more conservative than men, more inner-directed, and more religious, while men are more ethnocentric. No consistent differences in authoritarianism have been found.

An area in which sex differences stand out is attitudes toward school: girls consistently express a more favorable attitude toward school and teachers than do boys. This is probably due to several factors: girls do better in school and thus have more pleasant experiences there; they are given less freedom to express rebellion against school; and they are generally more docile and accepting of adult-controlled situations.

Two factors seem to be especially important in influencing the development of sex differences in attitudes. One of these is that girls, in general, are more interested in and sensitive to other people. As a result, girls tend to develop stronger, more rigid attitudes toward people. For example, Kuhlen (1960) has noted that adolescent girls make greater class and race distinctions than do boys, primarily because girls are simply more aware of such differences in people. Girls also tend to gain greater security from close personal relationships, which implies the existence of in-groups and out-groups, than do boys.

Intelligence also influences the development of attitudes, but it is not clear how it interacts with sex in this process. The research with Terman's gifted group suggests that, among highly intelligent persons, sex differences in political attitudes tend to be reduced. On the other hand, greater differences between men and women are found at the upper levels of intelligence in attitudes such as dogmatism. Apparently the relationship between sex and intelligence in the development of attitudes is a complex one, deserving of further study.

✄ ✄ VALUES. Values are generally less specific than attitudes and tend to last longer, but they are similar to attitudes in having a strong emotional basis. For the most part, men tend to put greater emphasis on values involving intellectual accomplishments and the attainment of power, while women tend to emphasize the more humanistic and aesthetic areas. There is, however, considerable overlap, so that it is not possible to consider any of these areas solely the province of one sex or the other.

✄ ✄ CHARACTER TRAITS. Sex differences in character traits are difficult to locate, since those behaviors related to a given trait may vary widely from one situation to another. Some generalizations may, however, be drawn from the research. First of all, the traditionally naïve, honest, morally pure girl is atypical. Girls have been shown to behave as dishonestly as boys, depending on the circumstances.

The second important conclusion is that the morality of girls depends more on the external situation and on the kind of test involved than does that of boys. Girls are more sensitive to what others think and tend to take less responsibility for their own actions.

Burton (1963, pp. 497–98) has suggested that girls typically appear more honest on verbal tests of honesty because such tests are more relevant for girls and therefore they are more inclined to falsify their responses:

It is . . . possible that the cognitive measures of acceptance of the moral code are mainly addressed to the areas of morality which are salient to girls who therefore are more motivated than boys to distort their responses. If this were so, girls would tend to appear more moral than boys on such tests which are not measuring lying but only cognitive acceptance of morality.

We must thus conclude that there are no major sex differences in moral behavior, and that such differences as have been observed are highly dependent on the specific situation involved and the kind of measurement employed.

❧ ❧ ❧ MOTIVATION. In accordance with differences in life patterns and in personality characteristics previously described, men and women also exhibit important differences in motives, needs, and life goals. In general, men are more strongly motivated by needs for achievement and sexual gratification, while women have stronger needs for emotional support from others, for love, and for security. Women also display stronger religious needs but feel more comfortable and less anxious concerning their religion than do men.

Sex differences in motivation are also evident in *life goals,* especially among young adults. Young men are motivated primarily by the desire to get ahead in their occupation, whereas young women, if unmarried, are primarily concerned with getting married and having children. This difference is especially evident when rural and urban groups are compared. Urban men have higher aspirations in both the educational and occupational areas than do rural men. Urban women also have higher educational aspirations than do rural girls, but there is no difference between them in occupational aspirations.

❧ ❧ ACHIEVEMENT NEED. The most heavily researched area of motivation in recent years has been that of achievement, and the results demonstrate that achievement motivation is a different phenomenon among girls than among boys. Among boys, achievement needs are closely related to a desire for power and status, but among girls such needs are related primarily to social acceptability. This means, in effect, that girls will strive to achieve if others expect it of them, but left to themselves will not generate achievement motivation from within.

Achievement motivation among girls is also peculiar in that girls who do demonstrate high achievement motivation tend to channel it into the "acceptable" female outlets—marriage and a family. This may have unfortunate outcomes, in that these women may seek outlets for their achievement needs through the accomplishments of their husbands and children. It would seem healthier for all concerned if women with fairly strong needs for achievement were encouraged to satisfy these needs more directly through their own accomplishments, but such behavior might run afoul of social stereotypes. In order to accomplish things for herself, a woman must not only have a strong achievement need but also a high degree of individuality.

This means that those girls who develop high achievement motivation, especially in intellectual areas, also tend to identify less with the traditional female sex role. In contrast to high-achieving men, these girls are more likely to come from wealthier homes and to have been at odds with their mothers during childhood. Nevertheless, their mothers somehow served as intellectual role models for the girls as they became older, and these girls thus did not slip into the traditional female pattern.

✣ ✣ ✣ SOCIALITY

✣ ✣ INTEREST IN PEOPLE. At all ages, girls are more socially oriented than are boys. This is evident in many areas: girls are more concerned about the welfare of other children, they play more social games, they are more interested in books about people, they are more interested in occupations dealing with people, they are more concerned about appearance and manners, they ask more questions about social relations, and they are more often jealous. Women are also better able to associate names with faces than are men, primarily because they pay more attention to such matters.

The reasons for this developmental difference are not fully established. Anastasi (1958) has suggested that it may be partly due to the girls' acceleration in language development, which enables them to communicate more easily with other people. But social pressures also probably enter in: girls are expected to be more sensitive to other people and to enter into interpersonal relationships with less inhibition.

Although girls are consistently more socially oriented, this interest in people is not necessarily translated into greater social activity. Sex differences in social activity are less consistent, and at some stages of development boys are actually more socially active than are girls.

Throughout development girls exhibit more interest in people, a difference evident as early as the age of 2, and consistently observed among nursery school children. As children grow older, sex-role influences begin to enter in, especially among boys, while girls are more interested in personal relationships and are less concerned with roles.

There is no firm explanation for this divergence. One possibility is that at this stage girls feel more secure in their sex role and therefore are freer to devote their attention to specific interpersonal relationships. An alternative hypothesis, however, is that girls develop a tendency to react to others rather than acting as individuals. Thus their behavior becomes "tuned" to what others expect, and their concern with understanding the needs and motives of others— especially of males—is greater. This is particularly evident in adolescence, when girls are more concerned with understanding boys than with understanding themselves. Calderwood (1963, p. 494) comments from his observations:

Much of the girls' discussion indicated their general attitude toward males to be one of manipulation. Much thought was given to how to get a boy to ask for a date, how to manage circumstances so that a boy will be required to act in a certain manner, or teaming up with Mother to "handle" Dad in difficult situations.

⚘ ⚘ SOCIAL ACTIVITY. Girls may well have greater social interest than boys, but social interest is not necessarily manifested in social activity. During childhood, girls are likely to be more socially active than boys, having more social contacts than boys of the same age. But in adolescence the situation is reversed, and boys are generally more socially active. Several factors seem to contribute to this change. For one thing, boys have more freedom to make and to maintain social contacts. They are less restricted, they can go more places alone or with a group of boys, and they can stay out later. In addition, heterosexual social activities are generally initiated by the boy. A girl may desire more social activity, but for many events she has to wait to be asked. A boy who is not dating, on the other hand, is probably doing so by his own choice.

Preadolescent boys typically have close-knit, well-organized groups, of which the gang is the most common example. Among girls of the same developmental status, such groups are less common. The girls' groups which do exist tend to be less well organized and to engage in fewer activities outside of parental supervision. One reason, presumably, is that girls are more closely supervised by their parents. In addition, girls tend to be more conforming and are less likely to engage in activities which are primarily "anti-adult."

⚘ ⚘ SOCIAL ACCEPTABILITY. In adolescence, both boys and girls are very much concerned with social acceptability (popularity), but it is sometimes difficult to determine just why one person is popular and another isn't. This is especially true among girls. Among boys, the criteria of acceptability are reasonably definite and consistent, generally based on athletic skill. This is perhaps unfair to those boys who don't possess much skill in this area, but at least they know where they stand in the group.

Girls, on the other hand, encounter a more complicated situation, inasmuch as the criteria of social acceptability change as they move through childhood. With increasing age, attractiveness and demure friendliness remain high as criteria for popularity, but submissiveness, docility, and timidity decline in value. At the fifth-grade level, a tomboy is just as acceptable as a "lady," but the acceptability of the tomboy decreases during adolescence.

It also seems that the commonly held notion that girls who get good grades in school are less popular has some truth in it, as far as dating acceptability is concerned, although cause-and-effect relationships are hard to determine.

❧ ❧ LEADERSHIP. Another characteristic of social development in adolescence is the emergence of leaders, and leaders within boys' groups are not like leaders among girls. Male leaders more often are seen by the rest of the boys as part of the group, or as pals, while the girls tend to perceive their leaders as different from the group, distant, and aloof. This makes sense when we recall that the kind of personality characteristics which are required to be a leader, such as dominance, are considered to be "masculine" traits. The girl who develops these traits probably does so at the expense of close relationships with other girls, with whom she now has less in common. In other words, a leader, whether male or female, is not "feminine."

❧ ❧ CONFORMITY. Women are also more susceptible to the influence of others in a social situation, as would be expected in view of their greater tendency toward conformity. They are less likely to rely on their own judgment when others disagree with them, although there are wide variations in this respect among women, as many husbands can testify.

It seems evident that the areas discussed in this chapter represent the greatest differences between men and women in our society. As opportunities for women become more nearly equal to those of men, many of these differences will probably diminish, but in the meantime they must be taken into consideration by those helping girls plan for the future.

The Homemaker

HOMEMAKING IS THE OCCUPATION OF CEREMONIAL FUTILITY.

✄ *Veblen*

THE MOST ACCURATE PREDICTION that can be made for a girl is that she will eventually be married. Nearly 95 per cent of all women marry sometime, and nearly two-thirds are married by the age of 21. Spinsters are becoming a vanishing race: the percentage of women in their early thirties who have never been married declined from 15 per cent in 1940 to only 7 per cent in 1960.

These statistics assume tremendous importance in light of the extent to which the event of marriage influences the lives of women. As married women, they are expected to perform certain duties and to limit their behavior to certain prescribed patterns, centering primarily on their role as wife and mother. The woman who deviates from the behavior expected of married women does so with considerable risk, not only to her relationships with others, but to her self-concept as well.

Most girls look forward to marriage, hoping and expecting to be married. Boys, of course, also expect to marry eventually, but the expectation seems to have greater impact on the girl. Marriage is, for boys, only one of many goals—one often relegated to secondary importance until other goals, such as education and a good job, have been achieved. For a girl, the goal of marriage very likely overshadows all others; it is the most important event in her life, and her hopes and plans for the future revolve around this eventuality. She finds it difficult to picture herself as anyone other than a "normal" housewife. Since, however, she cannot predict specifically whom she will marry she is unable to plan her life beyond marriage. The kind of person she marries will to a large extent determine the kind of life she will lead after marriage. This is one element contributing to the discontinuity of women's lives.

The amazing statistic that two-thirds of the women in this country are married by the age of 21 points up a source of concern to sociologists and educators: the adolescent bride. The prognosis for the marriages of persons in their teens is not good. Girls who marry at an early age tend to be less stable emotionally and to have poorer relationships with their parents, which leaves them poorly prepared for marriage. Ninety per cent of all married high school students are girls, although they usually marry boys who are no longer students. These girls, however, are not likely to remain in school for very long after marriage: the dropout rate for married girls varies from nearly 50 per cent among seniors to 83 per cent among sophomores. Public school administrators are very much concerned with the problem of married students and generally go to some lengths to discourage marriage before graduation, often to the extent of making it difficult for the married student to finish school.

At the other extreme are the women who never marry. These women tend to be more withdrawn in social relationships and to have a history of little heterosexual social activity; in short, they didn't have much to do with boys when they were young. In addition, they are likely to be concerned with social mobility, generally moving from a lower-class background to middle- or upper-class status. This has led Klemer (1954, p. 44) to conclude, "Women who try to move up in the social class scale by their own scholastic efforts may have difficulty in the marriage market."

✄ ✄ ✄ THE WIFE'S ROLE. The lives of most married women are a reflection of the expectations of their husbands, as evidenced by studies of factors which contribute to marital adjustment. Tharpe has surveyed the literature concerning psychological patterning in marriage and concluded (1963, pp. 101–2):

It seems that the maximally happy marital situation can be described as follows: husband and wife agree that he is as *he* wishes to be, namely, like his father; and as *she* wishes him to be, namely, like her's.

Tharpe thinks this occurs because the wife is more accommodating and the husband more rigid in his role needs. This is consistent with the discussion of how boys and girls differ in the process of development.

The wife's role may be structured severely by her husband's job, especially if he is in the sort of job that demands a great deal of his time and energy. This is more likely to be true of men in business or a profession, rather than those who can limit their involvement in their work to the 8-to-5 hours.

The role of wives of business and professional men is a sociological question which has not yet been extensively explored. Those studies which have been conducted suggest that the expectations made of wives are rather similar from one profession to another. The "successful" wife is one who organizes both her own life and the running of the home so as to further her husband's career. She limits her activity outside the home to social and community involvements which reflect favorably on her husband, and she avoids becoming immersed in such activities to the extent that she resists moving when her husband's career requires it. Since a man's success in business or a profession is often dependent on his willingness to move to take advantage of an opportunity for advancement, his wife is expected to live in the present and the future and to cut herself off from the past. This is especially true of the wives of business executives, who are successful to the extent that they do not get in their husband's way, by making demands on him that he has neither time nor energy to fulfill.

Obviously, few wives fit this pattern perfectly, which is probably desirable for the sake of their individuality. The perfect professional wife has little life of her own. Her husband's career comes first, and all else must be sublimated to it. Few women could play such a role without some feeling of frustration, and it seems unfair that society expects them to do so.

The current trend seems to be toward greater equality of the sexes in marital relationships and family roles. This means, on the one hand, that women are generally less tied to the home than they once were, which gives them greater freedom to develop interests and abilities in other areas. As this occurs, however, the husband must of necessity assume greater responsibility within the home in order to enable the wife to broaden her life. Many husbands profess to accept this philosophy, but there is reason to doubt that they really believe it.

The tradition is still strong that the husband's responsibility for supporting the family makes his contribution greater than his wife's. This has led men to feel that the family's life should be arranged to the husband's satisfaction. The husband must learn to recognize that if his wife is to be free to develop her own personality she cannot be a slave to him, but he may not be willing to relinquish his prerogatives without a struggle.

✿ ✿ ✿ HOMEMAKING AS AN OCCUPATION. Homemaking is the largest single occupational category in this country; although the ratio is declining, it employs more women than all other occupations combined. According to the Women's Bureau (1966a, pp. 8–9):

During a [typical] workweek in 1965, 50 per cent of all women were keeping house full time, and about 37 per cent were either full- or part-time workers. Most of the remainder were girls 14 to 20 years of age who were in school.

The importance of the homemaking role in the lives of women is tremendous. No boy can look forward to any specific occupation in his future with the certainty that a girl can expect to become a homemaker. But for all of its importance, numerous questions surround it. What, exactly, is a homemaker? What does she do? How demanding is it, as a job? What are the problems and what are the rewards?

Many persons probably would agree with Myrdal and Klein (1956, p. 25) that "running a home is an occupation incidental rather than essential to the state of being married. After all, it is done also by many unmarried women as well as by and for bachelors." Ferdynand Zweig (quoted by Zapoleon, 1956, p. 9) describes homemaking as "the most important and difficult profession any woman can have." It is this writer's opinion that homemaking, both as an occupation and as a role, falls somewhere between these views. It may not be the most challenging career for many women, but the full-time homemaker is certainly entitled to see herself as performing something more than an "incidental" job.

The major difficulty in discussing homemaking as an occupation is that it differs in many ways from what an occupation is normally considered to be. In simplest terms, the homemaker is responsible for food preparation, for housecleaning, and in most cases for child care, a description that hardly does justice to her role. In another sense, the most distinguishing feature is the emphasis on relationships between the homemaker and the other members of the family. She has the major responsibility for developing relationships with and among her children while maintaining a mutually satisfying relationship with her husband. It is likely that being a homemaker demands more of a woman *as a person* than would a more typical kind of job. On the other hand, it may not demand much of her in intellectual areas, in which she may be most competent. This will be discussed in detail later.

Homemaking is peculiar in terms of the hours required. In one sense, it is literally a full-time job; although the average homemaker spends about 7 hours a day in actual homemaking tasks, her work is scattered throughout a long day, with no point at which she can be sure of being able to withdraw entirely from her responsibilities. Few men hold jobs which demand the same kind of continual responsibility.

Demands on the homemaker vary according to the developmental stage of her family. Caplow (1954) has suggested that the housewife's career can be traced through three stages. The first is considered a *learning phase*. During the early part of marriage, before the children are born, only two persons are involved. The demands of food preparation and housecleaning are not great, the equipment is likely to be new, and the husband is usually willing to help. It is thus relatively easy for the wife to combine homemaking with outside employment if she chooses. The wife who does not work outside the home, but who tries to be a full-time homemaker during this phase, faces one of two potential dangers: she may become bored with her lack of responsibility and perhaps misdirect this frustration onto her husband or her marriage, or she may set housekeeping standards that will be difficult for her to maintain with the advent of children.

The second phase, according to Caplow, is one involving *intensive child care*. Since most young mothers have had relatively little experience in rearing children, they find these responsibilities exhausting. The total time covered by this phase varies, depending on the number of children and their spacing, but for most women it lasts between 10 and 20 years. During this period, the typical woman focuses most of her energies on her home, tends to abandon other interests and roles, and allows herself lower standards of housekeeping. Her husband assumes some responsibility for helping around the house. However, it is likely that this phase will coincide with her husband's struggle to get ahead, which may limit the amount of time he is able to devote to aiding his wife. As the children enter school, the homemaker has more free time for other activities, which will prepare her for phase three.

The third phase is characterized by the *declining work load* of the homemaker. By this time she probably is about 40 years of age with a great deal of useful life ahead of her; the demands and responsibilities of homemaking are receding, yet she has no real occupation. Although her "retirement" is not the abrupt kind which her husband will face in another 25 years, it is retirement nonetheless. And it has been thrust upon her. Still young enough to make other plans for herself, perhaps involving a shift in occupation, she may do this in a constructive and productive manner, or she may be unable to find her niche and just flit randomly from one activity to another, wasting and frustrating herself.

It should be evident that the major variable delineating these stages is the demands and responsibilities connected with child care. Young children require a great deal of the mother's time, but the demands on her time lessen as the children become better able to fend for themselves. When they reach the age that they are away from home a large part of the day she may seek other outlets for her interests and energy.

But what of the woman who works outside the home while her children are small? Where does she find the time for it all? The answer seems to be that she somehow compresses her housework into a shorter time span, so that the total amount of time she spends on housework and on her job is not a great deal more than the amount of time devoted to housework by the full-time housewife.

How does she manage this? There are several possible explanations, all of them speculative. The working woman undoubtedly has some help with her housework from her husband and the older children in the family and probably some hired help in addition. She may also set lower standards for herself in her home; since she gains personal satisfactions from her outside job, she has less need to achieve a high level of excellence in her housekeeping. Finally, it is likely that the woman who is able to combine being a wife and mother with outside employment is more efficient than the full-time housewife and thus gets more accomplished in less time. At any rate, having both a family and an outside job does not seem to add a great deal to a woman's working hours.

✄ ✄ PROBLEMS AND DEMANDS. Advertisement (David, 1958, p. 199):

Woman wanted who can help in house and home, 18-hour day, 7-day week, sleep in; coffee break occasionally; must have working knowledge of cooking, sewing, medicine, education, child welfare, elementary electricity, bookkeeping, and men. One who can work part time for money preferred.

This may be an exaggerated description of the occupation of homemaking, but it contains enough elements of truth to make it imperative that girls who plan to become full-time homemakers should have a realistic conception of what they are getting into. Too often girls have an idealistic picture of their lives after marriage, only to find too late that not only are many of their expectations not fulfilled, but that they also encounter frustrations and problems that they had not anticipated.

It will be claimed that in many ways the demands made of

homemakers today are not as exhausting as in previous generations. According to current propaganda, the modern homemaker is blessed with all manner of conveniences: prepared foods, laborsaving appliances, and more efficiently designed houses, to name but a few, all designed to make her life easier than her grandmother's.

To some extent this is true but it would be a mistake to consider that modern living has proved to be an unmixed blessing to the homemaker. As Reid (1947) has noted, the more complex way of living has in many instances simply replaced old problems with new ones. The price which the modern homemaker must pay for her myriad appliances is their lack of consistent performance and the difficulties which ensue when one fails to operate properly. And the increased trend toward urban living means that the time required to shop is much greater and requires more complex judgments than in the past. Whether the homemaker's life is better now than it was 50 years ago may be open to question, but there is no doubt that it is different.

What, then, are some potential problems and demands which the girl who plans to become a full-time homemaker may expect to encounter? The following list is not intended to be exhaustive, although the reader may find it exhausting.

Lack of Preparation. Many girls receive little formal training in homemaking before they plunge into it for themselves. Home economics courses offered by high schools have many limitations of scope, time, schedules, and student interest. A bright girl may operate on the assumption that she can casually pick up homemaking knowledge whenever she needs it, only to learn later that on-the-job training can be frustrating and embarrassing. A college curriculum in home economics usually is oriented toward the professional use of homemaking-related skills rather than to the occupation of homemaking itself.

Although most girls plan to marry and raise a family, few allow themselves to count on this as a certainty. Therefore they and their families expect the schools to prepare them for a job, in which they will probably remain for only a short time. In the process, the training in homemaking which will occupy the largest part of their lives for most girls is neglected.

Learning to become a successful homemaker is also complicated by the variety of skills required for the many roles involved. One woman may become a meticulous housekeeper, another an expert in child raising, a third a competent businesswoman who manages the family finances well, and a fourth a social asset to her husband. Each in her own way is successful, but for different reasons. The potential homemaker can be helped to develop her abilities in any of these areas, but it would be unrealistic to expect one person to attain a high level of proficiency in all.

The traditional pattern by which girls learn about homemaking from their mothers continues to be the predominant one, although it is becoming increasingly less effective as adolescent girls spend less time at home and as the demands on the homemaker change rapidly. The modern mother has at hand appliances and foods unknown to her own mother; these speed up the mechanics of homemaking, but do not adapt well to the training of daughters. An additional complication is the trend toward greater mobility, especially among young couples. When the new wife runs into difficulties, she likely cannot call on the help of her mother or of other relatives, simply because they may be hundreds or thousands of miles away.

All of this suggests that there is an increasing need to develop methods for acquainting young women with the principles and procedures of homemaking. To do so will require some alterations in attitudes and a willingness to view homemaking as an occupation as well as a role. Few would claim that the skills required in most occupations can best be mastered by blind trial and error, but we have been content to offer homemakers little better.

Disorganization of Time and Activity. Homemaking is an especially trying experience for the woman who likes to have her life well organized, who wants her plans undisturbed. Many of the homemaker's responsibilities are by their very nature spontaneous and unpredictable; her life must be geared to correspond to the demands of husband and children rather than to her own needs. Children are especially difficult to regiment—they seldom want drinks or get bloody noses at times convenient for their mothers. To be sure, during the day there are periods when they are not demanding, but these occasions arise only sporadically, seldom last long, and cannot be anticipated. The housewife with small children at home cannot plan to accomplish much during the day, which causes much of her work to pile up into the evening. Unlike many husbands, the wife has no secretary to act as a buffer between her and the demands of the outside world. It is therefore not surprising that a common complaint of housewives is that they never have time to themselves.

Low Status of Housework. It is a paradox that most girls aspire to become homemakers at a time when the job of housework has little prestige in our society. This is evident in the difficulty with which domestic help is obtained. Women do not want to do housework for others, even if the pay is good and the working conditions are pleasant, primarily because of the low status of the job itself. Another kind of evidence is seen in advertisements for household products. The common theme is that using the product—e.g., a dishwashing detergent—will enable the woman to appear as though she does *not* do housework. The implication is that the less a woman appears to be engaged in housework the more acceptable she is as a woman.

The drawback is that housework—which includes both house-cleaning and food preparation—is one of the major responsibilities of the homemaker. The other major component of her role is child care, which is important only for a limited period of time. The homemaker is thus in the position of having to devote a large share of her time to activities which are viewed by society, and perhaps by herself, as menial. So she must find some way of avoiding being seen as a person who does housework.

This problem becomes greater as she moves up the social scale and it may lead to the hiring of servants which in turn accentuates in her mind the low status of housework. This poses another dilemma, since to denigrate the value of housework—an important component of the homemaking role—might lead society to devalue homemaking in its entirety which would lead to the devaluation of women in their most common role.

Caplow (1954) suggests that many women solve this problem by emphasizing the *emotional* aspects of homemaking, which supposedly differentiate it from domestic service work. In reality, most women probably know that the difference is minimal, but they must maintain the fiction that it is important. Consequently, the woman who hires help so that she may work outside the home must be criticized by other women for neglecting her homemaking responsibilities, while the woman who hires servants so that she may have leisure time is acceptable since her continued presence in the household guarantees the emotional values.

✣ Lack of Demands on Abilities. No one has yet been able to establish any age or intelligence requirements for being a homemaker. A certain degree of maturity and intelligence are required to do a good job of homemaking, but even these levels are not necessarily high. Girls and boys are educated together, similar intellectual demands are made of them, and as we have seen they achieve equally well in school. Subsequently girls may hold a reasonably demanding job in which they perform well and from which they receive some personal satisfaction. Then they become homemakers, and the abilities which they have been encouraged to develop are no longer very important. Much of the knowledge which they have acquired is directly useful only on sporadic occasions, and for most of the day

there is no one with whom they can interact on an equal intellectual level. Thus homemaking can be viewed as an occupation which exerts few intellectual demands on women who prior to this time have been encouraged to develop their abilities.

Under such circumstances a woman may move in one of two directions. Many women, having set their goal in life as marriage and a family, seem to renounce any ambition for self-development once this goal is reached. Intellectually they go to sleep after leaving school. The result, according to Meyer (1956, p. 149), is that " . . . the sheer ignorance of American women is appalling." This is a source of frustration to many an educator who must stand helplessly by and watch all the hard spent effort to stimulate intellectual curiosity and to instill knowledge into the minds of his female students go rapidly down the drain as they succumb to the lethargy of being homemakers.

The homemaker need not, of course, stagnate intellectually, but the woman who tries to resist this trend will find herself fighting an uphill battle. Perhaps she herself honestly intends to maintain a reasonable level of intellectual competence, but from where is she to get encouragement and stimulation? From her immediate surroundings? Her children have not yet become stimulating intellectual companions, amusing and interesting as they may be in other respects. Even the most intelligent three-year-old has a rather limited conversational scope. Her friends? For the most part they are housewives like herself, most of whom have already, and perhaps happily, succumbed to domestic lethargy. To find other women who share her concerns she will have to go further afield, and she may not have enough energy left at the end of the day to make the effort.

Isn't her husband a potential source of intellectual stimulation? He might be, but chances are that he comes home exhausted from his job and prefers not to participate in lively conversation. The mass media? Television and radio have not distinguished themselves by the level of intellectual stimulation they provide at any time of the day, and especially not during the daylight hours. They are in business to entertain, not to educate.

Finally, she may turn to books for intellectual stimulation, but few people, male or female, enjoy reading without at least the occasional opportunity to discuss it with another person. In short, no avenue seems to provide a completely satisfactory solution to her problem.

In the face of such pressures, it is little wonder that the young wife and mother, harassed by a complexity of demands with which she feels she is not coping adequately anyway, neglects her mind and lets herself drift into a world of coffee klatches, discussions of children, quiz programs, soap operas, and women's magazines.

None will demand much of her in the way of intellectual effort, and she is well on the way to locking herself into a narrow existence.

❧ *Lack of Rewards.* Most occupations provide some means of rewarding superior performance, with the object of stimulating productivity and retaining competent employees. Among the more common rewards are increased pay, increased status via promotion, and fringe benefits such as vacations and insurance programs. It has long been an axiom of personnel management that the satisfied employee is one who feels that he is doing a good job and is being adequately compensated for it.

But what of the homemaker? Many readers will recoil in horror at the suggestion that the homemaker should—or even could—be motivated by incentives as crass as money or status. Surely, they will argue, she is fulfilling her responsibilities out of a sense of love and a desire to make life more pleasant for the other members of her family. According to this viewpoint, she obtains an inner satisfaction of an almost spiritual nature, much richer and deeper than that which money or promotion brings to a mere employee.

This picture is undoubtedly true for some women some of the time, but probably of very few women all of the time. To argue that women should be able to subsist entirely on such vague rewards is to deny that they are human beings, subject to needs for recognition and achievement of the same sort as are men.

Perhaps the picture of the self-sacrificing homemaker, rewarded only by the happiness she brings to her family, is more appropriate to other societies than to modern America. We have reduced the gap between the sexes in their upbringing and in their education. We have encouraged girls to develop achievement needs as well as needs for recognition. Can we then expect that, once they become homemakers, they will shed such inappropriate regalia? Indeed not. As Bruton (1947, p. 15) has stated:

Even the best mother resents the fact that she is never promoted, no matter how good a job she does; she never gets paid . . . ; and there is no social recognition of her achievements.

Her rewards of praise from her husband and children are often few and far between. The reactions that do occur tend to be negative, noting something which wasn't done properly rather than all the things that are, but which are taken for granted. It might help if husbands were educated to be more responsive to their wives' needs for recognition, but it is doubtful if this would entirely solve the problem.

Some women, frustrated by a lack of self-satisfaction but unable to recognize its true cause, may compensate by seeking to satisfy their frustrated needs for recognition through their children. One of the less pleasant aspects of this situation is the woman who is constantly pushing her children to greater and greater achievements. Surely some of this need to have her children in the spotlight must come from her own thwarted ambitions to be recognized as a significant person in her own right.

Social Isolation. One of the major frustrations of homemaking, the lack of intellectual stimulation, is caused in part by infrequent contact with other adults. This lack of adult contact is a social as well as an intellectual handicap. The feeling that the four walls of the home have become a prison is especially prevalent among young mothers, whose mobility is severely restricted by their responsibilities to their children. These women are truly in danger of going "stir crazy."

Often the major source of adult companionship for a wife is her husband, but this may be an unsatisfactory solution to her social needs. It is difficult for him to understand why her needs for conversation are so intense, why she wants to know every detail of his day at the office, no matter how trivial. The husband, who may spend a good part of his day talking with other people, has saturated his need for conversation and would rather be left alone to relax in peace and quiet. The outcome may be an argument, with neither person able to understand why the other is upset.

The casual social contacts between women of a neighborhood, subject to frequent interruptions by the demands of children or other responsibilities, are not apt to be very relaxing. The only common ground for social intercourse may be the fact that they live in the same neighborhood and happen to have children. Thus the rather limited exchanges which will result may not be very satisfying to any of the participants.

Dependence on Husband. Because of these and many related problems, the homemaker is forced to depend on her husband in numerous ways. The extent to which he can meet her needs may have an important bearing on the success of their marriage as well as on her own mental health. Many men are capable of recognizing and understanding these needs, and of meeting them; others are not. In the latter case the woman has only limited alternatives, most of which are not very constructive, and the result is likely to be a gradual separation of the lives of the husband and wife. Some marriages can adjust to this, but others can't. Could this be a reason why it is not uncommon to find marriages of twenty or thirty years' duration ending in divorce? Perhaps the children have held such a marriage together; when they have left home the couple realizes that the marriage itself has long since ceased to exist.

The full-time homemaker is, of course, also financially dependent on her husband. This is traditional, and one would not expect it to cause serious difficulties. Yet it serves to perpetuate the concept that the man is playing the more important role in the family and that the welfare of the family depends primarily on him. This perhaps is unfair to both husband and wife; it is certainly unrealistic and unnecessary.

Along with economic dependence, the homemaker is also dependent on her husband for her social status. Her primary role in society is as her husband's wife. Thus his status is hers also, and the only way she can raise her status is for him to raise his, or at least for her to act as though it is improving. Caplow (1954) observes that, as a husband's income rises, a higher proportion of it goes to his wife than to himself. He cites as an example that it is unlikely that a banker will spend fifty to sixty times as much on clothes as will his barber, but it is quite likely that the banker's wife will spend that much more for clothes than will the barber's wife. In a way, this is a carry-over from an earlier period, when a man displayed his wealth by the quality and quantity of his possessions, including his wives. Nowadays, he is presumably limited to one wife, but she is still a primary exhibit of his affluence and in this sense is considered as a possession.

❧ *Decline in Importance With Age.* Finally, we come to the problems of the middle-aged homemaker. The demands of homemaking, great when the children are young, diminish as they grow up, and when eventually they leave to establish homes of their own, her responsibilities for child care are at an end, except for occasional grandmotherly duties. She still has responsibilities for food preparation and household maintenance for two people, but these are not very demanding. She has more potential than her duties absorb.

Caplow (1954, pp. 265–66) has described the problem in the following way:

The general situation is highly unfavorable for the housewife in her middle years. In a culture which attaches extreme importance to striving and to individual productivity, the housewife at fifty is typically idle, with no economic need for employment but with a pressing psychological need to justify herself. At the least, she is constrained to give an appearance of difficulty to a job which has long since ceased to require serious attention or effort. Generally speaking, this group of women, with their unused energy transposed in various neurotic themes, are the most conspicuously maladjusted segment of the population.

This is a strong statement, perhaps, but it indicates what the house-wife can expect if she fails to prepare for her middle years.

✣ ✣ ✣ THE BRIGHTER SIDE. There are of course two sides to this issue, as there are to most. Despite evidence that the role of the homemaker has high "frustration potential," many women find it greatly rewarding. These are the women who are not es-pecially concerned with achievement and status but who are, instead, well satisfied with the approval of their husbands and children as indications that they are doing a good job and making others happy. In short, they fit the mold that society has decreed for all women. In many respects they are the fortunate ones.

Nor would everyone agree that homemaking is a wasteland of unused abilities. As a case in point, Terman and Oden (1959, p. 145) have this to say of the women in their gifted group:

[They] in the main are housewives, and many who also work outside the home do so more to relieve the monotony of household duties or to supplement the family income rather than through a desire for a serious career. There are many intangible kinds of accomplish-ment and success open to the housewife, and it is debatable whether the fact that a majority of gifted women prefer housewifery to more intellectual pursuits represents a net waste of brainpower.

This writer is inclined to think that Terman and Oden were being charitable in their evaluation of the contributions being made by the women in their study. Perhaps their own biases about women's roles are showing through.

There is another argument made in defense of homemaking which, while essentially subjective, is more difficult to refute. It is contended that criticisms of homemaking must be discounted be-cause they come primarily from women who are not full-time home-makers, and in some cases not even married. A statement by Stod-dard (1950, p. 19) is typical of such a position:

A running attack on the home is made by the speaking and writing non-homemaker—a futile business that plays off the desk-set against the sink but not the filing cabinet against the fireplace.

It is difficult to understand what the last part of that sentence is supposed to mean, since few persons would argue that homemaking and career occupations can be neatly balanced off against one another. Nevertheless, the charge that the critics of homemaking are not themselves homemakers has some validity, as does the im-plication that many of these criticisms are products of personal frustration rather than of sound, objective thought.

This writer, however, can see enough smoke in the pronounce-ments of the critics to believe that a fire must be smoldering some-where underneath, one which could easily get out of control if not attended to. Simply because some women find homemaking a con-genial occupation should not blind us to the realization that for many others it is little short of slavery, made even worse by the voluntary nature of the woman's commitment to it.

❧ ❧ ❧ ADJUSTMENT TO HOMEMAKING

❧ ❧ EXTENT OF DISSATISFACTION. Our major conclusion, then, is that homemaking presents many demands and frustrations, but that these are often outweighed by the rewards which it offers. It is up to the individual woman to determine which side is more im-portant to her: what she gets out of being a homemaker as opposed to what she has to give up for it. On the one hand, it seems evident that becoming a full-time homemaker represents an abrupt transi-tion for most women. The situation is well expressed in the follow-ing quotation from a young mother (quoted by Komarovsky, 1953, p. 106):

The plunge from the strictly intellectual college life to the 24-hour-a-day domestic one is a terrible shock, and it is no wonder that we stagger through the first few years of child-rearing wondering what our values are and struggling to find some compromise between our intellectual ambitions and the reality of everyday living.

We might therefore expect research studies of housewives to have uncovered a pile of latent dissatisfactions pushed under the emotional rug, but such has not been the case. If such dissatisfac-tions exist they are well repressed. Most housewives claim to be satisfied with their role in life, although the younger women are apt to complain about the harassments of rearing young children. Apparently as these women grow older they either seek other roles or else become adjusted to the more routine role of the housewife whose children are no longer underfoot all day.

❧ ❧ THE HOMEMAKER'S ROLE. There is danger in considering the "homemaking role" in the singular, as though all homemakers were alike. Obviously they are not. The woman who becomes a full-time homemaker has a number of subroles from which to choose, three of which have been described in some detail by Par-sons (1953).

The *domestic* role has the lowest status of the three, but is the safest since it emphasizes the values of fidelity and devotion to husband and children which society claims to be of highest importance. The community will approve of the woman who is domestic, even though it may have little respect for her as a person.

The *glamour* role is more dangerous but has several advantages. The woman who is concerned with gaining power and prestige does not have to struggle for them in an occupation but can instead gain satisfaction from outdoing other women in appearance and attractiveness to men. If she is successful—and there is always the risk of failure—she can feel superior and important. However, the role itself contradicts the moral codes and standards of society, as well as perhaps those of the woman herself. It is also difficult to adapt this role to increasing age. The "faded beauty" has long been a tragic figure in novels, which often mirror life with insight and accuracy.

For many women, the *good companion* role proves to be the most satisfying. This implies that the husband and wife work together as a team, interweaving their lives so that neither withdraws into a separate sector and maintains it as his own province. The major difficulty for women in this role is the lack of a single, prescribed pattern of behavior. Such a role requires more initiative and intelligence on the part of the woman than do the others, which in turn may have the virtue of forcing the woman to become more of an individual.

The homemaking role, then, provides some opportunity for a woman to express herself as a person, but within rather strict limitations. The needs of some women are adequately met as homemakers, and there is little reason why they should attempt to be otherwise. Many women, however, do not find the role of full-time homemaker to be enough for them, and they search for other alternatives. For some, employment provides an opportunity for self-expression. Others make use of community activities for the same purpose, often overcoming by enthusiasm their lack of education and experience. Our communities owe a great debt to the women of all ages who have assumed the responsibility and leadership for a variety of community improvement projects. If all women were expected to work for pay, this kind of effort would be lost to society. In any case, the woman who is dissatisfied with the role of full-time housewife has a number of alternatives available if she is willing to make the effort to locate them.

Women in the Labor Force

**A WOMAN SHOULD BE GOOD FOR EVERY-
THING AT HOME, BUT ABROAD FOR NOTHING.**

✄ *Euripides*

BOUT ONE-THIRD of the labor force in the United States is composed of women, and all indications are that this propor-tion will continue to increase in the foreseeable future. About 35 per cent of all women in this country of working age are in the labor force at any given time, and nearly half of all women spend at least part of each year working for pay. During the decade 1950–1960, women accounted for three-fifths of the increase in the labor force, a trend which is expected to continue.

✄ ✄ ✄ THE EMPLOYMENT PATTERNS OF WOMEN. The participation of women in the labor force differs in several respects from that of men. A most important difference is that few women are employed continually throughout their lives as are most men. The varying stages of a woman's life influence the likelihood that she will work and the length of time she will be available. Accord-ing to the Women's Bureau (1963, p. 56):

Most women work sometime during their lives, whether they marry or not. But marriage and the presence of children tend to curtail their employment, while widowhood, divorce, and the decrease of family responsibilities tend to attract them back into the labor force.

Thus most married women move in and out of the labor force, rather than remaining there consistently as do their husbands.

ℐ ℐ THE SINGLE WOMAN. The work pattern of single women is more consistent and resembles that of men to a large extent, but they account for only about 10 per cent of the total adult female population. The proportion of single women of working age who are employed nearly equals the employment rate among single men, and their work continuity is much more like that of men than of married women. The average single woman enters the labor force at about the age of 20, works for about 40 years, and then lives in retirement for about 13 years more. Thus her work continuity is very similar to that of a man, except that she can look forward to a longer period of retirement.

ℐ ℐ THE MARRIED WOMAN. The lack of employment continuity among women becomes evident when the employment patterns of married women are examined. Married women without children, who account for only about 10 per cent of all married women, have a work life of about 31 years, but many of them are in the position of being able to quit their jobs more easily than can single women because they can be supported by their husbands. Married women with children have a much more intermittent work pattern. Typically they work for about 4 years, then quit and have their children. If they then want to work, they re-enter the labor force at about the age of 30 and work for about 25 more years.

Marriage is thus an important determiner of whether a woman is likely to be employed, although the transition is not as abrupt as was once the case. Bell (1956, p. 91) describes the contrast in this way:

Only yesterday, historically speaking, when a girl married she left work, amid envious farewells of her office or shop mates. Today, a girl who announces she is being married is asked by her supervisor, "Are you taking a trip, or will you be back Monday?" Whichever the answer, it is becoming increasingly rare that she does not return at all.

A number of factors seem to have contributed to the high employment rate among newly married women. Chief among these is the presence of a high proportion of married women in our country at a time when womanpower resources are increasingly in demand, which requires employers to be willing to hire married women. Women are also marrying at an earlier age than before, resulting in a smaller supply of young single women for the labor

TABLE 6.1 ❧ Labor Participation Rates of Women by Age and Marital Status, 1961

| Age | Women workers as per cent of woman population | | |
	Single	Married*	Other
Total	44	33	42
14 to 19 years	26	28	42
20 to 24 years	77	32	58
25 to 29 years	79	29	60
30 to 34 years	81	29	63
35 to 44 years	77	38	72
45 to 54 years	82	42	70
55 to 64 years	69	29	52
65 to 69 years	36	11	24
70 years and over	13	3	7

Source: U.S. Department of Labor, Bureau of Labor Statistics: "Special Labor Force Report," No. 20; Women's Bureau, 1963, p. 42.
* With husband present.

market. In any case, society appears to be much more tolerant of the employment of wives than was the case a generation or two ago, to the extent that working wives now account for nearly 60 per cent of all women workers.

Despite this increasing trend toward the employment of women after marriage the fact remains that, once married, the typical woman does not plan to continue to work indefinitely. The antagonistic relationship which exists between marriage and employment is evident in Figure 6.1, which shows the trend in labor-force participation by marital status. Table 6.1 compares labor-force participation by both marital status and age and supplies evidence to support the conclusion (Women's Bureau, 1966a, p. 23), "When labor-force participation rates of single women and married women are analyzed according to age, it is evident that the probability of a woman's working is influenced more by marital status than by age."

The greatest single influence on employment rate among women seems, however, to be the arrival of children in the family. The employment rate among women with preschool children is about 25 per cent, which is significantly less than that for all women, but this proportion has been increasing at the rate of about 1 per cent each year for about 20 years. Most of these women, however, do not work full time.

As soon as their children are in school, many of the mothers return to work, and the employment rate jumps to about 40 per cent among mothers with school-age children. One reason may be that many women report less satisfaction from family relationships

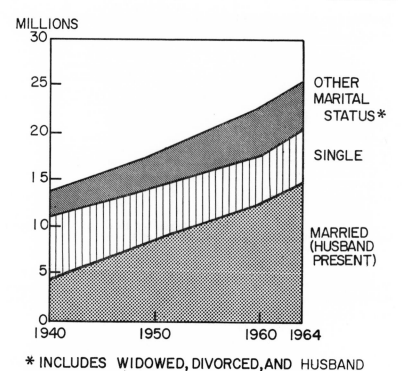

* INCLUDES WIDOWED, DIVORCED, AND HUSBAND
ABSENT FOR OTHER REASONS.

Fig. 6.1. Women in the civilian labor force, by marital status, 1940–1964 (U.S. Dept. of Labor; Women's Bureau, 1966a).

once their children are in school. It seems reasonable that school-age children do not require the amount of care by their mothers that they needed before they entered school, and that many women must therefore partially turn their energies elsewhere.

Of special significance is the sharp increase in a woman's interest in employment when her youngest child enters school, inasmuch as women are now having their children at earlier ages. The median age of the average mother at the birth of her last child is now about 26, as compared with 70 years ago when the median age was 32. This means that the average woman of today is only 32 when her last child has reached school age and still has a long, active life ahead of her.

These data hold true for women who are living with their husbands, but the picture changes when we consider those who are widowed, divorced, or separated. Since 400,000 women are divorced each year and there are almost 2 million in this country who have been divorced and have not remarried, this represents a sizeable segment of the female population. The employment rate within this group is 60 per cent, and they generally tend to congregate in low-paying jobs.

⋇ ⋇ JOB DISTRIBUTION. It is common knowledge that male and female workers are far from equally distributed throughout the various occupations. Some fields are considered to be the province of men, and women are accepted in them with great reluctance, if at all. Other occupations have been taken over by women to the extent that men will not attempt to enter them. Relatively few occupations employ both men and women in large numbers.

A comparison of the numbers of men and women employed in the major occupational groups is presented in Figure 6.2, while Figure 6.3 provides a comparison of sex representation in the major industries. Both figures show large differences between the numbers of men and women employed in various kinds of jobs.

Women workers tend to congregate in a relatively small number of jobs, as compared with men. Table 6.2 shows the number

TABLE 6.2 ⋇ The 25 Largest Occupations of Women, 1960 (Women 14 Years of Age and Over)

| Occupation | Women Employed | |
	Number	Per cent of total in occupation
Secretaries	1,423,352	97
Saleswomen, salesclerks (retail)	1,397,364	54
Private-household workers*	1,162,683	96
Teachers (elementary school)	860,413	86
Bookkeepers	764,054	84
Waitresses	714,827	87
Nurses, professional	567,884	98
Sewers and stitchers (mfg.)	534,258	94
Typists	496,735	95
Cashiers	367,954	78
Cooks (except private household)	361,772	64
Telephone operators	341,797	96
Babysitters (private household)	319,735	98
Attendants (hospitals and other institutions)	288,268	74
Laundry and dry cleaning operatives	277,396	72
Assemblers	270,769	44
Apparel and accessory operatives	270,619	75
Hairdressers and cosmetologists	267,050	89
Packers and wrappers*	262,935	60
Stenographers	258,554	96
Teachers (secondary school)	243,452	47
Office-machine operators	227,849	74
Checkers, examiners, inspectors (mfg.)	215,066	45
Practical nurses	197,115	96
Kitchen workers* (except household)	179,796	59

Source: U.S. Department of Commerce, Bureau of the Census: 1960 Census of Population; Women's Bureau, 1966a, p. 92.
* Excludes those listed separately by the Bureau of the Census.

of women employed in each of the 25 occupations which employ
the largest number of women, as well as the proportion of the total
number of workers in that field who are women. In almost all cases
women account for at least 50 per cent of the employees in these
occupations.

Although Figures 6.2 and 6.3 show clearly that the proportion
of men and women employed in various occupational groups and
industries is, in most cases, drastically unbalanced, they do not
show the extent to which there is job segregation by sex *within* the
occupational fields and industries. An outstanding example is the
professions. According to Figure 6.1, women account for a substantial proportion of persons in "professional" occupations. However,
most women who are employed in the professions are confined to a
small number of occupations, such as nursing, teaching, social work,
and library work. Teaching alone accounts for about 42 per cent of
all professional women.

Caplow (1954) believes that the evidence concerning sex ratios
in other occupational fields also is misleading. For example, in the
semiprofessional fields the number of women in entertainment and
the arts equals that of men. Women also predominate in ancillary
occupations, such as dental hygiene, whereas the technical trades are
limited almost entirely to men.

Few women are classified as farmers or farm managers, although
Caplow suggests that in many cases the wife actually manages the
farm for which the husband is nominally designated the operator.
In the category of proprietors, managers, and officials, however, men
outnumber women two to one, and the ratio increases with the level
of the job.

Clerical workers are predominately women, and men seem
willing to keep it that way. Recent expansions in business and government operations have created burgeoning needs for clerical
workers, a void which is being filled almost entirely by women.

Among craftsmen and foremen there are few women, but
among operatives the sex ratio is about equal. Domestic service
employs about 10 to 15 times as many women as men. There are
few women classified as laborers. In the service occupations there
is a sizeable proportion of women, but most of them work in restau-
rants or in beauty shops.

Women outnumber men in retail sales, if canvassers and travel-
ing salesmen are excluded. Most stores tend to use women in areas
where female customers predominate. A major exception is that
items of considerable weight or value are usually sold by men; it is
unusual, for example, to find women selling furniture or expensive
jewelry.

One must bear in mind that the data presented here are true

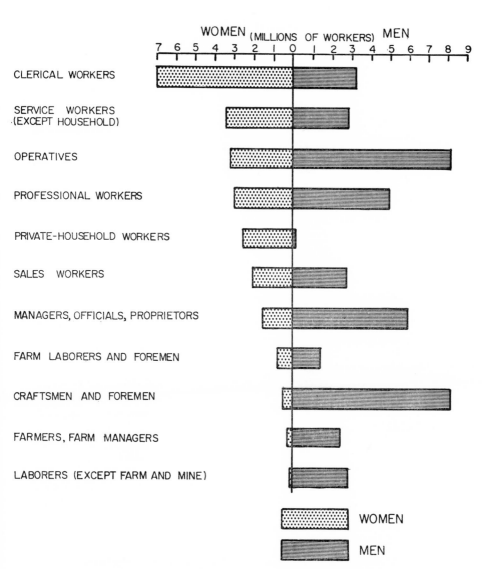

Fig. 6.2. *Occupational groups of employed men and women, April, 1962 (U.S. Dept. of Labor; Women's Bureau, 1963).*

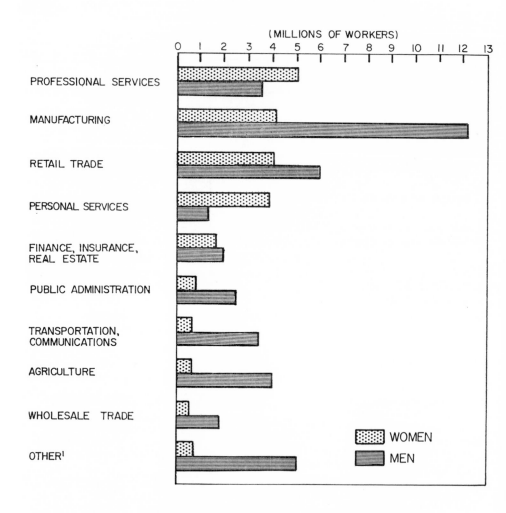

(MILLIONS OF WORKERS)

PROFESSIONAL SERVICES

MANUFACTURING

RETAIL TRADE

PERSONAL SERVICES

FINANCE, INSURANCE,
REAL ESTATE

PUBLIC ADMINISTRATION

TRANSPORTATION,
COMMUNICATIONS

AGRICULTURE

WHOLESALE TRADE

OTHER¹

WOMEN
MEN

¹INCLUDES BUSINESS SERVICES, ENTERTAINMENT AND RECREATION,
CONSTRUCTION, AND MINING.

*Fig. 6.3. Major industries of employed men and women, 1963
(U.S. Dept. of Labor; Women's Bureau, 1963).*

only for a specific point in time. The job picture is a fluid one, subject to day-to-day fluctuations as well as to long-term trends. Nevertheless, the general employment situation for women tends to change rather slowly, except for the advent of a major social force such as a depression or a war. In general, women are more likely to be employed in fields which have undergone recent expansion, such industries having a greater need for workers and being less bound by traditional prejudices. As evidence, the proportion of women in white-collar jobs, clerical occupations, sales, managerial, professional, and technical occupations increased during the decade of the fifties, while their proportion in service and factory jobs, which at one time accounted for most women workers, declined.

❧ ❧ ❧ RECENT HISTORY OF FEMALE EMPLOYMENT

❧ ❧ HISTORICAL TRENDS. The past half-century has witnessed important changes in the status of women in our society, changes which have been reflected in the labor force. The trend toward the increased employment of women is evident in Table 6.3, which describes the proportion of the labor force composed of women at various stages during this period.

For most of this period the change was gradual. It was World War II, with its sudden demands on manpower resources of all kinds, which gave women the opportunity to work outside the home under socially acceptable conditions. In 1940, only one-seventh of the married women in this country were engaged in some sort of

TABLE 6.3 ❧ Women in the Labor Force (Selected Years)

	Women Workers (14 Years and Over)		
Date	Number	Per cent of all workers	Per cent of all women
	Recent highlights		
April 1965	26,108,000	35	37
Start of sixties (April 1960)	23,239,000	33	36
Mid-fifties (April 1955)	20,154,000	31	34
Korean war (April 1953)	19,296,000	31	33
Pre-Korea (April 1950)	18,063,000	29	32
Postwar (April 1947)	16,320,000	28	30
World War II (April 1945)	19,570,000	36	37
Pre-World War II (March 1940)	13,840,000	25	28
	Long-term trends		
1930 (April)	10,396,000	22	24
1920 (January)	8,229,000	20	23
1900 (June)	4,999,000	18	20
1890 (June)	3,704,000	17	18

Source: U.S. Department of Labor, Bureau of Labor Statistics; and U.S. Department of Commerce, Bureau of the Census; Women's Bureau, 1966a, p. 6.

paid employment outside the home; the number has now increased to one-third.

Changes have also occurred in the age composition of the female labor force. The greatest increase is among women between the ages of 45 and 54, whose numbers rose from 24 per cent in 1940 to 50 per cent in 1965. By contrast, there has been only a slight increase in the proportion of women workers between the ages of 20 and 24, primarily because more young women within this age range are now attending college or marrying and having children.

The relationship of employment to the various phases of a woman's life is graphically illustrated in Figure 6.4, which compares the trend in 1890 with the current picture. In both instances, a jump in employment rate occurs between high school graduation and marriage, with a rapid decline thereafter. Beyond this point, however, the patterns diverge. Currently the employment rate increases again when the last child enters school. Figure 6.4 also shows that this stage is occurring earlier in women's lives now than was the case in 1890. Thus, at the turn of the century, the average woman lived for approximately 30 years after her last child had entered school, and for approximately 12 years after her last child had married. By contrast, the modern woman has a life expectancy of more than 40 years after her last child enters school and of about 25 years after her last child marries. She thus has a considerably longer period in her life when she does not have the full-time responsibility of children at home. This has certainly been a major factor contributing to the increased employment of women.[1]

The increase in the rate of employment among women which has been evident in our country for the past 70 years has not been consistently duplicated elsewhere. According to Myrdal and Klein (1956), the employment rate among women has remained constant in both France and Great Britain since 1900, the rate being about 50 per cent in France and 40 per cent in Britain. During this same period, it has increased in the United States from about 20 per cent in 1900 to about 40 per cent currently. This might suggest that a saturation point is being reached, since the employment rate among women in the United States is approaching that of other Western countries. Most experts, however, predict that the rate will continue to rise in this country and that it may begin to increase in other countries as well as they become more "Americanized."

Changes have taken place not only in numbers and percentages

---

[1] Employment among women has not, however, increased uniformly. Despite the over-all trend, increased educational and economic opportunity has actually served to *decrease* the employment rate among certain groups. For example, the National Manpower Council (1957) reports a sharp reduction in the employment rate among Negro women under the age of 20 and above 65, a trend which is probably in the best interests of society.

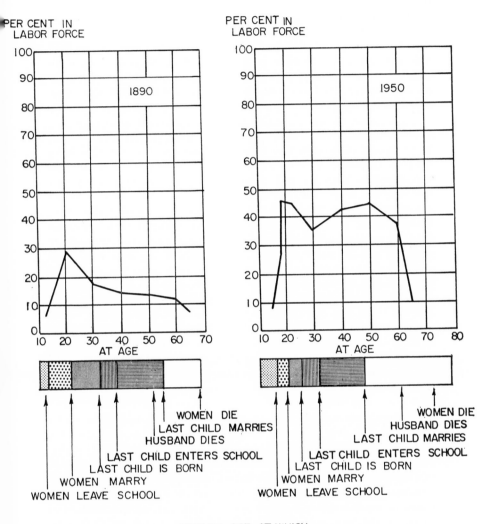

PER CENT IN
LABOR FORCE

1890

PER CENT IN
LABOR FORCE

1950

AT AGE

AT AGE

WOMEN DIE
LAST CHILD MARRIES
HUSBAND DIES
LAST CHILD ENTERS SCHOOL
LAST CHILD IS BORN
WOMEN MARRY
WOMEN LEAVE SCHOOL

WOMEN DIE
HUSBAND DIES
LAST CHILD MARRIES
LAST CHILD ENTERS SCHOOL
LAST CHILD IS BORN
WOMEN MARRY
WOMEN LEAVE SCHOOL

MEDIAN AGE AT WHICH ...

Fig. 6.4. Work in relation to significant stages in the lives of women, 1890 and 1959, showing median age at which these stages occur (National Manpower Council, 1957).

of women in the labor force, but also in their job distribution. In 1890, women who were employed outside the home were found for the most part in one of three occupational areas: teaching, factory work, or domestic service. Although teaching is still one of the most popular professions for women, it has also been opened to men, especially with the increase in high school enrollment during the past half-century. As a result, the proportion of public school teachers who are women has dropped from nine-tenths in 1890 to about two-thirds in 1965.

Similar influences have also served to alter the employment pattern of women working in factories. In the early days they were usually limited to unskilled or semiskilled jobs, the skilled jobs being reserved for men. These jobs were generally boring, required long hours, and paid little. It is thus not surprising that women have been eager to move into positions in which working conditions are more pleasant and the demands less stringent. The fields which have attracted them have been clerical and sales work. The clerical field in particular has shown rapid expansion: the number of women clerical workers has increased from 2½ million in 1940 to almost 8 million in 1965, the largest increase among women in any occupational group during this period.

Associated with these changes in the numbers of employed women have been striking alterations in the image of the "working girl." Smuts (1959) has presented a vivid picture of the typical 1890 working girl, one which can only be briefly summarized here. She generally came from a lower-class family and worked as a domestic or in a factory because of financial necessity. It was assumed that no girl would work by choice, and there was no conception that a woman could work outside the home and still be a "lady." Most employed women had only a grade school education, since at that time higher education for girls was designed to prepare them to be ladies rather than to train them for employment. Thus the working girl had little to offer her employer in the way of specialized skills and was useful only in menial jobs at low pay. Female employees were badly treated, since they had little training and could be easily replaced. Their job security was infinitesimal. The situation was not a great deal better for many men at that time, but they were likely to be more aggressive and to resent women who threatened to take away their jobs. Working conditions were generally poor, sweatshop conditions being not uncommon. This state of affairs led eventually to the passage of laws to protect women from unfair and unjust employers. The major exceptions to these poor conditions were the few professions, such as teaching, which were open to women.

The public, in 1890, not only frowned on women working outside the home, but it almost literally turned its back on them. Several forces conspired to produce these illogical but intense negative attitudes. Foremost among them was the belief that men and women were very different psychologically as well as physically, and thus their lives should follow different paths. The woman who worked was trying to behave like a man and must be severely punished for her transgression. Many persons also held the notion that any kind of physical labor was likely to be harmful to women. It must, however, be kept in mind that the kinds of jobs and the working conditions prevalent at that time did make employment physically more strenuous than it is today. It is also likely that many men objected to women working because of the threat to themselves both financially and psychologically.

Vestiges of these attitudes persist today, but women have made considerable headway against such barriers. The time may not be far distant when the public will ask why a woman is *not* working rather than why she *is*.

❧ ❧ REASONS FOR THE CHANGE. Why are women freer to work nowadays, and why are more of them working than ever before? A number of factors conspire to produce a situation which differs considerably from that of a half-century ago. Some of this change has been deliberately forced, but much of it was the result of other social changes which had this as one of their indirect effects. Some of the contributing influences are described below.

❧ *Shift From Rural to Urban Living.* During the first half of this century, our society shifted dramatically from rural to urban domination. With the decline of the family farm, it became more difficult for a woman at home to make a direct contribution to her family's economy. The farm wife was an integral part of the economic life of her family, working as a team with her husband to operate the farm. Her contemporary in the city likewise engaged in a variety of tasks within the home which contributed more directly to the welfare of her family than does the modern housewife. Thus the modern woman finds it difficult to gain a degree of satisfaction out of being a housewife comparable to that of the woman two or three generations ago.

A related factor is that women who want to earn money are less able now to do so within their homes than was once the case. Fifty years ago, most women who worked for pay did so within the home, while the modern woman who wants to earn money must generally look outside her home for a job. This shift has led Rollins (1963, pp. 226–27) to suggest:

The significant change for the 1960 earning wife may, therefore, be in the separation in time and space of earning and homemaking activities. Most earning wives in 1920 could coordinate their homemaking and earning activities because both were centered in the same place. Today, earning wives must perform their homemaking activities either before leaving for, or after returning from, an earning occupation. Thus, homemaking and earning activities today are competitive, whereas formerly they were complementary in the use of the homemaker's time and energy.

❧ *Growth of Industry.* The decline in farming has been paralleled by a rapid increase in industrial growth, which in turn has created a manpower demand that cannot be met by men alone. Women are needed to help run the industries on which our economy depends. This was most dramatically demonstrated during World War II, when women took the place of men in many industrial jobs which had heretofore been the sole province of men. Although following the war the need for the women's services was no longer as great, many women were reluctant to relinquish their jobs and slip meekly back into their homes.

Paralleling the great upsurge in industrial development are the shifts in emphasis on certain occupations which have facilitated the employment of women. The trend from heavy to light industry, along with increased automation with a comparable reduction in the demands made on physical strength, has served to break down many of the traditional barriers to the employment of women in industry. More and more, industries are coming to rely on brains rather than brawn.

❧ *Improved Working Conditions and Shorter Hours.* The gains made by the labor movement during the past half-century have also made it easier for women to hold jobs. Working conditions have improved and hours are shorter. A woman no longer must work in sweatshop conditions; she is well protected—some think too well—by state and federal laws restricting the hours and working conditions of women. The fact that the typical working day is only 8 hours and the typical work week only 40 makes it less difficult for a woman to assume the dual responsibilities of home and job. In earlier days the working girl who slaved at her job from the time she got up in the morning until she went to bed at night could hardly have made any contributions to a family. The dual combination is now not only possible, but quite common.

❧ *Laborsaving Devices.* Modern laborsaving devices make running a home less taxing than it once was, but they cost money, often more than the husband's income will allow. Many women prefer to earn extra money with which to purchase such conveniences rather than going without.

❧ *Emphasis on Education.* The expanded educational opportunities available to girls have served to make them less satisfied with their traditional homemaking role. There is considerable evidence that many women, having been encouraged by our educational system to think like men, find homemaking to be a relatively unstimulating way of life. They yearn for adult companionship and for persons with whom they can share intellectual interests. A job may meet these needs reasonably well.

❧ ❧ FUTURE TRENDS. Those who have been bold enough to venture predictions concerning future employment patterns generally agree that women will continue indefinitely to play an important role in the labor force. The National Manpower Council (1957) predicted that the proportion of women in the labor force, especially of those over the age of 30, will continue to increase for the foreseeable future. There is no reason to visualize any abrupt shift away from the employment of women. According to David (1960, p. 192):

Existing patterns of work outside the home are not likely, under any series of reasonable assumptions, to alter drastically in the near future. Careful projections indicate that adult women—most of whom will be wives and mothers—will play a critical role in the anticipated expansion of the working population.

More specifically, the future should witness an increase in the employment of married women as well as a concomitant increase in the average age of employed women, as more older women return to the labor force. It may also be anticipated that increases in the employment of women will come most rapidly in new and expanding industries.

Perhaps the most challenging and intriguing question concerns the potential changes in our society and economy which may result from the increased employment of women. Although no dramatic revolution is anticipated, it is surely reasonable to expect that our society and its institutions will undergo important modifications in response to the pressures exerted by a shifting labor pattern. But just how and where these changes will take place cannot be accurately predicted. The scope of the dilemma has been well stated by David (1960, p. 198):

> At present, all too little of a reliable nature is known about the implications which the new patterns of women's employment have for the meaning of work in the society, for the educational opportunities and experiences of the young, for the duration of marriage and the incidence of divorce, for the interpersonal relationships of husbands and wives both within and outside the family unit, for the parental role and functions of fathers, for family income and spending, for the availability of free time and the nature of leisure, for the character and adequacy of welfare policies and services for children, and for a host of other subjects.

Some would argue that answers to these questions will come with time and are best left to the future. Yet if outcomes of such changes can be predicted, even in a tentative way, it may be possible to meet them with more foresight than is usually allowed the victims of a major social upheaval. In a sense, the increased employment of women and the integration of women into the labor force is a new kind of industrial revolution, the consequences of which may be as far-reaching as those of the original event. As with the first industrial revolution, the results may not be entirely desirable for society. It is necessary that we anticipate the changes now and experiment with ways to meet them.

BARRIERS TO EMPLOYMENT. The question central to the employment of women is: What is standing in the way of the many educated and trained women who could be gainfully employed outside the home but who are not and probably never will be? Why aren't they?

There is no single answer. Instead, the woman who wants to work is confronted with a multiplicity of barriers which conspire to thwart her ambitions. Obviously, no woman runs into all of them, but it is likely that any woman who considers taking a job will encounter several. Whether she works will, in the long run, be a function of the strength of her own needs plus the number and strength of the barriers which block her path.

TRADITION. Nearly all women who want to work must somehow overcome the shadow cast by the traditional role women are expected to play. First of all, a married woman's place is in her home and, secondly, if she does work she must restrict her choice to certain "female" jobs. The first contention will be dealt with more thoroughly in a subsequent section. The second—that working women are acceptable only in certain jobs—is a strong one, although it no longer has a realistic basis. Most traditional job distinctions are the result of historical accidents rather than an outgrowth of real sex differences. They operate so as to prevent women from entering fields for which they might actually be well qualified. So long as a girl is willing to restrict her career plans to those fields which have been traditionally acceptable for girls—e.g., teaching and nursing—she will be given some encouragement by those around her, on the assumption that she will eventually become a wife and mother anyway. But woe to the girl who wants to enter a "man's" field. As Smuts (1959, p. 151) says, "She is likely to meet with skepticism, if not opposition, from friends, parents, and even guidance counselors."

This distinction holds true not only in the professions, but in skilled labor as well. Most industries have certain jobs that are reserved exclusively for men and others which are restricted to women, although such restrictions are usually governed by the desires of the male employees.

Major changes in this traditional pattern will have to take place on a two-way street. It is not enough to encourage women to enter occupations traditionally limited to men, and for the men to accept them there. Somehow, men must also be encouraged to enter fields which have traditionally been limited to women. If the movement were only in one direction—toward the men's jobs—the social consequences could be serious. For example, consider the situation in elementary education. Most elementary teachers are women. Some of them might, if originally given the opportunity and encouragement, have entered a field now restricted to men. But if this were to occur in the near future, where would our elementary teachers come from? To some extent, this gap would have to be filled by men. There is no reason why a man cannot be a good elementary teacher, but it certainly is counter to tradition.

Traditions change, of course, but the pace is slow. To some extent, our traditional attitudes toward female employment are undergoing important modifications, but many more are needed.[2] The problem must be approached from many different directions. One logical avenue is through employers. Women can only be accepted in jobs traditionally closed to them if they are given the opportunity, and this opportunity must come from those who do the hiring. The National Manpower Council (1957, p. 92) suggests:

Employers may be more prejudiced than they presume their customers to be. . . . Women would probably accept many jobs for

---

[2] Recent federal legislation concerning equal employment opportunities, stimulated primarily by the problems of racial minority groups in this country, prohibits job discrimination on the basis of sex as well as because of race or religion. If rigidly enforced, this could have important social implications, but it is doubtful if any such legislation will result in an immediate breakdown of the traditional sex distinctions in occupations.

which they are now considered unsuitable or in which they are thought to be uninterested, if more such jobs were open to them. . . . It is quite clear that many of the judgments about suitable or unsuitable jobs for women grow out of traditional attitudes and highly individual experience as well as a limited body of tested knowledge.

❧ ❧ ATTITUDES. Barriers of tradition merge with barriers of attitudes, tradition being the basis for many of the current attitudes concerning the employment of women. But the problem of attitudes is much broader, encompassing not only tradition but personal feelings as well. The importance of public attitudes in determining whether women will work outside the home is illustrated in the following statement by Terman and Oden (1959, p. 145), based on the experiences of Terman's group of gifted women:

The careers of women are often determined by extraneous circumstances rather than by training, talent, or vocational interest. Whether women choose to work and the occupations they enter are influenced both by their own attitudes and by the attitudes of society toward the role of women. These attitudinal factors also influence the opportunities for employment and for advancement.

There is abundant evidence that the general public views the working woman with disapproval which varies depending on the age of the woman's children and the financial status of her family. The working mother with school-age children is less strongly condemned than is the working woman whose children are of preschool age, and it is not so bad for a wife to work if her husband's income is inadequate to support the family.

The desirability of full-time employment for mothers of preschool children is open to question and will be discussed more fully in the following chapter. However, there is little if any rational reason to exclude a woman from employment because of the size of her husband's income. The attitude that a wife can work only if her family badly needs the money unfairly penalizes those women with professional training whose husbands earn enough for the family to live on. This is especially difficult for the female college graduate, inasmuch as her husband very likely also has a college education and in all probability earns an adequate salary. Many persons believe that this woman should stay home and let her expensive education rot while her uneducated counterpart, whose husband doesn't make a living wage, may be allowed to take a job. Small wonder that many housewives as well as many working women are dissatisfied with their lot. In both cases they feel they have been forced into their current status by circumstances not of their making.

Masculine Opposition. Although both men and women, as groups, tend to hold traditional attitudes toward working women, men tend to be more extreme in such beliefs. Since men hold most positions of power in both the vocational and academic worlds, women who want to work are constantly being thwarted by these attitudes. If the road to identity is to be smoothed for the female in our society, the male must adopt a more realistic and humane view of her.

It is difficult to say just why men are so strongly opposed to working women. Traditionally, they expect all women to be like their mothers, and the odds are great that their mothers were housewives. Regrettably, it also is likely that many men view the potential invasion of the labor market by women, and particularly the invasion of their own male-dominated occupations, as a threat. Just what is being threatened is not clear, but such a fear undoubtedly exists.

Much of this difficulty arises because few men know how to deal with women on an equal basis. From their point of view, men and women are two distinctly different kinds of persons and should stay in separate worlds. Even within the family, many men stress the division of responsibilities between themselves and their wives. Men profess, often with considerable smugness, that they "don't understand women," although it is implied that they are hardly worth understanding anyway.

This suggests that men resist the influx of women into their occupations because they don't know how to work with them, or at least think they don't. A business executive can deal with his secretary with little difficulty, since she's his subordinate (some would say "slave"), but he is panicked by the thought of having a woman as a colleague. Caplow (1954) suggests that part of the trouble is that interchanges among men tend to be aggressive, without causing hard feelings. When a woman is introduced into the group, the men feel that such interaction is no longer possible: since childhood they have been taught that fighting with girls is wrong, so they feel guilty when they do. Thus everyone behaves cautiously, and the spontaneity necessary for successful group interaction disappears.

Obviously, this situation is primarily a function of feelings and attitudes rather than of inherent sex differences. This is an awkward problem, one that must be met directly rather than avoided. Perhaps if men can grin and bear the influx of women into their occupations, they will get used to it. With practice, both men and women can learn to consider the other person as an individual rather than as exclusively male or female.

What has been said here about the attitudes of men toward working women is not a blanket condemnation of all men. Many of the leaders in the drive for equal rights for women have been men. Yet even some of these men have had their blind spots concerning women.[3] Perhaps the fairest conclusion is that no one is immune to petty bias. It would be difficult for men reared with certain beliefs concerning the proper roles of men and women in our society to question these beliefs, but that people can, and sometimes do, change their beliefs gives both men and women the possibility of improvement over their ancestors.

Feminine Opposition. Another surprising source of negative attitudes toward working women is other women. Many women look aghast at those members of their sex who violate the traditions by working outside the home, feeling most strongly when small children are involved; the working mother is more to be condemned than is the working wife.

A review of the history of the struggle for equal rights for women makes the current objections of some women to the employment of other women outside the home less puzzling. Women have long been divided among themselves as to the desirability of pressing for opportunities equal to those of men. Reasons for this are not clear. Some women probably simply echo the attitudes of their husbands. As we have seen, many girls make the shift from copying their fathers' attitudes to copying their husbands' with little inclination or opportunity to think for themselves.

But others have stronger reasons for being negative. Equal opportunity brings with it equal responsibility, which many women do not want. They are content in a passive role, basking in the reflected glory of the accomplishments of husband and children. They have never before thought of themselves as individuals, and

---

[3] A case in point is Ashley Montagu, a well-known anthropologist who has been a strong advocate of a better deal for women in our society through his book, *The Natural Superiority of Women.* In his book he does, however, make the following statement (Montagu, 1953, p. 177): "In general, evidence indicates that no mother should abandon her child for a job before the child is six years old." This statement is objectionable on two grounds. First, the "evidence" is far from conclusive, and certainly does not warrant such a sweeping statement. In addition, notice the use of the emotionally-loaded word "abandon." This in itself is enough to strike fear and guilt into the heart of any young mother who is considering the possibility of returning to work, even on a part-time basis. Thus Mr. Montagu, who professes to believe that women are entitled to the same rights and opportunities as men, proceeds to stack the cards in such a way that the mother of a young child has no choice but to stay home and take full-time care of her offspring. Mr. Montagu's biases seem to have gotten in the way of his common sense and his ability to interpret research evidence.

they feel it is too late to start now. Happy with their lives as they are, they resent the implication of the working woman that they might, and perhaps should, be different. To them, theirs is the only right way, and they must attack rather than support their sisters who attempt to break with tradition. They serve as examples for men who want to prove that the movement for equal employment opportunities for women is merely the result of the frustrations of a female "lunatic fringe." These men point to the contented housewife and say, "She represents the majority of women. See how happy she is." And the housewife agrees.[4] She presents a formidable enemy for the modern woman, all the greater for being able to disguise herself in the modern woman's clothes.

❧ *Employer Opposition.* The attitudes described permeate society in general, and the woman who works must be prepared to encounter them. Most of the damage, however, is psychological. They serve as barriers primarily because they make the atypical woman the subject of emotional attack as a result of her behavior. More direct barriers are the attitudes of employers, who are often reluctant to hire women for other than traditional jobs. Some practical bases for this reluctance will be discussed later, but at the moment we are concerned with the emotional reluctance based on the kinds of attitudes already described.

Employers are human and share the prejudices and biases of most of society; many of them feel that, over and above the practicalities of hiring or not hiring a woman for a specific position, it is morally wrong for a woman, especially a mother, to be working. Necessity may force them to hire women anyway, but they do so grudgingly, with perhaps a slight feeling of guilt for abetting what to them is an immoral practice. It's unlikely that in such a situation a woman will feel that working is pleasurable or that she is to be commended for engaging in it.

Most employers have difficulty, for this reason, in evaluating the performance of their female employees on the same basis that they would evaluate a man. This in turn presents problems for the woman who feels entitled to the same advancement opportunities as her male colleagues. To her it seems unfair that the fact that she is a woman is included in this judgment. But it will be. As Fuller and Batchelder (1953, p. 128) learned in their survey of women in administrative positions:

On the basis of all comments received, it may be concluded that the way in which women *behave* on the job rather than the way they

---

[4] A comparison with the racial situation in the South is obvious. In a sense, the contented housewife is the female version of "Uncle Tom."

perform the technical operations thereof is the chief determinant of their executive potential in the thinking of most superiors. . . . The principal task for women with executive aspirations seems to be *changing the attitude* both of *men* and of *other women* toward them, i.e., by themselves giving examples of fortunate rather than unfortunate job behavior [original italics].

In the final analysis, however, the most important attitude is that of the woman herself. In order to overcome existing barriers in her drive to establish herself as a nontraditional female, she must first of all believe in her own mind that she is doing the right thing *for her*. This is no simple task. She has been imbued since babyhood with the traditional concept of the female. She has had it impressed on her that the only acceptable way of life for a woman in our society is that of the full-time wife and mother. This concept has been given many names, the most recent being the "feminine mystique."[5] The woman who is secure in her own mind as to the kind of person she wants to be is better able to weather the slings and arrows of those who are trying to force her to be something else.

✿ ✿ SEX DIFFERENCES. Earlier chapters discussed in detail the major differences in abilities between men and women. Only a reminder to the reader is needed: in most areas, especially intellectual ones, the similarities between men and women are much more striking than are the differences.

Despite this, one of the major arguments used to justify differentiation between men's and women's jobs is that such jobs require different abilities, possessed to a considerably larger degree by one sex or the other. For the most part, evidence does not support this contention, although in a few instances it may have some justification.

Separation of the sexes in employment is evident in many areas. Data presented earlier concerning the employment rate of men and women in various occupational classifications show that some occupations are dominated by men and others by women. In relatively few instances do the numbers of men and women even approach equal balance. It is true that women have by now been employed in almost every occupational category, but in many of these a woman is found only rarely. Only the exceptional woman would dare to enter them in the first place.

Similarly, occupational segregation takes place within the same working area. Generally the men work in one place, on one kind

----
[5] See *The Feminine Mystique*, by Betty Friedan (1963), for a stimulating discussion of this problem.

of job, and the women in another, although the jobs may actually not be very different. Women are also handicapped in industrial situations by their lack of representation in unions and in apprentice positions. The difficulty which women have in entering a skilled-labor field is evidenced by the fact that women account for less than 2 per cent of all apprentices and about 20 per cent of all union members. Only about one-eighth of all working women belong to unions, as compared to one-fourth of the working men. To some extent, this condition exists because few women have been actively interested in unions. It results in most unions not being particularly sensitive to the needs of women employees, who make up only a small proportion of their total membership. Perhaps separate unions for women employees are needed.

Job segregation can be traced primarily to two major influences: tradition, already discussed, and confused beliefs about sex differences. These beliefs are, to a large extent, based on stereotypes which may have some general basis but which fail to consider individual differences.

One of the major arguments which employers use in defense of sex segregation is the contention that the greater strength and endurance of men make them more appropriate for certain jobs. This may have been important at one time, but physical differences between the sexes are no longer very relevant as determiners of job performance. With the advent of mechanization and automation, relatively few jobs require considerable physical strength for their performance. As Cassidy and Kozman (1947, p. 24) have put it, "A machine operates regardless of whether the hand that sets it in motion belongs to a man or a woman." The breadwinning role no longer puts a premium on physical strength; in fact, nowadays housework is often more strenuous than office work.

In the long run, the question of sex segregation in jobs is most important for its effect on the attitudes of women toward employment and toward themselves. Thus the elimination of sex segregation in jobs is simply one step in the broader fight for increased employment equality for women. As Klein (1950, p. 11) has stated:

The question whether in the competition for jobs women ought to specialize in fields which suit their feminine abilities and inclinations best cannot be answered in the affirmative, for women differ in their interests and temperaments as much as men do. To label some occupations masculine, others feminine, means to bar people of either sex from activities for which they may well be temperamentally suited and which they might accomplish with success. This exclusion is done not only at the expense of individual happiness but also to the detriment of human advance.

❧ ❧ LABOR COSTS. The question of the relative expense of employing men and women workers serves to complicate the picture. Many employers fear that the wholesale employment of women would increase their labor costs, primarily because women are less likely to be permanent employees. Especially hesitant is the employer who must sink considerable capital into the training of female employees, only to see them marry, move as their husbands' jobs demand, or become pregnant and leave the job before his investment is returned. The turnover problem is a real one and will be examined later in more detail. However, other anticipated costs of hiring women, such as a greater susceptibility to accidents or a need to provide special accommodations, are often the product of a misinformed imagination.

The other side of the coin is that women will generally work for lower pay than will men. This tends to balance out any increased costs of their employment and in some cases makes them more desirable employees, but the considerable agitation for "equal pay for equal work," enforced by legislation, may change this aspect. One wonders whether such requirements may not tend to reduce the employment opportunities for women in some areas.

❧ ❧ INCOME INEQUITIES. Lower average earnings by women is evident in Figure 6.5 which compares their wages with those of men in various occupations as of 1960. In most areas women earn approximately one-half as much as do the men. They do best, relative to men, in professional and managerial jobs, these being the only fields in which their income rose faster than that of men between 1939 and 1960. In general, however, the gap between the incomes of male and female full-time workers is widening.

An important determiner of income among both men and women is their amount of education. In 1965, women with more than four years of college earned almost one and one-half times that of college graduates, more than twice that of high school graduates, and five times that of women with less than a high school education. One explanation, of course, is that women who are motivated to seek additional education are likely to have a greater desire to make use of it once it is obtained.

Even advanced education, however, doesn't balance the incomes of men and women, although it helps. The median income of women workers with only a high school education is nearly two-fifths that of men with similar schooling; while among persons with some graduate work the women earn three-fifths as much as do the men.

There is little prospect for a closer approximation of equality of the pay of men and women employees in the near future. In

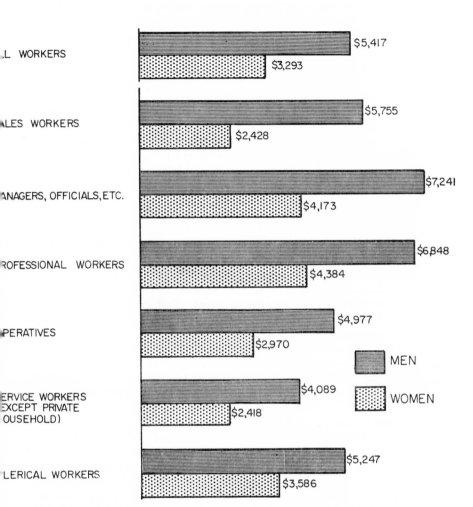

Fig. 6.5. *Average earnings (wage or salary income) of men and women workers, 1960 (U.S. Dept. of Labor; Women's Bureau, 1963).*

fact, the gap between the incomes of full-time male and female workers is steadily widening. Instead of catching up, women are falling further behind.

One reason for this discrepancy is that many women do not work full time. Thus when yearly incomes are compared, the average for all women who worked during the year will be misleadingly low. But this is not the whole story, since the gap exists among full-time workers as well.

Another commonly cited factor is that women are more often employed in lower-level jobs, because they lack job seniority and work experience and are less concerned with advancement. Unfortunately for women, those jobs in industry for which women are considered "suitable" usually pay less, which may be one reason why men shun them.

A third factor, however, is more controversial: To what extent do men and women receive equal pay for performing the same job? Comparative salary figures show that women are not paid as well as men for the same work, and many employers admit to having a double pay standard for men and women in the same job. On the other hand, it is argued that it is difficult, if not impossible, to determine the extent to which women are being discriminated against in pay. It is difficult to equate jobs, and two jobs which seem superficially to be the same may actually differ in the amount of responsibility and experience required. Thus to claim that women are paid less than men may really be to say that they are given less responsibility and that their services are deemed less valuable than those of their male counterparts.

Nevertheless, the issue of equal pay is an explosive one and has resulted in the passage of legislation to require equal pay for men and women in the same jobs. The federal government was the first major employer to formally recognize the importance of equal pay (in World War I) and it has been concerned since then with broadening this concept to all areas of the economy. However, it is doubtful if unequal pay is the most important cause of the income inequality between full-time men and women workers. The major reason is the job separation previously described, which forces women to limit their occupational aspirations to narrow areas in which, perhaps not by coincidence, the pay is seldom as attractive as that in occupations already preempted by men.

Another handicap to the woman worker is that the income of married women represents less profit than does that of a man. It has been decreed by custom that women are responsible for the care of the household and family. Since few persons, even women, are capable of managing two jobs simultaneously, the working wife must have help with her household duties. For this reason, working wives pay out between 25 and 50 per cent of their earnings for work-connected expenses. Some of these expenses—such as personal income tax, transportation, and meals—are directly related to the job itself, but others—including child care, prepared food, laundry, domestic service, and beauty parlor service—are incurred because the woman must pay for services which she might perform for herself if she were home all day. Many women avoid some of these expenses by working "overtime" at home, with some risk to their personal health as well as to family tranquility, but few women can work outside the home without incurring some related expenses, which in turn may discourage them from working at all.

More women might therefore be encouraged to seek outside employment if allowances for these expenses were made in the income tax laws. Only since 1954 have women been allowed to deduct child care expenses from their income tax, and even then the amount of deduction allowed is unrealistically small. Generally any tax breaks given to women are limited to those who must work out of financial necessity. Little help is provided the woman with professional skills who wants to work but whose husband earns an adequate income. In many cases, she may not be able to afford to work; the expenses may be too great. It is true that a desire for money may not be her major motive for working, but most people expect some financial return for their efforts.

In the long run, if we expect to encourage married women with professional skills to make use of these skills outside the home, we must make it financially more attractive to them, not only by paying them what they are worth but also by recognizing that it is costing them something to engage in this activity.

❧ ❧ LACK OF MOTIVATION TO WORK. One of the major differences between the life patterns of men and women is that married women have some choice in *whether* they will work outside the home. A man is concerned only with what kind of job to take, not whether to choose one at all, but his wife has several courses of action open to her.

Many women, given these alternatives, elect not to work, a decision reinforced by society's attitude that being a full-time wife and mother is the most important role a woman can play. Tomasson (1962) reports that, in Sweden, the birth rate is lower than in this country and most mothers work, although the economic conditions in that country do not differ greatly from ours, a discrepancy he attributes to a difference in attitude: in Sweden, working mothers have more status than housewives, while in our country their status is at best ambiguous.

It is difficult to assess the extent of motivation to work among women, but the very necessity of having to make this decision, against the grain of popular opinion, undoubtedly acts as a barrier for many women who might otherwise engage in outside employment. Women who are genuinely interested in their jobs and in advancing in them are handicapped by the low achievement drive among women in general. The exceptional ambitious female is not easily discernible from the majority, and is thereby likely to be ignored and shunted aside.

⚘ ⚘ TIME OUT FOR CHILDREN. It is unrealistic to expect that a woman will be able to stick to a career in the same way as a man, although a few do. The point at which most women quit their jobs is shortly before the birth of their first child. The difficulty is not that they quit—there are certainly many arguments in favor of this action—but that they may never go back to work, even when their full-time presence at home is no longer required by their families.

In addition to the reasons already examined as to why it may be difficult for a woman to re-enter the labor market, there is another which relates more directly to the gap in her vocational life caused by her child-raising responsibilities: the reluctance to take steps necessary to get back in. Her job skills are probably rusty, she is out of touch with the world of work, and she may be apprehensive at having to compete with the bright young girls fresh out of school. So, rather than make the effort, she avoids the issue by remaining a housewife. The intellectual and creative drives which carried her through high school and college and into a challenging job before marriage have been submerged too long in everyday trivia. For many women, these drives have been so well buried as to be undiscoverable, at least without more of an effort than they are willing to make. So they become housewives in spirit as well as title.

The Employed Woman

> What is the use of any social system in which women do not participate? In which their petticoat is not seen—where glossy ringlets cannot enter and make it paradise?
>
> ❧ *James Gordon Bennett, 1836*

DESPITE THE MANY BARRIERS which face the woman who considers employment, many women do choose to work. What causes them to come to this decision? The question is peculiar in that it is unique to married women. Men may be asked why they chose one job over another, but they are never asked why they work in the first place. But since many women do not work outside the home, it becomes legitimate to inquire why others do.

❧ ❧ ❧ REASONS WHY WOMEN WORK. There is a notable scarcity of evidence to determine why women choose to work outside the home; most of what passes for evidence is in truth merely speculation. A few studies have provided some suggestions.

Among women in high-level professional positions, many of whom are unmarried, the job plays a role in their lives similar to that in the lives of men: it satisfies their need for self-actualization and self-realization. Most married women, on the other hand, do not invest this much of themselves in their jobs. Not motivated for a career, they see their jobs as contributing to the welfare of their families. Financial rewards are most frequently cited by working women to explain their working, but many also work because they prefer a regular job to housework. According to Hoffman (1963a), the advantages of the job include a change of scene, a regular beginning and ending each day, an opportunity to interact with other adults, and more opportunities to make a creative contribution to society. Women who prefer to remain housewives apparently find compensating values in housework.

❧ ❧ FINANCIAL MOTIVES. Most married women, when asked why they work, will cite financial need as the major reason. Some claim to be contributing to essential living expenses of the family, others to improving the family's standard of living, and others to helping send their children to college. Few will say that they are working primarily for their own personal satisfaction or to maintain their job skills.

These claims are supported to some extent by evidence concerning the relationship between family income and the wife's employment. In general, working wives are more likely to come from low-income families, and the incomes of these families would suffer greatly if the wife were not working.

Nevertheless, there is some doubt that financial need is the major reason for the employment of middle-class wives, although even there the wife's income may significantly improve the family's standard of living. The ratio of the wife's income to the total family income varies little from one occupational level to another, and there is some evidence that the inverse relationship between the employment rate of wives and the income of their husbands is decreasing. It is therefore legitimate to question whether financial need is as important as most working wives insist.

One group for whom financial need is a major motive for working is mothers with small children. Whether a mother with small children will work is strongly related to the income of her husband, in a negative direction. Childless wives, by contrast, are about equally likely to work regardless of the level of their husbands' incomes.

How do families use the added income of the wife? According to Feldman (1958), there are several possible patterns: for savings or for major expenses; for immediate luxuries; or to compensate for the husband's low income in providing the necessities of life. In general, the third reason would be most commonly found among lower-class families and the second reason among the others. Apparently relatively few families view the wife's income as supplementary, to be saved for emergencies when she may not be able to work. The usual tendency is to spend it for things that the family would otherwise not be able to afford. Carroll (1962) suggests that the wife is probably working for some specific purpose, in order to buy something she particularly wants or to defray a major expense, such as a college education for a son or daughter; she rewards herself for working by spending the money for this purpose. In addition, whether she works full time or not, she is still able to work, which in itself acts as a financial reserve: if anything serious occurred to cause a strain on the budget she could go back to work. It is thus the wife's working *potential*, rather than her current income, which provides a "financial cushion" for many families.

The fact that many wives now continue to work after marriage until the first child is born increases the probability that they will later return to work in order to maintain the previously established spending patterns. As the first child and subsequent children arrive, financial demands may increase more rapidly than the father's income, so that in order to maintain the family's standard of living the wife may have to return to work, at least on a part-time basis.

Depending on the nature of the job in which she is engaged, the working wife has numerous expenses which she would not incur as a housewife. Among these are clothes (especially if she is in contact with the public), transportation, household help, and child-care expenses if she is a mother. When these are all deducted from her income, the remaining amount may be low enough to suggest that the stated motive of financial gain is largely a rationalization. On the other hand, many of these expenses may themselves be rewarding. For example, it is likely that working wives have a clothes advantage—both in quality and quantity—over their homemaking sisters.

What can be concluded about the validity of financial need as a motivator for working women? The chances are that it has been overstressed, especially for middle- and upper-class wives. Among the lower class, the income brought in by the wife may mean the difference between an adequate and inadequate standard of living. As the husband's income increases, however, this kind of financial need diminishes and eventually disappears, but their wives continue to work in about the same proportions, except for those with small children. The conclusion is therefore inevitable that other psychological factors are actually playing a more important role in this decision than is generally acknowledged.

Why, then, do so many women of all income levels insist that financial need is their major reason for working? Part of the answer may be that "financial need" is a state of mind, representing a gap between real and desired family income. In other words, many middle-class wives work in order to provide their families with a standard of living which seems to them to be desirable and perhaps necessary at their socioeconomic level.

A more realistic reason may be that, in our present stage of social change, financial need seems to be the most *acceptable* reason for working, or at least the most *understandable*. Therefore most women fall back on this to "defend" their working. They fear that society may not understand and accept a more personal motive, which actually may be closer to the truth.

The unanswered question is whether the women themselves recognize that "financial need" is a rationalization or whether they believe it to be true. Speculation about unconscious motives is risky, since there can be no proof one way or the other of their existence. In short, we need more evidence before we can draw any final conclusions as to what motivates women to work outside the home.

✣ ✣ ✣ VARIABLES RELATED TO THE DECISION TO WORK

✣ ✣ INTELLIGENCE. There is some evidence that, at least among college graduates, women who work outside the home tend to be brighter than those who don't. Nevertheless, the relationship between mental ability and employment among women is not striking. There is little indication that, in general, women with higher intelligence feel especially constrained to seek intellectual outlets in employment.

Some support for this conclusion comes from the experiences of the women in Terman's gifted group. As adults, in 1955, 50 per cent were housewives, 42 per cent had full-time jobs, and only 8 per cent worked part time. One-third of those with graduate degrees were housewives, as were 40 per cent of those who had had some graduate study and nearly two-thirds of those who had a bachelor's degree. It may be concluded that many of these women were making little direct use either of their abilities or of their education in their everyday lives.

✣ ✣ RACE. Comparison of the employment rates of white and non-white women in the United States shows striking variations. As of 1966, 45 per cent of Negro women and 38 per cent of whites were in the labor force, although the gap is narrowing. The major contrast comes when the employment rates of married and single women are compared. Among Negroes, the proportion employed is about the same among both married and unmarried, while among whites about one-half of unmarried females work, as compared with one-fourth of those married.

To a large extent these differences are reflections of variables other than race, such as socioeconomic status and amount of education. The median educational level among white women in 1965 was 12.1 years as compared with 9.2 years among nonwhites. Negro women, however, are just as likely to graduate from college as are Negro men, in contrast with the unbalanced sex ratio among whites. The largest proportion of working Negro women (60 per cent) are employed in service occupations, as compared with only about 20 per cent of white working women.

✵ ✵ RURAL VS. URBAN RESIDENCE. Women who live in urban areas are twice as likely to be employed outside the home as are those on farms or in small towns, although this gap seems to be narrowing. The employment rate among women also varies considerably from one city to another, due primarily to differences in the proportion of Negroes in the community as well as to the type of industry which predominates: proportionately more women are employed by light industry than by heavy industry.

✵ ✵ REGION. The employment rate among women is not consistent from one part of the country to another. This is partly due to differences in industry, but it is also an outgrowth of the traditions and mores within different sections. In the Northeast, for example, the employment rate among single women is high but among married women it is low. The opposite is the case in the South and West: few single women are employed, but the rate of employment among married women is relatively high. In all, women workers are concentrated primarily in the Middle Atlantic and North Central states.

✵ ✵ COUNTRY OF RESIDENCE. The pattern of employment among women also varies from country to country, and it should not be surprising to find that other countries do not necessarily agree with our way of doing things. Perhaps the most outstanding contrast with our society in this respect is the Soviet Union, in which sex differences in rate of employment as well as in occupational distributions are minimal.

Some idea of the extent of this contrast can be obtained from the following figures: in Russia, women account for about 50 per cent of all college students, 35 per cent of all engineering students, 70 per cent of all medical students, 35 per cent of all research workers, 75 per cent of all physicians, 70 per cent of all teachers, 35 per cent of college faculties, 45 per cent of workers in industry, and 60 per cent of workers on collective farms. This has been necessitated by the decimation of the male population during World War II, which forced women to assume many of the responsibilities normally allotted to men. The Russians, however, have apparently accepted this situation and it seems to be generally agreed that nearly all occupations are open to men and women on an equal basis.

This is not meant as a plea that the United States should blindly follow Russia's lead. It would be foolish to adopt a program simply because the Soviet Union has had success with it, just as it would be equally foolish to reject a program on the same basis. Nevertheless, it must be recognized that Russian society does not seem to have been adversely affected by the large-scale employment of women. In fact, by the effective utilization of their womanpower resources they have been able to produce many accomplishments which would probably have otherwise been beyond their reach.

ℐ *ℐ* *ℐ* CHOICE OF A JOB. Research concerning variables related to job choice among women is negligible compared to the amount of similar research among men. It is likely that women do not choose occupations for the same reasons as do men, but their exact motives remain obscure.

ℐ *ℐ* WOMEN'S CRITERIA OF JOB CHOICE. If it is true, as most women profess, that they work out of financial necessity, then it would seem logical that their working is not the product of a carefully considered life pattern but is instead determined by their immediate situation, making the choice of a job not determined primarily by special training or earlier plans but instead dictated by what is immediately available. This is obviously an inefficient way to choose a job, but it likely is the manner in which the majority of women enter the world of work. Even if they have special training and skills, they are limited in their choice of jobs by the locality in which they happen to live, especially if they are married.

Despite this, women do not necessarily choose their jobs blindly, but they seem to use different selection criteria than do men. Two major differences stand out: (a) women generally see a job in short-term, temporary perspective and are therefore less interested in long-term job characteristics such as retirement and opportunities for advancement; and (b) women are more sensitive to current characteristics of the job, such as the working conditions. For some women, none of the usual job preference factors are of high importance, and studies restricted to these would give a misleading picture. For example, among young girls an important determiner of job choice is the opportunity to meet eligible men. The job itself is of secondary concern.

Further evidence that men and women differ in their attitudes toward their jobs is seen in the tendency of women to avoid jobs which require a long-term commitment and considerable preparation. Parrish (1961) points out that 95 per cent of all working women are found in either short-term jobs requiring little skill or in long-term jobs requiring little-to-medium skill, with only the remaining 5 per cent in long-term jobs requiring high skill. He believes that women are becoming increasingly *less* interested in high-level careers; instead, most girls who intend to work after marriage plan to combine marriage with a job involving low skill rather than planning for a career. Parrish cites two reasons for this trend: (a) our expanding economy, which by providing higher pay for a shorter work week makes low-skill jobs more available and more practical for wives and mothers; and (b) increased barriers—such as the time, effort, and cost of obtaining an advanced degree—erected against employment in jobs requiring considerable skill.

Whether a woman remains on a job depends in part on how well satisfied she is with it. Research on job satisfaction among female workers has been infrequent compared to that among men, partly because it is recognized that women enter and leave their jobs in many cases for reasons other than personal satisfaction. From the research to date, we can conclude that women are generally less well satisfied with their jobs than are men and are more likely to quit if dissatisfied, and that older women are more satisfied than are younger ones, perhaps because they have more realistic expectations. Reasons for job dissatisfaction are difficult to locate among women, although it is evident that they tend to be more highly related to interpersonal variables and less to personal achievements than is the case among men.

Perhaps the soundest conclusion is that research concerning job satisfaction among workers must take sex differences into consideration, and men and women employees should not be combined into one group for analysis. The time may come when this will no longer be a problem but for the present, women workers have somewhat different reasons for working than do men, and these differences are reflected in their reactions to their jobs.

۶ ۶ SELECTION OF FEMALE EMPLOYEES. If women have relatively superficial reasons for choosing their jobs, employers have likewise not been very active in refining their selection techniques for women employees, inasmuch as few such studies have been reported in the literature. Perhaps employers feel that the turnover rate among women workers is so great that it is not practical to be concerned with selecting the best person for the job. It is true that continuance on a job is influenced by many factors in addition to skill and attitude toward the job. But as more women enter the labor force, and as outside employment for women becomes more acceptable, it may become necessary for employers and industrial psychologists to learn as much about the characteristics of their successful women employees as they now know about the men.

✲ ✲ ✲ DRAWBACKS TO HIRING WOMEN. Do women employees cause more headaches than they are worth? It is commonly assumed that women workers present problems: they are likely to quit after a short time, their absenteeism rate is high, and they are susceptible to accidents, all of which is complicated by the distressing tendency of young married women to become pregnant.

Since these assumptions restrict the job possibilities of women who want to work, their validity must be examined. There appears to be a great deal more smoke than fire, although some embers nevertheless remain, and there definitely is room for improvement. Some of the problems are beyond the control of the women themselves, but others are within their command and could be remedied by a concerted effort on their part.

✲ ✲ JOB TURNOVER. A decided sex difference is evident when the job turnover rates of men and women employees are compared. The hiring rate for women during the 1950's was approximately 15 per cent higher than that for men, while the total labor turnover was as much as 50 to 60 per cent higher among women, meaning that an employer could count on longer service from male employees than from females.

Since a woman's motivation for working varies considerably from one stage of her life to another, women move into and out of the labor force with a frequency which is distressing to those who must hire and train new employees. On the other hand, Wells (1955) points out that women's quit rates are more stable over a period of time than are men's, as the women's rates are tied more closely to personal and family variables and less to economic conditions.

The picture becomes a little brighter when details are examined. For example, the job turnover rate among women varies considerably by age, being greatest among young women who leave their jobs to get married or to have babies. Even those with small children who return to work may do so only on a temporary basis. But once the children are in school, and even more after they have left home, employment becomes more stable, so that the highest regularity of employment among women is found among those between the ages of 45 and 60.

There are indications that the job turnover rate among women is declining: the quit rates of women workers were only 30 per cent above those of men in 1950–55 as compared with 40 per cent in

1944–47. Several possible explanations are offered, including an increased interest in continuing employment among women, the greater availability of housework aids, the increased provision by industries of personnel workers to deal with problems of women workers, and the greater pressure to maintain a high standard of living. In addition, the influx of older women into the labor force has resulted in greater stability among women workers in general.

If this trend continues, the turnover problem will diminish in importance, although it is unlikely that women's employment will ever be as stable as that of men since their work motivations are different. But this higher turnover rate among women employees has advantages for the employer: it enables him to hire women for additional help on a short-term basis during seasonal peaks as well as to pay them lower salaries, since women are less likely than men to stay on a job long enough to move into higher salary brackets.

⤷ ⤷ ABSENTEEISM. Employers are also concerned about the problem of absenteeism, which they believe to be more extensive among women workers. Actually the difference in total amount of absences is not great, but the pattern differs considerably between the sexes. The rate of absenteeism among women workers is about twice that among men, but men lose more working days when they are absent, with the result that the number of days lost from work per year is about the same for men as it is for women.

Married women, however, are absent from time to time because of home responsibilities rather than illness. If both husband and wife work, it is generally assumed that if one of them is needed at home it will be the wife who will skip work. This is of course most likely to be a problem for a couple with small children, which explains why absenteeism among women is not related to age or marital status, but is related to the number of dependents.

It may be concluded that women do not take their jobs as seriously as do men. They are more likely to take time off when ill, albeit for shorter periods, and to relegate the job to second place in favor of family demands. It is difficult to argue that this is not in the best interests of society, although the individual employer might prefer that the job were given greater priority. Nevertheless, until women take their jobs more seriously they must expect to encounter job discrimination.

Employers must recognize that the absenteeism problem among women employees is largely caused by mothers with small children and that this reflects a conflict between full-time employment and child-care responsibilities. Many of these women might prefer part-time work to full-time employment if such opportunities were available, but part-time jobs are relatively scarce. If employers were to make more effort to adapt their jobs to part-time workers, the absenteeism problem could be reduced.

꒚ ꒚ ACCIDENTAL INJURIES. The injury rates among women in industry are generally much lower than among men. This may be due in part to greater care and caution among women, but it undoubtedly also reflects the fact that few are employed in dangerous jobs. On the other hand, women, who are more apt to be employed on a part-time basis or in seasonal jobs, have less opportunity to learn the job well, thereby increasing the risk of accidents. In any event, the employer need not be concerned that the hiring of women workers will result in increased injuries in his shop.

꒚ ꒚ PREGNANCY. Men employers tend to view the pregnant woman with awe and trepidation, although pregnancy among women workers is certainly no longer a novelty. A significant proportion of women workers become pregnant, and their presence on the job is difficult to ignore.

There are two ways to look at the relationship between pregnancy and employment: how the pregnancy affects the woman's job performance, and how her job affects her pregnancy. The first question is almost impossible to answer since it depends primarily on the nature of the job itself. A relatively sedentary job will probably continue to be performed with little if any loss in efficiency, while a job requiring considerable physical effort might be a handicap to a pregnant woman. The decision in each case must be made by the employer, but he should consider carefully whether he is deciding objectively.

The question of the effect of the job on the pregnancy is a serious one and can only be answered by a physician. Studies which have attempted to investigate this problem have typically become entangled in conflicting variables, thus allowing no general conclusions to be drawn. The best answer seems to be that this is a decision which must be made by the woman and her physician or by the company doctor. If they agree that she may continue to work after becoming pregnant, the employer should respect this decision unless he has good reason to believe that her job performance will be impaired.

Surveys of the effects of gynecological and obstetrical problems on work performance among women have concluded that there is little evidence that physiological changes such as the menstrual cycle and the menopause have any significant effect on the work performance of most women.

꒚ ꒚ LEGAL REGULATIONS. Whether legal restrictions should be called a problem is debatable, but many employers are reluctant to hire women employees because of the myriad regulations surrounding their conditions of employment. As a result of the exploitation of female workers during the last century, laws were enacted by both the federal and state governments to protect women from abuse, in the same manner that children were protected by child labor laws. Forty-three states and the District of Columbia have laws which regulate the number of daily and/or weekly hours of employment for women in one or more industries; 25 states prohibit the employment of women in certain industries or under certain conditions, and other state laws regulate rest periods, night work, and employment near childbirth. The Women's Bureau (1966a, p. 227) is on record as considering such laws to be important for the welfare of our country: "The Nation's best interests demand good labor standards for women, many of whom are mothers and homemakers as well as wage earners."

There is disagreement on the extent to which stringent regulations are needed. Many employers as well as many women themselves believe that women are capable of managing their own affairs and should be given the same rights as men to determine when, how long, and under what conditions they should work.

Restrictive legislation may have been necessary in a period when women were thought to be defenseless and in need of protection by men. Perhaps these archaic regulations are harmless and thus not a topic for concern, but to the extent that they prevent women from competing with men for jobs on an equal basis they are discriminatory and therefore unjust.

✄ ✄ ✄ WOMEN AS SUPERVISORS. Despite their prevalence in the labor force, women are not generally found in supervisory positions. There are several reasons for this, some of which involve attitudes and customs in employment as well as time-worn and often disproved assumptions about the characteristics of women.

✄ ✄ BARRIERS TO PROMOTION. Many women are barred from promotion by their own attitudes toward their jobs. Married women who feel that their first loyalty is to their families would not be willing to invest in the many requirements essential to promotion. They are also not free to pull up stakes and move to another part of the country if such a move were required for advancement and would be less stable in executive posts if their husbands were subject to moving. Their irregular work pattern gives them less job continuity and thus less experience to qualify for promotion.

A second handicap to promotion is that most women have little interest in being promoted, anyway. The low achievement drive of most women and their reluctance to assume responsibility, coupled with their desire to be one of the group and to do the accepted thing, means that it is the exceptional woman who is greatly concerned with getting ahead in her job.

The third barrier is that most employees, whether male or female, prefer to be supervised by a man rather than by a woman. To many men, having a woman for a boss seems to be psychologically threatening, as though they are somehow in danger of losing their masculinity. For this reason, women have great difficulty in attaining supervisory positions in fields in which male workers predominate.

But even in areas in which most of the employees are women, male supervisors are often preferred. Women often have trouble working for another woman and seem to get along more easily with a man as their boss. Much of this problem is probably simply the result of social stereotypes, but the difficulties are real enough to cause many employers to be reluctant to promote capable women to supervisory positions, even when the persons being supervised are mostly female.

There are, of course, many instances in which women are functioning quite well in supervisory positions, and these examples will undoubtedly continue to expand. In some fields, such as telephone companies and women's areas in department stores, women supervisors are the rule rather than the exception. But in other areas, the picture is not as promising. In professions such as teaching and library work, composed primarily of women, relatively few women are employed in administrative positions. This is especially evident in teaching, which employs more women than any other profession. Women account for 90 per cent of all elementary teachers but for only 50 per cent of the elementary principals, and the latter proportion is decreasing. This seems to be partly a function of community size, since the percentage of women principals varies from 38 in small urban school districts to 62 in large districts.

❧ ❧ IMPROVING CHANCES FOR PROMOTION. It is unlikely that the proportion of women supervisors will ever equal that of men. The achievement drive and desire to take responsibility is differentially taught to males and females from an early age. In addition, the home responsibilities of many women employees will continue to be a limitation. But beyond this, it seems likely as well as desirable that women will have more opportunity to assume more supervisory responsibility in the future than they have had up to the present time.

What can be done to facilitate this trend, in view of the reluctance of women to become supervisors? One suggestion is to bear in mind that the characteristics of a successful supervisor among women may not be the same as those among men. Women in leadership positions seem to have personalities different from those of women in general, while male leaders tend to be "one of the group." Leadership seems not to be a feminine characteristic, whether in an informal group or in a job situation.

A second possibility is that women may be helped to gain confidence as supervisors by putting a man in charge of the entire operation. Women seem to feel more secure when working for a man than for another woman, and a man may be able to delegate supervisory authority to women in such a way as to make it possible for them to be adequate as supervisors.

A third point is made by Moore (1960), who suggests that in order for women to move into administrative positions those who are already administrators (mostly men) will have to recognize their abilities and help them to develop. Capable administrators and supervisors do not grow spontaneously; they are generally nurtured and developed by someone in a higher position who recognizes their potential. Unfortunately, this is in most cases a man, and he naturally recognizes such potential more readily in another man than in a woman. In order to break this cycle, male administrators will have to go out of their way to develop administrative talents in their female employees.

❧ ❧ ❧ EMPLOYMENT PATTERNS OF OLDER WOMEN. The proportion of older women in the labor force has grown more rapidly during the past two decades than has that of any other segment of the population. In 1965, 41 per cent of women between the ages of 55 and 64 were in the labor force, as were 10 per cent of those 65 and older. Moreover, a higher proportioi was engaged in full-time employment than was the case among women workers in general.

Older women tend to be concentrated in a fairly narrow range of occupations, especially if they enter the labor force without recent specialized training or experience. The single most frequent occupation of older women is retail sales; other popular fields include clerical work, professional occupations, and service jobs. In addition, older women are frequently found in self-employed positions such as housekeepers or domestic service, practical nurses, etc.

Why does interest in outside employment increase so dramatically as women grow older? In one sense, this parallels a change in women's roles as determined by the discontinuities in their lives. As Kyrk (1956, p. 131) says, "The economic history of women is one of movement from one economic role to another with uncertainty as to how long she will fill either of them."

A woman's role problems often grow more acute as she moves away from being centered entirely on her family as the demands of the family become less intense. This may begin when her last child enters school, which now occurs at the age of 32 for the average woman. From this point on, her life becomes progressively either more dull or more diversified. Many older women therefore have difficulty determining what role they can most appropriately play and how to use their time and energies constructively.

In recent years the job performance of older workers has come under close scrutiny, as the great increase in numbers of older persons in our society has forced employers to reconsider their belief that young persons are to be preferred to older workers. There has been accumulated a large, consistent body of evidence to show that older persons generally do as well, if not better, on most measures of job performance. They do not, of course, have the speed and agility of a younger person, but such handicaps are balanced by the value of their experience and judgment and the care which they put into their work.

Another advantage of the older worker, which is especially noticeable among women, is the reduced rate of job turnover. This is to be expected, in light of the earlier discussion concerning the work patterns of women. A young woman is, in most cases, working only until she begins her family, at which point she drops out of the labor market for a time. The older woman, on the other hand, is more likely to stay with her job once she has returned to work and to be more willing to invest a significant amount of effort in it.

Generally, then, the evidence seems consistent that older women are desirable employees and that the employer is likely to get more out of them, both in length of service and performance on the job, than he is from younger women.

Thus far we have stressed that the job problems and performance of older women are in many ways similar to those of older men. However, even at the older ages some important differences remain.

In some ways older women are in a paradoxical situation in the job market. For some reason, their age is likely to be a greater detriment to their employment than it is for men. Women seem to be perceived as "old" sooner than men, perhaps because we have a stereotype of the elderly grandmother which does not include the idea of employment. Our society also tends to retire women at an earlier age than men, as incorporated in our social security laws which allow women to begin drawing their benefits at the age of 62 while their husbands must wait until they are 65. This is puzzling if we consider that, in all probability, the woman will live longer than her husband anyway, and will thus be saddled with a considerably longer period of retirement. It would thus seem more realistic to encourage the hiring of older women as well as older men, rather than to discourage it.

Perhaps one reason why employment among older women is frowned upon is the differences in training requirements between men's and women's jobs, as described by Belbin (1953, p. 181): "It is on fast, light work where age difficulties most characteristically occur that women are more frequently employed." He found that training difficulties start in the mid-twenties on operations involving small parts and fine control. Thus women may be handicapped by difficulties inherent in the kinds of jobs they normally fill, especially in industrial settings. Perhaps if these facts were recognized they could be incorporated into training in such a way as to minimize these handicaps.

The menopause, which most women undergo between the ages of 45 and 55, is an additional reason for the reluctance to employ older women. In actuality, for most women the menopause is a gradual process involving only mild physical reactions which should not be a detriment to performance on most jobs. Menopause itself, caused by changes in the sex hormones within the body, results in the cessation of menstruation, a somewhat less feminine appearance, and in some cases a temporary endocrine imbalance. It may cause a weight problem and it may make the woman more tired, necessitating opportunity for rest. But there seems to be general agreement that most of the changes associated with the menopause are not physical but psychological. What seems to happen is that during this period earlier problems become intensified, perhaps to the point where the woman is unable to cope with them adequately. In some cases psychiatric help may be necessary, but usually only of a short-term nature. With a few exceptions, the menopause should present no danger to a woman's performance on her job. In fact, a satisfying job in which she can expend her energies may help to reduce the frustrations and anxieties caused by the menopause by providing a woman with other outlets and experiences.

It is evident that older women can be successful and productive employees, and that their employment may benefit both their employers and themselves. There is, however, the problem of getting older women back into the labor market. It is not easy for a woman who has been a homemaker for a good many years to suddenly set out to find a job. She may need help, both in analyzing her own skills and abilities and in locating appropriate job opportunities. Society should encourage the development of counseling and placement services for the mature woman of a quality equal to those now available to young persons.

The Working Wife and Mother

Life in America is made up of a tissue of fictions that do not accord with reality, and the omnipresent "Mommie" is one of them which could very well be dispensed with.

✄ *Alicia Patterson, 1962*

THE EMPLOYMENT of women has become an accepted fact with diminishing debate as to whether it is appropriate. Our economy depends greatly on women as a source of labor, especially in jobs traditionally shunned by men as suitable only for women. It would be impossible to reverse this trend and to return to a world in which the labor force were composed entirely of men, if in fact such a condition ever existed.

The crucial issue concerning the employment of women is, therefore, whether women *with family responsibilities* should work outside the home. The working woman is an accepted part of our society, but the working wife—and, more importantly, the working mother—is still subject to criticism from many sides. Such criticism can arouse strong guilt feelings on the part of women themselves and probably limits the number of married women who seek employment outside the home. It is therefore important to examine carefully the effects of a woman's employment on her other roles, especially those of wife and mother.

Inasmuch as most research discussed in this chapter deals with differences between working and nonworking wives, we should consider whether this is a meaningful dichotomy. If it is found that working wives are different from those who don't work outside the home, or that they exert different kinds of influences on their husbands and children, what does this really tell us? Perhaps very little. Few if any investigators have studied such persons *before* they made the decision to work. Therefore there is no way of knowing whether differences between working and nonworking wives and their families exist *because* the women in one group are working and the others aren't, or are due to other important differences between women who choose to work and those who don't. This limitation must be kept in mind throughout the following discussion.

✻ ✻ ✻ EFFECTS ON THE HOME

✻ ✻ THE GENERAL PROBLEM. Even those writers who have most strongly advocated an increased emphasis on the working role of women have been forced to concede that the working wife and mother is subject to more stress and responsibility than is the unmarried working woman. In effect, the married working woman is trying to combine two roles, both of which may involve full-time responsibilities. As a result, she may find herself doing a poor job of each. The demands of her job may require a large output of energy, leaving her with less than enough to meet her home responsibilities. Thus the working wife must consider the effects of her working on her husband, her children, and herself.

This problem, of course, is not limited to women. Men must also strike a balance of some sort between their home and job responsibilities, and there are many sad cases of men who have not been able to do this successfully. The husband who spends too much time with his family may find that his chances for promotion are lessened because he's not putting in extra effort for the company. By contrast, the husband who devotes too much time to his job may find himself without a family at all. Neglect is a common complaint of wives in divorce actions.

But a man has at least two advantages over his wife in dealing with conflicting responsibilities. First, it is accepted that men should work outside the home. The wife who works, and who inevitably encounters some conflict in responsibility as a result, is handicapped in dealing with it constructively by the fact that society—and perhaps she herself—doubts whether she should be working in the first place. Thus, while the man can handle such a conflict without changing the basic structure of his life, the woman may attribute the conflict to the feeling that she is doing something basically wrong.

The second advantage for men is that it is acceptable for them to put their job first. Much as society may deplore the husband who neglects his family for his job, it has at the same time idealized the image of the hard-driving, successful business or professional man who overcomes all obstacles to get to the top of his field. Although exceptions do occur, it would be difficult for a man who spends a great deal of time with his family to make such a climb. We have no such idealization of the hard-driving woman who neglects her family in order to get to the top; she is a horrible caricature of a female, only to be deplored. A man may be criticized if he neglects his family too much, but when the rewards are gratifying enough, criticism is reduced to a point many men can ignore. The woman, however, has no such compensation. Society agrees that her first responsibility is to her family, and she may not question this.

Therefore it would seem that the major difference between working husbands and working wives is not in the conflict of responsibilities, which arise for both, but in the ways in which society allows them to deal with these conflicts, and in the extent to which they are able to view these conflicts as a necessary and inevitable part of assuming a dual role. In order to handle the dual responsibilities of home and job, therefore, the woman must first recognize that conflicts will inevitably arise, and she must feel some degree of freedom to resolve them along whatever lines seem most appropriate for her.

✤ ✤ SPECIFIC EFFECTS. Whether the wife works outside the home is certainly not the only variable which influences the structure of the family and the relationships among its members. First to be considered is the effect of the wife's employment on the husband-wife relationship and on the woman herself in her role as wife and mother.

✤ *Marital Adjustment.* There is no consistent evidence that working women are subject to greater marital dissatisfaction than are those who are full-time housewives. Research to date on this topic has produced inconclusive, and sometimes conflicting, results. One problem is that marital satisfaction is difficult to measure accurately. A woman's estimate of her degree of satisfaction with her marriage is influenced by her personal needs, by the way she perceives the interactions within the marriage, and by her ability to be honest with herself and with others about her feelings. Gover (1963) suggests that, inasmuch as it is conventional in our society to have a well-adjusted marriage and since working wives are less conventional than those who don't work, any tendency of the latter group to report greater marital satisfaction may be a reflection of their general need to be conventional rather than of a true difference. There is, in fact, some evidence that the satisfactions which the working wives derive from their jobs balance their dissatisfactions with their marriages, enabling them to tolerate a greater degree of conflict than those women whose lives are limited to their homes and families.

❧ *Power Structure.* While there is general agreement that the power structure of families in which the wife works outside the home is different from that in families with full-time housewives, it is difficult to determine whether the chicken or the egg came first. It seems reasonable to assume that the wife's working would directly affect the power structure of the family, inasmuch as she is absent from the home a great deal and, when home, has more intensive demands made on her time, necessitating that the husband assume responsibilities and make decisions which might otherwise be left to his wife. However, it is also likely that women who work outside the home have personality characteristics which would in any case contribute to the development of power structures different from those involving more conventional wives.

It is established that husbands of working wives participate more in household tasks, but there is no evidence of any consistent differences in decision-making patterns between families with working and nonworking wives although the employment of the wife is more apt to disrupt the power structure among the working class.

In any case, however, most working wives seem reluctant to exert their influence to an extent commensurate with their economic contribution to the family. Perhaps they sense that they must not alter the traditional roles too drastically, or perhaps they are satisfied not to have to bear a large responsibility for family decisions.

❧ *Role of Wife and Mother.* Most girls grow up with the idea that the role of wife and mother is the most important one for a woman to fulfill. What happens, then, to their perceptions of themselves in this role if they are working? The evidence suggests that mothers who work have more doubts about their adequacy as mothers than those who are full-time housewives, but this conclusion must be qualified by recognizing the nature of the situation.

For one thing, the woman's reason for working is a major factor in her feelings about herself as a mother. Women who have a true interest in their jobs tend to believe that their working has a favorable effect on their maternal role, whereas those who work out of necessity are more apt to be critical of their performance as mothers.

Perhaps even more basic to this question is the difficulty in assessing the validity of responses to this kind of question. When asked about their adequacy as mothers, do women report the way they *really* feel, the way they *think* they feel, or the way they think they *ought* to feel? One might speculate, for example, that women who work because they want to may report a favorable effect on their maternal role because of guilt feelings. Or perhaps the employed mothers in other studies who have reported more doubts about their adequacy as mothers are simply being more honest about their true feelings. Perhaps the nonworking mothers have similar doubts but, since they have invested themselves entirely in this role, they must deny the existence of such doubts. Whether any or all of these explanations is true is open to question, but they should at least serve to make one cautious in generalizing about the feelings of employed and unemployed mothers.

✤ ✤ ✤ THE HUSBAND'S ATTITUDE. Perhaps no single variable is as closely related to the effects of a wife's employment as is the attitude of her husband. A husband's influence operates in two ways: by determining whether his wife works at all, and, if she does work, by affecting the impact of her working on the family.

Many husbands prefer that their wives not work, for a number of reasons. Some believe that a working mother is detrimental to her children, others fear that having their wives working would be harmful to their own careers, while still others are simply disinclined to make the adjustments in their way of life that would be necessary if their wives were to work. The result is that many women are discouraged from working outside the home by the negative reaction of their husbands.

Some women, however, work despite their husbands' disapproval, but the results may be disastrous. Husbands whose wives work against their wishes tend to perceive more conflict in their marriages than do those husbands whose wives do not work or who work with their approval, although objectively the degree of conflict may be about the same. Apparently such a husband feels threatened by his wife's employment, and the fact that she continues to work despite his protests indicates to him that something is fundamentally wrong with their relationship. Perhaps he feels that his wife is working because of dissatisfaction with the marriage, which in turn may cast doubts on his own adequacy as a husband.

In contrast to the harmful effects of a husband's negative attitude toward his wife's employment is the beneficial effect that a positive attitude on the part of the husband may have for the whole family. In addition to allowing his wife the freedom to live a fuller life, the help which the husband gives in assisting his working wife with household tasks may improve family solidarity.

The wife who works against her husband's objections is likely to be fighting a losing battle. In order to successfully combine homemaking and an outside job, a woman needs the cooperation of her family, and especially of her husband. Among other things, this usually requires that the husband assume greater responsibility for household tasks, or at least that he be willing to tolerate a lower standard of household maintenance on the part of his wife.[1] The disapproving husband will probably do neither of these. Instead, he may try to sabotage her working by overreacting to any deficiencies in meeting her household responsibilities. Few women have enough confidence in the rightness of their decision to work to be able to withstand such pressure. If the wife continues to work, it is likely to be at the expense of her mental health and a satisfactory marital relationship. The only sensible alternative is for her to quit and to assume the role that her husband expects. Whether she can adjust her needs to this role is another question.

The importance of the husband's attitude leads us to wonder how and why husbands differ in this respect. Why do some husbands encourage their wives to work outside the home while others are in open opposition? One explanation is that these men have an honest difference of opinion as to the effects of a working wife on the family. Those who oppose their wives' employment may do so because they believe that their children would suffer. But the evidence suggests that many of these reasons are primarily rationalizations and that the true motives lie deeper.

Men tend to be self-centered. They would like their homes to revolve around them, and this is more likely to occur when the wife doesn't work. The husband of a working wife must adjust to the fact that his wife's schedule and additional responsibilities are such that his needs may not always come first. Most men have not been reared to accept this. In their minds, their wives should adjust to them because they are performing the more important role in the family. Thus an important prerequisite to a husband's approval of his wife's working outside the home if she wants is the feeling that her needs are just as important as his.

A second, but related, cause of difficulty is the reluctance of many husbands to lend a hand with household tasks, apparently out of fear that participating in such activities somehow makes them less masculine. Our society has developed an unflattering image of the hen-pecked husband, tied to the kitchen with an apron string, engaging in a multitude of women's tasks and being ridiculed by his friends and his children for not asserting himself. Boys learn from an early age that it is very bad to be called a "sissy," and many grown men seem to live in fear of a similar taunt.

Actually, though, the household tasks which the husband of a

---

[1] Perhaps the most sensible alternative is for the wife to hire outside help with her housework, but some husbands object to this on the grounds that they don't want a stranger prowling around their house.

working wife takes over are more likely to be those of a "masculine" nature anyway: mowing the lawn, repairing furniture, etc. In other words, in a family in which both the husband and wife work outside the home the role distinctions in household responsibilities are more likely to be traditional than in those families in which the wife is home all the time. If the husband is willing to help with the "feminine" tasks too, so much the better for his wife, but if not, she can probably use part of her income to hire outside help or encourage her children to take over some of these responsibilities.

 ✺ ✺ ✺ THE HUSBAND-WIFE RELATIONSHIP: A SUM-MATION. Despite these numerous problems, many women are able to work out a satisfactory combination of employment and family roles and responsibilities. Although it cannot be said that outside employment would be desirable for all women, it certainly is for many. Housework is not the only avenue by which a woman can satisfy her needs and gain a concept of herself as a worthwhile person. In fact, outside employment undoubtedly aids the emotional stability of some women who would have difficulty adjusting to the life of a full-time housewife.

Many of the problems that do arise can be overcome as serious attention is paid to them; for example, employers could recognize the dual responsibilities of working mothers by providing greater flexibility in working hours and conditions. Similarly, outside employment requires greater organization and efficiency on the part of the wife. To be successful, she must keep her household tasks simple, schedule chores so as to require the least effort, use laborsaving supplies and equipment, share time-consuming tasks with her family, hire help if needed, plan and shop ahead, and arrange her leisure for maximum relaxation. Obviously women will vary in the extent to which they can follow this prescription, but many are capable of doing it successfully.

The difficulty of solving this problem of the husband's attitude should not be underestimated. The intensity of opposition varies with individuals, and any change in point of view must be worked out carefully. This will be discussed more fully in the final chapter.

 ✺ ✺ ✺ THE MOTHER-CHILD RELATIONSHIP. The woman who desires to work outside her home may be deterred by the fear that her absence will have harmful effects on her children. Even stronger than the axiom that "a woman's place is in the home" is the belief that "a mother's place is with her children." A working mother is assumed by many to be guilty of neglecting her children, and deserving of severe condemnation for this.

One response has been an avalanche of pronouncements concerning the effects on children of maternal employment. For the most part these consist of emotional pleas by self-proclaimed experts for a return to the old-fashioned family, based on a great deal of honest concern but a minimum of evidence. Our purpose here is to try to uncover the grains of truth buried under the chaff of feeling by summarizing the findings and conclusions of research studies concerning this problem.

✄ ✄ EFFECTS ON THE CHILD. In general, research concerning the effects of a mother's employment on her children has produced little in the way of consistent, useful results. Typically the results are inconclusive or are so confounded by other factors as to be meaningless. Therefore those individuals who hold strongly to the belief that the employment of a mother is detrimental to the mental and physical health of her children have little in the way of firm evidence to support their position.

✄ *Adjustment.* Although a few investigators have found children of working mothers to be less well adjusted, most studies have typically failed to find significant differences in adjustment between children of working and nonworking mothers. However, there is some suggestion that children within these two groups may differ in the nature if not the number of their adjustment problems, with the children of employed mothers being more withdrawn and having fewer academic problems.

✄ *Juvenile Delinquency.* The belief that working mothers are a major cause of juvenile delinquency is not supported by evidence. Although some studies have found that children of employed mothers are more likely to become delinquent, others report the reverse. The reason for this confusion seems to be that the causes of delinquency are complex, and the influence of the mother's employment is important only in conjunction with other variables.

One of these variables is the education of the mother. According to Nye (1958), children of employed mothers who have higher education are less likely to be delinquent than are children of employed mothers with less education.

A second related variable is the regularity of the mother's employment. Children whose mothers are employed irregularly have a higher delinquency rate than those whose mothers work steadily. This seems to occur because the mothers in the first group work when their husbands are unemployed, and these husbands in turn are often emotionally unstable and "delinquent," which probably contributes more to the children's delinquency than does the employment status of their wives.

We may thus conclude that a relationship exists between the employment of mothers and juvenile delinquency, but the evidence does not allow us to infer that a mother's employment is a direct cause of the delinquent behavior of her children.

❧ *Personality Development.* A mother's employment status seems to have important influences on the personality of her children, especially in their development of *independence.* Although the pre-school child's degree of independence is not directly related to the employment status of his mother, it has been suggested that a desirable outcome of maternal employment may be an increased independence and self-reliance on the part of the child as he grows older.

This relationship is not a simple one, because a number of other variables interact with maternal employment to influence the development of independence. One is the degree of closeness between the mother and her children, especially her daughters. Daughters of women who work but who make an extra effort to spend time with them are judged to be independent and self-assertive, while those who seldom see their mothers tend to be more dependent on others. Also, girls whose mothers are satisfied with their roles, whether they are employed or not, are more independent than girls whose mothers are dissatisfied, the difference being greater among girls whose mothers are housewives than among those whose mothers work.

From these results we may conclude that girls whose mothers make an effort to maintain a close relationship with them and who, regardless of whether they are employed, are satisfied with their own role in life have a head start in the development of independence and self-reliance.

In addition to exerting some influence on the development of independence, the employment status of the mother has other effects on her child's personality development. Children of employed mothers, for instance, tend to develop stronger *achievement needs* than do children of full-time housewives, although underachievement is more often found among high-ability students whose mothers work.

We might also expect that a working mother would exert a strong influence on her child's perception of the woman's role, but this does not seem to be the case: children of working mothers perceive the female role little differently than do children whose mothers are not employed. There is some evidence that children of nonworking mothers tend to be more conservative in their perceptions of women's roles and that varying perceptions are more likely to occur among boys than among girls, but the most impressive finding is the lack of impact which a working mother has on her children's sex-role concepts, perhaps because many working mothers are dissatisfied with this role and communicate this dissatisfaction to their children.

On the basis of the varied evidence presented thus far, we can conclude only that the influences a working mother exerts on her children differ from those exerted by a nonworking mother, but that this may well be due to the kind of person she is rather than to the fact that she is employed. It is thus extremely difficult, if not impossible, to isolate any specific relationships between the employment of a mother *per se* and the characteristics of her children.

✢ ✢ RELATED VARIABLES. *Social class* influences the likelihood of a mother working outside the home as well as its effects on her children. The lower-class working mother will, of course, have a more marked effect on her family's standard of living than will a working mother of a higher level, but the lower-class working mother also has greater problems because she usually has more young children and fewer household conveniences. At this level, the employment of the mother is frequently a result of family instability, which in turn causes it to become associated with a higher rate of juvenile delinquency.

Among the middle class, a working mother presents fewer problems since the family can afford household conveniences and good child care. The working mother at this level is more likely to be working because she wants to and probably has a more challenging and interesting job, which contributes to making her employment a positive influence on her family.

The *age and sex of the child* are also determiners of the influence of maternal employment. It is commonly assumed that maternal employment will have more harmful effects on preschool children than on those who are of school age and away from home a large share of the day, but there is little evidence of specific differential effects by age. Only among adolescents has the mother's employment been shown to have positive effects, while working mothers with younger children are more likely to feel guilty about working. In general, however, the effects of maternal employment have not been found to be highly related to the age of the child.

The same is true with regard to the child's sex. Hoffman (1963b) says that a working mother seems to have positive effects on her daughter's self-concept but may have negative effects on her son, but the data to support this contention are not impressive. It is likely, moreover, that such influences also depend on the father's role within the family and his acceptance of his wife's outside employment.

The *reason* why the mother is working and the *satisfaction* which she derives from it are important variables. Dissatisfied working mothers engage in less desirable child-rearing practices and have more trouble with their children than do those who are satisfied with their jobs. Such differences are even more noticeable among satisfied and dissatisfied nonworking mothers, suggesting that employment of the mother who is dissatisfied with herself may improve her effect on her children.

Probably the most significant variable is the *meaning of employment* to the woman and her family, although its influence is difficult to assess. Yarrow (1961, p. 223) suggests that maternal employment may have a variety of meanings:

It may be a contributor to self-esteem, a focus of critical inner conflict, a personal competitive weapon, a means to economic survival or the attainment of social goals, an escape, or an involvement received supportively or hostilely by the significant people in her life.

It is obvious that women who stress one or another of these meanings will have different influences on their families.

⋇ ⋇ MECHANISMS OF INFLUENCE

⋇ *Mother-Child Separation.* Those who assume that maternal employment has certain important effects on the welfare of children must then concern themselves with the process by which these effects are produced. The physical separation of mother and child is one possible source of difficulty, and many authorities have concluded from the research to date that maternal separation invariably has very detrimental effects on the child. One of the foremost proponents of this point of view is Bowlby (1952, p. 11), who states:

What is believed to be essential for mental health is that the infant and young child should experience a warm, intimate, and continuous relationship with his mother (or permanent mother-substitute) in which both find satisfaction and enjoyment.

This viewpoint is by no means unanimous, inasmuch as the lack of controls in most of the studies concerning maternal deprivation must make one cautious in drawing conclusions from them. In such studies, many variables in addition to the actual separation from the mother are involved, so that it is doubtful if the effects attributed to this separation are caused by it alone. Conclusions based on studies of children permanently separated from their mothers are of dubious value in estimating the effects on a child of being separated from its mother for only a limited period each day.

❧ *Child-rearing Attitudes.* Contrary to what might be expected, maternal employment does not seem to be very highly related to child-rearing attitudes of the mother. Attitudes toward children seem to be influenced more strongly by other variables, such as the mother's education and her satisfaction with her current status, whether working or not.

Although employed and nonemployed mothers do not seem to differ much in their general attitudes toward children, it is nevertheless likely that they may emphasize different aspects of child training. Mothers who are professionally active tend to emphasize discipline and independence in their attitudes toward their children, while those who are more maternal play more of a protective, empathetic, and understanding role.

Two points need to be stressed. First, simply because two persons behave differently does not necessarily mean that one is right and the other wrong. Our knowledge concerning the "goodness" or "badness" of various child-rearing practices is still in a primitive stage, which means that it is difficult if not impossible in many cases to assert that one kind of practice is better than another. For example, is it better for a parent to be protective or to foster independence? Until we can give a definitive answer to such a question, we must accept the fact that different parents will raise their children differently. Perhaps this is just as well.

A second point, stressed elsewhere, is that the finding that working mothers treat their children differently than do nonworking mothers is not necessarily related to the fact that one group is employed and the other is not. Other variables, such as personality characteristics, may be producing both effects. In other words, the employment of the one group may not be causing the differences in the attitudes toward the child but may instead be a result of the factors which are producing these differences.

❧ *Amount of Time Spent Together.* On the surface, one obvious difference between the parent-child relationships of families in which the mother works and those in which she does not work is that the nonworking mother should be able to spend a considerably greater amount of time with her children. This variable has been the topic of considerable discussion but has not been subjected to analysis by research. Perhaps one reason for its neglect is that many experts doubt its importance in influencing the child. In one sense it's not the amount of time which the mother spends with her child that's important, but rather *what goes on during that time.* Many working mothers report that they are concerned about the amount of time they are away from their children, so they make an extra effort to spend time with them whenever possible. In this way, they may actually spend as much, if not more, *meaningful* time with their children than do mothers who are home all day.

However, the notion that working mothers have too little time to spend with their children may in itself be misleading. Housework formerly took up a great deal of time, so that the housewife may not actually have spent a great deal of time with her children after all. In addition, the current full-time job would have been considered only part-time a few generations ago, when the usual work week was fifty hours or more.

❧ *Child-Care Provisions.* It is generally agreed that the effect of a mother's outside employment depends greatly on the kind of arrangements which she makes for her children's care while she works. Many of the unfortunate outcomes of children with working mothers can be traced to inadequate provisions for their care. In many cases the children do not get professional care but instead are looked after by well-meaning but inadequately trained relatives or neighbors. Mother substitutes tend to be hired informally and to have no formal training in child care other than experience in rearing their own children.

Many psychologists feel that the area in which the greatest difficulty may arise when the mother works outside the home is in the conflicting attitudes and behaviors to which the child may be subjected by substitute parents. It is therefore important that the person who takes care of the child when the mother works is one whose attitudes are similar to those of the mother and whose discipline will be consistent with hers.

Unless the mother is fortunate enough to find a woman on whom she can rely to behave in a manner consistent with her own attitudes, the best source of child care is likely to be a day nursery. Such facilities are staffed by persons specially trained in child development, which means that the child is more likely to receive proper care in this setting than he would from the typical friend or relative. Research has indicated that professionally trained persons can provide care for children, even in infancy, such that the temporary separation from their mothers will have no harmful outcomes.

Likewise, evidence from other countries in which the employment of mothers is a more common occurrence and in which day nurseries account for much of the care of the children shows that such arrangements are successful and cause little or no difficulty for either the mother or the child. Thus the establishment and expansion of day-care centers throughout our country would permit more women to work and their children to be well cared for in the interval. Such arrangements would have the advantage not only of providing beneficial facilities for the child but also of helping to reduce the guilt feelings of the mother who worries that the care being given her child while she works is not all she would like. This concern in turn causes her to feel less satisfied with her employed role and to want to return to being a full-time mother as soon as possible.

One wonders, too, the extent to which the undesirable effects of maternal employment on children may be a reflection of society's tendency to criticize the working woman for "neglecting" her family. This anxiety and feeling of guilt may influence the woman's own attitude toward her husband and children, causing her to see them as a source of her difficulty. As society's attitudes broaden and the working mother can feel that she is doing the right thing both for herself and for her family, the effects of her employment will be more beneficial than they now are.

❧ ❧ A SYNTHESIS. There is no doubt that the question of the effects of maternal employment on children has long been of concern. We tend to take this concern for granted, but it has some important antecedents which explain its intensity (Stolz, 1960).

At one time, women worked for low pay under harsh conditions. The resulting concern of social reformers about the detrimental effects on children of mothers who worked outside the home under such conditions fostered the belief that there was something intrinsically wrong with the employment of mothers. The scarcity of jobs during the depression of the thirties made men resentful of working women, who cheated them out of employment. To force women out of the labor market, they inundated working mothers with propaganda that their children were being harmed. This reinforced the notion that mothers shouldn't work, in spite of the lack of evidence that employment of mothers is harmful to families.

Those who have investigated this problem in a careful and systematic way have agreed that there is a notable lack of meaningful differences between children of working and nonworking mothers. The results have been best summarized by Stolz (1960, pp. 772–73):

One is impressed with the number of different and opposing findings which research concerning the effect of maternal employment on children has produced. One can say almost anything one desires about the children of employed mothers and support the statement by some research study.

She goes on to point out that many of the studies suffer from lack of controls, and that in those studies which involve good controls and recent data (pp. 773–74):

. . . there was no statistically significant relation found between maternal employment and delinquency, adolescent adjustment, school marks in high school, and dependent-independent behavior of five-year-olds.

The lack of meaningful results from such research has led several experts to question the validity and importance of maternal employment as an independent variable in child development. Some have proposed that it be discarded on the grounds that the "employed mother" variable is too complex to be treated as a unit. Others, while acknowledging the complexity of maternal employment as a variable, believe something is to be gained from further research along these lines. Yarrow (1961, p. 224) presents a case for the latter point of view:

Maternal employment should open our eyes to the importance of studying certain maternal factors to which child development research has not given much attention. These are: variables in the life situation of the mother as a person, her identities as a woman, and the interaction of these factors with her mother roles.

It would seem that investigators in child development have been too quick to accept the traditional belief that maternal employment is an important variable in the development of the child. A more realistic view is that mothers differ from one another in many ways, and thus must have differential effects on their children. One of these differences is in the amount of time which the mother spends at home. This may have some influence on the child, but it seems unnecessary to single it out, in isolation from other variables, as *the* cause of differences between children. Again, we turn to Stolz (1960, p. 779) for a cogent summary:

After reading these studies, it looks as if the fact of the mother being employed or staying at home is not such an important factor in determining the behavior of the child as we have been led to think. It might be more profitable to focus attention on the psychological conditions within the family, especially on the personal characteristics of the mother and father and the kind of supervision and guidance which they provide, not only when the parents are at work but when they are at home as well.

It does not seem warranted to discard maternal employment entirely as a variable for further study, but it is necessary that the definitions be made more explicit and other variables be better controlled if the results are to have any meaning. At the moment, we can only say that employment of the mother has no clear-cut detrimental effects on the family as a general rule.

The emphasis which has been placed in this discussion on the possible harmful effects of maternal employment should not obscure the possibility that such employment may also have positive values for the family and for the mother. These values are discussed in the final chapter.

FULL-TIME VS. PART-TIME EMPLOYMENT. It has been stressed that the employed woman may be overburdened by her dual responsibilities of job and home, especially when her children are young and require considerable care. That many women recognize this by seeking only part-time employment is evident from data supplied by the Women's Bureau (1963) showing that 29 per cent of all working women in April, 1962, were employed part time, and over 60 per cent of all persons who usually work part time are women. In addition, many others who work full time do so only part of the year, so that a sizeable proportion of all women workers do not work the full year.

Many experts have extolled the virtues of part-time employment for women, stressing that women's lives require greater flexibility in their outside jobs. Many believe, along with White (1950, p. 120), that the traditional notion of the 8-hour day for every worker is unrealistic when women are considered:

> It is clearly in the interest not only of women but of the productivity of our economic system to break down this rigidity of thought about time-units of labor and to adapt each job to the unit which is most efficient for it and for society as a whole.

It would also be unrealistic to view part-time employment as the solution to all problems involving working women. While reducing some problems it increases others. For one thing, the occupations in which part-time jobs are more readily available are clustered on the lower end of the scale: food harvesting and processing, domestic service, and sales work are the most frequent in such areas. The better educated woman, therefore, is prepared for occupations in which full-time employment is more likely to be required and must choose between full-time work or none at all. The woman with less education, who works primarily for money and less for inner satisfaction, may be reasonably well satisfied with the part-time jobs available.

An additional difficulty is that hiring women for part-time work is more complicated, in some cases, and thus many employers are not interested in devising such opportunities. Part-time workers may, however, pay for themselves in the long run by lower job turnover, especially among middle-aged and elderly employees. The young woman who is employed full time will probably trade her job for marriage within a relatively short time, necessitating the hiring and training of a new person.

It would seem desirable, therefore, to create more part-time job opportunities for those women who are educated for professional jobs, but who do not at the moment want to embark on a career. It is likely that such women would be more interested in pursuing employment in their area of training if it could be done without undue disruption to their families or without placing too great a burden on themselves. Broader part-time employment opportunities might be one answer. At least it should be tried.

The Career Woman

> . . . a woman's emotional investment in her job is almost always secondary to her commitment to her family. Rob a woman of her work and she will undoubtedly feel deprived. But she won't feel destroyed. It's hard to imagine a play called *Death of a Saleswoman.*
>
> ❧ *Diana Trilling, 1960*

OF THE MANY WOMEN employed in our country, only a minority would consider themselves "career women." Exactly which women qualify for this label is a question. It seems safe to assume that most working women think of themselves as employed housewives rather than as career women, but the proportion of each is obscure. One reason for this confusion is that the term "career woman" has acquired an unpleasant connotation, suggesting a cold, aggressive, frustrated spinster, as celebrated in books and plays such as *Lady in the Dark.* Altogether it is a highly unflattering picture, and few women are eager to have the term applied to them.

What, then, is a career woman? A definition is difficult, but not impossible. To qualify, a woman must be engaged in an activity outside her family responsibilities for which she receives a salary. This activity should require a sizeable amount of education or training in preparation, so that it cannot be undertaken casually. It should provide an opportunity for advancement as skills and experience increase. Finally, a career implies that the woman's family responsibilities do not overshadow her job. They may be combined more or less equally, but the career woman must be prepared to subordinate responsibilities of a family, if she has one, so that her job will not suffer.

Despite their small numbers, career women play an important role in our society and their influence will continue to grow. It is well established that women as a group represent a major source of untapped abilities to meet our country's future manpower needs. Part of this need can be met by employed housewives, but in some areas women will be able to make important contributions only through careers. These are areas in which a lengthy period of education and training are necessary, requiring an investment which few persons would be willing to make without the expectation that they will have a career in that field. This is especially true in scientific areas, in which the amount of knowledge which must be acquired before a person can make an important contribution is increasing at a rapid rate. A woman who expects to devote her energies primarily to being a wife and mother can hardly be expected to invest the time and effort required for such an extensive education.

☙ ☙ ☙ THE DECISION TO SEEK A CAREER. The lack of extensive studies of career women makes it difficult to know at this point what factors are involved in the decision to seek a career. There is evidence that girls who plan a career are less well adjusted and have a poorer self-concept than those who intend to follow the traditional female pattern, but the cause-and-effect relationships must still be questioned. The woman who seeks a career, and especially the woman who is trying to move upward socially, encounters many obstacles in the form of negative attitudes by society, which may in turn produce some of the less desirable characteristics associated with this pattern.

The woman who seeks a career is undoubtedly "different," but how this difference relates to her decision to seek a career is uncertain. Perhaps she chose a career because her values were originally different; perhaps she is different because society forces her to be, once she has chosen a career; or perhaps other factors combine to produce both effects. In any case, the traditional picture of the hard-boiled, maladjusted career woman does have some basis in reality. Greater consideration needs to be given to ways in which women may embark on careers without running the risk of damaging their personality development.

Ideally, a career should play an important role in the personal development of a woman in much the same way it does for a man, by providing her with a means for expressing her individual potentials. This may be an important consideration to some women, and unimportant to others, but in any case a woman's career should add more to her life than it takes away.

To gain from a career the kind of satisfactions that are available to men, a woman must recognize she has several handicaps to overcome. Being a woman is itself a barrier to professional advancement, first because society views her with suspicion, and second because the characteristics which promote professional advancement are not apt to be compatible with the usual concept of femininity. Therefore the woman who wants to get ahead must run the risk of appearing "unfeminine" and thereby perhaps not achieving a concurrent goal of marriage. Boring (1951, p. 681) has described the situation thus:

Can a woman become a fanatic in her profession and still remain marriageable? Yes, she can, for I know some, but I think a woman must be abnormally bright to combine charm with concentration. These women make the synthesis by being charmingly enthusiastic.

The career woman must also accept the reluctance of society to give her full status as a woman since the role of wife and mother is lauded as a woman's most important accomplishment. People may tolerate, or even love, a bachelor, but the spinster is viewed with suspicion. The result is that the woman who elects to concentrate on her career and does not choose to marry finds it difficult to feel fulfilled as a person.

The alternative, that of combining a career with marriage, produces numerous problems too, particularly if the wife has a better job or makes more money than her husband. A secure, self-confident husband and a stable, sound marriage are required for such a differential to be tolerated comfortably. Such marriages do exist and many work out very well, but generally a husband and wife are so constrained by society's traditional attitudes concerning the role of each in a marriage that it requires considerable personal strength and maturity to overcome them and to achieve a mutually satisfying relationship based on the needs of both parties.

Perhaps an even more difficult problem is that of deciding which career—the husband's or the wife's—will determine where the family will live. In most cases, the husband's career will win out, but often at the sacrifice of a fine opportunity for his wife.

Most of the problems of the married career woman grow out of her dual responsibilities to her job and to her family. These are most likely to come into conflict when the woman has young children, since she is expected to assume more responsibility for their care than is her husband. One result is that many women trained for professional careers leave their professions when the conflict between family and job responsibilities becomes too great. For example, Rossi (1965a) has reported that, among women between the ages of 25 and 44, half the natural scientists, 30 per cent of the engineers, 35 per cent of the secondary school teachers, and 20 per cent of the physicians voluntarily leave their fields, as compared with 2 per cent, 1 per cent, 2 per cent, and 2 per cent respectively among the men.

Perhaps, however, this is only realistic. Some authorities have questioned whether any woman should try to be both a mother and a career woman. In effect, the professional woman is expected to handle two jobs—her outside job and her home—while her husband must handle only one. Some women can manage to do both, but they may be the exceptions.

Someone has said, "What the professional, working woman needs is a good wife." Since it is highly unusual to find a husband devoting himself to his wife's career, the most that a career woman can hope for, if she is married, is to have a cooperative and understanding husband. Even with such an asset, she will still be hard pressed to maintain a reasonable balance between her home and job responsibilities. Nevertheless, many women find that the personal satisfactions they gain from their dual roles are well worth the effort required to maintain them.

⚹ ⚹ ⚹ PROFESSIONAL CAREERS FOR WOMEN. The proportion of women who work outside the home is growing rapidly, but there is no corresponding upsurge in the proportion of women in professional fields in which a career commitment is necessary. As the population has increased the number of women entering the professions has also risen, but the ratio of women to men within the professions has changed little over the past half-century. The strong tradition that most professions are inappropriate for women has not yet been overcome. As Caplow (1954) has pointed out, women who enter professions are likely to concentrate in those specialties in which most of their clients are women—e.g., a medical specialty, teaching, or law—or in those in which they have little contact with the public, such as laboratory work.

One reason for the extremely unbalanced sex ratio is that it is still difficult for women to gain entry into many professions. This is partly due to the inertia of tradition, but also to evidence that large numbers of women fail to make long-term use of their specialized education and training. Reluctance to accept women into professional education programs and into responsible jobs is understandable in view of their high attrition rate, both during and after training. If women are to gain opportunities equal to those of men in the professions they must assume the responsibility of making constructive use of their preparation. As opportunities for women increase, it is up to them to take the initiative in demanding that doors be opened wider and then to make worthwhile use of the opportunities which are presented.

Whether women will take the initiative to enter the professions in greater proportions is, however, doubtful. Rossi (1965a) believes that in the future the proportion of women in professional occupations will probably decline as a result of increasing opportunities for women in second-level occupations, which do not require the degree of motivation or effort of the professions. As women marry at an early age, they find it advantageous to enter fields which complement their husbands' jobs rather than to undertake the struggle to carve out a career for themselves in a profession. Thus any future change in the direction of increased participation by women in the professions will first require social changes to develop motivation for such a goal among capable women.

The remainder of this chapter will consider opportunities for women in various career fields. This is not intended as a thorough survey of all possible professional opportunities for women but is designed instead to emphasize the variety of opportunities available to them.

ℐ ℐ EDUCATION. At first glance teaching seems to be a fine career field for women. It has traditionally been considered an appropriate profession for girls to enter, so that a girl who wants a career will encounter fewer obstacles if she decides to become a teacher than if she aims at a less traditional field.

ℐ *Public School Teaching.* Women outnumber men in teaching by a ratio of about two to one, although their proportion has been steadily decreasing. Table 9.1 shows the changes in the sex ratio among teachers during the decade 1957–67. It is evident that men are gradually moving into the profession in greater numbers.

It may be a mistake to consider elementary and secondary teachers as a single group, since they differ in personality characteristics and in motivation for entering the profession. The elementary

TABLE 9.1 ℐ Percentage of Women Among All Teachers in Selected Years, 1957–67

	Elementary	Secondary	All Levels
1957–58	87.2	49.6	73.2
1960–61	85.8	47.4	70.7
1963–64	85.5	46.1	68.9
1966–67	85.4	46.0	68.3

Source: National Education Association, 1967.

teacher tends to be more passive and orderly and to have had a close relationship with her mother as a child, while girls who become high school teachers tend to be more aggressive and to have had poor relationships with their mothers. On the basis of their research comparing college girls who planned to become elementary and secondary teachers, Wright and Tuska concluded (1964, pp. 9–10):

The motivation of grade school women might be explained as wanting to be like parents who were good, but different from teachers who disappointed them. The high school women, on the other hand, having found satisfactions in their relationship with good teachers, satisfactions that made up for the failings of their parents, wish to become like teachers who impressed them and different from parents who let them down.

Most girls who prepare to become teachers are not eager to make it a career. Teacher education programs typically attract girls who are bright but not brilliant, who make good grades, and who have rather vague, nonprofessional interests. Generally, they do not fit the pattern of career women.

Why, then, do so many girls choose to major in education in college if they do not plan to make it a career? In many ways, teaching is attractive for the girl whose primary goal is being married and raising a family. For one thing, teachers are always in demand, so that a teaching certificate is the next thing to a guarantee that a woman can find a job if and when it becomes necessary, regardless of the size of the community or the part of the country in which she may be living. A second advantage is that most teaching jobs require no preparation beyond the 4-year teaching certificate. A girl can go immediately into a teaching position without spending further time and money in graduate work or in a special training program. This is an especially important consideration for the girl who plans to marry soon after graduation. Finally, preparation for teaching seems to many girls to be suitably related to motherhood, since a teaching role is often stressed as one of the mother's major functions in the family.

The result is that few girls who prepare to become teachers actually have made a career commitment to teaching. Most girls view teaching as a short-term occupation or as an insurance policy rather than as a profession in which they will be employed for most of their lives. This explains why the average age of women teachers is eight years higher than that of men.

Most women who do become career teachers therefore fall into one of two categories: (a) unmarried women who have had to substitute their profession of teaching for marriage and children of their own; (b) older women who return to teaching with a career

commitment as their family responsibilities decrease. In neither
case, however, are they motivated by desire for a lifetime career
commitment to teaching as a profession.

Inasmuch as women compose a sizeable proportion of the teaching profession, the lack of a career commitment among most women
teachers has some unfortunate effects. Essentially it means that a
large proportion of the teachers who are being trained in our colleges will not devote a major part of their lives to teaching. Some
will never teach at all, some will teach until their first child is born
and never go back to it, while others may return later. In any case,
one can present a strong argument that the training of teachers is
one of the most wasteful undertakings in which our colleges and
universities are now engaged. Not only do many of those being
trained not intend to make enough use of their training to justify
the effort and expense, but they crowd the teacher-training programs to the extent that the quality of the training for those who
will make good use of it suffers.

In some ways, this lack of career commitment among most
women teachers makes it a frustrating profession for the girl who
is interested in a career. While teaching provides security without
much risk, it does so at the expense of the opportunity to gain
status and prestige as well as personal satisfaction by moving ahead
by one's own efforts. The range of salaries for women teachers is
improving—beginning salaries are competitive with those of many
other professions. But salary advancement tends to be geared to
mechanical criteria rather than to criteria which take individual
differences into account, and the salary ceilings in most schools are
too low to stimulate an ambitious person. The teaching profession
has avoided facing the issue that some teachers are better than
others and deserve to be rewarded more handsomely. Instead, a
naive picture is painted of the self-sacrificing, altruistic teacher who
wants no reward other than the smile of a student as he leaves her
room, with his feet firmly on the road to success and happiness. As
a result, the teaching profession tends to attract persons of both
sexes who are not strongly career oriented and who do not have
strong achievement needs. Whether this is good or bad is open to
question, but it is something which a girl who is considering teaching as a career should bear in mind.

Women teachers have few opportunities to advance into administrative positions, as evidenced by the fact that, despite the pre-
dominance of women in the teaching profession, most administrative positions are held by men. In 1963, for example, 77 per cent of
all principals in school systems with 300 or more pupils were men.
Women have a better chance to become principals in elementary
schools, since only 3 per cent of all high school principals are

women, but even at the elementary level their proportion is decreasing as more men move into teaching and administrative positions. Teaching as a profession is highly encumbered by tradition, and the ambitious woman would be well advised to look elsewhere for opportunities to use her talents for administration.

& *College Teaching.* College and university teaching provides more challenging intellectual opportunities for women than does public school education, although the situation is far from ideal. Women have long constituted a significant proportion of college faculties, a proportion that has not changed much over the past half-century, varying between 20 and 30 per cent during this time. More recently the proportion of women college teachers has been declining, having dropped from nearly 28 per cent in 1940 to 22 per cent in 1960. This has come about primarily because more men have entered fields which have traditionally been limited to women, such as home economics, while the barriers against women in male-dominated academic areas have been resistant to change (Bernard, 1964).

Any discussion of total populations obscures the fact that women college teachers tend to cluster in certain areas: 40 per cent of the faculties of teachers' colleges are women, as compared with little more than 10 per cent in the prestige private universities. Bernard (1964) attributes this to several factors: fewer women obtain the Ph.D.; fewer of those who do get doctorates have attended high-prestige schools; women have lower achievement drives; and women are less mobile geographically, being more closely tied to one locality by family demands.

Similarly, women tend to be concentrated at the lower levels of academic rank and to make less money than their male counterparts. Those in the higher ranks are found primarily in departments of education, home economics, and library science, and are more often in women's colleges than in coeducational schools.

As in public school teaching, administrative positions in the colleges go mostly to men, and there is no indication of change in the near future. In fact, the proportion of women in college educational leadership positions was lower in the mid-1960's than it was 25 or even 10 years before. In this respect, women seem to be advancing to the rear.

It is evident, therefore, that women who teach in college suffer by comparison in almost every respect with male faculty members. There seems to be a tacit agreement that women are to be allowed to compose a limited segment of a college teaching staff, but that they are to be kept in their proper place. Why is this?

Many women charge that they are discriminated against in the securing of academic positions and in advancement in these positions. The feeling is widespread that they are tolerated because they are needed to teach courses, but they are not part of the inner circles and they do not move within the academic community as freely as do men. According to Caplow and McGee (1958, p. 111):

Women tend to be discriminated against in the academic profession, not because they have low prestige but because they are outside the prestige system entirely and for this reason are of no use to a department in future recruitment.

On the other hand, Bernard (1964), in a study of academic women, found no evidence of any systematic discrimination in the hiring of women by colleges. She believes, however, that women who make a career of college teaching are handicapped in moving into top positions. This seems to support the contention of Caplow and McGee (1958) that women scholars are not taken seriously and cannot look forward to a normal professional career.

If discrimination is not the basic problem, other factors must then be involved. Several may be cited. One problem, to be discussed at greater length in a later chapter, is the low proportion of doctorates obtained by women. Bernard (1964) points out that the proportion of women on college faculties is limited by the proportion of doctorates obtained by women and by that criterion is actually somewhat higher than would be expected. In addition, women tend to get graduate degrees in areas in which the supply of college teachers is already fairly high, such as education and psychology, and not in fields in which college teachers are scarce, such as English, mathematics, physical sciences, and foreign languages.

A second difficulty is that there are at least two kinds of women on college faculties: those who have made a career commitment to college teaching, and those who live in the community and teach, perhaps only part time, as a convenient job. Surveys of women college teachers typically lump the two groups together, whereas only the first group can reasonably be compared with male faculty members.

A significant proportion of women college teachers do not view their job as a career; instead, they combine teaching with rearing a family or with other activities. Contrary to most male professors, many women have entered the profession more by chance than by choice. Small wonder that they do not advance as rapidly and do not attain the same status as do their male colleagues.

It is well known that, at the more prestigious colleges and universities, promotion is largely a function of scholarly productivity, and in this area women fall short. This may be a function of personality differences—as noted earlier, men tend to have stronger achievement drives and to be more creative. Complicating this, however, is the fact that men more easily obtain jobs in universities, in which productivity is more encouraged and in which more time for research and writing is made available. In any case, women are much less likely to gain scholarly reputations in their fields, with a resulting handicap in advancement.

Despite this rather discouraging picture, college teaching has some advantages over public school teaching for the woman who wants a career in education. Restrictions imposed by tradition are likely to be less severe in the college; even though the female college teacher may not be accorded an equal scholarly status with her male colleagues, she has the freedom to do pretty much as she pleases within her classroom, and women teachers are often well liked and well respected by their students and colleagues.

For the woman who wants to combine a part-time job with her home and family responsibilities, college teaching may offer some attractive opportunities. The public schools are reluctant to hire part-time teachers, preferring teachers who are full-time professionals and who will fit neatly into the total program of the school. Colleges, on the other hand, are more concerned with obtaining qualified persons to teach specific courses and they are not so reluctant to obtain the part-time services of well-trained women, especially for the staffing of elementary and stable undergraduate courses. This in turn may free a full-time faculty member, probably a man who doesn't enjoy teaching undergraduates anyway, to engage in more scholarly activity.

⁂ ⁂ SCIENCE. Despite the opportunities for qualified women scientists, only about 7 per cent of all scientists in the United States are women. One reason for the small proportion, perhaps, is that most available jobs are designed for full-time employees; women scientists who want to work part time are limited primarily to teaching positions.

⁂ *Physical Sciences.* A variety of job opportunities are available for women in the physical sciences. These women are most likely to be employed as chemists, although the ratio of women to men is highest within the field of astronomy. After an upsurge of interest following World War II, the number of women taking degrees in the physical sciences dropped until 1953; the growth rate since then has not kept pace with that for men. Because so few physical scientists are women, resistance to their employment is still to be overcome. It is therefore important that women interested in jobs in the physical sciences obtain degrees beyond the bachelor's level. For those women who enter the physical sciences the rewards are great, since starting salaries are the highest received by women in any field.

Women chemists are found in universities and government agencies, but most of them are engaged in industrial research. Nearly one-fourth of the professional research personnel employed by chemical and pharmaceutical laboratories are women, although the proportion varies greatly from one to another. This variation seems to be related to the kind of research involved, since women account for a much higher proportion of the personnel engaged in long-range research than of the personnel engaged in immediate research and development. Within these laboratories, the women tend to be concentrated in the more routine jobs. The turnover rates for men and women with B.S. degrees are about the same, but at the higher levels the women are more likely to leave than are the men.

Other areas within the physical sciences have not been studied as extensively as has chemistry, but it seems clear that the opportunities for women there are even more restricted. Women physicists, for example, are primarily engaged in college teaching, not necessarily out of choice. Women geologists are especially handicapped, since those who have family responsibilities cannot leave for long periods of time for field work. Their job opportunities tend to be limited to office jobs which in turn handicaps their chances for advancement. Since World War II, meteorology has grown rapidly and has attracted women, most of whom work for the federal government.

❧ *Biological Sciences.* In contrast to the physical sciences, a sizeable proportion of biological scientists are women, but they tend to be concentrated in jobs as research assistants or technicians rather than as full-fledged biological scientists. Between 10 and 20 per cent of all biologists are women, and they make up nearly 20 per cent of biology teachers in colleges as well as a large proportion of the personnel in state and local health departments. Fewer are employed in industry. The highest salaries are paid in nutrition, pathology, and pharmacology.

The future status of women in the biological sciences is uncertain. The rate of increase in the number of degrees awarded to women in the biological sciences has been rapid, but there are signs that this growth is slowing down. Biological science will probably continue to be a reasonably popular field for women, but there is no reason to anticipate that it will be taken over by women in the near future.

❧ *Science Technology.* Girls with scientific interests might do well to consider opportunities as science technicians. At present, few

women are employed in such jobs, partly due to employer prejudice but also because few women are trained for them. A wide
variety of technical jobs would be open to women with the appropriate training.

Salaries in technical jobs are usually good, since they are set by
the job and not by sex. On the other hand, there are fewer opportunities for part-time work in technical jobs than in the sciences,
and women technicians are unlikely to be moved into supervisory
positions, partly because such positions require production experience which women are not likely to have had. Nevertheless, the girl
who likes science but who does not have the ambition to get an
advanced degree in a scientific field would be wise to consider training for employment as a technician.

❧ *Conclusion.* Entrance of women into scientific careers seems to
be limited at present primarily by the attitudes of the girls themselves toward science as a career. Current demands for competent
scientists as well as the opportunities in this field for women impose
an obligation to find ways to encourage more girls to plan for careers
in science.

One drawback to a scientific career for many women is that
scientific knowledge is rapidly expanding, so that the woman who
takes time off from her career to rear children may find it quite
difficult to resume it at a later date. Perhaps this problem could be
alleviated by developing methods, such as meetings or short courses,
by which women who are not currently employed in their fields
could be helped to keep up with them. When they are ready to return to work, refresher courses might be helpful. Some of the programs in "continuing education" which have recently been initiated
around the country have included this as a feature, and the response
has been gratifying.

❧ ❧ MATHEMATICS AND STATISTICS. Women account for about 10 per
cent of all mathematicians in the United States and for about one-
third of all high school mathematics teachers. Although the number of women mathematicians is growing rapidly, their proportion
of the total is declining as men are entering the field at an even
more rapid rate.

Jobs are open to women at all levels and in all areas of mathematics and the pay is generally better than in science fields. Some
of the most promising opportunities are in the operation of electronic computers, for which many industries prefer women to men.
Although most women mathematicians continue to be employed in
educational institutions, the proportion of women who teach mathematics in college has not increased in recent years. There has, how-

ever, been a tremendous upsurge in the employment of women mathematicians by industry, with the largest numbers being hired by electrical manufacturing firms.

❧ ❧ ENGINEERING. There are fewer than 10,000 women engineers in the United States, which is about 1 per cent of the total engineering population, and it appears that this proportion is on the decline. During the decade 1950–60, the number of male engineers increased by 64 per cent, while the number of female engineers stayed about the same.

One reason for the lack of women engineers is that engineering schools have not been eager to admit women although they are becoming less restrictive and most will now accept girls. Chemical engineering is the most popular undergraduate engineering major among women, but among employed women engineers it ranks fourth, behind electrical, industrial, and civil. This suggests that many women engineers are not working in the field for which they were first prepared.

Employment prospects for women engineers are reasonably good, and beginning salaries are higher than in science and mathematics. The largest proportion of women engineers work for the government rather than for themselves, which may explain why few are licensed professional engineers. Industries in which women engineers are most welcome include airplane manufacturing, communications, and radio, television, and electronics.

❧ ❧ MEDICINE. Women account for about 6 per cent of all *physicians* in this country, a proportion which has changed little over the past fifty years but which seems now to be rising slightly. The most common specialties among female physicians are pediatrics, psychiatry, and public health, as women tend to choose specialties which are compatible with their family responsibilities. Women doctors are also much less likely than men to be in private practice.

Girls who consider medicine as a career may expect to be confronted by several barriers. One is the general attitude of society that women doctors are less competent than men. Medicine is still considered to be a man's field, but with the ever-increasing need for doctors this prejudice can be expected to diminish significantly. A second problem, which arises when a girl applies to a medical school, is the belief that girls are poor risks for training as physicians because they are likely to get married and not practice. There is some basis for such concern, in that married women physicians are less likely than are single women to be in active practice, although this difference is not great. In view of the time, effort, and expense which is invested in medical education, it seems unlikely that many women physicians would abandon their careers for the role of housewife.

A woman as a general practitioner might have some difficulty in managing a dual role, but with the increase in specialties, along with opportunities for group practice and for salaried positions with a regular schedule, the married woman doctor should have little difficulty integrating her career as a physician with her responsibilities to her husband and children.

Nursing as a career for women has much in common with teaching. Most girls who enter it do not plan to make it a career but view it instead as an "insurance policy," as training which will be useful in being a wife and mother, and as a field to which they may return on a part-time basis at some future date. In the latter respect, nursing offers more opportunities than does teaching, since part-time positions and work at odd hours can usually be arranged. However, nursing also resembles teaching in offering relatively few opportunities for advancement and is thus not the best field for a woman who has achievement ambitions or who wants to work on her own.

The choice of nursing as an occupation is often made for practical reasons rather than out of a strong dedication to the field. Many girls who cannot afford to go to college and who want some kind of professional training choose a nursing program as an alternative. These girls, if from a city, are usually from lower-class families; they are more likely to be middle class if from a rural area. Others, of course, enter a college program leading to a degree in nursing, thus combining a college education with preparation for nursing.

The outstanding characteristic of the interest patterns of nursing students is a strong social service interest, coupled with a fairly high interest in science and low interest in numerical and verbal areas. Nursing students are not dedicated to their work to the extent of men and women medical students, but instead show a fairly high degree of social interest and activity. This supports the contention that nursing students are not generally career oriented.

Several studies have attempted to predict success in nurses' training, but with conflicting results. A major difficulty seems to be the selection of a criterion of success: course grades can be predicted fairly well, but ward performance and completion of the course are not very predictable.

The shortage of nurses, acute in most parts of the country, is due not only to the lack of enough girls interested in becoming nurses in the first place, but also to the large number who retire from nursing to become housewives. Although the supply of nurses could probably be increased by modifications in training programs so as to enable more young women to finish their training, as well as making better use of part-time services of young mothers and older women, a substantial part of the attrition is probably due to the physical demands of the job. The work of the nurse requires a good deal of hard physical labor as well as unpopular working hours. Small wonder that only a minority of women have the need or dedication to make a career of it.

Women interested in medicine should also consider becoming *medical technologists.* As with nursing, medical technology is not generally considered as a career field but shares with nursing the advantages of providing part-time job opportunities as well as a valuable insurance policy. The major difference between the two is that nursing primarily involves service to patients whereas medical technology consists mainly of laboratory work. Persons in either profession work under the direction of physicians. Medical technologists should also be distinguished from laboratory technicians, who are less well trained and are qualified to perform more limited services for the physician.

Ninety per cent of all registered medical technologists are women. Salaries are adequate, comparing favorably with fields such as teaching which require comparable training. Employment opportunities are good and the need for qualified medical technologists is increasing. However, as with nursing, the opportunities for advancement are limited. A medical technologist may, by obtaining a master's degree in one of the biological sciences, become qualified for a supervisory position in a medical laboratory, but such jobs are more likely to go to the relatively few men in the field.

LAW. Only about 3 per cent of all lawyers are women, and this percentage seems to be declining. However, it is likely that most girls who prepare to become lawyers actually do make a career of it, since women law students share with their male counterparts a high interest in the expressive arts and are also career oriented.

It is surprising to find a larger proportion of women physicians than of lawyers, considering that girls tend to surpass boys in verbal ability in school as well as being more interested in verbal subjects and less interested in science. In addition, law school is less expensive and time-consuming than is medical education, which should make the former more attractive to girls. Somehow, however, law has acquired the image of a male profession and girls seem reluctant to enter it. Perhaps the fact that much of it is based on argument and contention makes it less compatible with girls' personalities. Closer inspection, however, reveals that there are many opportunities in the legal profession in areas other than direct trial work which might prove more attractive to girls.

Women lawyers are under no severe handicap in practicing

their profession. Their greatest problem, as with any lawyer, is getting established, and it is suggested that women may be able to do this more easily in small cities and suburbs rather than in large metropolitan areas. Opportunities for women lawyers are best in law specialties in which their contributions have already been recognized, such as real estate, domestic relations, problems of women and juveniles, probate work, and patent law. As compared with men, women lawyers are more likely to work in government agencies and are less apt to be self-employed. This may be due, in part, to the greater difficulty which women have in finding jobs in law firms.

Many women lawyers eventually become judges, a field in which women have made important contributions in recent years.

✸ ✸ PSYCHOLOGY. Psychology is a relatively popular career field for women, who account for about one-fifth of all professional psychologists. About 40 per cent work in colleges, one-third are employed in clinics, and about 15 per cent work in the public schools. Job opportunities are favorable, but most women psychologists feel that they are handicapped in advancement.

Women psychologists tend to have received their degrees later than the men and to have come from families with more education and of a higher status. Their reasons for choosing psychology as a career field are, however, no different from those of the men. Women psychologists are less professionally active than men, although the difference is not great.

✸ ✸ SOCIAL WORK. Social work, like teaching, is a profession which is traditionally considered to be a woman's field but which men are entering at an increasing rate. The proportion of women among social workers dropped from 70 per cent in 1950 to 60 per cent in 1965, and the increased male enrollment in social work programs indicates that this trend will continue in the foreseeable future. Women social workers are most commonly employed as caseworkers in direct service, while the majority of executive positions are held by men. This difference in authority and responsibility is reflected in salaries, with the median salary of male social workers being approximately $1,000 higher than that of females.

✸ ✸ BUSINESS. The field of business has traditionally been limited primarily to men, especially at the upper levels. Few of the large manufacturing corporations in the United States have women as directors or in major executive positions, and only about one-fiftieth of all business executives are women. Employers, however, are slowly becoming willing to hire women as potential executives, so all is not lost.

Fuller and Batchelder (1953) have suggested that the best opportunities for women who aspire to become executives are in small companies and in creative fields rather than in traditional industrial positions. Women are also more likely to succeed in staff rather than in line positions. This would include fields such as personnel and industrial relations, research, accounting and statistics, advertising, and branch operations. Government work also provides administrative opportunities for women.

One reason for the limited role which women have played in the business world may be that girls who major in business administration in college do not as a group have high scholastic ability, although they often do as well in their courses as their brighter male counterparts. Their interests, on the other hand, are similar to those of men in the same curricula. Noncollege business schools seem to attract girls for much the same reason as do the noncollege nursing schools: for vocational preparation. The girls who attend both schools are much alike in background, so that the choice of one school or the other seems to be made on the basis of minimal interest or perhaps the proximity of the school.

The stereotype of the female business executive is not a flattering one. She is usually pictured as cold, calculating, and unemotional, with a narrow range of interests. It is assumed that she is unmarried, since her devotion to the company is so strong as to eliminate the possibility that she might become attached to a husband and children.

As with most stereotypes, this one has a small kernel of truth surrounded by a thick shell of misconception and misunderstanding. Women executives tend to have a strong achievement drive and to be practical. They usually are able to organize well and are generally adaptable, energetic, confident, and sensitive to people. Many of these qualities are not characteristic of the typical woman, nor for that matter of the typical man. Perhaps it is for this reason that women in business have been looked upon as "different," which in turn may have led to the creation of a generally negative picture that in many cases bears little resemblance to reality. Actually, of course, women executives come in all shapes, sizes, and personalities, and any attempt to draw a composite picture is doomed to failure.

In some ways, the antifeminine stereotype of the woman executive seems to present a threat to women in executive positions, with the result that they begin to wonder what kind of persons they really are or ought to be. Frances Maule, in *Executive Careers for Women* (1961), describes opportunities for women in various business areas and also considers the kind of persons women executives are. To overcome the handicap that stems from the traditional picture of the "woman boss," Maule (p. 8) says she must ". . . present an appearance that conforms to the accepted portrait of the ideal woman. This means that she must be attractively feminine in her dress, conservative in her make-up, gentle in manner, soft of voice." But she must also give the impression that she has firmness and resolution and that she is rational rather than emotional.

Maule also advises that as a woman rises in the executive world she should spend more money on clothes and more time on her appearance—hair styling, facials, etc. She suggests that fashion magazines be used as guides to what the "rising young woman executive" should wear. *Mademoiselle* and *Glamour* regularly feature clothes appropriate for what *Mademoiselle* has called "the young lady tycoon."

This presents a picture of the woman executive as a person who must constantly be presenting herself as the epitome of several different and not very compatible roles. Perhaps it would be simpler and more realistic to suggest that the woman who wants a career in business can best move ahead by being herself. Certainly she should be encouraged to be feminine, but overdoing it, as Maule seems to recommend, may produce results even more negative than if she made no attempt at all to be feminine.

Several suggestions may be offered for women interested in business as a career. There is no best entryway into such fields, although some are more promising than others. Specific skills, perhaps more necessary for women than for men, might be obtained through college or business school training in business administration, personnel work, public relations, or accounting and statistics. The most common avenue in the past has been by starting as a secretary, but in view of the increasingly technical nature of business operations it is unlikely that this will continue to be a major entry for women into business.

Most graduate and professional schools in business administration accept women, although many have quotas of between 5 and 10 per cent of the total class. One of the few programs specifically designed to train women executives is the Harvard-Radcliffe Program in Business Administration.

Retailing is an area which women interested in business might do well to consider. Women compose close to one-third of the managers and officials in apparel and accessories stores, over one-fifth of those in general merchandise and variety stores, and more than one-fourth of the officials in department stores. Opportunities are good, perhaps better than in any other field of business, but advancement requires hard work and considerable time and may limit family and community activities.

Most girls who enter the business world do so, of course, as *secretaries* rather than as executives. Few intend to make it a career, but for the girl who wants a short-term job which can be adapted to later contingencies, secretarial work may be ideal. The skills can be learned in a relatively short time and the need for clerical workers is expanding, so that a trained secretary should have little trouble in finding a job. Part-time secretarial jobs are also available, and many women who have been trained as secretaries are able to do related work in their homes, thus combining outside employment and raising a family with a minimum of strain.

Perhaps the major disadvantage of secretarial work as a career is that it provides little opportunity for advancement. Over a period of time, a good secretary may assume many responsibilities in the management of the office in which she works, but she is unlikely to be given actual managerial responsibilities outside of the office itself. The girl who wants a career as a business executive would do better to enter the field in the same manner as a man, through advanced education in business administration.

CHAPTER TEN

The Education of the High School Girl

> Everywhere we hear the same cry, "Educate! Educate!" and the results have been far-reaching. . . . We have become brainy and unstable. . . . The removal of woman from the natural sphere of domesticity to that of mental labour renders her prone to degenerate and initiates a downward tendency which gathers impetus in her progeny.
>
> * *T. B. Hyslop, 1905*

THE OPENING QUOTATION suggests something of the feeling with which equal educational opportunities for women were resisted around the turn of the century. Education for women was condemned as a body blow to the traditional American way of life. Educated women were destined to become intellectual monsters, uncontrollable by the men who had breathed life into them. A woman's place was in the home, and the more education she acquired the more she would become dissatisfied with her role. The result would be chaos within the family.

To modern Americans such arguments seem naive, if not a little silly. During the past half-century, we have come to accept the belief that women *must* be educated, although we still disagree on how this can best be accomplished. In many ways, women are now better educated than men. According to the 1960 national census, women have an average (median) of 10.9 years of education as compared with only 10.3 for men.

The educational level of women, however, is more homogeneous than that of men. For the past century, girls have outnumbered boys among high school graduates, but many more men than women earn postgraduate and professional degrees. In any case, however, women are not suffering from lack of education, at least at the high school level.

Not only are girls more likely to graduate from high school than are boys, but they also tend to earn more credits, on the average. Among the academically talented, however, the situation is reversed and boys earn more credits than girls.

Despite the impressive proportion of high school graduates, many girls who have the ability to finish high school drop out before graduation. Most boys and girls who drop out of school attribute their departure to a desire to find a job or to a lack of interest in school. In addition, about one-fourth of the girls who quit school do so to marry, often under the pressure of pregnancy. Those who leave school before graduation tend to find jobs as private household or service workers or as operatives, while girls who graduate and don't go to college are more likely to take clerical jobs.

The major alternatives for the girl who has graduated from high school are, of course, college or a job, and about equal numbers choose each. About 8 per cent marry immediately after leaving high school, and about half of these become full-time housewives.

✄ ✄ ✄ EDUCATIONAL NEEDS OF GIRLS. Of major concern to many educators is not the *amount* but the *kind* of education which girls receive. Many feel that girls are not educated in a manner consistent with their future role in society. It is obvious that the life pattern of women is different from that of men, yet in many ways these differences are ignored in education. Girls are educated in much the same way as are boys, with the implicit assumption— contrary to fact—that they will enter the labor market after graduation and embark on a career. Society has done little to recognize and implement the preponderance of evidence that such education is not very relevant for most girls. Thus many girls emerge from high school poorly prepared for the role which they will soon assume—that of wife and mother. In many respects we seem to be educating women not wisely, but too well.

One reason is that, perhaps as a result of the struggle required to gain equal educational opportunities for women, too much emphasis has been placed on providing for girls an education equal to that of boys. As Alpenfels (1963, p. 42) has said:

The overriding aim of education for women in the United States has been to make it as good as that for men, [but] society thereupon makes different demands and no longer cares what women do with the education they have received.

This confusion is compounded by the conflicting demands made on girls in the typical school. On the one hand, they are expected to compete intellectually with boys and to assume equal academic responsibilities; on the other, they are expected to develop into women, adopting the traditional feminine role of subservience in which the man achieves success and his wife basks in his reflected glory. Thus coeducational classes exert conflicting pressures on girls with the result that many neglect their intellectual development in favor of attracting boys.

Because of this, some educators periodically argue that boys and girls should be educated separately. Research comparing coeducational classes with those in which the sexes are separated, however, has failed to locate significant differences in academic performance. Moreover, most girls prefer to attend school with boys, and it is likely that their social maturity is enhanced by the experience.[1]

One of the major problems, and perhaps the most serious, is that the direct application of a girl's education will be made, if at all, at some time in the distant future rather than in the present. A boy can see direct relevance between his current learning experiences and his plans for the future, after graduation, but a girl often cannot. Her immediate plans are centered on marriage and children, and except for home economics courses—which are not stimulating to many girls at this age—her school program for the most part is not very relevant to this. It is only later in her life, when her children are older and she has the time and motivation to expand her horizons, that her earlier education may become meaningful.

Thus a great problem for educators working with girls, according to Raushenbush (1961, pp. 265–66), is how to help them meet both their present and future needs:

The dominant fact is not that women are as able as men, but that the stages of women's lives are quite different from the stages of men's lives and that a system of education created for men and adapted to women will not do for their present needs. . . . We

---

[1] For those readers who may be unfamiliar with private girls' schools, an article in *Harper's* by LaFarge (1963) is recommended as a lively but critical description of five of the most prominent.

must consider what they might reasonably do in the middle years of their lives for which some preparation might be made now and toward which some preparation might be continued during the years when they are primarily involved with their homes and children.

⋇ ⋇ ⋇ CURRICULUM CHOICE IN HIGH SCHOOL. Whether a student is male or female plays a far more important role in determining choice of curriculum and of courses in high school than does any other characteristic, including ability. Some curricula, such as agriculture and industrial arts, are almost entirely male, while others, such as home economics and the commercial courses, are equally limited to females. The only curricula in which both sexes participate are general and college preparatory, with a slight majority of boys in each. Similar distinctions are found in specific courses, especially in math and science, in which boys predominate. Girls have some tendency to take more English and foreign languages than do boys, but the trend there is not so one-sided as for math and science.

⋇ ⋇ ⋇ POST-HIGH SCHOOL PLANS. High school girls tend to arrange their courses according to their plans after graduation, which are usually fairly definite. About 40 per cent of high school senior girls are training for employment after graduation as compared with only one-fourth of the boys.

This may appear to be a contradiction with the previous point that girls have greater difficulty than do boys in relating their educational experiences to their future lives. However, the explanation appears to be that most girls do not consider the job that they will take after high school graduation to be an important part of their future. For most, it is a way of bridging the gap between high school and marriage.

A higher proportion of boys than girls plan to attend college, and those girls who do have plans for college tend to aim at lower-level jobs after finishing than do boys. On the other hand, girls who plan on college are more likely than boys to have made a definite choice before entering college of both their major curriculum and their future occupation, particularly those planning to major in nursing or education, the most common fields for girls.

A peculiar feature of college planning among girls is that, in contrast with boys, girls reach a peak of interest in college between the ages of 11 and 14; their interest then diminishes during high school. Matthews (1960) explains this early peak as a "pseudo-career drive," which is displaced by marriage as the major life goal for most girls during later adolescence.

Interest in college among girls is strongly related to both ability

and family background, although the relationship between academic ability and the likelihood of attending college is slightly less
among girls than among boys. Social class, on the other hand, is a
better predictor of college intention among girls. Thus the lower-
class girl of high ability is much less likely to attend college than
is her male counterpart. Lower levels of family income also influence selection of occupation. As we shall see in a later chapter, girls have greater difficulty in financing their way through
college than do boys. Therefore the girl with high ability should
be encouraged early to plan for college, and her family should be included in the planning. It is also likely that federal and state programs designed to provide financial aid for college students who
come from low-income families may prove especially helpful to
girls.

✻ ✻ ✻ ACCELERATION. Flexibility in the rate at which students move through the public school program is increasing as research on various acceleration techniques shows that many are
feasible. Such procedures are psychologically more appropriate for
girls than for boys. One reason is that acceleration of a bright
girl increases the probability that she will be able to continue
her education to a point commensurate with her abilities and
still be young enough to marry and have children at the usual
age. In addition, acceleration is more sensible for girls since they
are developmentally accelerated anyway. The girl who is a year or
two ahead of her age mates chronologically will probably not be
far behind her class developmentally, whereas the accelerated boy
will be immature physically compared with the rest of his class.
This may explain why boys have more trouble adjusting to acceleration.

The logic seems irrefutable, but for some reason in practice
boys are more likely to be accelerated than are girls. This is probably a reflection of the greater attention paid by our society to the
education of boys. We tend to assume that it doesn't really make
much difference how effectively we educate girls since they are
destined to become housewives anyway. The obvious fact that
women's lives are much more complex than this means that society
must become equally concerned with the education of its daughters
as well as of its sons.

The College Girl: Who She Is and Why She's There

> A purely intellectual man is no doubt biologi-
> cally a deformity, but a purely intellectual
> woman is far more so. Bookishness is prob-
> ably a bad sign in a girl; it suggests artifici-
> ality, pedantry, the lugging of dead knowl-
> edge.
>
> ﾞ *David Starr Jordan, 1902*

THE COLLEGE GIRL is so much an accepted part of the modern
scene that it is hard to believe that a century ago few colleges
were open to women. The prevalent belief was that higher
education was of value only for men, and that it was a mistake to
educate women too well because higher education was not appropriate for the role they were expected to play.

The struggle by which women won the right to higher
education has been well described elsewhere. Out of this struggle
has emerged an educational pattern which in some respects has provided as many frustrations for girls as did the original closed-door
policy. The drive for higher education for women was closely associated with the feminist movement, which was based on the belief that
women were equal to men in every respect and that sex differences
should be minimized. Women's colleges, founded to provide women
with educational opportunities which were denied by the sexually

segregated men's schools, tried to copy the men's colleges as much as possible. Men's colleges had, in turn, been patterned on English models which were designed primarily for the education of gentlemen. Since the role of women in society was quite different from that of men a hundred years ago—and some important differences still exist—such a plan provided little in the way of useful education for most girls.

A more contemporary problem is that those persons responsible for the education of women do not agree on what kind of education is most appropriate for most girls. The major concern for many years was with gaining acceptance of the idea that women *should* have the right to higher education per se. Unfortunately, there was little concern with the use to which women would put this education once it became available, the implicit assumption being that women, once they became well educated and intellectually stimulated, would live happily ever after. In reality, many persons responsible for educating girls recognized the weaknesses of these assumptions and recently have taken a closer look at the current status of women's education, concluding that there is considerable room for improvement.

✄ ✄ ✄ FACTS AND FIGURES. College may no longer be a man's world, but men continue to dominate it. Nearly 40 per cent of all college students are women, although the proportion of girls declines steadily from the freshman year on. At the graduate level, the trend is more pronounced: 32 per cent of all master's degrees are awarded to women, but only 11 per cent of the doctorates go to them.

Among women college students, about one-sixth of the undergraduates and one-third of those in graduate school are married, but the proportion of married persons among female students is less than that among men.

The ratio of men to women among college students varies according to the kind of school under consideration. Women are most prominent in liberal arts and teachers colleges, less so in universities and technical schools. Approximately 31 per cent of all college women are in liberal arts colleges, 35 per cent are in universities, and 14 per cent are in teachers colleges; they account for 44 per cent, 34 per cent, and 52 per cent of all students in the three types respectively.

A rather surprising trend is that the proportion of women among all college students has been declining for many years, since reaching a peak of 47 per cent in 1920. From that point on, the ratio of women to men decreased steadily to a low of 30 per cent in 1950. Since then there has been a slight rise, to 35 per cent in 1956 and 39 per cent in 1964, suggesting that the trend may have been reversed. Similarly, the proportion of women recipients of doctor's degrees fell from 1 out of 6 in 1920 to 1 out of 10 in 1960 and seems to have stabilized there.

The decline in the sex ratio following 1920 was due primarily to a rapid growth in the number of boys going to college, rather than to a decline in attendance by girls. The proportion of all girls between the ages of 18 and 21 who are enrolled in college has risen steadily during this century to a current level of about 25 per cent. During most of the period described, the rate of increase among boys was considerably greater than that among girls, but this trend seems to be reversing itself. Between 1956 and 1961, the college population in general increased 32 per cent but the increase among girls alone was 44 per cent. If this trend is maintained, it should serve to bring the sex ratio closer to an even balance.

At the graduate level the sex ratio is even more one-sided since the proportion of girls receiving graduate degrees is considerably less than that among recipients of bachelor's degrees. It has been estimated that of all persons who have the ability to obtain a doctorate only about 37 per cent of the girls and 55 per cent of the boys even graduate from college, while only 1 out of 30 of the men and 1 out of 300 of the women continue through the Ph.D.

Educators are gradually becoming aware that many intellectually capable women in this country do not receive the amount of education for which they are qualified. There has as yet, however, been no great stride made in determining reasons for this state of affairs, which means that we are not yet in a position to do much about it. A few suggestions may be offered as starting points but they need to be corroborated by research. Ludeman (1961), for example, has suggested that girls are handicapped in pursuing higher education by several factors: (a) The early age of marriage means that many girls must take jobs as soon as possible. (b) Due to the rapid turnover in traditionally female occupations, especially clerical jobs, such jobs are readily available for girls with a high school education. Since most girls don't plan to work indefinitely anyway, they are satisfied with such jobs on a short-term basis. Indeed, many girls with college educations may settle for nothing better. (c) The feeling still prevails in our society that a college education is not as important for a girl as for a boy, so that a girl may have to exert extra pressure to get there at all; her motivation must be higher.

On the basis of these points, Ludeman suggests that several actions must be taken if this trend is to be significantly altered. Attempts must be made to modify parental attitudes toward the education of their daughters, so that girls may have the financial help and encouragement which their brothers enjoy. High schools will also have to do a better job of helping girls to plan their futures—a point frequently reiterated throughout this book—and colleges will have to do a better job of recruiting and retaining women students.

For these changes to occur, however, girls must demonstrate that they are entitled to equal treatment with boys by making more productive use of their educations. Up to now there has been some justification for the feeling that when a choice must be made to educate one of two children, it should be made in favor of the boy. He is more likely to need the education for future occupational advancement, and he is more likely to make productive use of it.

In addition, colleges will have to decide that it is worthwhile and desirable to attract and retain women students. At the moment most schools seem uncertain of this, and they generally tend not to make much effort to attract and hold bright girls. Perhaps this is related to the fact that the majority of the country's colleges and universities, and especially those which enroll large numbers of students, are run by men. Although these administrators are committed to the proposition that a college education is valuable for all persons with the ability to profit from it, they have a noticeable tendency to make a greater effort to attract and hold talented male students than they are willing to make for equally capable girls.

✣ ✣ ✣ WHY IS SHE THERE? Girls' reasons for attending college usually differ from those of boys. The latter are motivated largely by the requirement of a college education to enter a desired occupation as well as by the concomitant financial gain. Girls do not generally rate these motives as highly, although occupational goals may be more important than many are willing to admit.

Also, college is more an end in itself for girls than for boys. Girls see college more in terms of its potential benefits to them as persons, and are more likely to stress the academic aspects in describing their motives for attending. They often are vague as to the value which their college education will have for them in the future. They recognize that they are expected to emerge from college with a marketable skill, but this job is only a temporary measure until they marry and become housewives and mothers. Thus for most girls the "experience" of college is more important than the courses they may take.

College girls, whether they are willing to admit it or not, have a very specific goal in mind: to achieve propinquity to eligible young men. The intelligent girl who does not attend college has less contact with equally intelligent potential husbands. Most girls who go to college eventually marry college graduates, and one suspects that this is not just a casual by-product, but more a result of their having strived "as much for the acquisition of a bachelor as for a bachelor's degree." (C. Heilbrun, 1962, p. 35.)

Certainly the goal of finding a suitable marriage partner is an acceptable one as far as society is concerned, although it would be unrealistic to assume that this motive is limited to girls. Even though it may not be openly recognized, it is undoubtedly true that men look for wives in college just as girls hunt for husbands, but the motive is neither as intense nor as single-minded among the men. Vocational motives, important for college men, probably serve to dilute the marriage goal. In addition, society attaches less stigma to the unmarried male than to the unmarried female. Thus the need for the college man to be married, or at least committed to marriage, by the time he graduates is not as intense as the corresponding need among girls.

It is highly unlikely that this motive will be altered in the foreseeable future. Frustrating as it may be to educators, most college girls may be said to be in college not to pursue learning but to learn pursuing. That educators may question whether the college experience has any intellectual meaning to these girls is proposed by Carolyn Heilbrun (1962, p. 35):

The finding of a husband and the full use of one's mind are not, within a lifetime, mutually exclusive. But it is questionable whether either of these tasks benefits from being undertaken simultaneously with the other.

Others believe that girls can hunt for husbands and still have an academic orientation. Perhaps it would be best for college administrators to work with rather than against the recognized motive for most college girls: to find a husband. The teacher who tries to dissuade a female student from such concerns probably succeeds only in frustrating her by stimulating a feeling of guilt, with the result that the need becomes even greater.

❧ ❧ INFLUENCES ON THE DECISION TO ATTEND COLLEGE. Whether a girl chooses to attend college, and the specific college that she selects, are determined not only by what she hopes to get out of college personally but also by numerous other factors, many of which may be obscure to her.

❧ *Size of Hometown.* Although there is little difference between the percentage of rural and urban girls among high school seniors who plan to attend college, city girls are more likely to follow through with such plans and actually make it to college. On the other hand, those girls from small towns who enter college are more likely to finish than are those from either cities or rural areas.

✤ *Social Class.* Socioeconomic status seems to exert considerable influence on college attendance. Several studies agree that girls from the lower classes are less likely to attend college at all than are those from higher levels and are even less likely to graduate. The same holds true in graduate school, where the women tend to be of higher socioeconomic status than the men. One reason for this difference is undoubtedly financial: when a sacrifice is necessary it is much more likely to be made for a son than for a daughter. In addition, it is more difficult for girls than for boys to support themselves while in college.

However, the motivation element also plays an important role. The middle-class girl is expected to go to college, but the lower-class girl is expected to get a job after graduation from high school. This probably fits nicely with her future plans, so she has no reason to see college as of any potential value to her.

✤ *Family Influences.* A most important influence on a young person's decision to attend college is his relationship with his parents, although the exact pattern of influence is not fully understood. There is some evidence that boys who are close to their families are more likely to go to college than those who aren't, while the reverse is true among girls. This suggests that a girl's decision to enter college may reflect a rebellion against her family. However, when parental emphasis on college attendance is high, girls are more likely to plan to attend, whereas when it is low, boys are more likely to go. This is consistent with the belief that girls are more docile and conforming than are boys, but it seems inconsistent with the evidence previously cited.

One possible resolution of this dilemma is that there are two distinctly different patterns among girls who attend college. Some are there because college has been stressed in their families and their parents have insisted on it. These girls are likely to see little personal relevance in college, and their performance may thereby suffer. A second pattern, however, may characterize girls who attend college in opposition to their parents' wishes. These girls have had to make the decision for themselves, and they presumably have turned to college as a way of making something of themselves as persons. The danger is that their rebellion against their parents may become translated into rebellion against the school. Thus there is no guarantee that either pattern is a more desirable one for a girl to follow. The girl who is most likely to benefit from college is the one who is there because both she and her parents agree that it is desirable for her.

Other evidence of parental influence comes from studies relating father's occupation to college choice. As compared with boys, female college students are more likely to come from families in which the father's job is in the upper levels—professional, managerial, or sales. Whether the mother works does not seem to have any greater influence on girls than on boys in their decision to attend college, but the likelihood of a girl entering college is increased if her mother is a teacher.

✦ *Finances.* More critical for girls than for boys as a determiner of college attendance is the ability to meet the financial costs. Parents finding it difficult to send both a son and a daughter to college are reluctant to pay the additional costs of sending the daughter to an expensive school.

Girls find it difficult to obtain money for college from sources other than their parents. Summer employment and part-time jobs during the school year may supply funds for a substantial part of a boy's education. Similar opportunities available for girls generally pay less, so that a girl will have to work longer to make the same amount of money as a boy. Nevertheless, college costs the same for both.[1]

Girls are somewhat better off in winning undergraduate scholarships. At every aptitude level more girls than boys receive scholarships, although those awarded to boys tend to be for larger amounts. To some extent the former difference is probably due to the superiority of girls' high school grades, although it may also reflect a recognition by college officials that it is more difficult for girls to earn money of their own. Nevertheless, it is doubtful if national and local groups awarding scholarships and fellowships are making any special effort to encourage the education of women. The National Merit Scholarships are a prime example: only one-third of these are awarded to females.

At the graduate level the situation is cloudy. A wide range of fellowships is available to graduate students, and it would seem that girls are being overlooked. For example, according to figures for the fall of 1962, supplied by the American Association of University Women Educational Foundation, women accounted for only 27 per cent of Woodrow Wilson Scholars, $1\frac{1}{2}$ per cent of National Science Foundation Graduate Fellowships, and 12 per cent of National Science Foundation Summer Fellowships for Graduate Teach-

---

[1] This statement refers to the direct costs of education—tuition, fees, and books. In other respects, girls have some advantages and some disadvantages. At many schools, girls are required to live in university residence halls, at least during their freshman year. Boys often find it less expensive to live off campus, especially when cooking facilities are available. On the other hand, boys must bear the expense of most dating activities. Whether these differences balance in the long run is uncertain. Some couples eventually resolve the problem by marrying while still in school.

ing Associates. Bernard (1964), however, makes a telling point: women receive academic awards and fellowships in about the same proportion as they apply or are nominated for them. In some areas they are over-represented. The Woodrow Wilson Foundation, for example, while admitting that it tends to recruit more strongly among male students, awards about one-fourth of its fellowships to women. This seems generous, since the purpose of these fellowships is to encourage young persons to obtain a doctorate preparatory to entering college teaching, and the proportion of doctorates which are obtained by women is only about 1 in 10.

The primary difficulty in the awarding of scholarships and fellowships is the prediction of ultimate use of the education. When this criterion is stressed, women are bound to suffer since the odds are much greater that a man will eventually use his education productively. Thus it can be argued that girls are being treated more than fairly in the matter of financial aid, although many girls would undoubtedly dispute this view.

The great many students not eligible for scholarships must depend on loans to supplement the money which they and their parents can contribute to their education. Here, too, the girl is at a disadvantage. Her chances of obtaining a college loan are probably about as good as those of a boy in most cases, since the criteria are generally limited to need and grades, but a loan establishes an obligation which a girl may be unable or unwilling to contract. A male student can justify assuming a financial loan on the grounds that his college education will enhance his future earning power, making the gamble worthwhile. A girl, uncertain of attaining a career, has no assurance that she will make enough money after college to enable her to pay back the loan without putting undue strain on herself or her family, as financial gain is not likely to be a strong motive for a college girl in the first place. If she marries within a short time after college graduation, she would be in the position of having to ask her husband to assume the responsibility for paying off the loan. After all, few men want a mortgaged bride.

Intelligence. It is sad but true that many young people who have the ability to do college work do not attend college. Much has been written and spoken in recent years about the dangers to individuals and to society inherent in this ability loss, and considerable concern has been paid to its causes and potential cures.

This ailment is more acute among girls than among boys. According to a survey by Wolfle (1960) of students in the upper 30 per cent of ability (which is assumed to be the level required to do college work), 65 per cent of the men enter college and 45 per cent graduate, while among women of comparable ability only 50 per cent enter college and 30 per cent graduate. Other studies have confirmed this gap.

Differences diminish at the highest levels of ability. In Terman's gifted group, for example, 70 per cent of the men and 67 per cent of the women graduated from college and 67 per cent of the men and 58 per cent of the women went on to graduate work. As noted earlier, women in this group differed from women in general in their personalities and motivations, and these differences may have had an influence on their increased interest in education.

But just getting to college doesn't guarantee that a bright girl will use her ability constructively. Many of the factors which operate to dilute the academic motivation of the typical college girl influence the bright ones as well. The typical college girl, regardless of her ability, is not attracted to difficult courses, but instead feels it is more important to mold herself into the standard feminine image in order to enhance her chances of getting a husband. Alpenfels (1963, p. 40) has described the situation well:

In a thousand subtle ways, a young college woman learns that women are less capable, less intelligent, less serious, more emotional, and less important than men. It propels her toward "soft" courses, pushes her into "women's" occupations and away from science, and finally, closes the door on many kinds of work for which she may be well suited.

Thus the problem is not primarily one of getting bright girls interested in college, but rather one of getting all girls of college ability motivated for college *for academically appropriate reasons.* There is no simple definition of this, nor could one easily compile a list of reasons which would be acceptable to all, but certainly the girl's reasons should have some relationship to her development as an individual as well as to the goals and capabilities of the college. Without this in mind, any attempts to motivate girls to attend college will simply result in flooding our already overcrowded schools with girls who have little academic or intellectual reason of their own for being there.

✄ ✄ ✄ CHOICE OF A COLLEGE. After examining the reasons why girls choose to attend college, we must still question why those who go to college select one school over another. Several factors seem to operate in this choice, and they are not the same as those for boys.

In choosing a college, boys tend to stress such variables as the general reputation of the college, its physical facilities, and the cost, while girls put more stress on the academic standing of the college, a friendly atmosphere, its size (smaller preferred), its religious affiliation, and whether it is coeducational.

An additional factor which has a different influence on men and women is the distance between the college and the student's home. Girls are more likely to attend a college some distance away from home, if they can afford to, while men prefer a school nearby. This is consistent with White's (1950) suggestion that it is more important for a girl than for a boy to go to college away from home because the family will give the boy more freedom anyway. Since financial problems often force a girl to attend a college near home, however, it is not surprising that girls who live at home while attending college tend to have more difficulty in adjusting to school than do boys in the same circumstances.

✄ ✄ ✄ CHOICE OF CURRICULUM. Sex ratios vary considerably from one curriculum to another. Education is by far the most popular major for women, although its popularity is declining slightly. Many transfer to education from their original curricula, with the result that more than 50 per cent of all bachelor's degrees awarded to women are in education. Humanities and the arts account for about 20 per cent, with most of the others in the social sciences and the health professions. Besides the traditional fields of teaching, nursing, home economics, and library science, women also outnumber men in the undergraduate majors of sociology, English, and foreign languages. English is most often chosen by the brightest girls, while those with less ability gravitate toward education.

Perhaps the most notable trend over the past decade has been the increased proportion of women among majors in science and mathematics. The recent increase in the number of college students graduating with degrees in science and math has been due mostly to an increase in the number of women, although there is still room for many more women in these fields.

At the graduate level, the most popular fields for women are education, nursing, home economics, and library science. Nearly three-fifths of all master's degrees earned by women are conferred in education, as compared with two-fifths of men's, and while women account for only one-tenth of all doctorates awarded, almost one-third of these are also in education. Women are relatively frequent recipients of master's degrees in English, journalism, social sciences, and fine and applied arts, while at the doctoral level the fields with significant numbers of women receiving degrees, in addition to education, are the social sciences, biological sciences, psychology, and English and journalism. Since 1930, however, the proportion of women among recipients of doctorates in chemistry, biological sciences, economics, and mathematics has declined by 50 per cent or more.

General statements about sex differences in curricula obscure two important points: (a) such differences are not as consistent nor as great as one might expect, and (b) patterns vary from one kind of school to another. For example, there is little difference in the sex ratio among math majors in universities, but when men's and women's colleges are compared, women predominate in this field. By contrast, history and philosophy majors within small colleges are more commonly men, while women account for the majority of political science majors in small colleges. These patterns are not found in universities. The most significant general difference between the two types of schools, however, is that only a small proportion of the students attending liberal arts colleges are enrolled in curricula which emphasize training for a profession, while in the state universities such a program is characteristic of the majority of the students. This in itself defines one of the major differences between these schools, and it may be expected to continue.

The conclusion that can be drawn is that men and women who attend small, unisexual, liberal arts colleges tend to be less stereotyped in their choice of curriculum. The cause-and-effect relationships are difficult to isolate, but the differences definitely exist and are important for our understanding of choice of college major.

Sex differences in curriculum choice can thus be demonstrated, but relatively little is known as to the *reasons* for girls' specific choices. We know that girls tend to concentrate in certain curricula but we don't know why, nor can we explain why some girls choose curricula more typical of men. Certain variables need to be explored. Thistlethwaite (1963) addressed himself to this question in his analysis of the college performance of students who took the National Merit Examination in 1958, by relating factors in choice of college to choice of a major curriculum. Table 11.1 summarizes his results and suggests that these two variables are meaningfully related.

❧ ❧ ❧ NEEDS OF COLLEGE GIRLS. The modern college is concerned with meeting the needs of its students, but when the students are female it may be fighting a losing battle. The needs of girls in the late teens and early twenties are often incompatible with one another and, in some cases, incompatible with any sort of academic purpose.

On the one hand, as girls prepare for the role of wife and mother—which for many is the prime goal in life at this time—one

TABLE 11.1 ✤ Relationships Between Women's Reasons for Choice of a College and Choice of a Major Field

Reasons for Choosing a College	Most Likely Majors	Least Likely Majors
Educational standards	Political science Psychology Pre-med	Physical education Business
Course of study offered	Health professions Home economics Physical education	Sociology English Mathematics
Financial costs	Education Physical education	Political science
Close to home	Business Education	Political science Music
Small school	History Sociology	Health professions Journalism Pre-med
Prestige of the school	Psychology	Physical education

Source: Thistlethwaite, 1963.

would expect that a liberal arts education would be the most beneficial. The responsibility for transmitting culture from one generation to the next should motivate girls to learn about the world in which they live.

But opposing this is the expectation that a girl will graduate from college with a marketable skill. Companies are hesitant to train women, knowing that most of them will leave soon to marry and raise a family. Thus the college girl, while probably not planning on a career, must concern herself with being prepared for a job when she graduates. It is a tremendous challenge to colleges and universities which are educating women to work out means by which both needs may be successfully met.

As a first step, colleges could exert greater effort to help girls face the realities of their future lives by helping them develop self-respect and plan intelligently for their futures. The college girl not only needs realistic information from which she can develop her future plans, but she needs to be able to assimilate it in an atmosphere which recognizes the diversity of responsibilities and pressures to which she is being subjected and which allows her to work out her own unique pattern.

In addition to these general approaches, colleges might better meet the needs of their undergraduate women in specific ways.

Many of these have to do with increasing the flexibility of college programs to meet the needs of girls who are trying to coordinate their intellectual, occupational, and marital needs. The girl who marries before graduation and quits school without a degree may see her entire education go down the drain in the sense of having any direct value. In the job market the girl who has three years of college is scarcely ahead of the girl with none.

One suggestion which has been offered is that colleges should develop multidegree programs for women which could be covered at different rates of speed, so that the college girl might, for example, have something concrete to show for two years of work. The objection to such a program, in addition to the overburdening of already tightly stretched college resources, is that it would further encourage a trend toward vocationally oriented college programs which many think has already become too strong. Such a development also might undermine attempts to encourage girls to plan for careers requiring 4-year college degrees, which they can combine with marriage and family responsibilities.

Another kind of flexibility would be helpful to college women who marry and move away before finishing. Many still could and would finish except for traditional regulations which require that a student must obtain a substantial part of her college work—especially the latter part—at the college from which she is to obtain her degree. With a few exceptions, she cannot take her senior year elsewhere and then graduate from her original school, nor can she transfer her credits and graduate from her new location without losing many credits and having to take extra courses. For many young married women the project is too exhausting or too costly and they give up, the degree unfinished. It's hard to say whether they or society have suffered the greater loss. In any case, this rigidity has led many eminent educators to urge colleges to be more flexible in allowing girls to transfer credits and to complete their work elsewhere, and some schools seem to be taking these suggestions to heart. There are hopeful signs that such flexibility will be increased in the future.

Another important step which colleges could take to help more girls complete their education would be to provide more financial aid. This is especially important for married women students who thus would not have to quit school and take a job. Older married women could utilize this type of help, which would allow them to return to school while maintaining a family. In any case, the proportion of women students who obtain and use their college degrees could probably be substantially increased by an increase in financial assistance.

The special problems of married women students have been largely neglected by colleges. Most of the concern about married students has been focused on the men, with their wives and children seen as appendages. This attitude has its roots in the developments immediately following World War II when married students first became a significant part of the college population. It has continued, however, even though the original GI Bill of Rights has long since expired.

College administrators sympathetic to the needs of married women, especially those with children, are handicapped by the lack of sound information concerning these needs. Research on the needs and characteristics of married women students has been sadly lacking. In view of the increasing trend toward marrying at younger ages, colleges must expect that this problem will continue to grow, and they must take more definite steps to meet it constructively.

HOW SHOULD GIRLS BE EDUCATED? The longest and loudest debate concerning education for women is not *whether* they should be educated, but *how*. The problem arises out of the diversity of women's roles and the extent to which higher education for women should try to prepare girls to meet the various contingencies of the future. Numerous persons have taken strong positions, and for many it has become an emotional issue. There are no easy answers and perhaps no answer at all, in a final sense.

One point on which most experts seem to agree is that higher education for women should not try to duplicate that of men. The early women's colleges were developed to provide an education for women equal to that available to men, but their founders erred in assuming that equality meant "the same." We now recognize that the life patterns of most women are different from those of men, necessitating a somewhat different educational experience.

One of the harshest critics of male-oriented education for women has been Lynn White. In his book, *Educating Our Daughters* (1950), he deplored the typical educational program for women as designed to turn them into men, and he quoted a young mother to that effect (p. 18):

> I have come to realize that I was educated to be a successful man and now I must learn by myself how to be a successful woman.

He then went on to say (p. 48):

> If we are to rear our daughters to be proud that they are women, we must end our present peculiar habit of educating them as though they were men.

We can agree that women's needs in higher education do not parallel those of men, but there is still some doubt as to how far apart the sexes are in this respect and whether higher education for women should stress the differences or the similarities. Komarovsky (1953) believes some differentiation may be necessary in view of sex differences in interests and social functions, but that it is important to keep in mind that men and women differ little in most abilities. She also argues that overemphasis on differentiation in the higher education of men and women may have other unfortunate consequences (pp. 250–51):

The call for greater differentiation in the education of men and women comes at a time when marriage in the urban middle classes is already strained by the fact that husband and wife live in two separate worlds.

In her view, both men and women need educational experiences which will better equip them to understand and participate in the realm of life which has been traditionally reserved for the other sex.

In actuality, what is needed is neither a male-dominated curriculum for both sexes nor separate programs for each, but rather a curriculum applicable to both men and women. Such programs are already available, but colleges need to put more emphasis on them and encourage college women to take better advantage of them.

꙳ ꙳ SEGREGATED VS. INTEGRATED COLLEGES. The issue of segregated educational facilities is not confined to racial criteria, but includes colleges that segregate students by sex when they restrict enrollment to men or women only. Most schools are coeducational, enrolling students regardless of sex, although within them there may be a kind of partial segregation inasmuch as many curricula are composed almost entirely of men or of women.

It was only about 100 years ago that women began entering colleges and universities in appreciable numbers, and for a time they were restricted almost exclusively to those schools founded for that purpose. Most colleges and universities had been limited almost entirely to men, and, when they did respond to the demands of girls for equal educational opportunities, they tended to relegate their women students to second-rate, domestic curricula. Men's colleges, modeled on the European system, were viewed as the epitome of excellence in higher education, and the early women's colleges were frankly designed to emulate them. This form of education was not relevant to women's needs and has had a stultifying influence on women's education down to the present time.

Recent modifications of women's colleges have tended to bring their programs more into line with the real needs of their students, a trend which has been accentuated by the competition of the coeducational colleges and universities throughout the country.

One result is that the programs of the women's colleges have gradually allowed more emphasis on the arts and social sciences, fields in which girls are more likely to be interested. Concomitantly, the proportion of students in the women's colleges who major in such fields as sciences and modern languages—curricula in which the current need is being strongly emphasized—has actually declined throughout the past century. It may be surprising to learn that in 1865 a higher proportion of the students enrolled in women's colleges was majoring in the sciences than was the case in the men's schools. Since then, however, as girls have been given greater freedom of choice in their curricula they have tended to favor the more traditional women's fields.

Evidence is difficult to find to determine whether girls will obtain a better education at a college limited exclusively to women or at the more common coeducational school. Comparisons between students who have attended one type or the other are fruitless since the different kinds of schools attract different kinds of students in the first place. The women's colleges have been criticized for catering primarily to girls from upper income families; in recent years they have made a greater attempt to draw students from all socioeconomic levels, but most of their students still come from the upper strata.

Despite the lack of evidence favoring either the unisexual or coeducational system, many educators believe that girls can obtain a better education in a segregated environment in which they are free to develop their personal talents without the distraction of maintaining the usual feminine subservience to boys. The important question still unanswered is whether women's colleges provide an educational experience which realistically prepares girls for the future.

In any case, the trend of the times is against the women's colleges. In 1870, nearly 60 per cent of all females in college were attending schools limited excusively to women, but by 1957 the proportion had shrunk to only 9 per cent. As further evidence, no 4-year women's college has been founded since 1930, and the total number of women's colleges has declined from 78 to 53 since that date. Actually, this trend is not peculiar to the women's colleges, but seems rather to be true of colleges which limit their enrollment to one sex, whether male or female.

Newcomer (1959) has suggested several reasons for the overwhelming trend toward coeducation. One is that as colleges have become integrated into their communities the local residents have applied pressure for the admission of their own children, regardless of sex. Another is that young people of both sexes have come to prefer coeducational schools. Although it is unlikely that colleges devoted exclusively to the education of one sex will entirely disappear, the lines are becoming blurred. Even the most well entrenched have begun to lower the barriers. An outstanding example is the integration of Radcliffe and Harvard students to the point at which the distinction between them is for the most part only formal, a trend which is generally seen as having favorable results for both student bodies.

ả ả MAJOR APPROACHES. In addition to the debate concerning segregated or coeducational learning experiences, there has been considerable disagreement as to what should be emphasized in higher education for women. There seem to be three major alternatives, each of which has its advocates: (a) emphasis on homemaking skills and family education as preparation for the woman's role of wife and mother; (b) a firm grounding in the liberal arts; and (c) preparation for a profession. These are by no means mutually exclusive goals, but it is doubtful if all can be pursued with equal vigor at the same time; as a college chooses to stress one it must do so at some expense to the others.

ả *Emphasis on the Homemaking Role.* Those who urge that women's education should emphasize the learning of homemaking skills and preparation for being a good wife and mother do so with the belief that this role is the most important which a woman can play. They view with alarm the trends in modern society which are tending to undermine this theory and to make women dissatisfied with their lot. They believe that only a return to the traditional values of home and family can save our society, and that the colleges must take the leadership. De Luget (1958, p. 627) expresses it thus:

This training of the mind that home economics education pursues saves the woman from finding homemaking tedious and monotonous and thus endangering her culture and hampering the development of her personality.

One of the strongest supporters of this viewpoint has been Lynn White (1950), who believes that the typical educational curriculum for women is destroying their femininity and urges that girls be encouraged to concentrate instead on learning how to be good wives and mothers. His description of the joys and challenges of an education in home economics is enough to make a girl want to lay down her life for it, at least until the haze dissipates and she is once again able to see the homemaking role more realistically.

That some training in homemaking skills is desirable for the young woman seems irrefutable. But should this be the major emphasis of a college curriculum? Many would argue that preparation for homemaking is not in itself a scholarly activity, and thus should not constitute a college major per se. But, if she can be persuaded to take advantage of them, many elective courses related to food preparation and child care can be of value to the girl who will become a wife and mother.

College programs in home economics are not, in fact, intended to prepare girls to become homemakers. Instead, their graduates are expected to become professional home economists, in the best tradition of the land-grant institutions where such programs flourish. The girls themselves, however, often enter these programs with mixed motives, recognizing that despite the program's emphasis on professional rather than personal use of their education, they may learn a great deal which will be useful to them in their subsequent career as housewives. Persons responsible for conducting college home economics programs are thus faced with the dilemma of educating girls for a goal about which many have serious doubts.

We must conclude, therefore, that there is no legitimate way for a girl to prepare herself directly in college for becoming a housewife. She may obtain some indirect help, but homemaking preparation is not now, and probably never will be, a full-fledged academic major.

❧ *The Liberal Arts Approach.* The point of view that the college education of girls should emphasize the liberal arts also has its fervent advocates among persons responsible for educating girls. The case for liberal arts for women has been well stated by Gettel (1958, p. 260) in his inaugural address as president of Mt. Holyoke College:

The primary approach, in my estimation, is a comprehensive liberal arts education of the highest quality, consciously focused on developing the intelligent young woman's ability to learn for herself so that whatever she chooses to do, and whenever she wishes to do it, she will have the inner resources, the curiosity, and the mental ability to face and master new challenges.

The arguments for and against the liberal arts approach are numerous. On the positive side, women are required to be more flexible than men, since their life patterns are less predictable and are more likely to require readjustment. Presumably a liberal arts education provides the best resources to enable a woman to cope with her unpredictable future.

More important, however, is the belief that a liberal arts education can best help a woman prepare herself as an individual, not bound and gagged by society's concept of her role as a woman, as might be the case if all girls were forced into a family education program. As one educator has put it (Norris, 1954, p. 38):

> Women are human beings before they become mothers, educators, or professionals of any kind. Their education must enable them first of all to mature as human beings and to gain such intellectual and moral equipment as will enable them to find a purposeful outlet for their talents in whatever role they may be cast.

But the strengths of the liberal arts approach also reveal its weaknesses. The major difficulty is that, in contrast to other methods, a liberal arts program provides a girl with a fine education but with very little training. The question most often asked about such a program, especially for a girl, is, "But what good is it?" In this case, of course, "good" means job preparation, and the sad thing about a graduate of a liberal arts program is that she is not prepared to *do* anything in particular.

It is worth re-emphasizing a point made earlier, that although this problem exists for both male and female liberal arts graduates, it is more acute for the girl. She is less likely than her male counterpart to have either the time or money to continue her education into professional or graduate school, and she is not an attractive prospect for a business training program, which expects many years of service out of persons in whom it invests the time and effort of training. It is likely that the girl, if not already married by the time she graduates from college, has plans to marry in the near future. If her husband is also a liberal arts graduate he will probably continue his education, but it is doubtful if the couple will feel that both can afford to.[2] Someone has to get a job and earn money for the family to live on; the chances are good that the wife will draw the short straw, and probably with little complaint. The last thing she wants to do at this point is to outshine her husband.

Nor does a liberal arts education provide an adequate preparation for the woman who becomes a housewife. Although it may be argued that the housewife with a liberal arts background is better able to communicate with her husband and children, to participate

---

[2] As financial aid for graduate students increases at a rapid pace, it becomes more likely that both a husband and wife can obtain financial support for graduate education, so that the "either-or" choice may be unnecessary. On the other hand, the woman may not be motivated at this time to commit herself to a graduate program and may therefore still be forced to look for a job.

more fully in her community, and to make more constructive use of her leisure time, she is poorly prepared to deal with the day-to-day responsibilities and demands of homemaking. The real danger, however, is that a liberal arts education will cause the woman to become frustrated at the loss of the intellectual stimulation and challenge to which she became accustomed while in college, while providing her with no avenue of escape from her constricted life as a housewife.

Thus the liberal arts approach to educating women is an anomaly. In view of the uncertainty and discontinuity of women's lives it would seem to be the most sensible procedure, but in terms of the girl's needs immediately following college graduation it has the least to offer. It neither prepares her for a job nor for adjusting to the role of a housewife. To be adequate, therefore, a liberal arts education must be combined in some way with training of a more practical sort. Otherwise the woman may find herself to be educated not wisely but too well.

Preparation for a Profession. There is yet a third alternative, one which may be pursued alone or combined with either of the others: the girl may enter a program of professional education, designed to prepare her for a job after graduation. In most cases, the girls involved are not planning on a career, and most women's professions are not typically career fields; rather, they usually are fields which can be combined with home and family responsibilities and in which jobs are likely to be available wherever the woman lives.

Few educators have been eager to support professional preparation as an exclusive educational goal for women. They have, however, been willing to accept it when combined with either family education or a liberal arts program. Newcomer (1959), one of the advocates of the latter combination, sees the liberal arts program by itself as resulting in frustration for many of its graduates and therefore suggests that it be combined with a vocationally oriented program.

In many ways this seems to be the most reasonable approach, but it has some drawbacks. Any program which requires a girl to commit herself to preparation for a job in a specific field presents problems for her, since she may find it impossible to predict where or how she will be living after graduation. Many girls complete an educational program in preparation for a professional occupation only to find that they will be living in an area in which jobs in that field are not available. They then have the choice of (a) limiting themselves to being a housewife, (b) taking a job for which they were not prepared, probably one not requiring a college education at all, or (c) retracing their steps through college to get a "market-able" degree. None of these choices is very appealing, and all are likely to engender some degree of frustration and bitterness. The alternative is to limit the original choice of profession to a tradi-tionally "safe" field, one composed mainly of women and in which jobs are generally available.

A second drawback is that schools are not making it easy for their female students to achieve professional preparation within the limits of their life patterns. Special programs, for example, have been devised to enable students to accelerate their college work in order to obtain a master's degree with an emphasis on college teaching in a shorter-than-normal time span. Although such programs would seem especially suited to the needs of girls, enabling them to combine an undergraduate liberal arts major with a master's program to prepare them for a professional occupation, in practice girls have not been encouraged to enter them, apparently out of concern that the program's image might suffer. It is unfor-tunate that the schools which have adopted such innovations are more sensitive to the image of their program than to the needs of their students.

Some educators continue to question the advisability of en-couraging girls to plan to combine a career with a family, believing that the possibilities for combining a career with marriage and children are slight. In some respects this is true, but it is equally true that many girls who could manage such a combination success-fully do not consider it when planning their futures. Ultimately, of course, each girl must decide what is best for her as an individual, but all girls should have the opportunity to view all alternatives realistically so as to make the best possible choice.

✄ ✄ CONCLUSION. In summary, one must conclude that it is unre-alistic to attempt either to educate women the same as men or differ-ently from them. It is neither possible nor desirable to develop an educational program for "girls in general." Instead, an educational program must be developed for each girl on the basis of her needs and goals as a person. Rather than making assumptions about what girls should become as women, counselors, educators, and parents must allow them the freedom to choose the best path for themselves. It is true that society changes. Any young person, male or female, must be educated not for life as it is today, but for life as it may be tomorrow. This is the challenge which faces all of education, and it is a special challenge for persons responsible for the counseling and education of girls.

The Use and Abuse of Higher Education for Women

A MISS IS AS GOOD AS A MALE.

✄ *Bernice Fitz-Gibbon*

DESPITE THE CONFUSION and conflict which pervades the higher education of women, many girls do go to college and many of these get something worthwhile out of it. Insofar as grades are concerned, women students as a group do better than men, due primarily to the greater tendency of girls to conform to expectations. Among boys, achievement in college is related to definiteness of occupational goal, but no such relationship exists among girls who are apparently able to generate motivation to do well in college without the presence of a specific goal beyond college toward which they are working.

For this reason, it is rather difficult to locate characteristics which differentiate between more and less successful female students, although some progress has been made. In many ways, the successful students seem to be more conforming as well as more serious, more mature, and better organized. However, further research is needed concerning variables related to academic achievement among girls.

✿ ✿ ✿ ADJUSTMENT TO COLLEGE. The adjustment of young people to college has been the subject of considerable concern in recent years, although attention has been focused primarily on male students. Among girls, the transition from home to college may require some major shifts in self-concept and self-responsibility, and the struggle with the conflicting demands and pressures put upon them sometimes results in emotional problems. Most freshman girls are experiencing their first prolonged separation from their families and many are not well prepared for the transition. They find themselves pushed from the safety and security of their families into the demands of the college environment on what seems to be a "sink or swim" basis, and for many the process of learning to swim is an arduous one. To be sure, such demands are also made of boys at this age, but the shift is likely to be neither as sudden nor as dramatic for them.

Adjustment difficulties are often reflected in drop-outs, a problem of considerable concern to college officials. Among the college population in general, the drop-out rate for women is about the same as that for men, although girls who drop out are less likely to return later. At the upper level of ability, the attrition rate of girls is greater than that among boys, but this discrepancy disappears after the first two years of college.

In any case, men and women do not leave school for the same reasons. Women are less likely to leave because of academic failure, but they are more apt to leave voluntarily for nonacademic reasons than are men. Although both men and women students frequently cite financial reasons for leaving school, this is more likely to be a problem for the latter. Women are also more likely to leave school to marry or to take a job.

It is generally accepted that a girl is more likely to be in college for the value of the immediate experience rather than because of its importance in relation to her long-range goals. Boys, on the other hand, view college as a means to an end, generally to gain entrance into a desirable occupation. This motivational difference is reflected in drop-outs among men and women students. Whereas degree of satisfaction with initial career choice is highly related to retention in college among male students, there is almost no such relationship among girls. On the other hand, academic performance and retention among women students vary more from one school to another among colleges of the same type, so that whether a woman student will graduate from college depends more on the specific school she enters than is the case among boys. In other words, whether a girl sticks with college for four years depends on what she is getting out of it *right now,* whereas a boy who is dissatisfied with school may stay with it by keeping his eye on the *potential* value of a college education.[1]

Attrition is also more probable for girls who do not become involved in the life of the college. Girls who are engaged or going steady when they enter college, as well as those who have a history of social isolation, are unlikely to stay long. Women drop-outs are also more easily differentiated on personality measures than are men; they are characterized by being withdrawn and depressed as compared with male drop-outs who tend to be irresponsible and nonconforming. The importance of involvement for college women is also evident in the greater effect that college experience has on the attitudes of women who stay as compared with the men who remain.

In summary, it seems that men who leave college are generally immature and not yet willing to assume the responsibilities of college, whereas drop-outs among girls are those who have negative feelings about themselves and who have failed to become integrated into the college community.[2] Since girls in general become more involved in college life than do men, a girl who does not become involved is likely to rapidly become dissatisfied with school.

✻ ✻ ✻ EDUCATIONAL PATTERNS. Several attempts have been made to describe college girls in terms of different educational patterns. An outstanding example is the report by Donald Brown (1956), based on a series of studies of Vassar students and alumnae. The universality of his generalizations may be questioned on the grounds that Vassar does not represent a typical college experience for most girls, nor are the girls who go to Vassar typical in the first place, but nevertheless his analysis has something to offer persons interested in the process by which colleges turn girls into women.

Brown suggests that five patterns are evident among college

---

[1] This attitude on the part of college girls is exemplified by the story about the freshman girl who came to the office of the Dean of Women at the end of her second week in college, saying that she wanted to withdraw from school. The Dean tried to dissuade her, pointing out that the girl hadn't been there long enough to know whether she was getting what she wanted out of college. The girl, however, insisted that she had. Finally the Dean asked, "What did you come here for?" "Well," said the girl, "I came here to be went with and I ain't been yet!"

[2] This suggests that potential drop-outs among female students may be more amenable to counseling than are their male counterparts, inasmuch as the kinds of problems with which they are struggling—a lack of integration with the college community, coupled with doubts about their own adequacy and self-worth—are often dealt with successfully through counseling. Male drop-outs, on the other hand, being essentially immature and directionless, are not such good candidates for counseling and may instead profit more from other kinds of growth experiences before they are ready for college. Since male drop-outs are more likely to return eventually, they are not irrevocably lost.

girls. The first is a group of girls dominated by a *need for social activity and peer acceptance*—those primarily interested in having a good time in college. They come from upper-middle- or upper-class backgrounds and have attended private schools. Both their parents are well educated, and the girls identify strongly with them. They are closer to their poised, intelligent, socially active mothers than to their fathers, who are immersed in their jobs. For these girls, college is a step in the "grooming process"; they have no intellectual or vocational goals and are less likely than other girls to finish college. They are authoritarian, not introspective, and generally shallow as persons. They represent an outmoded kind of college girl and most schools are no longer tolerant of them.

The *overachievers,* who have only average ability but who work hard and do well academically, have well-educated mothers with high social aspirations and self-made fathers whom they greatly admire. Their high academic performance is due to conformity to their parents' expectations of them rather than to intellectual interests of their own. As adults, they become conventional suburbanites and are characterized by being authoritarian, traditional, and rigid.

By contrast, the *underachievers* come from happy, secure families in which they have positive relationships with their parents and identify more closely with their mothers. They are oriented primarily toward the role of wife and mother, and they are likely to marry soon after college and have several children. They are thoughtful, liberal, and not authoritarian. Despite their rather poor academic performance these girls show evidence of considerable intellectual growth while in college. Brown (p. 53) describes this pattern as ". . . a healthy integration of feminine role and intellectual aspirations at a minimum of cost." In short, they have used college to help themselves "grow up" and may be considered to be the best adjusted of the group in the sense that they have adapted realistically to their role as women.

The *high achievers,* those who have high ability and use it, are career oriented. They have little concern with the peer group but instead identify strongly with a professional role. They have a public school background and show early, intense intellectual interests. Their parents are not likely to be college educated, but their mothers are talented and domineering, which causes resentment between mother and daughter. These girls are unlikely to marry and eventually do have careers. Many develop role conflict problems after leaving college and may then seek psychiatric or psychological help.

The final group are called *seekers after identity.* These girls come from varied backgrounds and are in many ways different from one another, but they have in common a lack of emotional stability and a strong concern with their personal problems. Without counseling or therapy they get little out of their college experience, but they have the potential to do better with help.

Echoes of these patterns may be heard in a more recent conceptualization by Heist (1962), who suggests that college girls may be classified into one of four types: (a) *the directionless girl,* who has no real purpose for being in college and whose interests and behavior are primarily socially oriented; (b) *the future-oriented girl,* who is concerned with the utility of her college experiences and who looks for learning experiences which will have direct bearing on her job after college as well as on her ultimate role of wife and mother; (c) *the nonconformist,* who is trying to avoid falling into the typical female rut but who may not be very clear as to what she wants instead; and (d) *the scholar,* who is interested in learning for learning's sake.

Heist freely admits that these are only approximate categories and that many girls don't fit any of them. Unfortunately, he has not examined them systematically, so that we can only speculate as to what proportion of female college students would be described by each. It is likely, for example, that the second group—the future-oriented students—are the most prevalent, but this would certainly vary from one college to another.

Heist believes that girls in different categories are likely to have different kinds and degrees of educational motives. For example, he suggests that the future-oriented girls and the scholars are most likely to finish college, since they have more definite motives for study. The directionless girls, with no purpose, will eventually drift out, while the nonconformists may react against college as an attempt to force them into a mold which they want to avoid. The latter group can probably be salvaged if they can be persuaded to view college as an avenue through which they can achieve their potentials. Once graduated, the scholars and the nonconformists are most likely to continue on to professional or graduate school.

✻ ✻ ✻ AFTER COLLEGE. For most girls, college is part of the discontinuity of their lives. They may enjoy college, they may learn something from it, but they do not make direct connections between their college experience and their lives beyond college; the intellectual demands made on them bear little relationship to what they see themselves doing after graduation.

Educators are becoming increasingly concerned with the low level of intellectual ambition of the typical college girl. Parrish (1961, p. 60) has put it this way:

Our free and ever more affluent society is saying to talented women, "Don't take the high road to a career. It's long. It's tough. It's lonely. Take the low road. It's easy. It's short. It's more fun." Should we be surprised if so many take the low road? Talented American women do not use their brains because our culture tells them not to.

Most college girls, when asked about their plans for the future, emphasize their hope to marry and rear a family, in the good old American tradition. The fact that girls are going to college in greater numbers hasn't had much effect on this kind of thinking. According to Impellizzeri (1961, p. 12):

Early marriage has assumed a more and more important place in the plans of young women, and it has tended to depress the drive towards academic excellence at the higher education levels. Not only are more girls getting married instead of going to college, or leaving college in order to raise families, but so high a proportion of them get married as soon as they graduate from college that they are not interested in the possibility or utility of advanced or professional training.

Most educators seem, therefore, to take the attitude that "girls will be girls" and do little to help them resist the pressures of society to force them into the traditional mold.

For some girls, nevertheless, college does instill some doubts as to the validity of these plans by providing a vision of another way of life, but a vision so far removed from practicality as to make it very difficult for the girl to act upon it. Left to herself, she may be unable to find a way to integrate her intellectual interests with society's and her own expectations about the proper role for a woman, and with little help from those around her, she finds it easy to be carried along on the prevailing tide of tradition, unable to command her own destiny. Arlen (1962, p. 65), in describing the students at one woman's college, has said:

The Radcliffe girl, when confronted with the classic dilemma of (1) being "deeply interested" in Aztec anthropology, and (2) of assuming that in the natural course of things she will marry and have children, tends to stare sternly into the middle distance and take the view that everything will somehow work out.

The many conflicting pressures and expectations which interfere with a girl's desire to find herself as a person make it harder for her than for a boy to develop a clear sense of direction. Many girls simply take the path of least resistance, perhaps out of a desperate need to get the whole thing over with, which may be one explanation for the earlier age at which girls are now marrying.

Some educators, however, do not see the picture as entirely black. Raushenbush (1961), for example, suggests that counselors and educators should accept the fact that most college girls are going to marry shortly after graduation, if not before, and that during the early years of their marriage they will live "an adjunct kind of life." Somehow these girls must be helped to prepare themselves to make the most of those years, while at the same time anticipating that eventually their intellectual and creative urges will be reawakened. Before they enter their hibernation period, they should be encouraged to prepare a plan of action to meet the spring thaw.

✿ ✿ EDUCATION AND MARRIAGE. There is a strong feeling among many intelligent girls that too much education can handicap their chances of getting married. As Heist (1963) points out, the typical college girl is dissuaded from working for maximum education by the more immediate rewards of marriage, coupled with the fear that if she doesn't marry while she's young—i.e., in her early twenties— she'll never make it.

This concern cannot be lightly dismissed since some degree of relationship does exist between amount of education and likelihood of being married. The proportion of women college graduates who eventually marry is close to 90 per cent, only slightly below that of the population in general. The proportion of single women does, however, increase with amount of education, although the difference has been decreasing since World War II so that a college education need no longer be considered a handicap to marriage.

This suggests that surveys of marriage rates among female college graduates are likely to produce spuriously low results, since they include many women who graduated from college at a time when marriage for women with college degrees was much less common. It is likely that the age of marriage is somewhat higher for college graduates than for girls who don't go to college, especially among those who have educational goals beyond the bachelor's degree.

Another way of looking at the problem of marriage vs. education is to inquire why women with more education are less likely to marry even though the difference isn't great. The existence of such a relationship does not necessarily imply direct cause and effect. Glick and Carter (1958) suggest several reasons that seem to have some validity: the unmarried woman must hold a job, and if she is a college graduate, this will most likely be in a profession; in order to advance in her profession, or perhaps even to stay where she is, further education may be required; also the unmarried woman has much greater opportunity for advanced education since she is not circumscribed by the responsibilities of the young wife and mother. It would seem, then, that the increased amount of education characteristic of unmarried women may be a *result* rather than a *cause* of their unmarried status.

It should also be evident that women who have strong career goals may prefer not to marry, inasmuch as marriage and family responsibilities may not be compatible with advancement in a career. On the other hand, it is rather surprising to find, as Ginzberg (1966) has noted, that in this modern age in which women are freer to decide to remain single and in which the life of the single woman is fuller than in the past, a higher proportion of college-educated women are marrying than ever before. Apparently more women are trying to combine both career and family, rather than making a choice between one or the other.

Although women with college degrees may be slightly less likely to marry than those who have not graduated from college, divorces are less frequent among those who do marry. This may explain why the proportion of college women who are currently married and living with their husbands is little different from that within the general population.

The belief that women with a college education will have fewer children has led to the fear that the intelligence level of the population would decline as women became better educated. There is some basis for this concern in that the fertility rate among college-educated women has been lower than average as well as being below that of college-educated men. However, as in the case of the marriage rate, the difference is decreasing as college graduates are marrying earlier and are having more children than those who graduated many years ago.

❧ ❧ EMPLOYMENT. We can be reasonably certain that most women with college degrees will marry and will have children, but this they could have done without their college education. What about the direct use of their education in an occupation?

Not surprisingly, a college education increases the chances that a woman will work outside the home. During the first year following graduation, more than two-thirds of all women college graduates hold jobs, and most of the remainder are continuing their education. In many cases, the girl is only using the job to fill a hiatus between college and marriage or children. But at any one time, one-half of all women who have graduated from college will be employed outside the home, as compared with the national average of one-third. The proportion of college graduates who are employed is higher among all categories of women except for those with children under the age of six, and the difference increases considerably as the women grow older.

The chances are good that as the demand for manpower and womanpower, especially for persons with a college education, continues to grow, the trend toward greater employment of college-educated women will increase, also. Zapoleon (1961, p. 70) predicts:

Altogether, it is probable that there will be relatively more college graduates employed at a given time, especially among older age groups, but relatively fewer of them will remain continuously in the labor force.

Despite the relatively high rate of employment among women with college degrees, as compared with the general population, there remains the question of how efficiently these women are using their educations in their jobs. One would agree with Komarovsky's (1953, p. 287) statement that women college graduates who are employed "might as well be employed in occupations which give full play to their abilities and insure a comfortable standard of living."

Approximately 3 out of every 4 employed women college graduates are working in professional occupations, which is considerably greater than the proportion of less than 15 per cent among all employed women, but less than the proportion of male college graduates who enter the professions.

By far the most popular, teaching accounts for about three-fifths of all employed women college graduates. No other occupation has more than 10 per cent of employed women; those which include significant numbers are nursing, secretarial work, biological technology, and social and welfare work.

Whether a woman is employed in a job which is directly related to her college major depends a great deal on what she majored in, although women who continue their education beyond the bachelor's degree are more likely than men to stay in the field in which they got their first degree. Women who received their college training in education or nursing are almost certain to be in that field, if they work at all. The employment rate among music majors is highest of all because of the ease with which music teaching can be combined with home responsibilities. In other areas, the relationship is less striking, so that altogether only about two-thirds of all female college graduates obtain their first jobs in their major fields. For example, of women who have graduated with degrees in the biological sciences, only about half are employed as biological technicians and one-fourth as teachers on their first job; 40 per cent of the women graduates in business and commerce obtain their first jobs as secretaries and stenographers; and 60 per cent of female English majors find jobs as teachers.

Many college women are not making efficient use of their college educations, being employed in jobs only remotely related to their major fields and in many cases not requiring a college education for their performance. A major reason is that many girls graduate from college with no specific marketable skill. They may be said to be "college-bred and college-broadened, but not actually college-trained" (Kiell and Friedman, 1957, p. 91). They are thus forced to take routine jobs which present little challenge and which provide them with little opportunity to make use of their expensive education. Small wonder that the typical female college graduate seizes on the first opportunity to escape from her job into the secure haven of a home.

✄ ✄ ADVANCED DEGREES. The percentage of women college graduates who enter graduate school is about the same as that among men, and likewise they obtain master's degrees in about the same proportion. At the doctoral level, however, women are very much under-represented. The gap is less at the upper levels of ability, and women who receive doctorates are, on the average, brighter than their male counterparts in the same fields. Among the women themselves, those who are married and receive doctorates are brighter than the single women who obtain them, suggesting that marriage provides an additional hurdle for the intelligent woman who desires an advanced degree.

Although men and women enter graduate school in about the same proportion in which they graduate from college, they tend to do so for different reasons. The typical male views graduate education within the total perspective of his life plans, particularly if he has had his eye on a career in a certain field in which graduate or professional education is a prerequisite.

By contrast, a girl's early plans are generally tentative, contingent on when and whom she marries. Thus it is not surprising to find that her decision to enter graduate school has been made later and is more likely to have been influenced by her undergraduate experiences than is true for men.

This calls into question the reasons why girls choose to go to graduate school at all. One clue is that girls who are married or who plan to marry soon after graduation are less likely to plan on graduate school than are those who are still unattached, suggesting that many girls are marking time in graduate school until they find a husband. For them graduate school is simply an extension of their undergraduate experience, allowing them to remain in a relatively secure environment and to postpone the decision as to what they will do with their lives. In addition, the bright girl is perhaps more likely to meet eligible men in graduate school than in the professional world, especially if her bachelor's degree is in a field such as teaching, in which eligible men are relatively scarce. The female graduate student can thus hope that she will become attached to a man before she obtains her master's degree and has to make another decision. This may explain why the master's degree is more popular among women than the doctorate, the latter implying a professional commitment to a field as well as several years of concentrated effort.

This accounts for a significant number of female graduate students, but certainly not all. Many girls are academically motivated to go to graduate school, but even some of these may be suspect. Bernard (1964, pp. 59–60) suggests that bright female undergraduates often become attached to young male instructors, especially in small colleges, and are maneuvered into graduate school by them:

> The picture that comes through from the various studies is that of a bright young woman who has persisted in her studies far beyond other women, happy and at home in the college or university library or laboratories, who finds herself encouraged to continue into graduate work by a professor impressed by her ability, even, perhaps, offered a graduate scholarship or fellowship or assistantship, and who—without relinquishing hopes for marriage—accepts it, not because she purposively and planfully aspires to an academic career but because, at the moment, nothing more attractive offers itself.

This is not to overlook the girls who enter graduate school with a definite academic purpose in mind and who make good use of it, but it is meant as a warning that girls should critically examine their motives for undertaking graduate education. A graduate program demands a great deal of both the student and the department, and it is only fair that both should be willing and able to make a true commitment to it.

This raises the question as to the use which women make of advanced education. Studies indicate that, although they are less likely to use it directly than are men, their chances of being productively employed are considerably greater with an advanced degree than simply with a bachelor's. This does not, however, mean that graduate education acts as a spur to employment among women. It is more likely that women who are motivated to work are also motivated to get additional education, if only to enhance their job potential.

Women with Ph.D.'s are, of course, most likely to be employed, but they are not generally as productive in scholarly activities as are men with the same education. One handicap for women is domestic responsibilities, as we noted earlier, although men have family responsibilities and often manage to be productive too. Newcomer (1959) has suggested that a more important factor is that women are given less recognition for professional achievements than are men. In addition, women are likely to be assigned heavier teaching loads in most universities, thus freeing men to engage in more productive activities.

THE WASTE OF WOMEN'S EDUCATION. It is something of a paradox that, at a time when women are moving into the labor force in increasing numbers, they are also coming under growing attack for failing to make productive use of their education. Numerous writers have accused educated women of wasting their education by withdrawing into the home after graduation and never again entering the world of work, thus depriving society of the benefits of their knowledge and experience. This is of particular concern in areas such as teaching, for which the majority of those trained are girls who seem to feel little responsibility, in the face of severe teacher shortages, to use their education for the direct benefit of society.

A college education is expensive and few students entirely pay their own way, especially in state universities which are partially subsidized by public funds. It is therefore not surprising that many persons, both within and outside of education, are questioning whether a financial investment in a woman's education is worthwhile. This argument has been presented strongly by Myrdal and Klein (1956, p. 153):

> The more people capable of benefitting from a university education are able to do so, the better for society. However, as long as the number of places is limited, and as long as the cost of this education is borne largely by the public, those who administer the funds will regard it as their duty to insure that the money invested in education gives the maximum return. They cannot be blamed if they expect a social contribution from those who have had the advantage of a university education. Women who have been admitted to universities on equal terms cannot escape comparison with men in this respect and must not be surprised if the production of cultured and enlightened mothers—desirable as this may be—can only be regarded as a by-product, not as the main aim of university education.

Thus far this view has not seriously handicapped girls at the undergraduate level, where their chances of being admitted to most colleges and to most programs are as good as a boy's. At the graduate level, however, they are viewed with suspicion. Many graduate and professional programs for which members of both sexes commonly apply tend to discriminate against women, and many authorities believe they have good reason. Women are poorer bets than men to finish such a program, and those who do are less likely to use their education productively. A university feels some obligation not only to educate individuals but also to be of benefit to society; thus if an admissions committee must choose between a capable man and a capable woman for a place in its program, the choice can logically be made in favor of the man. The woman who is thereby rejected may, of course, be the exception who would have finished and would have made a worthwhile contribution, but her more casual sisters have prejudiced the committee against her.[3] Even female educators such as Newcomer (1959) and Bernard (1964) agree that this is a reasonable decision, under the circumstances.

One might question whether most girls who apply for college do so under false pretenses, in that they have no real intention of using their education productively once they have obtained the degree. Actually, most girls enter college with the intention of using the education later, but something goes wrong somewhere. Girls need not only encouragement to use their education constructively and directly, but also help in overcoming the barriers which arise to thwart their plans after graduation.

The female college graduate may have good intentions about making worthwhile use of her education, but she meets with many discouragements. Perhaps the greatest handicap for the married woman is a lack of job opportunities related to her college training in the area where she lives. As a result, those who do work are often employed in jobs considerably *below* the level of the jobs they held when they were first married. Part of the problem is undoubtedly that they have been away from their jobs for awhile, having and rearing children, so that when they try to return to their professions they are out of touch and must start in at a lower level, if indeed there is anything at all available. Small wonder that many women, under such circumstances, choose not to try.

As Carolyn Heilbrun (1962, p. 34) describes it, the young female college graduate encounters a situation something like this:

Graduating from college at an age entirely suitable to the life pattern of a man seeking his place in the world, [she] finds herself

---

[3] In this connection, the following quotation from Bernard (1964, p. 283) is appropriate: "Milton Eisenhower, president of Johns Hopkins University, has been quoted to the effect that it costs his university some $200,000 to train each professional woman biologist, a figure arrived at, no doubt, by charging her for the cost of training all the women who leave the profession."

launched, not into the world, but into domesticity. She progresses through diapers to the companionship of a three-year-old and the mothers of other three-year-olds, without privacy, without time to recollect herself, without time *to be* (author's italics). Ahead lie un-planned years for which she weaves nebulous schemes. She thinks that when her children are old enough she, like MacArthur, will "return." Too late she will discover that she is out of touch, out of training, and out of demand, and to be out of demand is to be ex-cluded from that public realm where excellence is honored.

An attack on this problem must be launched on many fronts. The girl entering college must be helped to plan her college curric-ulum so that it can be integrated into her life after graduation, even though the nature of that life is uncertain. The woman who has left college needs help in sustaining herself through the years of full-time child rearing, if she chooses not to try to combine this with a career, and to re-enter the labor market in her chosen field when her home responsibilities have diminished. We have for too long taken for granted the notion that girls simply graduate from college and live happily ever after. Many of them don't, and both they and society could benefit from a recognition of this problem and a willingness to meet it constructively.

⁂ COLLEGE PROGRAMS FOR THE MATURE WOMAN. We have seen that the college experience which women receive in their early twenties does not prepare them for their lives 10 or 15 years later. The result is that a large number of women return to college after the age of 30, either to obtain education and train-ing that they missed earlier or to revive and update early training which is now obsolete.

These women are important resources for society, since it is much more likely that they, at this time, will make direct use of their education than will the college girl in her early twenties. The older women are motivated to get a degree they can use. Their reasons for going to college are not as confused and conflicting as are those of the late adolescent girl. As a result, older women gen-erally outperform the younger ones.

In the face of this, it seems inconsistent that colleges would put roadblocks in the way of the older woman who wants to re-turn to school, but this is in fact what most of them do. Among the handicaps which the older woman faces is the loss of under-graduate credits which were obtained too long ago, the scheduling of classes at times which conflict with her family responsibilities, and age limits on many graduate and professional programs. Per-haps these problems cannot be entirely eliminated, but few schools have yet made a serious effort to minimize them and to give the re-turning housewife a break.

If colleges and universities are to educate effectively all those who can benefit, they must become aware of the educational needs of mature women. There is evidence that such an awareness is developing, although all too slowly, and examples will be described in the following chapter.

Mary Bunting (1961a, p. 109), a leading woman educator, has said, "We have never really expected women to use their talents and education to make significant intellectual or social advances." As long as this philosophy prevailed, the quality and appropriateness of education for women was of little concern to society. But now, with the growing recognition that women can make important contributions to society as well as to their families, the colleges and universities must take the lead in providing mature women with opportunities to further their education.

Toward Enlightened Planning

> Women think of themselves as individuals "just like anyone else," and it often comes as a surprise to them to find that their sex is very much in the minds of those who are observing or interacting with them. They might, under certain circumstances, forget they are women, but men do not.
>
> ❧ *Jessie Bernard, 1964*

T WO FORCES have been primarily responsible for hampering girls in their educational and vocational planning: pressures to assume the stereotyped role of the homemaker, and a failure on the part of persons guiding girls to recognize some fundamental differences between the developmental patterns of males and females in our society. As a result, much of what passes for vocational and educational guidance of girls has been at best of little long-term value, and has more often shunted them into a narrow existence.

Girls are entitled to the same opportunity as boys to plan their educational and vocational futures as individuals and, as adults, to carry out these plans in an intelligent, coherent manner. Given the traditional attitudes of society and of women themselves, however, this opportunity is denied many of them. There are signs that the traditions are breaking down, but unless the outcomes of this change are anticipated and controlled, the future may be no improvement on the past.

The changes taking place in the role of women in our society must be viewed within the context of the times. Evolution, not revolution, is the key to the future. Women as a group have made great strides during the past century; they must now concentrate on their development as individuals. The fact of being female cannot be ignored. Its psychological and sociological implications are enormous and will not disappear in the foreseeable future, if ever. But these implications can be modified and adapted to fit the needs and characteristics of the individual woman, just as they are for men. It is toward this goal that society must strive.

❊ ❊ ❊ THE MAJOR DECISIONS THAT GIRLS MUST MAKE

❊ ❊ VOCATIONAL CHOICE. Vocational choice for most girls does not represent the same kind of commitment as it does for boys, and such a choice is likely to be influenced by factors which have little to do with ability or potential satisfactions in a specific field. Nevertheless this decision is not to be taken lightly, and even though it has been suggested that it would be preferable to postpone a woman's vocational decision until after her children have been born and partially reared, this is seldom practical. Therefore, in view of the uncertainties which lie ahead for the typical girl, it is doubly important that any decision concerning her future be reached only after careful consideration of all relevant aspects.

What, then, should be considered in helping a girl to make a vocational decision? It must first be recognized that this choice, and its implementation, will be influenced by the role which the girl plans to play in her future family. Any vocational decision which a girl makes must be within the context of her future, a future which must of necessity remain somewhat vague. A boy can make his plans firmly, with the expectation that, given the required ability in his chosen field, he can mold his future to fit his plans. A girl, in most cases, cannot do this. She must expect to compromise, and she must plan accordingly. Otherwise her plans will very likely have to be discarded altogether as she meets with some future event which she failed to anticipate, and she is little better off than when she started.

This is not, however, the whole story. Regardless of the degree of commitment which a girl makes to her vocational plans, it is probable that their long-term fruition will come about only after a prolonged hiatus during her child-bearing years. Therefore it is especially important that a girl's vocational choice be closely related to her interests and personality characteristics, since she will need to maintain her vocational skills during a period of disuse. This is the major reason why a large number of women never go back to work in the field for which they were originally trained: their interest wasn't strong enough to sustain them during the fallow period, so that their skills have deteriorated and they lack the motivation to revive them. And, like men, women who are employed in jobs related to their interests are more satisfied with their jobs than those whose interests and jobs are not compatible.

✄ ✄ THE MARRIAGE-CAREER DILEMMA. Somewhere along the line a girl must make a tentative decision as to whether family responsibilities or a career will dominate her adult life. It is true, of course, that these can be combined, as many women have successfully demonstrated, but choices must be made and the girl will find that this question will begin to arise rather early. Most girls become concerned even while in high school with making some commitment in one direction or the other. On what basis can they be helped to make this decision?

There is evidence, first of all, that career interests among girls take shape by about the age of 14. It may thus be possible to give a high school girl some indication as to the strength of her career motivation by evaluating her responses to interest inventories. If her interests are similar to those of women in professions in which women are in the minority, she is probably oriented toward a career. If, on the other hand, her interests are similar to those of teachers, secretaries, and women in professions related to home economics, she will probably want to devote most of her life to her family.

Career-oriented girls also exhibit a personality pattern characterized by a concern with achievement, a strong self-concept, a willingness to take responsibility for themselves and others, and a willingness to work hard to reach a goal. In addition, they tend to be intelligent, to come from homes in which the mother is employed, and to have had a strong emphasis placed on academic achievement by their parents.

The drawback in most research on this problem is that it is based on the *plans* of young women rather than on outcomes. Long-term studies are badly needed to compare the developmental patterns of career women with those of full-time housewives, as well as with women who are combining both roles, to provide truly useful information for girls who are trying to make decisions about their futures.

✄ ✄ ✄ TOOLS AND TECHNIQUES TO AID PLANNING. Enlightened planning requires knowledge of oneself as well as knowledge of the world which one will be entering. Although there are many sources of such information, professional counselors are often best equipped to help a person gain the information and develop a self-concept necessary to make a mature, satisfying plan for his life. To achieve this, counselors often utilize psychological tests and sources of information about jobs and educational opportunities, helping the client integrate this information through counseling into something personally relevant and meaningful.

The effectiveness of this process depends a great deal on the quality of the available tests and information. Unfortunately, the quality of tests and information used with girls is not nearly as good as that used with boys. This is due partly to the more confused nature of educational and vocational careers of girls, but it also reflects the attitude prevalent in our society that the guidance of girls is less important than that of boys.

⅍ ⅍ PSYCHOLOGICAL TESTING OF GIRLS: CURRENT PROBLEMS. Most psychological tests used in educational and vocational guidance have been validated primarily with boys and men, and the information which these tests provide girls is neither as broad nor as accurate as it is for boys. A number of problems exist in the use of psychological tests with girls, which must be confronted and solved if girls are to obtain meaningful information from tests in the same way as do boys.

⅍ *Lack of Tests for Girls.* As compared with the tremendous amount of time, effort, and money expended on the design of psychological tests for use with boys, the amount expended on girls has been miniscule. With a very few exceptions, the tests available to counselors for use with girls are adaptations of tests which have proven useful with boys, on the assumption that girls ask the same questions about future plans and have the same kinds of life patterns as boys. This assumption is known to be untrue in many cases, but test designers have not yet faced up to this fact. The prevailing attitude seems to be that girls are fortunate to have a few crumbs thrown their way in the form of separate normative data or, in a few instances, a separate form of an existing test. They do, however, have a right to something more.

⅍ *The Question of "Sex Norms."* Most standardized tests provide separate normative data for males and females, on the assumption that this provides more specific information than would a single set of norms and that predictions can thereby be more meaningful. There is a growing tendency, however, to question this assumption and to wonder whether the publication of separate sex norms may not instead serve to maintain an overly rigid conception of job possibilities for both men and women by making it difficult to obtain realistic comparisons with persons in fields dominated by the opposite sex. In view of the important implications of this question for the development of psychological tests for girls, the argument is worth examining in some detail.

The point of view that sex norms are necessary for greater accuracy has been defended most ably by Wesman (1949) on the grounds that, inasmuch as boys and girls tend to separate into different curricula and jobs anyway, combined sex norms would provide misleading information for members of both sexes. He cites as an example the tenth-grade norms for the Mechanical Reasoning section of the Differential Aptitudes Tests (DAT). On a combined scale, a boy with a raw score of 40 would be close to the 75th percentile, as compared with only a 50th percentile on the scale for boys alone. Since his competition in mechanical curricula will come primarily from boys, a comparison with boys alone would be more realistic. Wesman provides similar examples for girls on the Clerical, Spelling, and Sentences tests of the DAT, and concludes (p. 227):

It is clear from these data that to the extent that competition in any curriculum or vocation comes predominantly from a single sex, separate sex norms are needed for test score interpretation.

He also suggests that students who plan to enter a curriculum not typical for that sex—e.g., a girl who wishes to enter a mechanical field—should be compared with norms for the opposite sex.

Others have argued to the contrary, that sex norms are useless, if not misleading, and should be eliminated. This argument has been most cogently presented by Bauernfeind (1956) in a reply to Wesman's article. Bauernfeind questions the rationale on which separate norms are reported, pointing out that boys and girls do not live in two separate worlds so that it is not reasonable to consider their cultures to be a great deal different. He suggests that if separate norms must be presented, it would be helpful to use more meaningful distinctions, such as socioeconomic status, instead of sex.

Bauernfeind also disputes Wesman's argument that sex norms are necessary for fields in which one sex predominates. He points out that no norms are completely realistic since the actual subgroup with which the individual must compete will change from one time to another. The assumption that fields which are currently limited primarily to one sex or the other will continue indefinitely to be limited in itself reduces the probability that they will broaden.

From the point of view of enlightened planning for girls, two aspects of this argument are especially pertinent. The first is that it would be highly desirable to compare each young person, male or female, with the exact group with which he will have to compete in the future. For example, a test of college ability may provide an estimate as to the level at which a girl may expect to perform in college, but allowances must be made depending on whether she is aiming at Vassar or at a two-year "finishing school." The same is true in many other areas. Presumably a professional counselor could also be expected to take into consideration the fact that a person who intends to enter a specific curriculum will probably be competing primarily with those who already show a reasonable amount of ability in that area. With this in mind, it seems unnecessary to make a special point of separating scores by sex, especially since such distinctions are not made for other relevant, and perhaps more important, variables.

This, however, only says that such separation is not very helpful and probably not worth the trouble. A second point is that it can, in fact, be dangerously misleading. This comes about when a student fails to take into account the meaning of a score based on separate sex norms. A typical example would be a girl who scores above the 75th percentile on a test of mechanical reasoning or on the mechanical scale of an interest inventory. Many will immediately jump to the conclusion that she would be successful in a mechanical field. Obviously this is an unwarranted assumption, since the girl's competition will not come from other girls, but instead from boys, most of whom have more mechanical knowledge than she. Wesman anticipated this problem by suggesting that the girl, in such a circumstance, be compared with boys' norms. But this is easily overlooked, and there are many cases in which important decisions about the future have been made on the basis of such misleading evidence. It is questionable therefore whether such information is worth the risk. In the long run the student, with the aid of a competent counselor, can probably get more meaningful information from combined normative data and is less likely to be misled by them. Or, if more specific comparisons are desired, the relevant criterion group can be isolated for study. In any case, the inescapable conclusion is that the routine presentation of sex norms should be banished as archaic and perhaps actually discriminatory.

✿ ✿ THE SEARCH FOR WOMEN'S VOCATIONAL INTERESTS. It is generally agreed that interests should play an important role in vocational choice, and interest inventories are therefore a staple of vocational counseling. This procedure has proved quite useful in helping boys make vocational decisions, but it has not been nearly as successful with girls.

One problem is that relationships between job choice and personal interests are not as evident for women as for men, which is not surprising in view of the lack of career commitment prevalent among girls. Girls, in other words, make vocational decisions for reasons which may be at best only tangentially related to their personal interests. Their reasons for a particular choice are typically based instead on short-term considerations.

A related difficulty is the lack of specific interest inventories designed for use with girls. In view of the problems described above, psychologists have been slow to develop special inventories for girls. A few attempts have been made in this direction, but they have not been commercially successful. Those inventories which are available for use with girls have been adapted from interest inventories widely used with boys. The two inventories which are by far the most frequently used are the Kuder Preference Record and the women's form of the Strong Vocational Interest Blank. Their value with girls is limited, but in the absence of anything better they are worth examining more closely.

The most obvious drawback to the use of the Kuder with girls is the scarcity of evidence concerning the validity of the various forms for females. In addition, however, the interpretation of scores in relation to job or curriculum outcome is hazardous.

The problem discussed earlier concerning the misleading separation of male and female norms becomes especially significant with this inventory. For example, it is difficult to know how to interpret a high score on the Mechanical scale for a girl, and likewise a low score on the Artistic or Musical scales may not necessarily indicate a lack of interest in these areas. In general, therefore, the Kuder must be held to be of doubtful value for use with girls at any level.

Kuder has also published the Occupational Interest Survey (Form DD), in which the individual's responses are compared with those of persons in a variety of occupations, with occupational scales reported separately for men and women. Of the 35 female scales, almost half (17) appear to be duplicated in title on the men's form, although the norm groups were restricted to one sex or the other. In addition, scores are reported for women on 20 of the 79 men's scales, apparently arbitrarily chosen as fields in which women might conceivably be employed. Although this procedure appears to be based on the recognition that sex distinctions in occupations are cloudy, it seems at best unwieldy and potentially misleading. Kuder does not satisfactorily explain why he chose to separate men and women for normative purposes in the first place. His decision to do so only serves to complicate the vocational planning of girls and to perpetuate the myth that men and women live in two different worlds.

In contrast to the Kuder inventories, the Strong Vocational Interest Blank for Women (SVIB) has been the subject of a considerable amount of research. It was devised in the same manner as the men's form, with norm groups composed of women employed in various occupations. The major difficulty with the use of the women's form has been the lack of differentiation among women's interests. For this reason the scales on the women's form are not generally presented in groups, as they are for the men, although Strong made some attempt at such an organization.[1] In general, women tend to score high in the group composed of physical education teacher and nurse and in the group made up of housewife, office worker, and stenographer-secretary. These are generally considered to be noncareer occupations and would seem to be characteristic of women whose main goal in life is marriage and a family. This in turn makes it difficult to differentiate such women into various occupational groups, since their occupational interests are, in general, low.

Whether the women's form of the SVIB does in fact differentiate among occupational groups in the same manner as does the men's is open to question. Apparently it differentiates reasonably well among groups of college women in different curricula, but it doesn't predict very well in which fields they will eventually be employed. A woman's work history is influenced by many factors, of which job-related interest is only one.

Although Strong (1955) insisted that separate forms and profiles were necessary for men and women on the grounds that their M-F scores differ considerably, several studies have indicated that a single form might do just as well for high-ability, career-oriented women, who are more apt to be interested in fields composed primarily of men.

This suggests that the girl who is undecided as to the strength of her career ambitions might learn from the women's form whether

[1] In a memorandum dated March, 1966, Dr. David Campbell, Director of the Center for Interest Measurement Research, University of Minnesota, describes the plans of his organization for revision of the women's form of the Strong and suggests that the women's scales be organized according to the following groups:
  I. Music: music teacher, music performer
  II. Verbal-Linguistic: artist, author, librarian, English teacher
  III. Social Service: social science teacher, YWCA secretary, social worker, psychologist, lawyer
  IV. Sales: life insurance saleswoman
  V. Business-Clerical: buyer, business education teacher, stenographer-secretary, office worker
  VI. Domestic: elementary teacher, housewife, home economics teacher, dietitian
  VII. Health-related Services: physical education teacher, occupational therapist, physical therapist, nurse
  VIII. Medical Sciences: physician, dentist, lab technician
  IX. Physical Sciences: math-science teacher, engineer

she is similar to noncareer-oriented women, as indicated by high scores on the housewife and related scales, or whether she has interests in common with those of women in career fields. If she is definitely not career oriented, the women's form may give her some help in choosing a stopgap occupation, although its value in this respect is limited since the interests of women in such occupations are relatively undifferentiated.

The girl who is definitely interested in a career occupation, on the other hand, will probably obtain more relevant information from the men's form, especially if she is considering fields in which men predominate. A comparison of her interests with those of men in those fields would probably be more relevant for her than would a comparison with the few women in them.

When in doubt, a girl should take both forms. She can thereby get a more complete picture of her interests in relation to those of both men and women in a variety of occupations, as well as obtaining an assessment of the strength of her career motivation.

OCCUPATIONAL INFORMATION. Another tool often used in vocational planning is occupational information to help the client gain insight into the world of work. Here again girls are handicapped, since most occupational information is designed for use with boys. The information available for girls is generally limited to the traditional female occupations, and little is provided for girls who are interested in other fields. Even less is available for use with older women who want to return to the labor force.

There are some encouraging signs that this deficiency is finally being recognized, although the steps taken thus far have been only tentative. The largest source of information concerning occupational opportunities for women are the booklets issued by the Women's Bureau of the U.S. Department of Labor. Some, unfortunately, are not up to date, although the Bureau frequently revises them, and they tend to be limited to fields which employ primarily women. Other sources of special interest to women are described in the Appendix.

A beginning has been made in the development of occupational information for mature women, but much more is needed. A promising approach is the compilation of information related to a specific geographical area, since older women are usually limited in job choice by their place of residence. These women also need information on how to prepare for and locate a job, a need which is often overlooked in the information provided them.

GUIDANCE COUNSELING. Professional counselors are most readily available to young people in high school and college. It is at this stage of development that crucial decisions about the future must be made, and efforts of counselors have been directed primarily toward helping young people make appropriate decisions and develop as individuals. The counseling needs of persons beyond school age have been largely ignored.

Even during high school and college, however, the counseling which girls receive is often of dubious value. Girls who are in the process of choosing a college or a first job do not necessarily need *more* counseling than they now receive, but they need counseling more appropriate to their interests and problems.

Not all girls would, of course, make good use of enlightened counseling, but neither do all boys. There is some evidence, though, that girls who seek counseling are different from boys who do: the girls tend to be more introverted and career oriented, whereas the boys are more extraverted and want definite answers to specific questions. This supports the argument that the counseling needs of boys and girls are not identical.

The need for enlightened guidance is not limited to girls who are becoming adults, for many women do not develop realistic educational and vocational plans until they have married and have borne children. Then they are free to look beyond their role of wife and mother to a more varied existence and to plan realistically for the remainder of their lives. Many could profit from counseling services at this point, but at the present time few services for adults are available.

In some respects, the need for counseling is greater among adult women than among men, whose lives have more continuity. There appears to be a growing realization that counseling facilities for adults are needed, but this awareness has not yet been translated into action in most parts of the country. If women are to make good use of their abilities, they need this kind of help, and counseling facilities for adults must be developed quickly to meet this need.

❧ ❧ ❧ WOMEN IN THE WORLD OF THE FUTURE. It is foolish to wonder whether the role of women *should* change. That it is changing is a fact, and no amount of hand wringing and head-shaking will reverse this trend. The relevant question, instead, is: "How can this change in role be constructively absorbed by society?"

The answer must come from many sources. Many elements of society must adapt willingly to the trend of the future, or be shunted aside into obsolescence as the role and needs of women evolve. Only a few of the social changes which must take place can be mentioned here, but they should provide some idea of the complexity of the task ahead.

❧ ❧ CHANGES IN THE WORLD OF WORK. The large influx of women into the labor force, already an increasing stream, can be expected

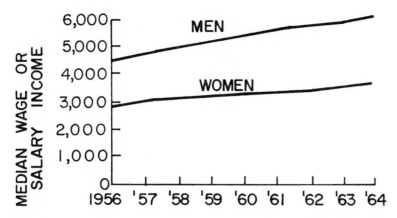

Fig. 13.1.   Wage or salary income of year-round, full-time workers, by sex, 1956–1964 (U.S. Dept. of Labor; Women's Bureau, 1966a).

to become a flood in the not-too-distant future. Up to now, most employers have made only stopgap provisions to meet the needs of their female employees, as though hoping that if ignored they will soon disappear. At the same time many of these same employers, perhaps without realizing it, have come to depend on women to fill many crucial positions, so that if by some chance women were suddenly to leave their jobs and return to their homes, the effect on the economy would be disastrous. It therefore behooves employers to admit that women workers are here to stay and that they deserve to be treated as well as men. This means the following improvements must be made:

✣ *Better Wages.* The wages of women employees are increasing, but the wages of men are rising faster, so that women are falling behind in relative income (see Figure 13.1). Many factors conspire to produce lower incomes among women, as discussed earlier, but when all else is accounted for it is still evident that women are often not paid as well as men for essentially the same job. This inequity must be corrected.

✣ *More Part-Time Jobs.* Many women with special training and skills would like to work, but not on a full-time basis. A sizeable pool of potential employees remains to be tapped by employers with the imagination to design jobs to enable women to work part time, perhaps by allowing two or more women to share a job, or perhaps by adjusting working hours to coincide with the time when more women are free to work. Many so-called "full-time" jobs do not actually require a full-time person, and the employer who insists on rigidly retaining this requirement may be discouraging many potentially valuable employees.

One example in which part-time job opportunities might help to alleviate a serious shortage of workers is in teaching. A large proportion of those trained as teachers are women, especially at the elementary level, and the turnover is great. The teaching profession, however, has been reluctant to encourage the development of part-time elementary teaching jobs, on the grounds that this is "unprofessional" and that children will suffer by having to change teachers in the middle of the day. At the high school level, where the students change teachers for each subject, there has been less resistance, and part-time job opportunities are becoming available. By contrast, a strong inertia still opposes such a trend in the elementary grades, although there is little if any research to support the contention that having two teachers is detrimental to a child's development. Logically, it would seem that a child in a class of 20 students taught by two part-time teachers will probably learn more than the same child in a class of 40 taught by one full-time teacher. Actually, no one knows how many women trained as teachers would be interested in teaching on a part-time basis, especially at the elementary level. On the basis of what is known about women's employment patterns it seems likely, however, that there is a sizeable untapped source of trained teachers in this category. This example is only one of many which could be cited, but it serves to point up the need for more information and more creative thinking on the part of employers who need the skills that women have to offer.

✣ *Child-Care Provisions.* Mothers of young children do work, and more would like to if they could be certain that their children were being well cared for during that time. Most employers have ignored this problem, perhaps feeling that to do otherwise would imply that they were encouraging mothers to abandon their children. As a result, those mothers who work anyway, whether by necessity or choice, find it difficult to make satisfactory arrangements for their children.

The only sensible solution is for employers to admit that many of their female employees have small children and to cooperate in helping find adequate care for them. This might be accomplished through a community agency, or the company might provide the service itself. A few companies already provide nursery services, staffed by trained child-care workers, to care for small children while their mothers work, and many others could certainly follow their example. Such a program should result not only in better care for the children of working mothers, but also in a reduction of guilt feelings of the mothers themselves.

❧ *Revised Working Conditions.* The world of work has traditionally been a man's world, with women admitted only if they were
willing to adapt to a male-oriented society. As the numbers of
women workers have increased, however, their willingness to adapt
has diminished and pressures for changes in working conditions
have risen. Employers must recognize that working conditions
which prove satisfactory for men may not be accepted by women
and may have to be modified accordingly. For that matter, male
employees frequently change their concept of acceptable working
conditions, as evidenced by the presence of working conditions as a
major issue in many strikes. Employers who make a real effort to
determine the working conditions desired by women will be ahead
in attracting the increasing numbers of women who will enter the
labor force in the future.

❧ ❧ CHANGES IN SCHOOLS AND COLLEGES. Educational institutions,
too, have been slow to adapt to the needs of the modern woman.
Traditional education of girls has not included the expectation that
they will use their education in a productive way. But more and
more they want to do so, and schools and colleges must redesign
their curricula and programs to provide girls and women with the
kind of education which makes optimum use of their interests and
abilities.

❧ *More Flexibility in High School Programs.* Girls should be encouraged to take courses in line with their abilities and interests
rather than being restricted to the traditional female program. Many
girls, for example, have the ability to do well in science courses but
are often discouraged from them because such an interest is not
ladylike. Even earlier, in the elementary grades, subtle distinctions
begin to be made between subjects which are "appropriate" for
boys and for girls. These distinctions are often based on tradition
rather than on true differences in ability and should be de-em-
phasized.

At the same time, teachers and administrators must recognize
that most girls will eventually marry and raise a family, although
they may combine this role with employment. This means that
any girl, no matter how bright, will probably need to learn something about homemaking. Opportunities should be provided for
more bright girls to participate in home economics courses, rather
than relegating to them those girls who are not in the college preparatory program. Preparation for college is important, but so is
preparation for life.

❧ *More Flexibility in College Curricula.* The comments just made
apply equally well to curriculum planning for girls in college. Most

girls should plan for some combination of two roles: homemaking and employment. Many college programs at present do neither very well, with the result that many girls make little or no use of their college education in their subsequent lives. The ideal curriculum for a girl would provide challenges commensurate with her intellectual abilities and interests, while at the same time providing her with skills to aid her in her future homemaking role.

Colleges should also accept the trend toward early marriages, which means that many girls marry before obtaining their degrees and, if their husbands graduate before they do, will probably leave school to move to a new community. In order that they can finish their degrees, transfer of credits should be made more flexible, and restrictions should be waived which require a substantial number of credits to be obtained at the school from which a person graduates. Such changes should result in more young married women finishing their degrees and making productive use of their education.

❧ *Development of Programs for the Mature Woman.* Most college programs are designed for young people. This makes sense for men, since only rarely does a man return to college during his middle years. But many women, with free time and a new sense of purpose, want to return to school when their children grow up and need less of their attention. Few colleges make it easy for them.

In recent years this problem has been recognized, and steps are being taken to do something about it. A number of universities have established programs specifically designed to meet the needs of women with families who want to continue or complete their education. Many of these programs have been developed with the aid of foundation funds, with the hope that they will prove valuable enough to their universities and their communities to be able to operate eventually on their own.

Two pioneering programs will serve as examples: the Minnesota Plan for the Continuing Education of Women, and the Radcliffe Institute for Independent Study. The Minnesota Plan was established in 1960 with a grant from the Carnegie Corporation and has a 3-pronged purpose: (a) to help undergraduate women plan for their multiple roles of the future; (b) to help young married women maintain their intellectual interests and continue their education during the period of high family responsibilities ("rust proofing"); and (c) to provide education and guidance for the mature woman who wants to return to the labor force ("rust removal"). Among the special services which the program provides to meet these objectives are the provision of scholarships for women who want to return to school, child-care facilities, special seminars and courses, and counseling services.

The success of the program is shown by the fact that during its first 3 years nearly 1,300 women were enrolled in some phase. Not all aspects, however, have been equally successful. The first phase—that of trying to encourage undergraduate women to view their future roles realistically and to plan accordingly—has had disappointing results. As might be expected, most of the girls (with some rewarding exceptions) have not been eager to take a cold, hard look at themselves 10 or 20 years in the future. They have resisted attempts to challenge their romantic outlook on life. By contrast, the other phases have been well received and the program is making great strides in its work with adult women. Other schools in large communities are setting up programs modeled on the Minnesota plan, with modifications appropriate for their particular institution and locality.

The Radcliffe Institute for Independent Study has a considerably different approach. It is designed to provide opportunities for women with high ability to engage in research or other creative activity without the pressures of home and family which have made it difficult for them to do the kind of work of which they are capable. A small number of women (about 20) are appointed annually as "associate scholars" at Radcliffe. They are provided financial aid to hire services at home to release them for creative work, and they are given a place to work and free run of the university. These scholars are stringently selected on the basis of past performance and some degree of assurance that they will make productive use of the time and money provided them. They must have a Ph.D. or "the equivalent in achievement," which in the case of literature and the arts may not include a college degree at all. Although aimed at a much more select group than the Minnesota plan, the Radcliffe program seems to be meeting a different kind of need very effectively.

Two additional programs may be mentioned as indications of the breadth of attack on the problem. Seven New York colleges have organized a series of workshops, called the Seven Colleges Vocational Workshops, for women between the ages of 30 and 60 who want to find "meaningful work" outside their homes but who do not necessarily want to embark on full-scale careers. These workshops, designed for 50 to 60 women at a time, meet for a half-day a week for 8 consecutive weeks. The program consists of speakers who provide information concerning jobs, small-group discussions, and field trips, all emphasizing occupational fields with particular opportunities for women. The results of the first series were encouraging: the women reported not only aid in finding a job or entering a training program but also in clarifying their thinking about themselves and improving their family relationships. Such programs could conceivably be organized by other schools which do not have the personnel or the facilities to establish a program as elaborate as that at Minnesota or Radcliffe.

Some attempts are also being made to increase the flexibility of training programs in specific fields to accommodate women who might otherwise be unable to complete them. A case in point is the psychiatric residency program at New York Medical College. Several modifications have been made in the traditional year-round program to make it easier for women with children to complete a psychiatric residency. Among these modifications are a change from the usual year-round program, which takes 3 years to complete, to a nine-months program covering 4 years. Steps have also been taken to reduce the demands of night and weekend work without diluting their experience or antagonizing other residents. The medical profession has not, in general, been among the leaders in the development of flexible training programs. It is therefore especially gratifying to see programs such as this. Similar innovations could undoubtedly be instituted in the training programs of other professions so as to make them more attractive to women.

These examples, and many others which could be cited, demonstrate that it is possible to design programs for the mature woman and that such programs will be popular. It is difficult to state specifically what the women get out of such programs. Some, of course, are seeking training or retraining for employment, and this need is rather easily met. Others, however, simply want to keep up with what's going on in the world and resist the pressures to stagnate. Women who complete these programs generally become more self-accepting, as well as more productive members of society. Such results are surely worth the effort expended by both the colleges and the women themselves.

❧ ❧ CHANGES IN THE ATTITUDES OF MEN. Men exercise a great deal of control over the lives of women—as fathers, as husbands, and as employers. Their attitudes toward women must become more enlightened if women are to make optimum use of their own resources.

❧ *Recognition of Women as Individuals.* Men tend to view women as living in a world apart. The typical male says he "doesn't understand women," with the implication that it is hardly worth the trouble. To many men, women are the secondary sex, and equality is a meaningless concept. Men must, however, learn to accept women as equals, to recognize that they differ in abilities and interests as much as men themselves do, and to help them make the most of these differences.

❧ *Acceptance into "Men's Fields."* Many occupations are closed to all but the most aggressive and highly motivated women because they have traditionally been limited to men. Men are moving into women's fields in increasing numbers, but the men themselves have resisted movement in the opposite direction. Such attitudes and behaviors are discriminatory, in that they restrict the freedom of a woman to seek the job for which her training and interests best qualify her. It was for this reason that discrimination on the basis of sex was made illegal in recent federal civil rights legislation, although it will take time for the law to be effectively enforced. It would be preferable if men would willingly admit women to the fields which have for so long been closed to them.

Husbands of Working Wives. Perhaps the single most important determiner of whether a wife works outside the home, and if so whether she is happy with her dual role, is the attitude of her husband. Many men object to their wives' working, for a number of reasons. Part of the problem is simply inconvenience to themselves: if a man's concept of the wife's role includes the responsibility for arranging the household to accommodate her husband, the full-time housewife can more easily fill this need. But part of the cause in many cases is a fear that a wife's employment signifies that her husband is inadequately supporting his family. At lower-class levels this may be true, but among the middle class it is probably not. Nevertheless, many a man feels that his masculinity would be threatened if his wife were to take a job.

In order to deal with this fear realistically, a man must come to realize that whether his wife works need not affect his own feelings of masculinity. He must recognize that his wife's needs are as important to her as his own are to him, and that they must have mutual respect for each other's needs. If household tasks are distasteful to the husband, he might expect that they may also be distasteful to his wife; he might therefore understand why she may prefer to work outside the home on a job which she enjoys while hiring someone to do her housework. Most husbands aren't forced to continue indefinitely in a job which is repugnant to them, but many thoughtlessly insist that their wives should. In order for such a change to take place, however, women must also be willing to hire outside help with their housework. For many women this is difficult, even if they are working themselves, because of the feeling that this is their responsibility and that they are somehow neglecting their homes if they don't do their own housework, even though they may hate it. The result, if they are also holding down an outside job, is that they press their husbands into service on a task which neither of them enjoys, with a predictable outcome which in turn is blamed on the fact that the wife is working rather than on the true cause.

The husband might also consider that having a working wife

may be of advantage to him. For one thing, a working wife is likely to run a better scheduled and more efficient house because she has to. One result is that household tasks are more likely to be done on time rather than being put off indefinitely. Secondly, the working wife is more willing to spend time at home in the evening with her husband. Many housewives feel cooped up during the day and can hardly wait for their husbands to come home so that they can get out of the house. The husband, however, tired from a long day on the job, is not apt to be enthusiastic about going out. The upshot is that the wife either goes somewhere alone while the husband stays home, or she stays home with him and feels frustrated and hurt.

A third advantage for the husband of a working wife is that she is likely to be a more interesting person to live with. Many housewives are not very interesting people, even to their own husbands. Whether this is important to the husband may be questionable in some cases. Perhaps he gets enough intellectual conversation at the office and merely wants to be left alone in peace and quiet at home. The housewife's situation, however, is much different. She gets relatively little contact with other people, especially of an intellectually stimulating nature, and is almost entirely dependent on her husband for this. The working wife, on the other hand, not only can satisfy some of these needs on her job but can become also a more interesting person both to herself and to her husband.

❧ ❧ CHANGES IN THE ATTITUDES OF WOMEN. Perhaps the barrier most restricting the development of women as individuals is the attitude of women themselves. The process by which a girl acquires a concept of herself as a female was traced in an earlier chapter, and it was noted that the attitudes and personality characteristics traditionally associated with the female role do not lend themselves easily to the development of individuality. They especially handicap a girl in competing in the world of work and encourage her to limit herself to a simpler and less demanding way of life.

❧ *Women Must Earn Equality.* As a result, only the atypical woman is willing to expend the effort required to establish a career for herself. Many girls begin with a vague career goal in mind, but this goal dissipates quickly and they settle for the role of housewife. This is evident in the number of girls who do not finish educational programs or business training programs. Small wonder that colleges and employers have been reluctant to invest time and effort in girls, especially at the advanced levels of education. They know that many girls who are admitted to a program will not finish it, and that many who do finish will use their training for so short a time as to hardly have been worth the trouble. The failure of women to recognize an obligation, both to themselves and to society, to make productive use of their education and training has produced a cynical attitude on the part of men responsible for that training. Only the women themselves can demonstrate that their attitudes have changed and that they are willing to accept the responsibility implied in the education provided them.

ॐ Greater Expectations of Themselves. Girls must also be taught to expect more of themselves than the limited role which tradition has set down for them. They must seek opportunities to develop themselves as persons, not to the neglect of their family responsibilities, but coordinated with them. Girls must recognize that the role of wife and mother is of great, but not sole, importance. They have an obligation to themselves to develop as persons as well. The future will likely bring increasing opportunities for combinations of various roles, and women must be prepared to take advantage of these opportunities.

ॐ More Careful and Realistic Planning. At whatever their stage of development, girls and women contemplating further education should consider carefully their immediate plans in relation to their goals for the future. It is obvious that many girls do not attempt to relate their present educational experiences to their future goals. If education is to be effective, it must meet the needs of women more adequately. As colleges and universities show a willingness to modify their programs with this in mind, women must prove that they will take advantage of these modifications by planning to make use of them. Persons helping women to make educational plans may have to nudge them in this direction.

ॐ ॐ CHANGES IN SOCIETY

ॐ Care for Young Children. Many mothers of young children who would like to work outside the home, at least on a part-time basis, are deterred from doing so by the concern that their children will not receive adequate care during their absence. Some work anyway, perhaps out of necessity, and with resulting negative effects on the child. Society has a responsibility to provide help for these women, perhaps through community-sponsored child-care facilities or perhaps through the development of services in which trained older women can take care of a child in the child's own home. In any case, it no longer seems reasonable to continue on a hit-or-miss basis, hoping that mothers will find adequate care for their children and knowing that in many cases they won't.

⁂ Providing Girls With Realistic Models. Most girls, when faced with the necessity of combining a career and a home, find little help available from persons around them. Much of one's ability to play a role successfully comes from observing and imitating the behavior of others already successful in this role. Society, however, has not provided many visible examples of women who successfully combine a career with the role of wife and mother. Certainly many women are doing this, but their performance has not been highlighted. Girls who are planning their future roles need to become acquainted with women who have developed combinations successfully, to see that such roles are possible and to learn how they are managed. These women should be visible in schools, in business, and in any other areas in which they can be seen by girls. Too often a girl knows only the role of her mother (probably a housewife) and of a few professional women who may be absorbed in their careers to the exclusion of everything else. To her the choice seems to be either one or the other. That a combination is possible and often desirable needs to be stressed in the most realistic way possible: by providing actual examples from which girls can learn.

⁂ More Enlightened Parents. Basic attitudes about sex roles are learned first in the family, and those learned there form the basis for the interpretation of subsequent experiences. The increased flexibility in women's roles which has been predicted must be learned through teaching and example in the family. As women become more flexible in their planning for themselves, and as they become more accepting of themselves in these various roles, they should be able to pass this enlightened attitude along to their children. Their husbands, too, should gain an appreciation for the variety of roles that women can play, and the value of each, from the examples set by their mothers. Succeeding generations should witness a growing breadth of women's roles, as women come to share the variety of choice open to men in our society.

⁂ ⁂ ⁂ THE RESEARCH FRONTIER. Despite the mountain of research studies on which this book is based, there are glaring gaps in our knowledge about women's roles and how they affect society. Enumerated here are some areas in which more research is needed before definite prescriptions can be offered.

   How important is sex-role identification? As long as society stresses a strong distinction between the male and female roles, sex-role learning is not difficult for most children. But as these distinctions become blurred, as they must when women move more fully into what has been the "man's world," children may have increasing difficulty in developing a sense of personal identification. The stress here should be on *may*. The extent to which the learning of one's sex role depends on the specific activities of one's mother and father is not known and should be established. Also uncertain is the part that one's sex-role identification plays in his over-all adjustment. It is known that serious adjustment problems are often accompanied by sex-role confusion, but the cause-and-effect relationships are unclear. If, however, society is to encourage the complete emancipation of women, more must be learned about the potential effects of such a trend on the development of children.

What are the effects on small children of a mother's absence from home? At first glance it may seem that this question has already been studied to death, but the results to date have been only equivocal. The difficulty in obtaining a clear set of answers does not, however, invalidate the importance of the question. It simply means that more sophisticated approaches must be found for its study.

Comparisons of working and nonworking mothers have proved of little value and should probably be abandoned as a means of determining effects of maternal employment on a child's development. Women who work are different from women who do not work, and the variable of employment itself may not be very relevant. The questions to be answered must be more specific and more sophisticated, based when possible on a theory of child development rather than on random brainstorms. Stolz (1960) has suggested that in further research on the effects of maternal employment the conditions of employment and unemployment should be defined more clearly; the effects on the family of different kinds of occupations should be studied; characteristics of the mother should be better controlled; and the behavior of the child should be defined by better criteria. To this list can be added the suggestion that future research concentrate on the process of mother-child interaction and the influence of periodic separation on this interaction. The effects themselves are probably less important than understanding the ways in which these effects are produced.

An increased knowledge of the relationship between short-term maternal separation and child development will not, ultimately, dictate whether mothers of small children should or should not work. Mothers, as individuals, are too diversified to allow any single specification to be applied to all. More importantly, however, further knowledge in this area would help reduce the potential negative effects of separation, or for that matter of the possible negative effects of continual mother-child interaction. Perhaps a child can get too much of a good thing as well as too little. In some cases, a mother's employment may have positive effects on the entire family. More must be learned about the kind of women for which this is most likely true, and the conditions under which the positive effects will be optimized.

What are the characteristics of women who successfully combine several roles? Many women probably cannot concentrate on more than one role at a time and do it well. These women would be well advised to select the one they feel is most important to them for the immediate future—whether housewife or employment—and invest most of their energies in it. This is not to say that they should avoid the other entirely, but they should expect to relegate it to a definite second place in their lives.

Other women obviously can combine two or more roles and perform each of them well. Little, however, is known as to the relevant characteristics which differentiate the latter group from the former. Moreover, increased knowledge in this area might suggest characteristics to be emphasized in the development of girls so that their chances of being able to handle several roles are increased.

How can women gain acceptance in male-dominated fields? Women are often prevented from obtaining a job suited to their interests and capabilities by the reluctance of men to accept women into fields which men have traditionally dominated. Often the discrimination is most severe among the woman's potential colleagues. Like the white person who agrees that Negroes should have equal rights but wouldn't want to live next door to one, many men who accept the principle that women have an equal right to jobs for which they are qualified rebel at the suggestion that they accept a woman as a colleague. Some reasons for this resistance were discussed earlier. The problem now to be faced is how to persuade men to become less threatened and less resistant, other than through the force of law. This appears to be a fertile research field for persons interested in the study of interactions within groups.

How do attitudes concerning women develop, and how can they be altered? The focus here would be on understanding the nature of attitudes toward women in various roles: the woman as housewife, as career woman, as mother (working or nonworking), etc. If women are to freely choose a life pattern, attitudes toward women in certain of these roles must become more positive. We must learn how these attitudes develop, what influences them, and at what stages of development they are most malleable.

What kinds of guidance do women need at various stages of development, and how can this guidance be more effectively provided? Modern guidance is aimed primarily at boys, with girls being helped rather as an afterthought. Research is needed to establish the guidance needs most common at the different stages of a woman's life, as well as the most effective means of providing guidance to meet these needs. Likewise, better tools, in the form of tests and occupational information, are needed for persons counseling with girls, if girls are to receive guidance of the quality now available to boys.

✻ ✻ ✻ RECAPITULATION. The most predictable thing about the future is that it is unpredictable. The world of today will not be the world of tomorrow, although it provides us with glimpses of tomorrow. At best, we can extrapolate from the trends of the recent past and plan as best we can to meet the challenges of the future.

Such extrapolations have two important implications for women. First, they foretell an increasing need for better use of our human resources. Society's demands for the efficient utilization of abilities will grow, and the pressure will be felt especially by those with above average skill and training in needed areas. No group, not even women, will be exempt. All must contribute, or all will suffer the consequences.

This trend parallels the movement toward increased recognition and respect for individual differences. It is becoming more accepted that people first of all are *individuals,* and that their membership in a socially distinct group—whether classified by race, social class, or sex—is of lesser importance than their uniqueness as individuals. Women are even now profiting from the attention being paid to such other "minority" groups as Negroes and members of the working class, and the benefits will continue to accrue.

The picture presented here is one of hope and opportunity but not yet one of fulfillment. Women have the opportunity to develop as individuals as never before in our history. Whether they will take full advantage of this opportunity cannot yet be determined. To do so, they will need the help of those who shape their lives: parents, teachers, husbands, and employers. For the girl to have true freedom to develop as an individual, she needs the support of all of these persons.

More specifically, several modifications within our society are necessary, some of which have already begun. Girls must be encouraged, first, to develop a broader concept of the woman's role as they grow up. Role change lags behind social change, but as more women move into jobs on an equal footing with men, their children should develop more modern attitudes toward the role of women in our society.

Second, girls need help in anticipating their needs when their children are no longer small and to make their high school and college plans accordingly. This means that they will need the help of enlightened teachers and counselors who are not themselves bound by traditional stereotypes. Initial attempts to persuade girls to see their future in a more sensible perspective have not met with enthusiastic receptions, but further tries must be made. Even if most girls reject such help for the time being, those to whom it is meaningful will probably be the influential women of the next generation.

This means, too, that girls must be encouraged to question the traditional narrow range of occupations suitable for women. They must, instead, be given the opportunity to discover the fields which are most appropriate for them as individuals, in light of their plans for the future. Some of the traditional women's occupations, such as teaching, are not always adaptable to part-time work, while others, such as secretarial work, provide few opportunities for persons with career ambitions. The girl should be encouraged to emphasize in her planning her individual needs and goals and to avoid being frustrated by tradition.

Emphasis must be given to helping the mature woman get back into circulation once her family no longer requires her full-time attention. This may involve several approaches: an upgrading of earlier education or training, education in a new area to which her interests have shifted, or simply guidance as she re-enters the labor market and competes with young women fresh out of school. At the present time the resources for mature women are few and unevenly distributed. There is a great need for a more systematic means of helping the mature woman come to terms with herself.

Society is constantly changing, but society does not usually welcome change. Change is resisted, and few improvements are won without a struggle. Women fought for legal rights equal to those of men, and won them. There remains, however, a personal equality which is more difficult to obtain because it requires changes in attitudes, not in laws. And this change must be evident in the attitudes of women toward themselves, as well as of men toward them. The rewards of being an individual are countered by the risks. Presumably for most persons the rewards are greater, but for those who have not known individuality, the first steps are hesitant. Once begun, however, the march is not likely to be halted. Like it or not, women as individuals are here to stay. They should be treated accordingly.

✄ ✄

Appendices

Introduction: Revolution in a Man's World

❧ ❧ ❧ A NEW CHANGE. The 1963 symposium, *The Potential of Women,* has been published under the editorship of Farber and Wilson (1963).

❧ ❧ ❧ THE STATUS OF THE MODERN WOMAN. Research by Fernberger (1948) and by Sherriffs and Jarrett (1953) has shown that college students tend to view women as possessing more negative characteristics than men.

Among those psychoanalysts who have suggested connections between women's anxieties and society's restrictions on the role of women is Thompson (1953).

❧ ❧ ❧ THE WOMANPOWER GAP. Estimates of the projected need for women workers come from the Women's Bureau (1966a).

Among those writers who have stressed the importance of making better use of women in the labor market are Kaltenborn (1958), Wolfle (1964), and Rossi (1965a).

The Girl Grows Up

❧ ❧ ❧ PHYSICAL DEVELOPMENT. Sources of detailed information concerning the physical development of girls include Shuttleworth (1937, 1939, 1949a, 1949b); Tuddenham and Snyder (1954); Horrocks (1954); and Krogman (1955).

It is not necessary that menstruation come as a complete surprise either to the girl or to her parents, since there are earlier indicators of the onset of the physical and physiological changes which will lead to it. Reynolds and Wines (1948), from a study of 49 girls in the Fels research group, found that the first appearance of pubic hair and the beginning of breast development appear at about the same time (approximately 11 years of age, on the average) and about 2 years before first menstruation.

Shock (1943) has described the physiological changes which accompany puberty.

Many of the physical and physiological changes associated with puberty are influenced by body hormones, which are responsible for the development of many sex-appropriate characteristics. For detailed information concerning the process by which these hormones operate, the reader is referred to discussions by Shock (1944), Beach (1948), and Hamburg and Lunde (1966), as well as the volume edited by Beach (1965). The extent to which the male and female sex hormones, androgen and estrogen respectively, influence the development of sex-related characteristics beyond those which are physical in nature has not been established.

Evidence of an inverse relationship between age of reaching puberty and final height among girls comes primarily from the Oakland Growth Studies, reported by Bayley (1943b).

Several studies have investigated the relationship between age of reaching puberty and the interests and personality characteristics of adolescent girls. Stone and Barker (1937) compared premenarcheal and postmenarcheal girls between the ages of 132 and 182 months, equated for race, age, and social status. They found that the postmenarcheal girls scored slightly higher on the Otis Intelligence Test and gave more mature responses on the Pressey Interest-Attitude Test and the Sullivan Scale for Measuring Developmental

Age in Girls. Based on an intensive analysis of a small sample of boys and girls, More (1955) concluded that early-maturing girls are seen by their peers as warmer, more friendly, more pleasant, more emotionally stable, more forceful, more assertive, better groomed, and more calm than girls who mature late. No such differences were found among the boys. Jones and Mussen (1958), on the other hand, reported fewer differences between early- and late-maturing girls on the Thematic Apperception Test than they had obtained in a previous study involving boys. They did find, however, that the late-maturing girls tended to score higher on negative characteristics and to show a greater need for recognition.

❧ ❧ HEALTH AND PHYSICAL DEFECTS. The male sex begins with a numerical advantage, since the sex ratio at birth favors boys. Data for 1960 show that the number of births in this country that year included 2,179,708 boys and 2,078,142 girls (U.S. Public Health Service, 1961a). At all stages of development, however, females are more likely to survive (Shuttleworth, 1949a; U.S. Public Health Service, 1961b).

Most studies agree that physical defeats are more common among men. An exception is a report by Lund, Yeomans, and Geiges (1946) that Philadelphia school girls showed a higher incidence of diseases and defects than did their male counterparts. This study, however, is limited to only one sample of children and does not negate the overwhelming evidence to the contrary.

The evidence concerning the higher ratio of left-handedness among boys has been documented by Enstrom (1962).

Studies of sex differences in sensory defects include those by Loch (1943), Reymert and Rotman (1946), and Corso (1959). The study by Scully (1947) is typical of those that have found color blindness to be more common in males, but others (Pronko *et al.*, 1949; Bowles *et al.*, 1949) have failed to find the expected sex difference. Studies involving school children have found more eye defects among girls (Eames, 1939; Ely, Kephart, and Tiffin, 1950), although several crucial variables have not been well controlled.

❧ ❧ ❧ PSYCHOLOGICAL DEVELOPMENT

❧ ❧ THE GIRL AND HER FAMILY. The belief that many parents would prefer their first child to be a boy is not a myth. Based on questionnaires given to college students, Dinitz, Dynes, and Clarke (1954) found that, if they were to have only one child, 92 per cent of the men and 66 per cent of the women would want it to be a boy. For the first child of several, 62 per cent of the men and 50 per cent of the women preferred a boy. On the other hand, one boy may be enough. Sears *et al.* (1957) found that mothers exhibited less warmth toward a new baby boy if there was already a boy in the family, but there was no change in attitude toward girl babies.

Findings by the Sears group that mothers tend to be more permissive with sons and demanding of daughters are substantiated by several other studies. Hubert and Britton (1957) investigated the treatment of 50 children during their first 2 years and found the mothers to be more restrictive and demanding of their daughters, although the mothers also seemed to enjoy girls more and to be more relaxed with them. Similarly, Rothbart and Maccoby (1966) reported a study in which parents responded to a child's voice which was ambiguous but was labeled as either male or female. They found that fathers were more permissive toward girls, while mothers were more permissive toward boys.

The process by which dependency develops is not entirely understood, since studies which have attempted to deal with it have produced conflicting results. In a study of forty preschool children and their mothers, conducted by Sears and his co-workers (1953), it was found that punitiveness on the part of the mother tended to make girls more dependent but boys less so. The girls' dependency was in turn more likely to generalize to women teachers than was the boys'. The investigators also felt that the mothers tended to emphasize nondependency more with their preschool daughters but that they later reversed their policies and stressed dependency more with the girls.

These findings, however, are contradicted by the reports from the Fels longitudinal research studies (Kagan and Moss, 1962) involving 89 children studied periodically from infancy to adulthood, which concluded that dependency is much more stable for girls than for boys. The investigators believe that this occurs because girls are consistently rewarded for dependent behavior, while independence for boys is stressed more at some stages of development than at others. They also found a high relationship between dependency in childhood and dependency among adults (Kagan and Moss, 1962, pp. 56–57): "Girls who were highly dependent on female adults during Period III [ages 6 to 10] established a passive and dependent relationship with their husbands or boy friends during early adulthood."

Several studies have established that the interaction between parent and child depends greatly on the sex of each. Emmerich (1962) administered to 306 parents a questionnaire concerning responses to children's behaviors. He found that the mothers were more nurturant toward their children than were the fathers, and that parents exerted more power over the child of the same sex. Droppleman and Schaefer (1963) questioned seventh graders about their relationships with their parents. The girls reported receiving more love, affection, and nurturance from both parents, while the boys reported receiving more hostile, negative treatment. Generally, the boys reported being more controlled by their parents, although this may be due to greater self-control on the part of the girls.

One area in which mothers seem to influence their sons more than their daughters is in the development of abilities. As evidence of early differences in this respect, Moss and Kagan (1958) have reported the results of two studies concerning the relationships between the extent of the mother's concern with her child's achievement, as estimated by ratings of interviews, and the child's performance on an intelligence test. The correlations between achievement ratings of the mother and the child's I.Q. were, for boys, .42 and .41 at age 3 and .27 and .08 at age 6. Among girls, the correlations were .07 and .16 at age 3 and .01 and .09 at age 6. This suggests that there is some degree of relationship between the extent of the mother's concern for achievement and the child's intelligence-test performance among boys, at least at age 3, but not among girls. Perhaps this is consistent with the considerably greater emphasis put upon the abilities of boys in our society. It is likely that three-year-olds, not yet having developed a high degree of personal motivation to do well on tests, are more responsive to their mothers' pressures than are six-year-olds, who generate their own motivation.

Girls have stronger emotional relationships with their families than do boys. One kind of evidence comes from a study by Winch (1949), who found that, among college students, the degree of parents' marital happiness correlated positively with the love which the girls had for their parents and the extent to which they were likely to submit to their parents, but no such relationships were found among boys.

Evidence for increased conflict between adolescent girls and their parents during the teens comes from interpretations by Liccione (1955) of TAT stories written by 250 girls between the ages of 9 and 17. He found that the girls had more themes involving conflict with their mothers than with their fathers, but also more themes involving interactions of all sorts with their mothers.

Parent-adolescent conflict seems to be a continuing phenomenon from one generation to another. In 1952, Ramsey and Nelson (1956) replicated a study originally published in 1939 concerning the degree of family adjustment among high school juniors and seniors. The only difference between the two groups was a lessened sense of obligation to the family expressed by the girls in 1952. Since these two studies were only 13 years apart, the results do not actually reflect similarities or differences between generations. The suggestion from these data that girls may be tending toward a weaker feeling of obligation toward their families might be more noticeable in a comparison of two separate generations.

The general conclusion that family relationships do not change much from one generation to another is also supported in a study by Bath and Lewis (1962), in which they found that young adult women who reported conflicts with their parents in various areas when they were teen-agers indicated that their attitudes toward these behaviors were now becoming more like those of their parents. Presumably as parents of teen-age daughters in the future they will repeat the same conflicts that they experienced with their own parents. These conflicts arise, then, not so much because succeeding generations become progressively more liberal in their attitudes but rather because people become more conservative as they grow older.

Emancipation from the family occurs much more readily among boys. Among college students, for example, Sherman (1946) found that nearly three-fourths of those judged "most emancipated" were men. Sherman (1946, 1948) has also found that, among college women, those who are more emancipated are likely to be older, more intelligent, more emotionally stable and self-sufficient, and to come from larger families, but to be less sociable and gregarious than the less-emancipated girls.

❧ ❧ DEVELOPMENT OF THE APPROPRIATE SEX ROLE. The distinction between sexual inversion and homosexuality has been discussed by Brown (1958a). Evidence supplied by Kinsey et al. (1953), that homosexuality is more frequent among men than among women, supports the notion that males are more likely than females to adopt the inappropriate sex role.

Much of the evidence that the male role is more preferred by children comes from research with the It Scale for Children, described by Brown (1958b). The It Scale involves the presentation to the child of several ambiguous figures for which he chooses activities which he thinks they would prefer. His choices are presumably indications of the sex role which he is projecting into the figures. Sex differences in role preference have been found with the It Scale with children as young as 3 years (Hartup and Zook, 1960), although the degree of difference at this age is less than among older children. Similar results have been obtained by DeLucia (1963) using a Toy Preference Test.

A study with contradictory results has been reported by Lansky and McKay (1963), in which the It Scale scores of kindergarten girls were found to be more feminine than those of boys the same age were masculine. The investigators suggest that earlier studies may reflect experimenter bias. However, in view of the preponderance of evidence in the opposite direction, as well as the small size of the sample in the latter study—20 boys and 16 girls—it must be concluded that preference for the male role has not been disproved.

Fauls and Smith (1956) report that preschool children choose sex-appropriate play activities in accordance with the preferences which they assume their parents would express. The parent-child interaction, however, is complicated by being two-way: Lansky (1964) has demonstrated that the sex-role concepts of parents may change over time, depending on the sex of their child as well as his or her stage of development.

A number of studies support the view that children develop a reasonably accurate concept of sex-role distinctions at an early age. Vener and Snyder (1966) asked children between the ages of $2\frac{1}{2}$ and 5 to name the sex associations of 44 household and task objects. Although the older children made fewer errors, all children showed a reasonably accurate discrimination. Emmerich (1959b) analyzed the projective drawings of children between the ages of 3 and 6 and found that both boys and girls perceived the mother as more facilitating than the father. Landreth (1963) questioned four-year-olds in Berkeley, California, and Wellington, New Zealand, as to the more appropriate parent to play various roles in relation to the child. In both groups, the mother was more often chosen for both care and companionship roles, with a greater difference among the American children. Sex-role perceptions quickly shift to the child's own age level. Tuddenham (1952) found in a study of elementary school children that even in the first grade girls were perceived as docile and feminine, while boys were seen as aggressive and masculine.

Kohlberg and Zigler (1967) compared bright and average children between the ages of 4 and 8 on several sex-role measures and found that on most, the bright children were advanced in their sex-role attitudes.

Social class influences on sex-role development are evident in a study by Rabban (1950), in which children between the ages of 3 and 8 from the upper-lower and upper-middle classes were asked to indicate sex-role awareness and preferences through play activity. A major finding was that lower-class children were more aware of sex-appropriate behavior than were middle-class children of the same age, with the difference being more striking among the girls. Likewise, Hartley (1961) found that middle-class girls between the ages of 8 and 11 were more traditionally feminine in their perception of the adult female role than were lower-class girls, although the middle-class girls were more apt to reject domestic activities as preferred for themselves.

Sex-role development may also be influenced by the size of the family and the sex of the child's siblings. Rosenberg and Sutton-Smith (1964b) have analyzed the differential effects on sex-role development of being an only child or having one or two siblings, according to the sex of the siblings.

Anthropological evidence as to variation in sex roles among various cultures, and its effect on personality development, has been presented by Mead (1939) and by Milner (1949). Romney (1965) has suggested possible relationships between sex-role development and variations in the structure of households in different societies.

In a study reported by Barry, Bacon, and Child (1957), two judges rated various aspects of socialization in 110 different cultures and concluded that there were few sex differences in the treatment of infants. As the children grew older, consistent sex differences common to many cultures became evident: the girls were pressured to be nurturant, obedient, and responsible, while the boys were expected to achieve and to be self-reliant. The same report includes an observation by Spiro of an Israeli kibbutz in which an attempt was made to minimize sex-role differences. The attempt failed because the primitive living conditions put a premium on physical strength for the functioning of the community.

Although most authorities (e.g., Brown, 1958b; Lynn, 1959, 1966; Hartley, 1964) agree that early identification with the mother is of considerable importance in sex-role development, a minority report has been filed by Johnson (1963). She contends that the mother plays a neutral role toward children of both sexes, so that the father becomes the most important influence on the development of sex-role concepts. This comes about through his differential treatment of his son and daughter, being expressive and rewarding toward the girl and demanding and instrumental toward the boy. The theory is intriguing, but in the face of considerable evidence and opinion to the contrary it must be rejected at this point in favor of one which stresses the importance of the mother's role.

Evidence that preschool girls identify more strongly with their mothers than do boys comes from studies by Sears, Maccoby, and Levin (1957) and by Hartup (1962).

Brim (1958), in a study of preadolescents, found that girls of that age are more feminine than the boys are masculine, and that the boys are really more "antifeminine" than truly masculine in their behavior.

Studies by Schoeppe (1953) and by Gray and Klaus (1956) agree that, in adolescence, girls are more likely to identify with their mothers than boys are with their fathers.

Whether working mothers tend to produce nontraditional sex-role concepts in their daughters is uncertain. On the basis of a thorough review of the research on this topic, Stolz (1960) concluded that whether the mother works outside the home has little effect on the daughter's identification and role perception, with the exception that girls whose mothers work are more likely to plan to enter a profession than are daughters of nonworking mothers. Hartley (1961), however, reports that girls whose mothers are employed demonstrate greater egalitarianism toward women's roles than do the daughters of full-time housewives, and Minuchin (1965) found that girls from less traditional backgrounds tended to engage in less sex-typed play and to have a weaker commitment to a sex role than did girls from traditional homes.

The extent of role conflict among adolescent girls is suggested by a study by Frank *et al.* (1951) of 300 adolescent girls in which they found evidence of numerous disturbances centering on role conflict, the resolution of which was more difficult for girls with high intelligence and middle- or upper-class backgrounds. The conflict between tomboyish and feminine behavior, often evident among adolescent girls, has been discussed by Gray (1957).

Evidence that college women often feel compelled to fake inferiority to men, especially in the intellectual area, comes from a study by Wallin (1950).

✄ ✄ SOCIAL DEVELOPMENT. From a review of the literature, Mussen and Martin (1960) concluded that popularity and prestige among peers in childhood are associated with taking on the role and behavior appropriate to one's sex.

Faust (1960) compared developmental status with prestige among 731 girls in grades 6 through 9. During the sixth grade, prestige was associated with being neither ahead nor behind the other girls in development, but in the later grades those girls who were developmentally accelerated gained greater prestige.

Personality characteristics associated with popularity among high school girls have been studied by Marks (1954) by comparing those girls rated as having high and low social acceptability on a sociometric test. The acceptable girls were found to be more sociable, more involved with people, more outgoing and impulsive, more flexible, and more feminine, while the less acceptable girls had higher intellectual and cultural interests.

Evidence that social acceptability is more closely related to social relationships among girls than among boys comes from a study by Schoeppe, Haggard, and Havighurst (1953). They compared 16-year-old boys and girls and found that, whereas the boys gained popularity by being altruistic and fair and by having positive attitudes toward other boys, the girls' popularity was associated with the ability to get along well with the opposite sex. This is substantiated by Calderwood's (1963) report that girls are more concerned about understanding boys than boys are with understanding girls.

Douvan and Kaye (1956) report that girls begin dating at an earlier age than do boys, but Lowrie (1952) found no such difference. This question remains open.

✸ ✸ ✸ PLANNING FOR THE FUTURE. Reports of the vocational plans of girls have been presented by Berry (1955), Douvan and Kaye (1956), Empey (1958), and Simpson and Simpson (1961). Evidence that the vocational plans of girls are often unimaginative and unrealistic comes from research by Ginzberg *et al.* (1951) and by Siegel and Curtis (1963). In a study of college freshmen, Darley (1962) found that women were about as likely as men to have made a specific occupational choice when they entered college, but the choices of the women were much more likely to be in relatively low-status fields and to be stable throughout college.

Hewer and Neubeck (1964a) asked entering freshmen at the University of Minnesota about their beliefs and attitudes concerning employment for women. Both the men and women students agreed that, although it was all right for a woman to work so as to buy things for her family, a normal woman would have no need to seek outlets outside her home. At this stage, at least, both the men and women are planning on a very traditional family pattern.

Morgan (1962) compared career women and nonworking women, all college graduates, on self-ratings and role conceptions. The career women viewed themselves as more different from the typical woman than did the noncareer women.

Several studies (Hoyt and Kennedy, 1958; Vetter and Lewis, 1964; Parker, 1966) have found that college girls who are career oriented can be differentiated from those who are marriage oriented by several scales on the women's form of the Strong Vocational Interest Blank. Typically, the career-oriented girls score higher on the "professional" scales—author, lawyer, physician, etc.—while the homemaking-oriented girls score higher on scales such as housewife, office worker, and nurse. Also in the area of interests, Astin and Nichols (1964) found that, among National Merit Scholars, women students planning to enter medicine and law had more masculine interests and values than did men entering these fields.

Hoyt and Kennedy (1958) and Vetter and Lewis (1964) also agree with White (1959) that career-oriented girls tend to have a poorer self-concept and to have lacked a close relationship with their families as adolescents. This is substantiated by Simpson and Simpson (1961), who found that career-oriented girls tend to model themselves after professional persons rather than after friends or members of their families, and by Schneider's (1962) finding that the career-oriented girls tend to aim at adult roles considerably different from those which their mothers have played.

✄ ✄ VOCATIONAL DEVELOPMENT OF GIRLS. Research studies concerning the process by which girls make vocational choices, based on current theories of vocational development, have been few and far between. Davis, Hagan, and Strouf (1962) analyzed descriptions of occupational choices written by sixth graders according to Ginzberg's theories and found that the proportion of girls who had made a "tentative choice" was considerably larger than the proportion of boys who had reached this stage (74 vs. 41 per cent).

Mulvey (1963) has reported a study of women between the ages of 37 and 47, based on Super's approach. She was able to relate degree of adjustment to career pattern and found that most well-adjusted women had a career pattern midway between housewife and full-time career. She concluded that personal contentment was associated with: (a) satisfaction with career pattern and with job; (b) working at a job of high level, of the feminine professional orientation, and in the field of general culture (largely teaching); and/or (c) active participation in volunteer activities. Low state of morale was associated with: (a) the "married state," marked by discontinuities of widowhood, divorce, etc.; (b) working at a job of low level; and (c) little or no participation in volunteer activities.

Matthews and Tiedeman (1964) have found strong relationships between marriage-career attitudes among women and their life style, as indicated by curriculum choice and by life plans. They conclude that the degree of commitment to a career drops considerably from junior high to high school, and that one deterrent to a career commitment among girls is the belief that men disapprove of a woman who has ability and uses it productively.

Norton (1953) compared the vocational interests and job patterns of male and female teachers and found that the women had developed their vocational interests at an earlier age and had more homogeneous interests. In addition, the women were more likely to remain in teaching rather than shift to another profession.

Sex differences in job preferences were established many years ago in the pioneering study of children's interests by Lehman and Witty (1936), and more recent evidence (Edmiston and Starr, 1948; Dixon, 1958; Empey, 1958; Sorenson and Morris, 1962) is consistent with their findings.

Singer and Stefflre (1954a) report that girls are less likely than boys to view a job as a means of satisfying their personal needs. Despite this, several studies (Singer and Stefflre, 1954b; Eyde, 1962; Astin and Nichols, 1964; Wagman, 1965) agree that, in choosing an occupation, girls put more emphasis on personal comfort and social service and less on power and esteem than do boys.

Sex and Abilities

THIS CHAPTER is based on research which is primarily relevant to educational and vocational planning. More extensive surveys of the literature concerning sex differences have been published by Terman and Tyler (1954), by Anastasi (1958), and by Maccoby (1966b). The reader is also referred to the volume edited by Maccoby (1966a) for an annotated bibliography of research concerning sex differences.

Evaluation of research on differences between males and females requires some recognition of the methodological problems involved. These have been analyzed thoroughly by Anastasi (1958), from which the following discussion has been abstracted.

One difficulty concerns the comparability of male and female samples. At the high school level a comparison of boys and girls in an intellectual area will produce misleading results since high school boys of low ability are more likely to drop out of school than are low-ability girls. The question of equality of sampling is one which must be raised in connection with any study which attempts to draw conclusions concerning sex differences.

Another major problem is that of the overlap of groups. In any study of group differences, attention may be focused on either (a) the amount of difference between the mean scores of the two groups on the characteristic under consideration, or (b) the extent of overlap between the two groups on the characteristic. Comparisons of males and females, in which large numbers of both groups may be studied, can thus result in the location of significant mean differences for a characteristic for which the overlap is nonetheless great. This would mean that, although the average scores for males and females might differ significantly, simply knowing that a person is male or female would provide little information about his or her probable level of performance in that particular characteristic.

Sex differences are not limited to the United States. Vernon (1960) has noted that sex differences in intellectual abilities are in the same direction among British children as among American.

⚬ ⚬ ⚬ SEX DIFFERENCES IN INTELLIGENCE. The case for eliminating sex differences on the Stanford-Binet has been stated by McNemar (1942, p. 42) in speaking about the 1937 revision:

One who would construct a test of intellectual capacity has two possible methods of handling the problem of sex differences. (1) He may assume that all the sex differences yielded by his test items are about equally indicative of sex differences in native ability. In this case separate norms for the sexes will be necessary if the means for total scores on the battery show appreciable discrepancy for the sexes. (2) He may proceed on the hypothesis that large sex differences on items of the Binet type are likely to be fictitious in the sense that they reflect sex differences in experience or training. To the extent that this assumption is valid he will be justified in eliminating from his battery the test items which yield large sex differences, and by this method may be able to dispense with separate norms. The authors of the new revision have chosen the second of these alternatives and have sought to avoid using test items showing large sex differences in per cents passed.

This approach, however, has not been accepted with equanimity by all psychologists. Many, such as Brown and Bryan (1957), argue that to eliminate such differences eliminates an important source of information concerning individuals and is unrealistic in view of the different experiences and expectations of males and females in our society. A similar view has been presented by Sarason and Gladwin (1958), who argue that, if sex differences are to be omitted, other group differences should be treated likewise.

The Scottish studies of intelligence reported in Chapter 3 were preceded by a study in the early 1930's, in which the Otis Advanced Test was administered to all children in Bath, England, who had been born between certain specified dates in 1921 and 1924 (Fraser Roberts, Norman, and Griffiths, 1935). The total sample, including 1,336 boys and 1,217 girls between the ages of 9½ and 13½ years, yielded only small and unreliable differences between the sexes. Similar results were obtained in a subsequent study of all Scottish children born on certain dates in 1926 (Macmeeken, 1939).

Results of other studies of sex differences in intelligence have been inconclusive. Dunlop (1947) reported a significant sex difference in favor of girls among 12,000 Canadian fourth graders, but the actual difference was only one IQ point. By contrast, Tozer and Larwood (1953) found no significant sex differences among 9,000 students in a British university. Fitt and Rogers (1950) obtained a significantly higher IQ for girls on Scale III of the Cattell Intelligence tests among 600 college students, and Lewis (1945) found that girls scored significantly higher on the Kuhlmann-Anderson. These are representative of the many studies which could be cited.

The standardization data for the 1937 revision of the Stanford-Binet Intelligence Scale have been reported by Terman and Merrill (1937).

Analysis of standardization data of the Wechsler Intelligence Scale for Children (Seashore, Wesman, and Doppelt, 1950) and of the Wechlser Adult Intelligence Scale (Wechsler, 1958) have not located any consistent sex differences in IQ scores. Other studies, however, have revealed sex differences on the subscales of these tests. Among the numerous studies which have shown sex differences on the Wechsler Intelligence Scale for Children are those by Miele (1958), Darley and Winitz (1961), and Gainer (1962). Similar studies with the Wechsler Adult Intelligence Scale include those by Miele (1958), Wechsler (1958), and Shaw (1965). On the WISC, males are consistently superior on the Comprehension subtest and females on Coding. On the WAIS, males are superior on Information, Arithmetic, Picture Completion, and Block Design; females do better on Similarities and Vocabulary and are markedly superior on Digit Symbol.

Factor analytic studies of girls' performance on intelligence tests have been conducted by Mellone (1944) and by McCall (1955), with inconclusive results.

Influences on the development of mental ability present an inconsistent pattern. Honzik (1963) reports data from the Berkeley Guidance Study which show that, by the age of 3, the IQ's of girls are significantly correlated with those of their parents, but the correlations between boys and their parents do not reach significance until the age of 5. She cites a number of supporting studies which confirm this finding and concludes that the results reveal a sex difference in the rate of maturation of mental ability. On the other hand, Bayley and Schaefer (1964) report correlations between maternal behaviors and the IQ's of children of various ages, from the Berkeley Growth Study. These correlations show fairly consistent relationships, beginning rather early, between boys' IQ's and behaviors of their mothers, but inconsistent relationships for girls. They conclude that the mother-son relationship apparently has a more long-term effect on the development of intelligence than does the mother-daughter relationship, and that later IQ's of boys but not of girls can be predicted to some extent from early maternal behavior.

Studies by Bennett (1932) and Johnson (1952) have shown that boys in institutions or special classes for the mentally retarded typically score higher on intelligence tests than do girls in the same groups, suggesting that girls of low ability are more apt to be kept in the regular classroom.

Data from the extensive longitudinal study of gifted children begun in the 1920's by Terman have been reported by Terman (1925) and by Terman and Oden (1947, 1959). A much more limited study by Hollingworth (1942) of children with IQ's over 180 included only 31 children, of which 16 were girls and 15 were boys.

During high school, the Stanford-Binet scores of Terman's group dropped on a retesting, as would be expected because of statistical regression, but the girls' scores dropped more than did those of the boys. This may be a reflection of the tendency of bright high school girls to minimize their intellectual ability in order to be popular and socially accepted.

Other studies have confirmed Terman's findings of increased sex differences in favor of men in adulthood. Bradway and Thompson (1962) have reported data from a retesting 25 years later of 59 women and 51 men between the ages of 27 and 32 who were part of the 1937 Stanford-Binet standardization sample. Although the women in the group originally scored higher than the men, the males had increased their scores more over the 25-year period, primarily because of little increase among women of high ability.

One of the earliest and most popular factored intelligence tests in this country is the Primary Mental Abilities Tests, developed by Thurstone. Several studies of sex differences on this set of tests have agreed that girls are superior on Word Fluency, Reasoning, and Memory, while boys excel on Spatial Ability (Hobson, 1947; Havighurst and Breese, 1947; Herzberg and Lepkin, 1954; Koch, 1954; Meyer and Bendig, 1961). Less conclusively, girls seem to be superior on the Numerical, Verbal Comprehension, and Perceptual Speed tests.

Only slight sex differences have been located on the General Aptitude Test Battery, developed and used by the United States Employment Service. Boys tend to score higher in spatial aptitude and girls in clerical aptitude and manual dexterity (Ohio State Employment Service Testing Staff, 1949; Droege, Crambert, and Henkin, 1963).

Sex differences are also evident on the Differential Aptitudes Tests (Bennett, Seashore, and Wesman, 1952). Boys are consistently superior in Spatial Relations and Mechanical Reasoning, whereas girls are consistently ahead on the Clerical, Spelling, and Sentences tests. At the younger ages there is little sex difference in Numerical Reasoning and Abstract Reasoning, but by the eleventh or twelfth grade the boys are decidedly ahead. This suggests that sex differences on these measures may be primarily a reflection of differential interests and experiences rather than of actual ability.

A study by Templin (1958) suggests that sex differences in intellectual areas may be decreasing. She compared the level of general information of kindergarten children with the results of a similar study conducted 26 years previously. She found not only that the contemporary children scored higher than the earlier group, but also that there was less difference between boys and girls in the current group. Inasmuch as information-type items are a common feature of many intelligence tests, one might expect sex differences on these kinds of items to be decreasing, bringing the total scores of boys and girls closer together.

ACADEMIC ACHIEVEMENT. Data from numerous studies show that girls get better grades in high school and continue to do well in college (Fifer, 1952; Summerskill and Darling, 1955; Northby, 1958; Heimann and Schenck, 1958; Berdie *et al.*, 1962; Darley, 1962).

There is also consistent evidence that girls are not superior on standardized tests of academic achievement (Parsley *et al.*, 1963), or on college entrance tests (Darley, 1962). In science in particular, the discrepancy is especially striking: Among high school students, boys do considerably better than girls on tests of science ability and achievement (Grobman, 1964) as well as winning more science contests and scholarships (Edgerton and Britt, 1944; Edgerton, 1947; Edwards and Wilson, 1958). The Project Talent survey (Flanagan, 1964) has reported that twelfth grade girls do little better than those in the ninth grade on tests of knowledge in science and math.

Those who hope that the increased emphasis in recent years on science and math education may attract more girls into these fields will be disappointed by an analysis by Poffenberger and Norton (1963). They conclude that the incentives instigated within the schools appeal primarily to boys, and that the trend has thus far not had much influence on girls. They believe that this is consistent with the evidence concerning achievement motivation provided by the research of McClelland and his associates.

On standardized achievement tests, boys are generally superior in social studies and science, girls are superior in verbal areas such as spelling and English mechanics, and there is no consistent sex difference in arithmetic achievement (Stroud and Lindquist, 1942; Traxler and Spaulding, 1954). Similar patterns are found on the college entrance tests, such as the "College Boards" (College Entrance Examination Board, 1950) and the Graduate Record (Osborne and Sanders, 1954), both of which include several subject-matter areas. Although 55 per cent of the students who were selected to compete in the first National Merit Scholarship Testing Program were girls, 69 per cent of the scholarships went to boys (National Manpower Council, 1957).

R. Carter (1952) has supplied evidence that men teachers in high school tend to give lower grades than women teachers, so that the high school boy is handicapped even when he has a teacher of the same sex. By contrast, in a previous study G. Carter (1948) found that women *college* teachers were harsher in rating students than were male teachers, although teachers of both sexes rated girls higher than boys. A related finding is that males in science courses are penalized by their teachers in grading, whereas females are rewarded (Cline, Richards, and Needham, 1963).

Boys are also at a disadvantage in the classroom because teachers expect more trouble from them and therefore tend to disapprove of their behavior more (Meyer and Thompson, 1956). This is especially evident beyond elementary school, when there is less personal contact with the teacher (Rundquist, 1941).

Evidence concerning sex differences in risk-taking behavior, which may be related to school achievement, comes from a study by Slovic (1966). He presented children between the ages of 6 and 16 with a task in which they could make a series of selections from a covered board. If a correct choice were made, the child would win a prize, but a choice of the one incorrect spot would cause him to lose everything. The child was free to quit at any time and keep what he had earned. This meant that as the number of successes increased, the risk of losing everything also increased. By the age of 11, boys were more inclined than girls to take risks and keep going longer. As a result of quitting at the right time, girls were more successful, which the author suggests may be related to their superior school performance.

At the college level, Erb (1961) reports that the grades of girls are related to conformity, with the high conformers getting better grades. There seems to be no such relationship among boys.

✦ ✦ UNDERACHIEVEMENT. According to a study by Shaw and McCuen (1960), underachievement among boys is evident as early as the first grade, but not until the sixth grade among girls.

Personality variables appear to be related to underachievement, but their manner of relationship is not the same for boys and girls. Among girls, high achievement is associated with high scores or ratings on social characteristics and behaviors, meaning that the achieving girl is socially active, conventional, and dominant, but not necessarily more popular with boys (Keislar, 1955; Roberts, 1962). Such characteristics are not as highly related to achievement among boys.

At the college level, attempts to relate underachievement to MMPI scores have generally met with little success (Zeaman, 1956), although Clark (1953) has developed an MMPI scale which seems to predict underachievement among college women fairly well.

Among female college students, those who are achieving well express more positive feelings toward themselves and greater self-acceptance than do the underachievers (Malloy, 1954; Vacher, 1963). However, at the high school level this pattern is less consistent and tends to be more characteristic of underachieving boys than of girls (Shaw, Edson, and Bell, 1960).

Anxiety also seems to be related to achievement in different ways among boys and girls. According to a study by Phillips (1962), increased anxiety causes lower achievement among girls and higher achievement among boys. Social class, however, is also involved in that middle-class girls are likely to be most highly concerned about school achievement and to suffer the greatest detrimental effects from anxiety, while anxiety interferes least with the academic achievement of lower-class boys.

The relationship between achievement and personal needs is seen to be rather complicated when sex differences are considered. In a study of high school students, Pierce (1959) concluded that achievement among boys is related to degree of personal involvement in the task, while among girls it is determined more by the extent to which they value achievement in general. He noted that high-achieving girls were characterized by wanting credit for their achievement more than did the boys. This is supported by a study involving college students (Todd, Terrell, and Frank, 1962) in which personal needs were found to be related to underachievement among boys but not among girls, leading to the conclusion that girls, unlike boys, can satisfy their social needs without academic damage. Heilbrun (1963a), however, has reported finding more frequent relationships between underachievement and scores on the Edwards Personal Preference Schedule for girls than for boys, again among college students. It may be concluded, therefore, that achievement among boys is related to general achievement needs more closely than among females, and the female under-achiever is characterized by immaturity and rebellion.

Several investigations have been concerned with determining the role of parental influence in underachievement. Despite the use of the same research instrument, the Parent Attitude Research Inventory (PARI), these studies have not produced consistent results. Pierce (1959, 1961) found that mothers of high-achieving boys scored low on the authoritarian-control factor, while mothers and fathers of high-achieving girls scored lower on the democratic scales. From this he concludes (Pierce, 1961, p. 29),

. . . that high achievement in girls is associated with more strict authoritarian controlling attitudes in both fathers and mothers, with the mother's influence of major importance.

Pierce's explanation is that girls, in addition to being more conforming than boys, can justify educational achievement more easily because they can identify with the parent of the same sex, who values such achievement, whereas boys tend to rebel covertly against domineering mothers by underachieving.

Shaw and Dutton (1962), however, found that mothers of female underachievers scored *higher* on "authoritarian-control" on the PARI than did mothers of achievers; no differences were found among mothers of male students. They conclude that, as compared with mothers of female achievers, mothers of underachievers are more dependent, more dominant, more in need of respect and dependency of their children, more fearful of their own hostile impulses, and can't tolerate aggression by their children.

At the college level, the evidence is more clear-cut that female underachievers have more dominant mothers and are more dependent on their families (Malloy, 1954; Teahan, 1963).

⚘ ⚘ VARIABILITY. The most persuasive evidence supporting the contention that males are more intellectually variable than females comes from a Scottish survey of mental ability (Fraser Roberts, 1945), based on an extremely large, random sample. Although the results show no sex difference around the mean, the males in the sample, who comprised 50.6 per cent of the total group, accounted for 55.2 per cent of those scoring 70 or above (out of 76 items) and 62.7 per cent of those scoring below 10. The author estimates that the extreme 10 per cent of boys are matched in ability by only 8.65 per cent of girls, the extreme 5 per cent of boys are matched by 4 per cent of girls, and the extreme 1 per cent of boys are matched by two-thirds of 1 per cent of girls. These figures, if accurate, could support an explanation of sex differences in achievement that would not depend wholly on cultural factors.

⚘ ⚘ PREDICTABILITY. There is a large body of evidence that the academic grades of females can be predicted more accurately than can those of males, especially at the college level. Among the studies which have demonstrated this are those by Abelson (1952), Berdie, Layton, and Swanson (1954), Jacobs (1959), Lewis (1962), and Brown (1962). An extensive discussion of this phenomenon has been presented by Seashore (1962), based on a number of studies for which such information was available.

⚘ ⚘ ⚘ SEX DIFFERENCES IN SPECIFIC ABILITIES

⚘ ⚘ VERBAL ABILITY. Girls are superior on the language usage tests (Spelling and Sentences) of the Differential Aptitudes Tests (Bennett, Seashore, and Wesman, 1952). Boys, on the other hand, are slightly superior in Verbal Reasoning, although boys would have some advantage anyway due to the biases in sampling of high school students.

McCarthy (1930) has reported that at 18 months, 14 per cent of the boys and 38 per cent of the girls make comprehensible verbal responses, while at 24 months the percentages are 49 and 78 respectively.

Cameron, Livson, and Bayley (1967) have reported data from a longitudinal study which indicate a substantial correlation between early infant vocalizations, as measured by items from an infant intelligence test, and later intelligence among girls, but no such relationship among boys. In another longitudinal study, Moore (1967) found that language is a more important factor in the mental development of girls than of boys.

Studies of speech defects show that they are much more common among boys (McCarthy, 1954; Everhart, 1960). Anastasi (1958) has summarized research by various investigators reporting sex ratios among stutterers of between 2:1 and 10:1, while Dunlap (1944) has reported a sex ratio of 20:1 among stammerers; in all cases, boys predominate.

In a survey of 8,000 stutterers and former stutterers, Milisen and Johnson (1936) found that the ratio of boys to girls was greater among *former* stutterers than among those currently afflicted, leading them to conclude that boys are more likely than girls to outgrow stuttering. On the other hand, Schuell (1946) has cited research which shows an increase in the sex ratio of stutterers up to the age of 30. Schuell (1946, 1947) has presented an extensive analysis of the problem of stuttering, concluding that boys are more likely to become stutterers due to their slower rate of verbal development and the resulting frustration and anxiety.

Evidence for girls' superiority in reading ability comes from a variety of studies, including those by Samuels (1943), Jackson (1944), Mitchell (1962), Ames and Ilg (1964), and Weintraub (1966). Wilson (1939) and Hughes (1953) report that the sex differences disappear by the fourth grade, but Gates (1961) and Flanagan *et al.* (1964) have found sex differences continuing into high school. Gates (1961) also found that the amount of difference between boys and girls remained about the same at all ages, which he interpreted as ruling out a maturational explanation and suggesting environmental stimulation as the major determiner.

Gansl (1939), Thorndike and Gallup (1944), and Schulman and Havighurst (1947) have all failed to find any consistent sex differences on vocabulary tests. A contrasting view, however, comes from an extensive study conducted by Dunsdon and Fraser Roberts

(1955, 1957), in which 4 vocabulary tests were administered to all children in Bristol, England, whose birthdays fell on the first day of each month and who were between the ages of 5 and 15, a total of 980 boys and 967 girls. The boys were found to be significantly superior on all 4 tests at all age levels, the difference increasing from 5 months at the age of 6 years to nearly a year by the age of 14. More recently, however, the results of Project Talent, an extensive survey of high school students in the United States, have indicated that sex differences in vocabulary performance are primarily a function of the subject matter sampled by the words rather than a true difference in ability (Flanagan *et al.*, 1964).

Preston (1962) compared students in grades 4 and 6 in both Germany and the United States. In America, the girls were ahead of boys in reading achievement in both grades, while the reverse was true in Germany. The investigator believes this discrepancy is related to the preponderance of male teachers in German elementary schools. Davis and Slobodian (1967), however, failed to find any differences in the behaviors of teachers toward first-grade boys and girls during reading instruction.

The belief that one reason for girls' superiority in the development of verbal ability is their closer interaction with their mothers is supported by a study by Ferguson and Maccoby (1966) concerning relationships between abilities and interpersonal relations. As compared with girls who were low in verbal ability, those who were high showed closer relations with adults but more distant relations with their peers.

✻ ✻ MECHANICAL ABILITY. Evidence for male superiority in mechanical ability comes from normative data for the Minnesota Mechanical Ability Tests (Paterson *et al.*, 1930), the Bennett Test of Mechanical Comprehension (Bennett and Cruikshank, 1942), and the Mathematical Reasoning Test of the DAT (Bennett, Seashore, and Wesman, 1952).

Based on their studies of infants, Gesell *et al.* (1940) have reported that there is little observable sex difference in motor and mechanical behavior among preschool children.

Allison (1956) compared mechanical test scores of Navy enlisted men and women and found that the males scored higher on achievement measures, as expected. On new tasks, however, the women equalled the men on pencil-and-paper tests as well as on performance tasks, although in the latter situation the women required slightly more training time. Allison concluded that women can achieve a higher learning score than men of comparable *measured* mechanical ability.

Portenier (1945) found that, among a group of college women, performance on a test of mechanical aptitude was fairly highly related to academic aptitude, suggesting that mechanical ability is not a special ability among women.

Evidence that the reliability and validity of typical tests of mechanical ability are lower for women than for men comes from studies by Doppelt and Bennett (1951) and by Mollenkopf (1956). To overcome this problem, special mechanical aptitude tests for use with women have been devised. These include the women's form of the Bennett Test of Mechanical Comprehension (Bennett and Fry, 1943), composed of items from Forms AA and BB which do not discriminate against women. The authors report a split-half reliability coefficient of .77, but no validity data. Rimland and Steinemann (1958) have described the development of a Women's Mechanical Test for use with Navy women, adapted from the Navy Mechanical Aptitude Tests.

Although there is no evidence that sex differences in mechanical aptitude have an innate basis, the performances of men and women on such tests are strikingly diverse. As an indication of the extent to which such performance is sex-linked, Lee (1952) compared the performance of male and female college students on the Bennett Test of Mechanical Comprehension, the Minnesota Clerical Test, and the Terman-Miles Masculinity-Femininity test. The per cent of overlap between the sexes was 22 on the mechanical comprehension test, as compared with 46 on the clerical test and 10 on the M-F test. In addition, the correlation between the scores on the Bennett and M-F test for the combined groups was .57, which is higher than most validity data reported for the Bennett. These data led the author to conclude that mechanical comprehension is a masculine characteristic among women, and that the Bennett might be used as a disguised measure of masculinity-femininity.

❧ ❧ NUMERICAL ABILITY. Martin (1951) reports a study in which children between the ages of 3 and 7 were compared as to quantitative expression and number ability. Boys were more likely to describe stimuli in terms of quantity, but girls were superior on the test of number ability.

On the norms for the Numerical Reasoning Test of the DAT, male superiority is not strongly evident until the high school years (Bennett, Seashore, and Wesman, 1952). Similarly, the Project Talent studies found no sex difference in arithmetic reasoning and math ability in the ninth grade, but by the twelfth grade the boys were clearly superior (Flanagan et al., 1964).

Evidence that attitudes play an important role in math achievement comes from a study by Aiken and Dreger (1961), in which a Math Attitude Scale was related to math grades and numerical ability among college freshmen. Scores on the scale were positively correlated with grades in a basic math course for women but not for men, while performance on the DAT Numerical Ability test was more highly related to scores on the attitude scale for men than for women.

ℳ ℳ PERCEPTUAL SPEED. In a pioneering sudy, Schneidler and Paterson (1942) found important sex differences among both high school students and adults on several tests of perceptual speed, in all cases favoring the females.

Normative data for the Minnesota Clerical Test (Andrew and Paterson, 1946) show women to be greatly superior to men, as do the normative data for the Perceptual Speed test of the DAT (Bennett, Seashore, and Wesman, 1952) as well as a perceptual speed test in the Human Talent Project (McGuire, 1961).

ℳ ℳ SPATIAL RELATIONS. Normative data from the DAT (Bennett, Seashore, and Wesman, 1952) and the Minnesota Paper Form Board Test (Likert and Quasha, 1948) show that boys are superior to girls in spatial relations once adolescence is reached.

On the basis of a factor analysis of a large number of tests, Michael, Zimmerman, and Guilford (1951) concluded that a greater verbal element is evident for girls in tests of spatial relations. Ferguson and Maccoby (1966) found that high spatial ability is associated with inappropriate sex typing among children of both sexes, which means that girls with high spatial ability have a stronger masculine identification.

ℳ ℳ MEMORY. Girls do better than boys in memory tasks involving objects and words, but less well in number memory (Duggan, 1950; Sommer, 1958). Likewise, girls are superior on the Information subtest of the Wechsler-Bellevue (Sommer, 1958) and the picture memory items on the Stanford-Binet (McNemar, 1942).

ℳ ℳ ARTISTIC ABILITY. Girls outperform boys on tests of art judgment, at least by the ninth grade (Barrett, 1950), and they continue to improve during adolescence while boys' scores during the same period may actually decline (McLeish, 1951).

ℳ ℳ MUSICAL ABILITY. In an extensive survey of studies involving the Seashore tests of musical ability, Farnsworth (1931) reported no evidence of consistent sex differences. Likewise, Gilbert (1942) found no sex differences in musical ability when degree of musical training was equalized.

ℳ ℳ SPATIAL ORIENTATION. Although Witkin's findings of greater field dependence among women are generally accepted, they have not been confirmed in all cases. One failure to confirm has been reported by Stuart *et al.* (1965).

⁂ ⁂ SCIENCE APTITUDE. Lesser, Davis, and Nahemow (1962) report the development of the Hunter Science Aptitude Test, to measure scientific aptitude among elementary school children. In their study, with only a small sample, boys exceeded girls on both forms of the test as well as on a composite science-achievement test, but none of the differences were statistically significant.

⁂ ⁂ ⁂ PROBLEM SOLVING AND CREATIVE THINKING

⁂ ⁂ PROBLEM SOLVING. Sex differences in problem solving have been the subject of several studies. Morgan (1956) found no significant sex differences on a test of logical reasoning, while Sweeney (1953) reported that women had greater difficulty in problem situations in which application of new principles was required. Using the Luchins volume problem and Maier's 2-string problem, Guetzkow (1951) demonstrated that women have greater difficulty in overcoming a mental set than do men.

Several studies aim more specifically at determining the conditions under which women have greatest difficulty. Carey (1958) found that the problem-solving ability of women could be improved by excluding men from the group being studied, and Milton (1957, 1959) found that reducing the masculine content of the problems improved women's scores. Hoffman and Maier (1966), however, failed to confirm this. They did find that women performed better for female experimenters and were more responsive than men to special instructions designed to stimulate motivation, although the latter was true only when the instructions were presented by male experimenters.

Performance on problem-solving tasks may also be related to the kinds of answers which are allowed. Maier and Burke (1967) concluded from a study involving various kinds of problems that men and women tend to choose different kinds of incorrect alternatives, so that the availability of certain alternatives may tend to distract women from the correct answer more than men.

⁂ ⁂ CREATIVITY. Evidence concerning sex differences in creativity among grade school children is conflicting: Torrance (1963) found boys to be superior, while Klausmeier and Wiersma (1964) found little difference. Torrance did note, however, that any sex difference may be disappearing as parents and teachers become more aware of the importance of fostering creativity in all children. There seems to be more consistent evidence that, in adolescence, boys do better on tests of creativity than do girls (Torrance, 1961; Flanagan *et al.*, 1964).

Helson (1965, 1966) has reported research concerning the development of creativity among girls, conducted at the Institute of Personality Assessment and Research. The results are limited by being based on the retrospective activities and interests of girls judged to be creative as college students, but they suggest that strong imaginary and artistic interests in childhood lead to creative achievements in late adolescence. She found no definite relationship between creativity and masculinity among the girls studied, but did find evidence that those who produced more had fathers who expected more of them and were more intellectual.

✻ ✻ ✻ MOTOR ABILITIES. According to Gesell *et al.* (1940), in tests conducted with children between the ages of 3 and 6, girls made more errors in walking on boards and walked more slowly at all ages. Sex differences were also noted in ball throwing by the age of 4, both in ease of throwing and in accuracy of direction. Boys were also noted to begin building block towers at an earlier age.

An extensive series of studies by Espenschade (1940) has demonstrated that during adolescence sex differences in motor performance become increasingly greater. She found the greatest difference in the distance throw in the sophomore year, in which less than 10 per cent of the girls were within the boys' range and none reached the boys' mean. Girls tended to do relatively best on tests of balance and control, the balance test being the only one on which girls showed significant improvement during adolescence. Boys, on the other hand, improved in all areas.

Among college students, women are superior in learning simple motor tasks (Archer and Bourne, 1956; Bendig, 1959), although research by Hodgkins (1962) suggests that women reach their peak performance in reaction time and speed of movement earlier than do men.

Girls show an early and continued superiority in manual dexterity. On the Purdue Pegboard, the raw-score equivalents (number of pins inserted during a specific time interval) for nearly all percentiles under all conditions is higher for women than for men (Science Research Associates, 1948). The same is true for the O'Connor Finger and Tweezer Dexterity Test: according to data cited by Super and Crites (1962), women score lower than men (scores being the amount of time required to complete the task) at all percentile levels.

Sex differences are less consistent on tests of large-muscle coordination. Most popular is the Minnesota Rate of Manipulation Test, which consists of two parts: (a) placing round blocks in round holes, and (b) turning the blocks over before placing them in the holes, both scored for speed of response. Some investigators (Teegarden, 1942; Cook and Barre, 1942) have found women to be slightly superior on one or both parts, while others (Tuckman, 1944) found men to be slightly faster, although the latter result may have been contaminated by unequal differences in intelligence and job experience.

Evidence concerning sex differences in reaction time and eye-hand coordination is inconsistent. Jones and Seashore (1944) found that girls exceeded boys in reaction time during adolescence, while Hodgkins (1963) has reported that males are superior at all ages from childhood into old age. The latter study did find, however, that women maintained their peak speed in reaction time longer than did men.

Jones and Seashore (1944) report no reliable sex differences for spatial eye-hand coordination and bimanual coordination, while Buxton and Grant (1939) and Ammons, Alprin, and Ammons (1955) have found boys to be significantly superior in temporal eye-hand coordination during adolescence.

Whatever the eventual outcome, girls do seem to start out with an advantage in coordination. Sapir (1966) tested 50 kindergarten children on 9 perceptual-motor tests and retested them 9 months later. In both cases, girls scored higher on all subtests, although boys showed more improvement during the 9 months, suggesting that the difference at that level is largely maturational.

Research concerning sex differences in strength has been summarized by Jones (1944, 1949) and will not be detailed here.

The Female Personality

❧ ❧ ❧ INTERESTS. For more detailed descriptions of research concerning sex differences in interests, the reader may refer to summaries by Terman and Tyler (1954), Roe (1956), Anastasi (1958), and Mussen and Martin (1960). Sex differences in a variety of interest areas have also been reported by Kuder (1956) and by Flanagan *et al.* (1964).

❧ ❧ DEVELOPMENT OF INTERESTS. In a pioneering study of interests by Lehman and Witty (1927), one of the major findings was that boys' play was more active and vigorous and involved more muscular dexterity and skill; it also tended to be more organized and competitive. Girls, on the other hand, tended to prefer sedentary, conservative, and restrained activities. Lund (1944) has reported that boys continue to be interested in physical activity throughout adolescence, but that girls' interest in such activity drops sharply once adolescence is reached.

Sex differences in amount and kinds of comic books preferred have been described by Butterworth and Thompson (1951), and sex differences among children in preferred books have been described by Andersen (1948).

Many girls are interested in subjects, such as science and math, which are generally considered to be "masculine." According to research by Flood and his associates (Flood and Crossland, 1948; Flood, 1950), boys and girls who prefer a certain academic area, such as science, do so for approximately the same reasons.

Communality in interests between the sexes during adolescence has been noted in a study by Fleming, Digaria, and Newth (1960), and the lack of consistent sex differences in interests during the later years has been reported by Strong (1943).

In a study of first-grade children, Tyler (1951) found a negative correlation between masculinity and "helping adults with work," which suggests the beginning of a major sex difference in preferred activities. In research with children in the Fels group, Kagan and Moss (1962) found a relationship between sex-role interests in childhood and adult sexual anxiety among the men, and no such relationship among the women.

Tyler (1964) reports that the interest patterns of girls are related to their eventual decision to concentrate on a career or a family role as an adult. She says (1964, p. 224):

We can conclude that girls' career interests begin to take shape at or before the age of 14 and that there may be some temperamental factors that precede them. Girls who develop such interests make less feminine choices in first grade but are indistinguishable from the others on this basis at later stages. This group of *Career* girls scored more feminine on the final Strong test than did the comparison group. Interests of this kind seem to develop only in girls average or above on mental ability tests.

✿ ✿ STABILITY. Kagan and Moss (1962), in their studies of the Fels longitudinal group, report that boys show more consistent patterns of sex-typed interests during their development than do girls. On the other hand, both Fox (1947) and Rosenberg (1953) concluded from research with the Kuder Preference Record that girls tend to develop a stable and mature interest pattern earlier than do boys, with the major modification among high school girls being a shift toward greater social service interests in the later grades.

Another approach to the question of stability is to investigate the extent to which interests are similar from one generation to another. Several studies have attempted this, with reasonably consistent results (Harris, 1959; Jones, 1960; Rosenberg and Sutton-Smith, 1960). In general, the similarities in interests between the generations are more striking than are the differences, although certain differences have been found. Sex differences appear to be decreasing with succeeding generations, among both children and adolescents, which Jones (1960) attributes to the expansion of girls' interests during the past generation so as to include some previously masculine areas.

✿ ✿ INTEREST FACTORS. An early factor analytic study by Crissey and Daniel (1939) reported three major interest factors—interest in people, a language factor, and a science factor—derived from the responses of men to several interest inventories. Women were found to exhibit the same factors plus another, labeled by the investigators as "interest in male association," which could also be considered as a sort of noncareer interest factor. In another early study, Darley (1941) reported a factor analysis of the women's form of the Strong Vocational Interest Blank, which yielded factors which he labeled as technical, verbal (linguistic), business contact, welfare, and nonprofessional.

Among children, interest factors are less well differentiated.

Tyler (1955) conducted a factor analysis of the responses of ten-year-olds to the Interest Inventory for Elementary Grades, by Dreese and Mooney, and found that each sex had a strong tendency to repudiate activities identified with the opposite sex. In addition, the girls' interests were more homogeneous. The major factors influencing the boys' preferences were (a) awareness of inappropriate activities, (b) antisissy interests, and (c) antiwork interests; among the girls the major factors were (a) antiactivity interests, (b) antiaggression activities, and (c) rejection of inappropriate activities. It is obvious that at this age interests are determined more by what the child dislikes than by what he likes.

☙ ☙ RELATED VARIABLES

☙ *Abilities.* Both Tyler (1951) and Krippner (1961) have reported studies in which the interests of first-grade children were related to their scores on the Primary Mental Abilities tests. Both investigators found significant correlations between abilities and interests among boys but not among girls.

In research with Terman's gifted group (Terman, 1925; Terman and Oden, 1947, 1959), the correlation between the scholastic interests of children in the gifted group and those of a control group of average intelligence was .72 among the boys but only .16 among the girls. In the case of activity interests, on the other hand, sex differences were the same in both groups, although the gifted of both sexes were accelerated in play interests. Twenty years later, sex differences within the gifted group in avocational and reading interests were quite evident, while by midlife the interests of the men and women had again become fairly similar.

☙ *Social Class.* Data concerning social class differences in interests among adolescent girls come from a survey by Douvan and Kaye (1956).

☙ *Family Composition.* A study by Sutton-Smith, Roberts, and Rosenberg (1964) showed that girls with older brothers tend to develop a greater interest in economics than do other girls.

☙ ☙ ☙ PERSONALITY AND ADJUSTMENT. Sex differences in emotional behavior are evident in lower animals as well as among humans, as evidenced by Hebb's (1946) study of chimpanzees.

Several studies involving the doll play of preschool children (Bach, 1945; Pintler, Phillips, and Sears, 1946; Sears, 1951) agree in finding that girls tend to be more affectionate while boys are more hostile and aggressive. In an extensive longitudinal study of the behavior problems of children, covering the same group from 21 months to 14 years, MacFarlane, Allen, and Honzik (1954) concluded that boys were more overactive, demanding of attention, jealous, competitive, dishonest, selfish, and had more temper tantrums, while the girls were more reserved, fussy, timid, shy, fearful, oversensitive, somber, moody, and engaged in more thumb sucking. Studies of college students by Darley (1937) and by Byers and Mather (1950) agree that men at this age are better adjusted than women. Manosevitz and Lanyon (1965) found that, among college students, women report more fears than do men, the difference being general rather than specific to certain areas.

♣ ♣ EMOTIONAL STABILITY. Maxwell, Lemere, and O'Hollaren (1958) conducted an extensive study of private hospital alcoholic patients between the years of 1935 and 1955 and reported an increase in the proportion of female patients during this period. Based on a study of a small group of female members of Alcoholics Anonymous, Fort and Porterfield (1961) reported that alcoholism among women is more closely related to other personality difficulties than it is among men.

Information concerning the sex ratio in suicide attempts in adolescence comes from a report by Tuckman and Connon (1962). Information concerning trends in the development of ulcers comes from a report by Kezur, Kapp, and Rosenbaum (1951).

♣ ♣ EMOTIONAL STABILITY. Maxwell, Lemere, and O'Hollaren dence that girls display more *anxiety* than boys. For example, girls score significantly higher than boys on the Children's Form of the Manifest Anxiety Scale between the fourth and sixth grades (Castenada, McCandless, and Palermo, 1956). Similar sex differences have been obtained with college students (Sinick, 1956; Bendig, 1959) as well as in other cultures (Sarnoff *et al.*, 1958). There is some evidence, however, that the tendency for women to score higher than men on the Manifest Anxiety Scale is at least partly due to differential sex-role expectations in responses to the items (Jahnke, Crannell, and Morrissette, 1964).

Anxiety seems to be more closely related to personality variables among girls than among boys. L'abate (1960) found that girls who were judged more anxious were also rated as more dependent. Sarason *et al.* (1958b) found that girls with high anxiety also had higher achievement drives, while no such difference was evident among boys. The high-anxiety girls also tended to make more favorable impressions on their teachers, although there was no relationship between anxiety and school performance, while the boys with high anxiety tended to perform better than those with low anxiety. Russell and Sarason (1965) have also found that women with high "test anxiety" are more handicapped in problem solving than are men at the same level.

Evidence concerning sex differences in reactions to stress situations is conflicting. On one side is the report by Carrier (1956) that stress in an exam situation has a more detrimental effect on the performance of women than of men, as well as Uhr's (1959) finding that under simulated dangerous situations women drivers make less appropriate and less safe responses than men. Apparently the notion that women are poorer drivers than men is not entirely a myth, at least under stress conditions, although one explanation may be that women have less driving experience.

On the other side of the picture, Paivio and Lambert (1959) report a study of college students' responses to projective pictures which suggests that men are more likely to experience "stage fright" than are women.

Evidence that boys exhibit more *aggression* than girls comes from reports by Sears (1951), Clark (1952), Archer (1961), and Berkowitz (1962). Weinstein and Geisel (1960) have found evidence that parents treat their sons and daughters differently in ways which lead to differences in the development of aggressive behaviors.

Irvine (1957) reports a study which demonstrates that boys tend to be more *domineering* and authoritarian than girls, while Janis and Field (1959) have shown that girls are more easily persuaded to change their opinions and their goals.

Research concerning sex differences in *introversion and extraversion* has been reported by Gray (1946, 1948).

Greater frequency of displays of *affection* by girls has been found in a study by Koch (1955).

Self-confidence. Bennett and Cohen (1959) report a study which shows that women tend to see themselves as less adequate and capable than men. On the other hand, research in the late elementary grades (Perkins, 1958) and among ninth graders (Taschuk, 1957) found that at both levels the girls were more self-accepting than the boys.

A study by Slovic (1966), described in the previous chapter, found that girls tend to be more cautious in risk taking but, as a result, tend to do better because they are less likely to take great risks.

Masculinity-Femininity. Among current interest and personality inventories which contain masculinity-femininity scales are the Minnesota Multiphasic Personality Inventory (Hathaway and McKinley, 1951), the Guilford-Zimmerman Temperament Survey (Guilford and Zimmerman, 1949), the California Psychological Inventory (Gough, 1957), and the Strong Vocational Interest Blank (Strong, 1943; Strong *et al.,* 1966). Specific M-F instruments include an adjective check list by Berdie (1959), and a scale devised by Rosenberg and Sutton-Smith (1959) based on games most commonly recognized by boys and girls. Special M-F indices have been developed for the Wechsler Adult Intelligence Scale (Wechsler, 1958), for the Kuder Preference Record (Overall, 1963), and for the MMPI (Aaronson, 1959), although Maine and Goodstein (1966) failed to confirm that Aaronson's index could discriminate between males and females in a college population.

Terman and Miles (1936) reported that M-F scores were positively related to scores on tests of mechanical ability among men but not among women. This was confirmed by Lee (1952), who found that, among college students, scores on the Terman-Miles M-F test correlated +.57 with scores on the Bennett Test of Mechanical Comprehension, but —.22 with the Minnesota Clerical Test and +.12 with the ACE examination. Since the correlation between the Bennett and the M-F test is higher than most of the validity coefficients reported for the Bennett, the author concludes that the Bennett could be used as a disguised measure of masculinity-femininity.

The evidence concerning the relationship between M-F scores and age is not consistent. Terman and Miles (1936) report that males reach their peak masculinity score while in high school and from then on become more feminine, so that sex differences on M-F scores decrease with age. Kelly (1955), however, failed to confirm this in a 21-year follow-up study in which the M-F scale on the Strong Vocational Interest Blank was included. Both the men and women showed a shift in the masculine direction during this period. Several factors must be considered in comparing these results, including the difference in the instruments used to assess masculinity-femininity as well as the educational and intellectual superiority of Kelly's group. For example, there is some suggestion from Kelly's study that, among the men, the college group tended to have higher M-F scores when younger and to suffer less decline with age than was true of those with less education.

Evidence that masculinity-femininity may involve several dimensions comes from studies by Aaronson (1959) and Tyler (1960).

Gough (1966) has reported that the Femininity scale of the California Psychological Inventory differentiated males from females with reasonably high accuracy within samples from the United States, France, Italy, Norway, Turkey, and Venezuela.

Heston (1948) compared M-F scores from the Strong Vocational Interest Blank, the Personal form of the Kuder Preference Record, the MMPI, and the Heston Personality Inventory. He reported intercorrelations based on a small sample of college students ranging between .41 and .73, the highest being between the Strong and the Kuder. Barrows and Zuckerman (1960) compared performance on the M-F scales of the Guilford-Zimmerman Temperament Survey, the MMPI, the Strong, and the Kuder, based on a large number of white-collar workers. The correlations were all in the low thirties. Klopfer (1966) intercorrelated M-F scores from the MMPI and the Strong for two groups of women and obtained correlations of .48 and .41. Nichols (1962) intercorrelated M-F scores of college students from the MMPI, the Heston, the VC Attitude Inventory, the Guilford-Martin Personality Inventory, the California Psychological Inventory, the Terman-Miles M-F Test, and the Strong, and obtained correlations ranging from nearly zero to around .80.

⋇ ⋇ BEHAVIOR PROBLEMS. Bentzen (1963) has reported that the majority of pupils referred by teachers as behavior problems are boys, and that this is related to the greater amount of frustration encountered by boys in school.

Data concerning sex differences in frequency and type of delinquent behaviors among juveniles have been presented by Wattenberg and Saunders (1954) and by Gibbons and Griswold (1957).

⋇ ⋇ ⋇ ATTITUDES AND VALUES

⋇ ⋇ ATTITUDES. In an analysis of responses of several hundred students to attitude items during the years 1937–41, Ferguson (1945) concluded that women were more humanitarian but had more rigid attitudes toward religion and toward censorship. The greater tendency of females toward conservatism was corroborated by Kallen (1963) among high school students and by McConnell and Heist (1962) among college students, while Kosa and Schommer (1962) found that female Catholic college students are more religious than their male counterparts. Finally, Plant (1958) reported that female college students are less ethnocentric than males, both before entering college and after two years of college.

There is some disagreement as to whether there is a sex difference in authoritarianism. The classic work in this field, by Adorno and his associates (1950), reported no consistent sex differences on the authoritarianism scales. A subsequent study by Bendig and Hountras (1959), however, has suggested that men tend to be more authoritarian than women, although one may question whether a group of college psychology majors is a sample from which one can draw meaningful conclusions concerning the development of such a complex characteristic.

Evidence that girls have more favorable attitudes toward school and toward teachers comes from studies by Moore and Holtzman (1958), Josephina (1959), and McGuire (1961).

Within Terman's gifted group, no significant sex differences in political preferences or in frequency of voting were noted when they were young adults, nor were there any differences in average scores on a conservatism-radicalism scale, although the men tended to be more variable on the latter measure (Terman and Oden, 1947). By middle age things had changed a little, and the men were slightly but significantly more conservative than the women (Terman and Oden, 1959). Anderson (1962) reported that sex differences in dogmatism are more evident among persons of higher intelligence.

✺ ✺ VALUES. On the Allport-Vernon-Lindzey Study of Values, standardized on college men and women, the men score slightly higher on the Theoretical, Economic, and Political scales while the women are slightly higher on the Aesthetic, Social, and Religious scales. Despite the fact that these differences are significant, they are not numerically large and there is considerable overlap between the sexes on each scale (Allport, Vernon, and Lindzey, 1951). Similar results have been obtained for high school seniors (Traxler and Vecchione, 1959), as well as for members of two generations of the same families (Fisher, 1948).

✺ ✺ CHARACTER TRAITS. Evidence that boys and girls differ little in over-all level of moral behavior comes from studies by Hartshorne and May (1928) and by Hartshorne, May, and Maller (1929).

Aronfreed (1961) asked sixth-grade children to complete stories in which a child committed an aggressive act with no reasonable provocation. The girls were more inclined to emphasize external responsibility in their reactions and to be more dependent on external imitation of moral actions. Aronfreed concluded (pp. 233–34):

Sex differences . . . seem to reflect . . . the variability in the extent to which moral consequences occurring in the child's actions are nevertheless dependent on the support of the external environment.

✺ ✺ ✺ MOTIVATION. On the basis of TAT stories related by college students, Lindzey and Goldberg (1953) concluded that men showed higher sex needs, while the women showed greater need for security. Bennett and Cohen (1959) studied the needs of persons between the ages of 15 and 64 and found that women are more motivated by a need for love and security and less by needs for personal attainment than are men. Evidence that women have stronger religious needs than men comes from a study by Allport, Gillespie, and Young (1948).

The needs of women seem to be strongly related to their cultural background, as evidenced by Ghei's (1966) finding of many differences in scores on the scales of the Edwards Personal Preference Schedule when American and Indian women were compared.

Evidence that young women are motivated primarily by a desire to get married and have children comes from a study by Kuhlen and Johnson (1952). Middletown and Grigg (1959) report that, although urban girls have higher educational aspirations than do rural girls, they do not differ in occupational aspirations.

The lack of strong occupational aspiration among girls may be related to the finding by Walter and Marzolf (1951) that girls in general have a lower "level of aspiration," which enables them to predict their performance more accurately than do boys, who make more reckless predictions.

❧ ❧ ACHIEVEMENT NEED. Research on achievement motivation has been stimulated primarily by the work of David McClelland and his associates. Much of their work has been summarized by McClelland in *The Achievement Motive* (1953). The usual procedure in these studies involves the presentation of projective pictures, containing scenes which might be viewed as representing achievement-oriented situations, to groups of subjects under varying conditions. In some cases, the subjects are "relaxed," but at other times the test situation is preceded by a competitive task designed to arouse achievement needs which it is assumed will be projected into the stories.

One of the variables which seems to influence the extent to which such needs can be aroused is the sex of the subject. Studies by McClelland's students (Veroff, 1950; Wilcox, 1951; Field, 1951) lead to several conclusions concerning sex differences in the arousal of achievement needs: (a) Although men show a significant increase in projective themes involving achievement under conditions designed to arouse achievement needs, little change is found among women. (b) The failure to obtain differences among women in "relaxed" and "achievement" situations seems to be because the women present high achievement themes under the relaxed conditions, so that there is little room for an increase. (c) Both men and women project more "achievement striving" into pictures containing men than into pictures containing women.

From these data, McClelland (1953, p. 181) concludes:

> The data unequivocally support the hypothesis that women's [need for achievement] is tied up with social acceptability, men's with leadership capacity and intelligence. . . . If you want to arouse [need for achievement] in men, refer . . . to their leadership capacity and intelligence. . . . If you want to arouse [need for achievement] in women, refer . . . to their social acceptability. The reasons for this sex difference are not altogether clear, although we have a little evidence that it may be related to the greater importance of dependence on others for women and independence for men.

The study of achievement needs among girls is further complicated by numerous discrepancies between achievement motivation, as determined by the technique described above, and actual performance in achievement situations. Several examples may be cited: (a) Girls who achieve well in high school score *lower* on achievement motivation than do equally intelligent, low-achieving girls (Pierce and Bowman, 1960). (b) Girls who are *not* motivated for college score *higher* on achievement motivation than those who are highly motivated (Stivers, 1958). (c) Girls who marry and don't continue their education score *higher* than those who go to college (Pierce, 1961). In each case, the reverse pattern exists among boys.

How can this strange relationship be explained? For help in answering this question one must look to studies which have approached the problem from a different angle. Lesser, Krawitz, and Packard (1963) compared achieving and underachieving girls on the McClelland test situation and found that the achievement score of the achievers increased significantly with pictures containing *females,* while the achievement score of the underachievers increased with pictures containing *males.* This suggests that girls who achieve best in school are those who identify more closely with women. In support of this, French and Lesser (1964) found that the achievement-motivation response to pictures containing *male* figures was greater when preceded by conditions designed to arouse intellectual concerns, but that under conditions designed to arouse concerns about the woman's role, the achievement-motivation response was greater to pictures containing *female* figures.

Girls who develop high achievement motivation in relation to intellectual goals are characterized by a lower degree of identification with the traditional female sex role (Kagan and Moss, 1962).

In contrast with men who have high achievement needs, such girls come from families in the higher income brackets and frequently from broken homes (Veroff *et al.,* 1960). Another important contrast is that high-achieving men are likely to have been overprotected by their mothers during childhood, while women with high achievement needs have experienced hostility from their mothers during childhood (Kagan and Moss, 1962).

Hill (1966) has related autobiographical information of college students to their scores on the two achievement scales of the California Psychological Inventory. He reports that girls who score high on Ac (Achievement via conformity) are happier and better adjusted than their counterparts among the boys.

✸ ✸ ✸ SOCIALITY. Goodenough (1957) has reported that sex differences in interest in other people are evident among nursery school children, and Winkler (1949) has found that girls are more interested in personal relationships than are boys and less concerned about learning roles.

According to Jones (1958), early-maturing girls are less socially active during adolescence than other girls, while the reverse is true among boys.

Evidence that the criteria of social acceptability among girls change between childhood and adolescence comes from a study by Tuddenham (1951). He concludes (p. 276):

It is suggested that the problem of securing group approval for a boy is one of conforming to a clearly defined group of traits for which he may or may not possess the requisite strength and motor skill. For a girl, the problem is more one of adapting to a continuously changing set of values which are never as closely defined as they are for the boy.

Keislar (1955) compared high school juniors of equal intelligence and found that, among the girls, those with high grades were rated as more influential but less popular with the boys.

In a comparison of leaders with followers within unisexual high school "cliques," Marks (1957) found that the boys' leaders scored higher than their followers in acceptability, athletic leadership, popularity, prominence, and social interests, while leaders among girls scored higher than the followers in athletic leadership, attractiveness, popularity, prestige, prominence, style setting, scientific interests, and nonconforming interests.

Tuddenham (1958, 1961) has conducted several studies involving the use of a distorted group norm, a situation in which the majority within a group agrees with a wrong perceptual judgment, in an attempt to influence the judgment of the subject. Among children, college students, and adults, females yield more readily to group pressure in this situation, although there is greater variability among the performances of the females than among the males.

Evidence that girls respond more readily to verbal conditioning comes from a study by Baer and Goldfarb (1962).

The Homemaker

EVIDENCE that married women are expected to conform to certain well-defined roles within the community comes from a study of a rural Minnesota community by Beilin and Warner (1957). They conclude (p. 342): "A well-adjusted woman's role is defined in terms which characterize her as gracious, charming, and as happy and successful as wife and mother."

Data concerning marriages among high-school girls come from reports by Landis and Kidd (1956) and by Moss and Gingles (1959). Information concerning women who never marry has been presented by Klemer (1954) and by Doty and Hoeflin (1964).

✤ ✤ ✤ THE WIFE'S ROLE. Two major groups of wives of professional men which have been studied intensively are the wives of business executives and of ministers. Warner and Abegglen (1956) studied the wives of 8,300 top business executives. Several possible roles were specified, including an independent career, working cooperatively with the husband, being involved in civic and social activity, or devoting herself to her home. The last two were the most common, and the community-centered role was the most successful. The investigators reported that the wives were expected to run the household so as not to interfere with the husband's career and were not to expect much of him at home, even sexually. The successful wives were able to focus on the present and not become too involved in the community, so that they were free to break their ties and move when the husband's job required it. In a subsequent, less extensive survey, Helfrich (1961) substantiated these expectations, with emphasis again put on the wife's contribution to furthering her husband's career.

Despite the difference in the occupations of their husbands, ministers' wives present patterns rather similar to those of the wives of business executives, according to a study by Douglas (1965). On the basis of an extensive survey of a large sample of wives of ministers in a variety of denominations, he found several reasonably consistent types: (a) the teamworker, who works closely with her husband in his ministerial responsibilities; (b) the wife with strong religious convictions who stays in the background; (c) the wife who stays in the background because she feels useful to her husband there; (d) the wife who isn't involved with her husband's work and doesn't care one way or the other; and (e) the wife who rebels against the demands she feels are made on her as a result of her husband's occupation. Although studies have yet to be made of the wives of men in other professions, logic suggests that similar patterns probably exist there, too.

❧ ❧ ❧ HOMEMAKING AS AN OCCUPATION. A French study, described by Myrdal and Klein (1956), reported that the average work week of housewives varied between 47 and 74 hours. In families with no children the wife spent 61 hours per week on household activities; with 1 child the amount jumped to 79 hours, increased to 89 hours with 2 children, and to 100 hours with 3 or more. The same study also found that women who worked outside the home spent only 6 to 8 hours more per week on *all* work (outside job *plus* household activities) than did full-time housewives with children.

Among those persons who have discussed problems inherent in the homemaking role are Bassett (1940), Parsons (1953), Caplow (1954), and Myrdal and Klein (1956).

❧ ❧ ❧ ADJUSTMENT TO HOMEMAKING. Falk (1966) has reported the results of a job satisfaction questionnaire administered to a group of female college graduates. Housewives in the group were more satisfied with their present "occupation" than were working women, although the working women believed they were using their college education to better advantage.

Gass (1959) has reported a study of the attitudes of a group of middle-aged housewives. (Although the report is vague as to the composition of the group, one can infer that they were Jewish clubwomen, which may limit the generalizations to be made from the findings.) The outstanding characteristic of these women was a passive attitude toward homemaking; they found it neither highly satisfying nor frustrating. They did not obtain any great satisfaction from having raised children, and they were pleased that they now had a minimum of responsibilities. Although a number indicated dissatisfaction with their use of leisure time, others admitted that they wasted a great deal of time and enjoyed it. The author concluded that most of these women were reasonably content as they were and that their creative and productive desires were not strong enough for them to be seriously frustrated.

According to a study of women's participation in voluntary

community activities by Rothe and Mewark (1958), women who are not employed outside the home are more likely to participate than are those who are working, although the extent of participation of the former group is limited by child care responsibilities. The extent of participation is also positively related to the woman's amount of education as well as to the participation rate of her husband.

The meaning and function of voluntary women's organizations may also vary a great deal, depending largely on social class. On the basis of a study of women's organizations, Moore (1961, p. 598) concluded:

Participation in [voluntary] associations is different and performs different functions in the middle and upper classes. For the middle class its functions are primarily to help adapt the woman herself to changes in the family life-cycle in a minimally disturbing way; for the upper class it plays a role of significance to the entire class.

Women in the Labor Force

THE MOST COMPLETE DATA concerning the employment of women in the United States are presented in the *1965 Handbook on Women Workers,* compiled by the Women's Bureau of the United States Department of Labor (1966a).

❧ ❧ ❧ EMPLOYMENT PATTERNS OF WOMEN. Most of the data presented concerning the employment status of married women comes from the *1965 Handbook on Women Workers* (Women's Bureau, 1966a). Supplementary data concerning the employment rates of mothers have been presented by David (1960) and by Zapoleon (1961).

Weiss and Samuelson (1958) have reported a national survey of women concerning activities which made them feel useful and important. Among other things, they found that the proportion of women mentioning satisfactions from family relationships decreased after the children reached school age.

Data concerning the employment patterns of women by occupation and industry come primarily from the *1965 Handbook on Women Workers,* with supplementary data from Hauser (1962).

❧ ❧ ❧ RECENT HISTORY OF FEMALE EMPLOYMENT. An extensive history of female employment in the United States has been presented by Smuts (1959) from which some of the discussion here has been adapted.

Data concerning the proportion of school teachers who are women have been supplied by the National Education Association (1965).

Rollins (1963) has compared employment of wives in 1920 and in 1960 within the same city and found that most of those who worked for pay in 1920 did so within the home. She concludes that many women who work outside the home now do so because the means by which housewives contributed to the family income in 1920 are no longer available.

Several studies have established that the employment of women, especially of mothers of young children, is frowned upon

by the general public. Glenn (1959) interviewed married women
in a small Georgia town as to whether they approved or disapproved of women working under various conditions. Generally,
employment was more acceptable for married women with no children, while those with preschool children were discouraged from
working. Conyers (1961) interviewed 18 managers and found that
they generally objected to hiring mothers with young children, believing that their place was at home. Hewer and Neubeck (1964a)
questioned college freshmen concerning their attitudes toward the
employment of women. The students had generally conservative
responses, believing that a normal woman should not have to find
satisfactions outside her home.

As evidence for pay inequalities, Baer (1962b) has noted that
in 1960 the median income for persons with a bachelor's or master's
degree in chemistry was $9,000 for men and $6,000 for women;
men with a Ph.D. earned $11,000 and women $9,000. Thus a
woman had to have a Ph.D. in chemistry to earn a salary equal to
that of a man with a master's degree. Likewise, Baer (1963b) cites
studies by the Bureau of Labor Statistics which show that in 5 out
of 6 office jobs in one city women averaged less pay than did men,
and that among bank tellers with less than 5 years experience
women averaged $5 to $15 less per week than men. In the same report, Baer cites a Women's Bureau survey of employers in which
one-third admitted having a double pay standard for male and female office workers.

Information concerning the work-connected expenses of working women comes from a study by Clover (1962) and from the
Women's Bureau (1966a). Karzon (1956) has reported on the working woman's need for greater lattiude in income tax deductions.

The Employed Woman

❧ ❧ ❧ REASONS WHY WOMEN WORK. Walt (1962) interviewed 50 women employed by the government concerning their attitudes toward their work careers. Many of these women were unmarried and living alone. She concluded that their jobs satisfied their needs for self-actualization and self-realization. Hartley (1960b) interviewed 40 working mothers concerning their attitudes toward their jobs. Most of the women viewed their employment as a way of serving their families and considered their husbands to be the major and responsible breadwinner in the family.

A valuable attempt to determine the relationships between work values and employment among women has been made by Eyde (1962). One of her major contributions is the development of a Work Values Scale for use in the analysis of differences between employed and nonemployed women. Her subjects were college seniors and alumnae from an Eastern women's college; the seniors indicated whether they planned to work in the future and the alumnae described their actual work experience. Eyde found that work motivation was easier to predict for the alumnae than for the students, suggesting that the motivation of the former group was more realistic and more personally oriented. In addition, a comparison of the work values of the two groups indicated that, with increasing age, work values changed from an emphasis on a desire for independence and achievement to a desire for variety, self-expression, and social experiences.

Most of the women surveyed by the Women's Bureau (1952) reported financial need as their main reason for working. Few said that they were working primarily for their personal satisfaction or to maintain their job skills. Carroll (1962) has reported an analysis of data from the 1950 Survey of Consumer Expenditures by the Bureau of Labor Statistics. Families with working wives had above-average incomes, but without the wife's job the incomes of these same families would, as a group, have been below average. Those women who were employed contributed an average of 27 per cent of the total income of their families; those employed full-time contributed 38 per cent. However, the ratio of the wife's income to the total family income was constant across occupational levels. The Women's Bureau (1966a) has also reported data which show an inverse relationship between the rate of employment among wives and the income levels of their husbands, although Nye (1963b) reports that this relationship is decreasing.

Among those who have questioned whether financial need is as important as has been claimed are Bell (1956) and Feldman (1958). Sobol (1963) found no relationship between future work plans of women and the income of their husbands.

Both the National Manpower Council (1957) and Zapoleon (1961) have reported a negative relationship between frequency of employment among mothers with small children and the income of their husbands.

Nye (1963b) has reported that, despite the lack of an impressive relationship between the husband's income and frequency of wife's employment across all economic levels, there is a definite relationship within occupational levels.

✱ ✱ ✱ VARIABLES RELATED TO THE DECISION TO WORK. Rossman and Campbell (1965) have reported that, among a group of college graduates surveyed several years following graduation, the women who worked outside the home tended to be more intelligent than those who were full-time housewives.

Data concerning the employment rates among nonwhite women come from the National Manpower Council (1957), Zapoleon (1961), and the U.S. Bureau of the Census (1966).

Data concerning the employment rates among rural women come from Caplow (1954) and the National Manpower Council (1957). Data concerning the geographical distribution of women workers come from the Women's Bureau (1966a).

Data concerning the employment of women in the Soviet Union come from Derthick (1958), Murphy (1959), and *Life* Magazine (July 28, 1961).

✱ ✱ ✱ THE CHOICE OF A JOB. Baudler and Paterson (1948) asked high school and college students to rank 29 women's occupations according to their relative status. The rank order from highest to lowest was: physician, artist, registered nurse, journalist, symphony music performer, high school teacher, designer, commercial artist, secretary, buyer, elementary teacher, practical nurse, dancer or musician, stenographer, dressmaker, sales person, office machine operator, show card writer, hairdresser, sales clerk, telephone operator, factory sewing machine operator, factory operative, servant, waitress, and laundry worker.

In a similar study, Tuckman (1950) reported data from high

school and college students in Montreal, who ranked women's occupations according to social status, earnings, and working conditions. The social status rankings were quite similar to those reported by Baudler and Paterson. There was, however, considerable variability in estimated salaries, with men estimating higher than women. The correlation between social status and estimated earnings was found to be higher than the correlation between social status and actual earnings. There was also a wide variability in estimated working conditions, with again a high correlation between this variable and perceived social status.

Jurgensen (1947, 1949) has conducted two studies in which male and female job applicants ranked 10 job factors in order of importance to them. In both studies, the men ranked security, advancement, and benefits higher than did the women, while the women ranked working conditions higher than did the men. McGregor and Knickerbocker (1941) reported a study in which blue-green lighting was introduced into a plant in hopes that it would reduce eye strain. The men's productivity increased but that of the women went down. On being questioned, the women reported that they thought the new lighting made them look "ghastly," which in turn had a negative effect on their productivity.

Several studies have been concerned with the job satisfaction of women workers. Hulin and Smith (1964) measured the job satisfaction of male and female employees in three companies and found that the women were generally less well satisfied with their jobs. The same investigators (1965) found that the job satisfaction of men could be related to several independent variables, but this was not the case among women. They concluded (Hulin and Smith, 1965, p. 215):

It seems that as a minimum condition investigators must draw distinctions between male and female workers when discussing functional relationships between job satisfaction and other variables.

Hulin (1966) reported that female clerical workers who indicated low job satisfaction had a much higher probability of leaving the job during the succeeding months, in a city in which the labor supply was short. Centers and Bugental (1966) compared male and female workers on job motivations and concluded that, although there were no consistent sex differences in emphasis on intrinsic or extrinsic motivators, the women tended to stress co-workers more and the men stressed opportunity to use their talent and skill.

Bolanovich (1944, 1948) has reported two studies dealing with the selection of female engineering aides. In the first, he found that performance in a training program showed positive correlations in the fifties with the ACE math score, the Wonderlic Personnel Schedule, and previous grades in school, but was not correlated with interview ratings or the Kuder Preference Record. He also found that a combination of the ACE math score and previous grades produced a multiple correlation of .61 with performance in training. In the second study, he reported the development of an interest measure which predicts continuation on a repetitive assembly job with some success.

DRAWBACKS TO HIRING WOMEN. Data concerning the job turnover rate among women workers have been reported by the Women's Bureau (1966a). Data concerning absenteeism have been reported by Wade (1955), Spiro (1960), and the Women's Bureau (1966a).

Naylor and Vincent (1959) found no relationship between absenteeism and age or marital status among 2,000 clerical workers, but a positive relationship between absenteeism and number of dependents was evident. Hinkle *et al.* (1960) report that women are more likely to take time off from work when ill, although for shorter periods than men.

Data concerning injury rates among women workers have been reported by Spiro (1960).

Erickson and Hansen (1952) have reported that between 30 and 40 out of every thousand women workers become pregnant each year.

A study by Balfour (cited by Baetjer, 1946) of the effects of employment on pregnancy found a greater than normal rate of premature births among mothers who worked longer than 6 months during pregnancy, although the cause-and-effect relationship is obscure.

Surveys by Baetjer (1946) and Nadelhoffer (1960) agree in finding little relationship between the menstrual cycle or menopause and the work performance of women.

Descriptions of the various legal restrictions on the employment of women may be found in publications of the Women's Bureau (1961d, 1966a).

WOMEN AS SUPERVISORS. Wolfle (1954) has reported a study by the Women's Bureau, in which several hundred women in higher level positions in business and industry were asked what position they would like to hold 5 years in the future. Only 40 per cent hoped to be promoted or in some way to get ahead in their jobs. The majority preferred to remain where they were or to transfer to a similar job elsewhere.

Livingstone (1951) questioned several hundred women employees concerning their reasons for not wanting to be promoted. The most frequent explanations given were lack of self-confidence, domestic responsibilities, a desire to remain a part of the group, and the lack of a relationship between promotion and their self-esteem.

Hardin, Reif, and Heneman (1951) administered an attitude and job preference blank to both male and female department store employees and found greater similarity between male supervisors and male employees than between female supervisors and female employees. This finding is similar to a study described in an earlier chapter concerning the characteristics of leaders among adolescents (Marks, 1957). The leaders among the boys were looked upon by the other boys as "one of the group," whereas the leaders among the girls were viewed by the other girls as being on a higher level. The conclusion was drawn that to be a leader among girls requires to some extent a rejection of the typical "female" pattern, which may also be true of job supervision.

Rossi (1965b) has reported a study by the President's Commission on the Status of Women in which federal employees were asked whether they would prefer to be supervised by a man or a woman. Most of the men preferred a man, some didn't care, and almost none preferred a woman. Among the women employees, about two-thirds didn't care, and most of the rest preferred a man.

Livingstone (1953) analyzed 10 companies which were having difficulty in recruiting women as supervisors and compared them with a company in which women were eager to become supervisors. She concluded that in the latter company, where a man was given responsibility as manager of the entire section, the women supervisors worked for him and used him as a sort of "father-figure."

✺ ✺ ✺ EMPLOYMENT PATTERNS OF OLDER WOMEN. Data concerning employment rates among older women have been reported by Zapoleon (1961) and by the Women's Bureau (1966a). Information concerning occupations of older women workers comes from Pearce (1949), Kyrk (1956), the National Manpower Council (1957), and the Women's Bureau (1966a).

Neugarten (1956) has reported a study in which the concepts of women's roles held by older women were analyzed by projective tests. The "young woman" was seen by these women as bland, passive, and tied to her mother. The "married woman" was seen as collaborating with her husband, having more feelings, and identified with her husband rather than with her parents. They saw the older woman as strong, deep, self-confident, inner-directed, dominant, yet dependent on younger people. Data were also obtained from a group of men of the same age, with somewhat different results. The men saw the young woman as dependent, bland, and dominated, generally similar to the picture drawn by the women. But the men saw the older woman as opposite to themselves: emotional and authoritarian. An important additional finding was that the older women tended to view being an older woman in a positive light.

In a study conducted in a manufacturing company in the early 1940's, involving an analysis of the separation records of 1,600 women over a period of 14 years, Smith (1952) found that women over 45 were less frequently discharged and were more frequently rated high in ability, job attendance, and attitude than were the younger female employees. Gadel (1953) reports a comparison of full-time and part-time employees within the same company, the full-time being in their early twenties and the part-time having an average age of 41. There were no differences between the groups in production records, comparative ratings, or supervisors' estimates of learning ability, but the older group was rated more satisfactory by their supervisors and showed higher satisfaction with their jobs. The latter finding is explained by the factors which the two groups stressed as bases for job satisfaction. The older group looked for security, supervision, prestige of the company, and reasonable hours, requirements which were more realistic and more likely to be satisfied than those sought by the younger workers, such as type of work, working conditions, pay, compatible co-workers, ease of commuting, and advancement.

A study reported by the Bureau of Labor Statistics (1960a) of 6,000 office workers in comparable clerical jobs, of whom 85 per cent were women, showed little variation in man-hours by age except for a lower performance among the youngest group due to lack of experience. However, considerable variation within age groups was found. Exceptionally high performance records were reported for women between the ages of 45 and 65 in jobs such as typing, sorting, and filing. The report concludes that mature women are more consistent in their job performance than are younger workers, while the quality or accuracy of the work at different ages is about the same. According to a study of applicants for clerical positions, older applicants also have more favorable personality characteristics (Thumin and Wittenberg, 1965).

Stanton (1951) analyzed the work experience of 3,000 part-time employees in a midwestern department store. During the period studied, the women under 30 were available for work an average of 103 days, as compared with an average of 412 days by those over 60. In addition, merit wage increases were obtained by 57 per cent of those over 60 but by only 11 per cent of those under 30.

Discussions of the effects of the menopause on women have been presented by August (1956) and by MacFarlane (1956).

Differences in the retirement patterns of men and women have been explored by Palmore (1965), based on data from a 1963 survey by the Social Security Administration. He reports that higher-paid men are less likely to retire than are those with lower income, primarily because their jobs are more interesting and there is less compulsion on them to retire. No such relationships exist among women workers, although women are much more likely to retire voluntarily than are men.

The Working Wife and Mother

✻ ✻ ✻ EFFECTS ON THE HOME

✻ ✻ MARITAL ADJUSTMENT. Research concerning the effects of the wife's employment on marital adjustment has produced conflicting results. Studies in which working women rated themselves as less satisfied with their marriage than did comparable groups of non-working women include those by Powell (1963b) of mothers of adolescents, by Gover (1963) of working-class women, and by Rossman and Campbell (1965) of college graduates. On the other hand, Warren (1959) reported that working wives had a higher marital adjustment score than those not working among a group of college graduates. Finally, studies by Locke and Mackeprang (1949) and by Nolan (1963b) failed to locate significant differences in marital adjustment when working and non-working wives were compared.

In a study by Nye (1959b), employed mothers reported more marital conflict than did those who weren't working, but there was no over-all difference in marital happiness, suggesting that other satisfactions balanced marital dissatisfactions for the working wives. Nye (1961) has also found that poor marital adjustment is more likely to be associated with employment of the wife if either the husband or the wife is dissatisfied with the wife's working, or if the family is of low socioeconomic status.

✻ ✻ POWER STRUCTURE. Studies by Blood and Hamblin (1958) and by Hoffman (1960) agree that husbands of working wives participate more in household tasks than do husbands whose wives do not work outside the home, but that the actual power structure doesn't vary much. Heer (1958, 1962), however, has reported that husbands have more influence on decisions in families in which the wife doesn't work, especially at the working-class level. Also, there is more disagreement as to the power structure among working-class families in which the wife works.

✻ ✻ ROLE OF WIFE AND MOTHER. Sears, Maccoby, and Levin (1957) reported that employment prior to the arrival of the first child had no negative effect on the attitude toward having children or on the shift to a housewife and mother role among the women in their study. In a study by Feld (1963), women who worked outside the home reported more doubts about their adequacy as mothers than did those who didn't work, and Kligler (1958) found that women who worked because of a real interest in their jobs were more likely to report that their working had a favorable effect on their role as mothers than were women who worked out of financial necessity.

Nye (1963d) reports a study in which working and nonworking mothers of school-age children were compared on a satisfaction questionnaire involving 7 areas. He concluded that the working mothers were more satisfied with their jobs than nonworking mothers were with housework.

❧ ❧ ❧ THE HUSBAND'S ATTITUDE. Among the variables which Weil (1961) found to be related to current work status and future work plans among a group of young mothers were the husband's attitude toward his wife's employment, his willingness to help with child care and household chores, the educational or training level required in the jobs held before marriage, and whether the wife had continued to work after marriage.

Axelson (1963) compared the attitudes of husbands of working and nonworking wives. Those whose wives did not work felt that a working mother was detrimental to her children, that having their wives working would be harmful to their own careers, and that they would not be inclined to make adjustments in their way of life so that their wives could work.

In a study of cases seen by the Marriage Council of Philadelphia, Gianopulos and Mitchell (1957) concluded that the husband whose wife works against his wishes tends to perceive more marital conflict than does the husband whose wife does not work or works with his approval, although the actual amount of conflict was judged to be about the same in all three groups. As a result, in families in which the husband disapproved of his wife's working, the husband and wife tended to perceive many areas of marriage differently.

❧ ❧ ❧ THE MOTHER-CHILD RELATIONSHIP. Among the many summaries of research concerning the effects of maternal employment on children, the most useful are those by Stolz (1960) and by Siegel and Haas (1963).

❧ ❧ EFFECTS ON THE CHILD. Burchinal and Rossman (1961) found no significant relationship between maternal employment and personality scores, school achievement, school absences, school activity, or community activity of their children. Nolan (1963a) reports similar results as well as the finding that adolescents with employed mothers were rated *more* favorably and showed *better* academic achievement and peer acceptance than those whose mothers didn't work.

❧ *Adjustment.* Essig and Morgan (1946) reported that adolescent girls whose mothers worked showed poorer adjustment than those whose mothers were not employed. Stolz (1960), however, has criticized this study on the grounds that a number of variables, including socioeconomic status, were not controlled. Studies by Hand (1957) and by Nye, Perry, and Ogles (1963) failed to locate significant differences in adjustment between children of working and nonworking mothers.

Rouman (1956) analyzed the problems of children sent to a school guidance department by their teachers and found that those with employed mothers had proportionately more withdrawing behavior and fewer academic problems than those whose mothers didn't work.

❧ *Juvenile Delinquency.* Nye (1959a) compared adolescents whose mothers were and were not employed. He found no significant differences in educational achievement or anxiety, but found that the children of employed mothers were more likely to be delinquent. By contrast, in a study of 52 middle-class families Bandura and Walters (1959) found that 9 of the 26 boys in the delinquent group had employed mothers, as compared with 12 of 26 in the nondelinquent group.

Evidence that children whose mothers work irregularly have a higher delinquency rate than those whose mothers work steadily comes from research by Glueck and Glueck (1957).

❧ *Personality Development.* Siegel *et al.* (1959) compared matched pairs of young children whose mothers did and did not work. No significant differences were found in the independence level of the children.

Douvan (1963) found that the daughters of working mothers, who had little time to spend with them, were judged to be less independent than other girls, as evidenced by their tendency to go steady more frequently and to have more difficulty finding things to do with their time. By contrast, the daughters of mothers who worked part time and who seemed to have made an extra effort to spend time with them were judged to be independent and self-assertive. Similarly, Yarrow (1961) found that girls whose mothers were satisfied with their role, whether they were employed or not, were more independent than girls whose mothers were dissatisfied, the difference being greater among girls whose mothers were house-wives than among those whose mothers worked.

Evidence that children of employed mothers have higher achievement needs than those whose mothers are not employed comes from research by Powell (1961, 1963a). Frankel (1964) has reported a study of gifted students in a New York City high school in which 80 per cent of the low achievers had employed mothers, as compared with 50 per cent of the high achievers.

Duvall (1955) questioned kindergarten and first-grade children concerning women's roles. There was little difference between the children of working and nonworking mothers in their perception of women's roles, although the children of working mothers showed greater preference for the mother working. Hartley (1960a) ob-tained similar results, but found some tendency toward perceived differences among the boys but not among the girls. She also found that the majority of children thought that their parents were un-happy at having to leave their children to go to work, while the children of working mothers were slightly more likely to believe that the mother was unhappy.

☙ ☙ RELATED VARIABLES. McCord, McCord, and Thurber (1963) report data from a study of lower-class boys begun in the 1930's, which show maternal employment to be associated with a higher rate of criminality among unstable families.

Evidence that the mother's satisfaction with her role has an important influence on her child-raising practices comes from a study by Yarrow (1961).

☙ ☙ MECHANISMS OF INFLUENCE. Heinicke (1956) compared chil-dren of working mothers who were kept in a day nursery with children in residential nurseries who were temporarily separated from their parents. Within a few days, the latter group had become more disturbed and resistant than were the children in the day nursery.

Among the studies which have failed to locate a relationship between the work status of mothers and their attitudes toward raising children are those by Powell (1961, 1963a) and by McCord, McCord, and Thurber (1963), while Nye (1963d) has reported that full-time working mothers have more favorable attitudes toward their children than do those who do not work outside the home. Yarrow et al. (1962) found that a mother's employment status has little effect on her child-rearing practices, provided that she is in the role she prefers.

A study by von Mering (1955) shows that mothers who are employed tend to emphasize discipline and independence in raising their children, while those who do not work are more protective, empathetic, and understanding.

✤ *Child-Care Provisions.* According to a survey by the Bureau of the Census of the child-care arrangements of full-time working mothers with children under 12, the children of 56 per cent of the women were cared for by their fathers, older siblings, or other relatives; 20 per cent by nonrelatives, usually neighbors; 16 per cent by group facilities; and 8 per cent cared for themselves (Lajewski, 1959). Perry (1961) has confirmed that mother substitutes generally have no formal training in child care.

Evidence that having more than one mother figure during infancy is not harmful comes from research by Gardner, Hawkes, and Burchinal (1961), and Mace (1961) reports that children in Russia who are cared for in day nurseries so that their mothers may work show no ill effects.

Data concerning the part-time employment rate among women come from the Women's Bureau (1963, 1966a).

Nye (1959a) reports that full-time employed mothers were more likely to have a college education and to be of higher socioeconomic status than other women, while there was little difference between unemployed mothers and those who worked part-time in this respect.

The Career Woman

MOST STUDIES of working women have not differentiated between career women and employed housewives, presumably because of the lack of firm criteria by which to make this distinction. Some suggestion of what career women may be like comes from a study of women in the 1948 edition of *Who's Who* (Kiser and Schachter, 1949). Of the 2,400 women studied, 72 per cent had attended college and 55 per cent had graduated; 40 per cent were unmarried and 41 per cent of those who were married had no children. A subsequent study of women in the 1962 edition of *Who's Who* (Frank and Kiser, 1965) showed that few changes had taken place during the 14-year interval, although the latter group showed a trend toward a higher rate of marriage and fertility.

❧ ❧ ❧ THE DECISION TO SEEK A CAREER. Ellis (1952) compared a group of unmarried career women who were occupationally mobile—i.e., whose occupations were considerably higher than those of their fathers—with women who were classified as "nonmobile," and concluded that the mobile group had undergone more humiliating childhood experiences, had experienced more rejection by community and parents, had fewer friends, and had more psychosomatic symptoms than those who stayed at the same class level.

Roe (1960) has considered the relationship of women's personal needs to satisfactions derived from employment, using Maslow's hierarchy of needs as a basis. She points out that many of the needs which Maslow has postulated—such as the need for belongingness and love, the need for information, and the need for beauty—can be satisfied within the context of being a wife and mother, while others, such as the need for self-esteem, can be met by a job which is secondary to her housewife role. However, Roe suggests that the highest need in the hierarchy—the need for self-actualization—could be best served within the context of a career.

❧ ❧ ❧ PROFESSIONAL CAREERS FOR WOMEN

❧ ❧ EDUCATION. Data concerning the sex ratio among teachers have been reported by the National Education Association (1967).

Swanson and Berdie (1961) found that girls in the College of

Education at the University of Minnesota compared favorably in scholastic ability with girls in the other colleges, confirming Thiede's (1950) results at the University of Wisconsin. Votaw and Moses (1956) found that women students in a teachers college made higher grades than did the men. Both Anderson (1952) and Mitchell (1957) have reported that girls majoring in education tend to have nonprofessional interests.

Scandrette (1962) administered the Edwards Personal Preference Schedule to elementary and secondary school student teachers. The elementary teachers scored higher on deference, order, and affiliation, and lower on autonomy and aggression than did the norm group; the secondary teachers scored higher on order and dominance and lower on affiliation and succorance. Nance (1949) reported that both men and women education majors scored more feminine on the MMPI and the Strong than did noneducation majors; among the women education students, the music students were most feminine and the secondary education majors least.

Wright and Tuska (1964) asked 2,650 college women who planned to become teachers to recall who among their mother, father, and teachers was most important in 20 childhood relationships. In general, the teacher was viewed as most important, the father as least. High school trainees recalled positive relationships with their teachers, while grade school trainees recalled teachers as interfering. By contrast, grade school trainees recalled their mothers as a strong positive influence, while high school trainees recalled their mothers as uninteresting and ineffectual. Fathers were recalled by high school trainees as less successful than others, and by grade school trainees as a positive influence.

Durflinger (1963) compared women students who graduated in education with those who started there but switched to other majors. Those who changed majors had higher academic ability and scored lower on the following Strong scales: housewife, home economics teacher, dietitian, physical education teacher, nurse, and dentist.

White (1967) found that higher career commitment among beginning female elementary teachers was associated with having had a working mother, having come from a working-class home, having worked their way through school, and being married.

In a survey of beginning teachers, more than two-thirds of the women reported that they planned to leave teaching eventually, of which more than half "hoped" to return later (Mason, Dressel, and Bain, 1959). According to the National Education Association (1964a), the average age of women teachers is 8 years higher than that of men.

Kuhlen (1963) has reported that satisfaction with teaching is much more dependent on need satisfaction among men than among women, but that neither male nor female teachers are strongly career oriented.

Data concerning the proportion of women in administrative positions in education have been reported by the National Education Association (1963b, 1964b).

St. John (1965) has reported the results of a questionnaire survey of the attitudes of parents of school children toward women teachers. Fathers were more restrictive of women teachers than were mothers, and they tended to expect behavior from women teachers which they didn't expect from other employed women.

Data concerning the proportion of women among college teachers have been presented by Parrish (1962), by Bernard (1964), and by Dunham and Wright (1965).

Eckert and Stecklein (1961) surveyed 700 Minnesota college teachers, of whom 27 per cent were women, concerning their job motivations and satisfactions. As compared with the men, the women had made a more tentative career choice, regarded college teaching less favorably as a personal goal, and were more influenced by external circumstances (such as encouragement by professors or unsolicited job offers) than by job-related factors in entering the field. The authors concluded that most women are too modest to aspire to become college professors.

❧ ❧ SCIENCE. According to the National Science Foundation (1964), only 7 per cent of the scientists who completed the National Register of Scientific and Technical Personnel in 1964 were women.

Information concerning women in physical science occupations comes from the Women's Bureau (1959a), from Parrish (1965), and from Bolt (1965). Parrish (1965) found that employers were reluctant to hire women for laboratory positions and were also reluctant to employ them on a part-time basis, although those companies which did had had satisfactory results.

Information concerning women in the biological sciences comes from the Women's Bureau (1961a) and from Rossi (1965b), while information concerning women as science technicians comes from the Women's Bureau (1961c).

❧ ❧ MATHEMATICS AND STATISTICS. Information concerning women in mathematics and statistics comes from the Women's Bureau (1956c) and from Rossi (1965b).

❧ ❧ ENGINEERING. Data concerning women engineers come from Torpey (1962), from Wolfle (1964), and from Rossi (1965b). Information concerning the employment characteristics of women engineers comes from Barth (1954), Bolt (1965), Hill (1965), and the Society of Women Engineers (1963).

⚹ ⚹ MEDICINE. Information concerning female physicians comes from Williams (1946, 1950), from Kosa and Coker (1965), and from Rossi (1965b). In the mid-1940's, Lowther and Downes (1945) reported that 82 per cent of the married women graduates of 7 medical schools were still professionally active, and there is no evidence that this figure has changed much since then.

Data concerning the backgrounds of nursing students have been presented by Berdie (1954) and by Berdie and Hood (1965). The interest patterns of nursing students have been studied by Triggs (1948), by Healy and Borg (1953), by Mitchell (1957), and by O'Neil and Madaus (1966). Among the studies which have attempted to predict success in nurses' training are those by Gunnell and Nutting (1957), Garrett (1960), Kirk, Goodstein, and Cummings (1961), and Haney, Michael, and Gershon (1962). Church (1953) has offered some suggestions as to how the number of nurses might be increased.

Information concerning medical technologists comes from the Women's Bureau (1954).

⚹ ⚹ LAW. Information concerning women lawyers comes from the Women's Bureau (1958) and from Parrish (1961), and Mitchell (1957) has studied the interest patterns of women law students.

⚹ ⚹ PSYCHOLOGY. Data concerning the proportion of women psychologists employed in various kinds of jobs come from a study by Fjeld and Ames (1950), and information concerning their careers comes from a study by Bryan and Boring (1947).

⚹ ⚹ SOCIAL WORK. Data concerning female social workers come from a report by Baker (1965).

⚹ ⚹ BUSINESS. Information concerning women as business executives comes from reports by Fuller and Batchelder (1953) and by Hamill (1956). Evidence concerning the academic ability of girls majoring in business administration comes from a study by Watley and Martin (1962), while Mitchell (1957) has studied the interest patterns of female business students. The backgrounds of girls who enter noncollege business schools have been analyzed by Berdie (1954) and by Berdie and Hood (1965).

Hamill (1956) has reported a study by Social Research, Inc., of 60 successful female executives, from which it was concluded that their common attributes were practicality, organizational skill, sensitivity to people, adaptability, high energy, high confidence, and a strong achievement drive.

A study by Gurr (1956) of 36 successful women executives revealed certain similarities in abilities and personal characteristics, but also wide differences in some areas.

Information concerning opportunities for women in retailing comes from the Women's Bureau (1959b).

The Education of the
High School Girl

CENSUS DATA concerning average educational levels of men and women have been reported by Hauser (1962). According to the National Manpower Council (1957), 57 per cent of all 17-year-old boys and 63 per cent of the girls graduated from high school in 1956, while the National Education Association (1963e) reports that 53 per cent of the high school graduates in June, 1962, were girls.

According to a government report entitled, "What High School Pupils Study" (quoted by Baer, 1963b), 77 per cent of high school girl graduates in 1958 earned at least 16½ credits, as compared with only 64 per cent of the boys. Conant (1959) reported that, within the academically talented group (upper 15 per cent) in the 22 high schools he surveyed, the boys tended to earn more credits than did the girls.

Information concerning high school drop-outs among girls comes from the Bureau of Labor Statistics (1960b) and the National Education Association (1963e).

❧ ❧ ❧ THE EDUCATIONAL NEEDS OF GIRLS. Sutherland (1961) compared boys and girls in both coeducational and segregated (unisexual) schools in Ireland on a standardized achievement test. The boys in the coeducational schools did better than those in boys' schools, but the girls in coeducational schools did less well than those in girls' schools. Tagatz (1966) found no evidence of achievement differences between coeducational and segregated sex groupings in the first and second grades, and the teachers preferred the coeducational classes. Fisher and Waetjen (1966) compared coeducational and segregated eighth grade classes within the same school. They found no significant differences in English achievement and slight evidence of superiority for the coeducational classes in Reading Vocabulary. In a study of ex-grammar school pupils in England, Dale (1966) found that both the men and women graduates of coeducational schools were strongly in favor of them.

Graduates of men's schools also favored their kind of experience, but graduates of women's schools were less pleased with their experience.

❧ ❧ ❧ CURRICULUM CHOICE IN HIGH SCHOOL. Cass and Tiedeman (1960) related eighteen variables to choice of curriculum (college preparatory, general, commercial, home economics, industrial arts, and agriculture) among high school freshmen in Maine and concluded that sex was 6 times more influential than any other variable, including ability, in determining curriculum choice. The industrial arts curricula were composed entirely of boys, the home economics courses contained only girls, the commercial students were almost all girls, while no girls were found in agriculture programs. The general and college preparatory curricula had approximately equal sex ratios, although the Project Talent survey has subsequently reported that at the twelfth grade level a slight majority of students in both programs are boys (Flanagan *et al.*, 1964).

Cass and Tiedeman also reported that several variables differentiated between boys in agriculture programs and those in industrial arts, but none differentiated between girls in home economics and those in commercial courses. The factors which lead girls to choose one or the other of these programs are obscure.

Data collected by Conant (1959) in his national survey revealed decided sex differences in enrollment in various sequences of courses. The major finding was that boys take a great deal more math and science than do girls in high school. For example, within the 22 schools which he studied, the percentage of boys who took at least 3 years of math ranged from 55 to 100, with a median of 90; the percentage of girls taking the same amount ranged from 0 to 85, with a median of 40.

❧ ❧ ❧ POST-HIGH SCHOOL PLANS. Berdie (1954) found that between 60 and 70 per cent of the high school senior girls in his survey reported that their major goal was to become a housewife within 10 years.

A study of Minnesota high school seniors by Berdie and Hood (1965) revealed that 45 per cent of the boys and 37 per cent of the girls planned to attend college following graduation. In the Project Talent survey of 90,000 high school seniors, the percentages were higher: 53 per cent of the boys and 46 per cent of the girls planned to attend college immediately, while 73 per cent of the boys and 53 per cent of the girls said they planned to attend eventually (Flanagan *et al.*, 1964). Subsequent follow-up of this group revealed that 49 per cent of the boys and 35 per cent of the girls actually attended college immediately (Flanagan, 1964).

On the basis of a study of seniors in three Florida colleges, Miller (1960) concluded that girls are more likely than boys to choose both their occupation and major before entering college.

Both Cutright (1960) and Matthews (1960) have reported that more girls are interested in college between the ages of 11 and 14 than later.

Studies by Flanagan et al. (1964) and by Berdie and Hood (1965) agree that ability is a better predictor of college plans among boys than among girls. According to the National Manpower Council (1957), only 66 per cent of the boys and 54 per cent of the girls in the top 30 per cent of high school seniors in ability were in college preparatory curricula in the mid-1950's.

Studies by Cutright (1960) and by Berdie and Hood (1965) have shown that socioeconomic variables predict college plans better for girls than for boys. Berdie and Hood (1965) also report that girls from small towns and farms are likely to attend a nursing school or business school instead of college if money is short.

✺ ✺ ✺ ACCELERATION. Among those with IQ's over 170 in Terman's gifted group, the boys were 3 months ahead of the girls in average grade placement by the eighth grade, 4 months ahead by high school graduation, and 9 months ahead by college graduation (Terman and Oden, 1947). Similarly, only 25 per cent of the students chosen for the Ford Foundation program for special admission to college following the eleventh grade were girls (Fund for the Advancement of Education, 1957).

In a study of children who had been accelerated in elementary school, Weinstein et al. (1966) found that 32 per cent of the girls and 62 per cent of the boys had had some difficulty in adjustment, which supports the observation by Terman and Oden (1947) that the male accelerates in their gifted group had more problems in adjustment than did the females.

Early studies by Engle (1935) and by Terman and Oden (1947) found that girls who were accelerated had no subsequent advantage in scholastic achievement or occupational status over those who proceeded at the normal rate, although such an advantage was observed for the boys who were accelerated. A more recent study by Flesher and Pressey (1955), however, of female college students accelerated during World War II showed that, 10 years later, the accelerates were twice as likely to have earned further degrees, as compared with a matched group who were not accelerated, as well as more likely to be currently employed.

The College Girl: Who She Is and Why She's There

A GOOD DESCRIPTION of the history of higher education for women has been presented by Newcomer (1959).

≉ ≉ ≉ FACTS AND FIGURES. Data concerning the numbers and proportion of women among college students come from Cass (1961) and the Women's Bureau (1966a). Estimates of the proportion of capable persons who actually obtain the doctorate come from the National Manpower Council (1957).

≉ ≉ ≉ WHY IS SHE THERE? Studies of girls' motives for attending college have been conducted by Hopwood (1954), Iffert (1958), and Irish (1962). In a study by Whithey, McLeod, and Swinehart (quoted by Douvan and Kaye, 1962), adults were asked for their conceptions of the function of college in our society. Thirty-two per cent mentioned marital benefits for girls, as compared with only 3 per cent who thought it would benefit boys in this way. Haller and Sewell (1957) found no difference in educational aspiration between rural and urban Wisconsin high school seniors, but Berdie and Hood (1965) report that city girls are more likely to actually go to college. Mueller and Mueller (1949) report that, of girls who enter college, those from small towns are most likely to finish, and that girls from the lower class are not likely to attend college and even less likely to graduate than are girls from higher income families. Stivers (1959) has also found a slight tendency for college-motivated high school girls to come from the higher social classes. Bernard (1964) reports that women in graduate school tend to come from higher income families than do the men.

Both Rose (1956) and Lane (1961) have found that girls who are more likely to attend college are those who are not very close to their families, while the reverse is true among boys. Bordua (1960), however, reports that, when parental emphasis on college attendance is high, girls are more likely to plan to attend, whereas when it is low boys are more likely to go. Hewer and Neubeck

(1962) have reported that female college students tend to come from families in which the father is employed in an upper-level occupation, while Berdie (1954) found that the likelihood of a girl entering college is increased if her mother is a teacher.

Thistlethwaite (1963) reports that boys tend to get larger scholarships for college than do girls, and Baer (1963a) reports that only one-third of the National Merit Scholarships are awarded to girls. Figures concerning graduate fellowships awarded to women also come from Baer (1963a). Information concerning Woodrow Wilson fellowships comes from the Woodrow Wilson Foundation (1961).

Havighurst (1960) has reported that, in the fall of 1960, 16 per cent of the men and 27 per cent of the women in the upper two quartiles of ability were not in college, and Stalnaker (1961) has noted that, among those students who had scored in the upper one-third of the National Merit Exam, only 77 per cent of the girls entered college as compared with 87 per cent of the boys. Data concerning Terman's gifted group come from the report by Terman and Oden (1959).

Based on data from a survey of 120,000 students entering 250 colleges, Werts (1966) concluded that, among low-ability students, boys are more likely than girls to enter college, but that there was no difference at the upper levels of ability. The same relationship was true for social class, with more boys than girls entering college from the lower levels but the difference decreasing at higher levels.

✷ ✷ ✷ CHOICE OF A COLLEGE. Reasons why girls choose one college over another have been explored by Holland (1958, 1959) and by Stone, Kennedy, and Danskin (1963).

✷ ✷ ✷ CHOICE OF A CURRICULUM. Most of the data concerning enrollment of girls in various college curricula comes from the Women's Bureau (1966a).

According to the Project Talent research, the more intelligent girls tend to major in English in college, while those with less ability are more likely to become teachers (Flanagan, 1964).

In a study of the curriculum choices of National Merit semi-finalists, Nichols (1964) reported that between 1956 and 1963 the girls showed an increased interest in biology, math, and social sciences and a lessened interest in medical technology, education, journalism, and home economics as majors. The *Science News Letter* (December 30, 1961) reports that the increase in the number of college students graduating with degrees in science and math has been due mostly to an increase in the number of women majoring in these fields. According to Parrish (1961), the proportion of women receiving doctorates in science and math has declined by 50 per cent since 1930.

Newcomer (1959) reports a study in which comparisons were made between the majors of students in 6 large state universities and those in 8 small liberal arts colleges for men and women separately (4 of each sex). There was little difference in the sex ratio among math majors in the various universities, but within the colleges, women tended to predominate in this field. History and philosophy majors within the small colleges were more commonly men. The majority of the political science majors in the small colleges were women, while in the universities the majority were men.

Isaacson (1964) examined the relationship between curriculum choice and achievement need and found among male students a tendency for those with higher achievement orientation to select majors of intermediate difficulty, but no relationship among women.

✿ ✿ ✿ NEEDS OF COLLEGE GIRLS. Among the educators who have urged colleges to be more flexible in handling the credits of female students are Newcomer (1959), Habein (1960), and Blackwell (1963).

✿ ✿ ✿ HOW SHOULD GIRLS BE EDUCATED? Information concerning women's colleges comes primarily from Newcomer (1959). Both White (1950) and Norris (1954) have presented strong arguments in favor of educating women in separate colleges designed for them alone. Arlen (1962) has described the amalgamation of Radcliffe and Harvard.

Among those who have opposed the view that women's education should stress the homemaking role are McBride (1947), Loutitt (1951), Mueller (1954a), and Mendenhall (1960). Among those who have favored a liberal arts approach to the education of girls are Komarovsky (1953), Roberts (1953), Dement (1960), Mendenhall (1960), and Mead (1961b).

Carmichael (1964) has reported on the MA-3 programs, available in many universities, in which talented undergraduates aim for a master's degree with emphasis on college teaching as a future occupation, and their work is telescoped accordingly. As of the fall of 1963, the enrollment in these programs was about equally divided between men and women, although requests for admission came more frequently from women. The schools argued that they had to limit the number of women admitted so that the program would not become identified as a woman's program.

The Use and Abuse of Higher Education for Women

✣ ✣ ✣ ADJUSTMENT TO COLLEGE. Summerskill and Darling (1955) have reported that women students get better grades than do men; and Weitz and his associates (Weitz, Clarke, and Jones, 1955; Weitz and Colver, 1959) have found that college men who declare a major do better than those who are undecided, while no such relationship exists for the girls.

Evidence that the more successful female college students tend to be more serious, more mature, and better organized than the others comes from studies by Kuaak (1956) and D. Brown (1960).

There has been little research concerning the characteristics of girls who are most likely to have adjustment problems in college. Heilbrun (1960, 1962a) reports that girls with strong needs for autonomy, succorance, and change, as well as those who have identified more strongly with their mothers than with their fathers, are apt to have greater difficulty in adjusting to college, but this is about the limit of the available evidence.

Evidence that the drop-out rate for men and women college students is about the same comes from research by Darley (1962), Summerskill (1962), Thistlethwaite (1963), and Flanagan (1964). Astin (1964) reports that girls who drop out are less likely to return than boys. Thistlethwaite (1963) and Astin (1964) have found a greater frequency of drop-outs among high-ability girls than among high-ability boys, but Darley (1962) reports that this discrepancy disappears after the first two years of college.

Numerous studies (Summerskill and Darling, 1955; Darley, 1962; Thistlethwaite, 1963; Astin, 1964; Flanagan, 1964) agree that girls are less likely than boys to flunk out of college but are more apt to leave for nonacademic reasons. Among these reasons, the most common are lack of money, desire to marry, or desire to work instead (U.S. Office of Education, 1957a; Thistlethwaite, 1963; Astin, 1964; Flanagan, 1964).

Astin (1964) has found that satisfaction with initial career choice is related to retention in college among men but not among

women, and Darley (1962) has reported that the school entered
plays a more important role in continuation in college for girls
than for boys.

Hood (1957) has reported that girls from small towns, those
who are engaged or going steady when they enter college, or those
who have a history of social isolation are more likely to drop out;
Aiken (1964) adds poor high school grades as another indication.
On the basis of performance on the Minnesota Counseling Inventory, F. Brown (1960) found that drop-outs among female
students were more deviant than were drop-outs among the males.
The male drop-outs tended to be irresponsible and non-conforming,
while the female drop-outs tended to be withdrawn and depressed.
Lehman, Sinha, and Hartnett (1966) found that females who stayed
in college showed a more marked attitude change after 4 years than
did those who dropped out, while both groups of men changed
about the same amount. Williamson *et al.* (1954) and Summerskill
and Darling (1955) agree that girls are more likely than boys to
participate in activities in college, so that failure of a girl to become involved in college life makes her more of a deviant than it
would for a boy.

♪ ♪ ♪ EDUCATIONAL PATTERNS. The Vassar studies, one of
the best-known approaches to the analysis of educational patterns
among college women, have been presented by Sanford *et al.* (1956).

Differences in educational patterns may also be reflected in
attitudes toward various kinds of courses, an assumption which
forms the basis for a study reported by Lewis, Wolins, and Yelsma
(1967). Junior and senior undergraduates in the College of Home
Economics at Iowa State University, as well as first-year alumnae,
were asked to give their reactions to 17 courses included in the
Home Economics core curriculum. On the basis of their responses,
6 factors were located and were defined in terms of the courses loading most heavily on each. These factors were: (a) a general factor;
(b) human relations (high positive loadings by the introductory
psychology and sociology courses, negative loadings by laboratory
courses); (c) English (high loadings by freshmen English courses);
(d) science vs. arts (positive loadings by chemistry and foods courses,
negative loading by art); (e) general attitude toward home economics
courses (high loadings by all introductory home economics courses);
and (f) an intellectual factor (positive loading by chemistry, negative loading by physical education).

♪ ♪ ♪ AFTER COLLEGE. Christensen and Swihart (1956) asked
senior women at Purdue University to state their role preferences
at various periods following graduation. All wanted to be married

within 5 years, and 90 per cent wanted to be full-time housewives up to 10 years in the future.

✄ ✄ EDUCATION AND MARRIAGE. Data concerning the percentage of college women who are married is inconsistent. Havemann and West (1952) found that only about 70 per cent of their sample of about 4,000 college women were married, but Bowman (1949) and Lyle (1957) have both reported figures close to 90 per cent, and a survey by the Women's Bureau (1966c) of college women 7 years after graduation found that 85 per cent had been married within that time.

On the basis of an analysis of data from the 1950 Census, Brunner and Wayland (1958) reported that the proportion of single women increases with amount of education, except for a low marriage rate among illiterates, and Ginzberg et al. (1966) found that 28 per cent of a group of women who had attended graduate or professional school were still single 12 years later. Freedman (1962), however, reports that this relationship has been decreasing since World War II.

In different samples of women college graduates, Chervenik (1955, 1956) and Leopold (1959) found that one-third were married within 6 months following graduation. In Terman's gifted group, the proportion of women who were married was somewhat below that of the general population in 1940, but by 1945 the marriage rate was equal to that of the general population (Terman and Oden, 1947).

Studies by Havemann and West (1952) and by Brunner and Wayland (1958) agree in finding that the divorce rate among female college graduates is lower than average. Brunner and Wayland (1958) report that the fertility rate among college-educated women is below average, and Lauriat (1959) found that the fertility rate among college men is higher than among college women. Several studies (Brunner and Wayland, 1958; Smuts, 1959; Lauriat, 1959), however, agree that the fertility differential between women who have and have not been to college is decreasing, since college graduates are now having more children than they used to.

✄ ✄ EMPLOYMENT. Data concerning employment rates among college-educated women come from Chervenik (1955), Lyle (1957), Zapoleon (1953, 1961), and the Women's Bureau (1963, 1966a, 1966c).

✄ ✄ ADVANCED DEGREES. Data concerning women receiving advanced degrees come from Bernard (1964). Harmon (1965) has found that women who obtained doctorates between 1959 and 1962 had done better in high school and had higher IQ scores than men who obtained doctorates in the same field, and that married women were superior to single women in intelligence. In an analysis of post-graduation activities of National Merit Scholars, Nichols and Astin (1966) found that 87 per cent of the boys and 69 per cent of the girls entered a graduate or professional school.

Gropper and Fitzpatrick (1959) have reported that women who enter graduate school tend to make this decision later than do men and to have been more influenced by their undergraduate experiences. Davis (1964) reports that girls who are married or who plan to be married soon after graduation are less likely to plan on graduate school than are those who are still unattached, and that the decision to enter graduate school is less highly related to ability among women than among men.

Schletzer (1963) has reported a survey of graduates from the graduate program in psychology at the University of Minnesota between 1953 and 1962, of whom 28 per cent of the master's degrees and 16 per cent of the Ph.D.'s were earned by women. She found that 65 per cent of the women were working full time and another 24 per cent part time.

Two studies of graduates of women's colleges shed some light on the question of the use which women make of the Ph.D., although these women may not be typical of women Ph.D.'s from other universities. A survey in the early 1950's of 258 Ph.D.'s from Bryn Mawr (Bliss, 1954) showed that 95 per cent had been employed at some time during their lives, and that 75 per cent of those of working age were currently employed; 60 per cent were in college or university teaching, with most of the remainder in administration, scientific research, or school teaching.

A similar survey was made of Ph.D.'s from Radcliffe College (Radcliffe Committee on Graduate Education for Women, 1956), of whom more than one-third were employed as college teachers. Of the 175 who were married, 31 were employed full time, 29 part time, 32 were "temporarily unemployed," and 41 were classified as "nonworkers." These groups seemed to differ in a number of ways. The full-time workers were generally a young group and seemed to have little difficulty in combining family and career responsibilities. By contrast, the part-time workers and the temporarily unemployed felt that their children had interrupted their careers; they were concerned with a marriage-career conflict, which they had apparently not resolved to their satisfaction. As far as productivity is concerned, 13 per cent had published at least one book or between 10 and 19 articles, but 21 per cent had published only one or two articles and 29 per cent had never published at all.

❧ ❧ THE WASTE OF WOMEN'S EDUCATION. Among those writers who have criticized educated women for not making worthwhile use of their education are Sanders (1960), Rice (1961), and Friedan (1963).

Stephenson (1960) questioned women students in an elementary education program concerning their post-graduation plans and found that 82 per cent planned to be married and working 5 years after graduation, but a 5-year follow-up revealed that only 40 per cent were both married and employed.

Hornung (1955) surveyed 100 faculty wives at the University of Indiana, with an average age of 39 and an average of 4½ years of college. Most reported that they disliked housework, yet only 23 per cent were employed, primarily due to lack of job opportunities related to their college training. Two-thirds felt that their college education had been of little practical value for them, and one-fourth said they would change their college major if they were to do it again.

❧ ❧ ❧ COLLEGE PROGRAMS FOR THE MATURE WOMAN. Halfter (1962) compared women undergraduates over the age of 40 with women between the ages of 18 and 25. The average performance of the older women was above the mean for the younger women in nearly all curricula, although there was no difference in high school performance.

Toward Enlightened Planning

✣ ✣ ✣ THE MAJOR DECISIONS THAT GIRLS MUST MAKE

✣ ✣ VOCATIONAL CHOICE. In a study of female college graduates, Warren (1959) found that job satisfaction was greater among women who held jobs in line with their interests, who were working because they wanted a career rather than out of financial need or boredom, who were working in a field related to their college major, and whose undergraduate major and interests were compatible.

✣ ✣ THE MARRIAGE-CAREER DILEMMA. Tyler (1964) has reported a longitudinal study of interests comparing the patterns of twelfth-grade girls with career and noncareer goals. She found that these girls could, by the eleventh grade, be differentiated on the Strong Vocational Interest Blank, with a greater difference on the scales related to business than on those related to homemaking, but that there were few consistent differences between the two groups prior to high school. The career-oriented girls did show more masculine interests in the first grade, but this difference disappeared later, and the career-oriented girls actually scored more feminine on the Strong by the end of high school. The career-oriented girls also scored higher on ability tests, a finding confirmed by Rezler (1967).

Differences between career-oriented and homemaking-oriented girls on the Strong Vocational Interest Blank have also been established by Hoyt and Kennedy (1958) and by Vetter and Lewis (1964). Personality characteristics of the two groups have been investigated by Hoyt and Kennedy (1958) and by Tyler (1964), and background characteristics have been described by Kosa, Rachiele, and Schommer (1962), by Zissis (1962), and by Vetter and Lewis (1964).

✣ ✣ ✣ TOOLS AND TECHNIQUES TO AID PLANNING

✣ ✣ PSYCHOLOGICAL TESTING OF GIRLS. The Minnesota Interest Test for Girls has been described by Tyler (1941), and Drinkwater (1960) has reported an interest inventory related specifically to physical education for women. Montague (1960) factor analyzed the responses of 200 women college students to a 300-item interest inventory consisting of reactions to job titles, school subjects, job tasks, etc. The factors obtained included mathematics, entertainment, art, human welfare, biological and physical science, business, written communication, and agricultural-outdoor.

In a study of the Kuder Form D, a forerunner of the Occupational Interest Inventory which was limited almost entirely to occupations in which men predominate, Hornaday and Kuder (1961) found that the keys developed for men differentiated equally well among women in 9 of 10 occupations, the exception being the librarian key. In a factor analysis of women's responses to the same inventory, Schutz and Baker (1962) reported a factor structure similar to that obtained previously with men.

General data concerning the performance of women on the Strong Vocational Interest Blank have been summarized by Darley and Hagenah (1955).

Dunteman (1966) has reported that a multiple discriminant-function analysis of the scales on the women's form of the SVIB differentiated successfully among students majoring in occupational therapy, physical therapy, medical technology, nursing, and education. Harmon (1967) classified women in a longitudinal study according to whether they had worked since college and for how long. Except for a small group of single women who had always worked, the groups of employed women could not be differentiated by their Strong responses while in college in terms of the jobs they had held since.

Seder (1940a, 1940b) compared the interest patterns obtained on both the men's and women's forms of the SVIB by women physicians and life insurance saleswomen and found that they were similar on the two forms. Stewart (1959) analyzed the responses of National Merit Scholars to the men's form of the SVIB and found that the interest patterns of the males and females were more alike than was the case among other college students, although the women had a much lower M-F score. On the other hand, McCormack (1954) found that female social workers showed different patterns on the male and female forms of the SVIB.

⁂ ⁂ OCCUPATIONAL INFORMATION. The best sources of up-to-date information concerning occupational opportunities for women are the booklets issued by the Women's Bureau of the U.S. Department of Labor. They deal with specific occupations, or occupational areas, for both college-educated girls and for those with only a high school education.

Other sources of information which girls may find helpful include a series of leaflets describing opportunities in business, published by the Harvard-Radcliffe Program in Business Administration under the title *A Profile of Jobs for Women;* career leaflets appropriate for high school seniors or beginning college students, as well as booklets for adult women, published by the Women's Program of the New York State Department of Commerce, 230 Park Ave., New York City; and a booklet, *Job Opportunities for the Woman College Graduate,* published by the Midwest College Placement Association and available for $3.00 from the Executive Secretary, P. O. Box 2197, West Lafayette, Indiana.

A beginning has also been made in the development of occupational information for mature women. As an outgrowth of the Radcliffe Independent Study Program, White (1964) has edited a collection of information concerning job-hunting procedures and job opportunities for educated women in the Greater Boston area. The specific information is, of course, of immediate value only to women living in or near Boston, but the format might serve as a model for similar projects in other urban areas.

꙰ ꙰ GUIDANCE COUNSELING. Skager and Weinberg (1967) compared high school students who did and did not utilize counseling services. Among the boys, those who sought counseling were more often other-directed, wanting clear clues for guidance in making their plans. Other-directed girls, however, were primarily concerned with being married and having a family and therefore made less use of counseling. The inner-directed girls, by contrast, were more career-oriented and sought counseling help with their career plans.

An example of a counseling program for older women is that described by LaFollette (1956) at the Women's Service Exchange of the Madison, Wisconsin, Vocational and Adult School.

꙰ ꙰ ꙰ WOMEN IN THE WORLD OF THE FUTURE

꙰ ꙰ SCHOOLS AND COLLEGES. A publication by the Women's Bureau (1966b) entitled *Continuing Education Programs for Women* lists 90 colleges and universities which offer special programs of interest to women, varying from short courses to full degree-oriented programs. Dennis (1963) has edited a conference report, *Education and a Woman's Life,* which contains descriptions of some of the more extensive programs, including those at the University of Minnesota, the Kansas City branch of the University of Missouri, Rutgers, Sarah Lawrence, Radcliffe, and Brooklyn College.

The Minnesota Plan for the Continuing Education of Women has been described by Senders (1961, 1962) and by Schletzer (1963). The Radcliffe Institute for Independent Study has been described by Bunting (1961a, 1961b) and by Smith (1962). The Seven Colleges Vocational Workshops have been described by Cronin (1963), and the psychiatric residency program of the New York Medical College has been described by Kaplan, Kaplan, and Freedman (1964).

Denmark and Guttentag (1966) compared women who completed the Adult Continuing Education Program at Queens College with a group who indicated interest but did not enroll. They found that the women who completed the program showed a decreased gap between ratings of present self and ideal self, while the others remained about the same.

Bibliography

Aaronson, B. Age and sex differences on MMPI profile peak distributions on an abnormal population. *J. Consult. Psychol.*, 1958, *22*, 203–6.

———. A comparison of two MMPI measures of masculinity-femininity. *J. Clin. Psychol.*, 1959, *15*, 48–50.

Abel, H., and Sahinkaya, R. Emergence of sex and race friendship preferences. *Child Develpm.*, 1962, *33*, 939–43.

Abelson, R. Sex differences in predictability of college grades. *Educ. Psychol. Measmt.*, 1952, *12*, 638–44.

Abrahms, A. Industry views its elderly workers. In *Birthdays Don't Count.* Legislative Document No. 61. Albany: New York State Leg. Comm. on Problems of the Aging, 1948, pp. 141–62.

Adorno, T. W., *et al. The Authoritarian Personality.* New York: Harper, 1950.

Aiken, L. The prediction of academic success and early attrition by means of a multiple-choice biographical inventory. *Amer. Educ. Res. J.*, 1964, *1*, 127–35.

———, and Dreger, R. The effect of attitudes on performance in mathematics. *J. Educ. Psychol.*, 1961, *52*, 19–24.

Albjerg, Marguerite. Why do bright girls not take stiff courses? *Educ. Forum*, 1961, *25*, 141–44.

Allison, R. B., Jr. Mechanical ability: comparisons of test scores for Naval enlisted men and women. *USN Bur. Nav. Pers. Tech. Bull.*, 1956, No. 56–5, p. ii.

Allport, G., Gillespie, J., and Young, Jacqueline. The religion of the postwar college student. *J. Psychol.*, 1948, *25*, 3–33.

———, Vernon, P., and Lindzey, G. *Study of Values: Manual of Directions.* Boston: Houghton Mifflin, 1951.

Alpenfels, Ethel. The "world of ideas"—do women count? *Educ. Rec.*, 1963, *44*, 40–43.

Alpern, M. L. The ability to test hypotheses. *Sci. Educ.*, 1947, *30*, 220–29.

Amatora, Sister Mary. Free expression of adolescents' interests. *Genet. Psychol. Monogr.*, 1957, *55*, 173–219.

———. Interests of pre-adolescent boys and girls. *Genet. Psychol. Monogr.*, 1960, *61*, 77–113.

Amatora, Sister Mary. Home interests in early adolescence. *Genet. Psychol. Monogr.*, 1962, *65*, 137–74.

Ames, Louise, and Ilg, Frances. Sex differences in test performance of matched girl-boy pairs in the five-to-nine-year-old age range. *J. Genet. Psychol.*, 1964, *104*, 25–34.

———, Metraux, Ruth, and Walter, R. *Adolescent Rorschach Responses.* New York: Paul B. Hoeber, 1959.

Ammons, R. B., and Ammons, H. S. Parent preferences in young children's doll-play interviews. *J. Abnorm. Soc. Psychol.*, 1949, *44*, 490–505.

———, Alprin, S., and Ammons, Carol. Rotary pursuit performance as related to sex and age of pre-adult subjects. *J. Exp. Psychol.*, 1955, *49*, 127–33.

Anastasi, Anne. *Differential Psychology.* (3rd ed.) New York: Macmillan, 1958.

———, and D'Angelo, R. A comparison of Negro and white preschool children in language development and Goodenough Draw-a-Man I.Q. *J. Genet. Psychol.*, 1952, *81*, 147–65.

Andersen, E. E. Sex differences in timidity in normal and gonadectomized rats. *J. Genet. Psychol.*, 1941, *59*, 139–53.

Andersen, Esther. A study of leisure-time reading of pupils in junior high school. *Elem. Sch. J.*, 1948, *48*, 258–67.

Anderson, C. C. A developmental study of dogmatism during adolescence with reference to sex differences. *J. Abnorm. Soc. Psychol.*, 1962, *65*, 132–35.

Anderson, Mary. A descriptive study of values and interests of four groups of graduate women at the University of Minnesota. Doctoral dissertation, Univ. of Minnesota, 1952.

Anderson, Rose. Reported and demonstrated values of vocational counseling. *J. Appl. Psychol.*, 1949, *33*, 460–73.

Andrew, Dorothy, and Paterson, D. G. *Minnesota Clerical Test: Manual.* New York: Psychological Corporation, 1946.

Appley, M. and Loeller, G. Conforming behavior and personality variables in college women. *J. Abnorm. Soc. Psychol.*, 1963, *66*, 284–90.

Archer, E. J., and Bourne, L. E. Inverted-alphabet printing as a function of inter-trial rest and sex. *J. Exp. Psychol.*, 1956, *52*, 322–28.

Archer, R. H. A preliminary study of hostility: the hostility ratio. *Psychiat. Quart.*, 1961, *35*, 562–74.

Arlen, M. J. The girl with the Harvard degree. *N. Y. Times Mag.*, June 10, 1962, pp. 16–17, 63–65.

Arns, Josephine. A factorial analysis of the vocational interests of two hundred adult female students. Doctoral dissertation, Temple Univ., 1958.

Aronfreed, J. The nature, variety, and social patterning of moral responses to transgression. *J. Abnorm. Soc. Psychol.*, 1961, *63*, 223–40.

Astin, A. Personal and environmental factors associated with college dropouts among high aptitude students. *J. Educ. Psychol.*, 1964, *55*, 219–27.

———, and Nichols, R. Life goals and vocational choice. *J. Appl. Psychol.*, 1964, *48*, 50–58.

August, H. E. Psychological aspects of personal adjustment. In Irma Gross (ed.), *Potentialities of Women in the Middle Years*. East Lansing: Michigan State Univ. Press, 1956, pp. 87–104.

Axelson, L. J. The marital adjustment and marital role definitions of husbands of working and nonworking wives. *Marr. Fam. Living*, 1963, *25*, 189–95.

Bach, G. R. Young children's play fantasies. *Psychol. Monogr.*, 1945, *59*, No. 2.

Baer, M. F. Women in federal government. *Personnel Guid. J.*, 1962, *40*, 416. (a)

———. Washington flashes. *Personnel Guid. J.*, 1962, *40*, 672–73. (b)

———. Uncle Sam's women workers. *Personnel Guid. J.*, 1962, *41*, 208–9. (c)

———. Washington flashes. *Personnel Guid. J.*, 1963, *41*, 392–93. (a)

———. Washington flashes. *Personnel Guid. J.*, 1963, *41*, 500–501. (b)

Baer, P., and Goldfarb, G. A developmental study of verbal conditioning in children. *Psychol. Rep.*, 1962, *10*, 175–81.

Baetjer, Anna. *Women in Industry: Their Health and Efficiency*. Philadelphia: W. B. Saunders, 1946.

Baker, Elizabeth. *Technology and Woman's Work*. New York: Columbia Univ. Press, 1964.

Baker, Mary. Personnel in social work. In H. L. Lurie (ed.), *Encyclopedia of Social Work*. New York: National Association of Social Workers, 1965, pp. 532–40.

Ball, J. C. Comparison of MMPI profile differences among Negro and white adolescents. *J. Clin. Psychol.*, 1960, *16*, 304–7.

Bandura, A., and Walters, R. *Adolescent Aggression*. New York: Ronald Press, 1959.

Barr, M. L. Sex chromatin and phenotype in man. *Science*, 1959, *130*, 679–85.

Barrett, H. O. Sex differences in art ability. *J. Educ. Res.*, 1950, *43*, 391–93.

Barrows, G., and Zuckerman, M. Construct validity of three masculinity-femininity tests. *J. Consult. Psychol.*, 1960, *24*, 441–45.

Barry, H., Bacon, M., and Child, I. A cross-cultural survey of some sex differences in socialization. *J. Abnorm. Soc. Psychol.*, 1957, *55*, 327–32.

Bartemeier, L. The children of working mothers: a psychiatrist's view. In National Manpower Council, *Work in the Lives of Married Women*. New York: Columbia Univ. Press, 1958, pp. 173–82.

Barth, Emma. Opportunities for women in engineering. Paper

read at Educ. Dept., Congr. of Engin. Clubs, Pittsburgh, Nov., 1954.

Bassett, M. One hundred and twenty-eight mothers consider our family pattern. *Bull. of Fam. Res. and Educ.*, 1940, *1*, No. 5.

Bath, J. A., and Lewis, E. C. Attitudes of young female adults toward some areas of parent-adolescent conflict. *J. Genet. Psychol.*, 1962, *100*, 241–53.

Baudler, Lucille, and Paterson, D. G. Social status of women's occupations. *Occupations*, 1948, *26*, 421–24.

Bauernfeind, R. H. Are sex norms necessary? *J. Counsel. Psychol.*, 1956, *3*, 57–63.

Bayley, Nancy. Sexual maturing in adolescence as a basis for determining percentage of completed growth. *Child Develpm.*, 1943, *14*, 5–46. (a)

——. Size and body build of adolescents in relation to rate of skeletal maturing. *Child Develpm.*, 1943, *14*, 51–90. (b)

——. Some psychological correlates of somatic androgyny. *Child Develpm.*, 1951, 22, 47–60.

——. Consistency of maternal and child behaviors in the Berkeley Growth Study. *Vita Hum.*, 1964, *7*, 73–95.

——, and Bayer, Leona. The assessment of somatic androgyny. *Amer. J. Phys. Anthrop.*, 1946, *4*, 433–61.

——, and Schaefer, E. S. Correlations of maternal and child behaviors with the development of mental abilities: data from the Berkeley Growth Study. *Monogr. Soc. Res. Child Develpm.*, 1964, *29* (6), 1–97.

Beach, F. *Hormones and Behavior.* New York: Paul B. Hoeber, 1948.

——. (ed.). *Sex and Behavior.* New York: Wiley & Sons, 1965.

Beardslee, D., and O'Dowd, D. Students and the occupational world. In N. Sanford (ed.), *The American College.* New York: Wiley & Sons, 1962, pp. 597–626.

Becker, Esther. Office manners—the gals talk back. *Personnel J.*, 1948, *27*, 218–22.

Beilin, H., and Werner, Emmy. Sex role expectations and criteria of social adjustment for young adults. *J. Clin. Psychol.*, 1957, *13*, 341–43.

Belbin, R. M. Difficulties of older people in industry. *Occup. Psychol.*, 1953, 27, 177–90.

Bell, D. The great back-to-work movement. *Fortune*, 1956, *54* (1), 90–93, 168–72.

Bell, R., and Buerkle, J. The daughter's role during the "launching stage." *Marr. Fam. Living*, 1962, *24*, 384–88.

Bendig, A. W. Extraversion, neuroticism, radicalism and tendermindedness. *J. Consult. Psychol.*, 1958, 22, 292.

——. College norms for and concurrent validity of Cattell's IPAT anxiety scale. *Psychol. Newsletter, NYU*, 1959, *10*, 263–67.

——, and Hountras, P. T. Anxiety, authoritarianism, and student attitudes towards departmental control of college instruction. *J. Educ. Psychol.*, 1959, *50*, 1–8.

————, and Vaughn, C. Extraversion, neuroticism, and motor learning. *J. Abnorm. Soc. Psychol.*, 1959, *59*, 399–403.

Bennett, A. A comparative study of subnormal children in elementary schools. *Teach. Coll. Contr. Educ.*, 1932, No. 510.

Bennett, E., and Cohen, L. Men and women: personality patterns and contrasts. *Genet. Psychol. Monogr.*, 1959, *59*, 101–55.

Bennett, G. K., and Cruikshank, Ruth. Sex differences in the understanding of mechanical problems. *J. Appl. Psychol.*, 1942, *26*, 121–27.

————, and Fry, D. E. *Test of Mechanical Comprehension, Form W-1.* New York: Psychological Corporation, 1943.

————, Seashore, H., and Wesman, A. *Differential Aptitudes Tests: Manual.* (2nd ed.) New York: Psychological Corporation, 1952.

Bentzen, Frances. Sex ratios in learning and behavior disorders. *Amer. J. Orthopsychiat.*, 1963, *33*, 92–98.

Berdie, R. F. *After High School—What?* Minneapolis: Univ. of Minnesota Press, 1954.

————. A femininity adjective check list. *J. Appl. Psychol.*, 1959, *43*, 327–33.

————, and Hood, A. B. Personal values and attitudes as determinants of post-high school plans. *Personnel Guid. J.*, 1964, *42*, 754–59.

————, and Hood, A. B. *Decisions for Tomorrow.* Minneapolis: Univ. of Minnesota Press, 1965.

————, and Layton, W. L. *Minnesota Counseling Inventory, Manual.* New York: Psychological Corporation, 1957.

————, Layton, W., and Swanson, E. A follow-up of the junior tests used in the Minnesota State-Wide College Testing Program and a survey of scholastic aptitudes in Minnesota colleges. (mimeo.) Univ. of Minnesota, Student Counseling Bureau, 1954.

————, et al. *Who Goes to College?* Minneapolis: Univ. of Minnesota Press, 1962.

Berkowitz, L. *Aggression: A Social Psychological Analysis.* New York: McGraw-Hill, 1962.

Bernard, Jessie. *Academic Women.* University Park: Penn. State Univ. Press, 1964.

Bernreuter, R. G. *The Personality Inventory: Percentile Norms.* Stanford, Calif.: Stanford Univ. Press, 1938.

Berry, Jane. Life plans of college women. *J. Nat. Assoc. Deans of Women*, 1955, *18*, 76–80.

Bettelheim, B. Growing up female. *Harper's*, 1962, *225* (1349), 120–28.

Bieliauskas, V. J. Recent advances in the psychology of masculinity and femininity. *J. Psychol.*, 1965, *60*, 255–61.

Bienenstok, T. The peer culture of youth and the school. *Educ. Forum*, 1954, *18*, 312–19.

Bilash, I., and Zubek, J. The effects of age on factorially "pure" mental abilities. *J. Gerontol.*, 1960, *15*, 175–82.

Black, J. D. MMPI results for fifteen groups of female college students. In G. Welsh and W. G. Dahlstrom (eds.), *Basic Readings on the MMPI in Psychology and Medicine*. Minneapolis: Univ. of Minnesota Press, 1956, pp. 562–73.

Blackwell, A. M. A comparative investigation into the factors involved in mathematical ability of boys and girls, Part II. *Brit. J. Educ. Psychol.*, 1940, *10*, 212–22.

Blackwell, G. W. The college and the continuing education of women. *Educ. Rec.*, 1963, *44*, 33–39.

Blair, G. M. Mentally superior and inferior children in the junior and senior high school: a comparative study of their backgrounds, interests, and ambitions. *Teach. Coll. Contr. Educ.*, No. 766.

Bledsoe, J. C. Sex differences in Mental Health Analysis scores of elementary pupils. *J. Consult. Psychol.*, 1961, *25*, 364–65.

Bligh, H., and Reeves, Barbara. Curriculum choices and post-high school plans. Paper presented at Amer. Educ. Res. Assoc., Chicago, Feb., 1963.

Bliss, Eleanor. Bryn Mawr studies its Ph.D.'s. *J. Amer. Assoc. Univ. Women,* 1954, *48*, 14–16.

Blood, R. O. The husband-wife relationship. In F. I. Nye and Lois Hoffman (eds.), *The Employed Mother in America*. Chicago: Rand McNally, 1963, pp. 282–305.

———, and Hamblin, R. The effect of the wife's employment on the family power structure. *Soc. Forces*, 1958, *36*, 347–52.

Bolanovich, D. J. Selection of female engineering trainees. *J. Educ. Psychol.*, 1944, *35*, 545–53.

———. Interest tests reduce factory turnover. *Personnel Psychol.*, 1948, *1*, 81–92.

Bolt, R. H. The present situation of women scientists and engineers in industry and government. In Jacquelyn Mattfeld and Carol Van Aken (eds.), *Women and the Scientific Professions*. Cambridge, Mass.: M.I.T. Press, 1965, pp. 139–62.

Bonney, M. E. Sex differences in social success and personality traits. *Child Develpm.*, 1944, *15*, 63–79.

Bordua, D. J. Educational aspirations and parental stress on college. *Soc. Forces*, 1960, *38*, 262–69.

Boring, E. G. The woman problem. *Amer. Psychologist*, 1951, *6*, 679–82.

Bowlby, J. *Maternal Care and Mental Health*. Geneva: World Health Organization, 1952.

Bowles, J. W., *et al.* Another experiment in pursuit of "color-blindness." *J. Psychol.*, 1949, *28*, 265–71.

Bowman, H. A study of Stephens College alumnae. *J. Higher Educ.*, 1949, *20*, 429–31.

Brachman, H. M., and Costello, C. G. Cultural and sex differences in extraversion and neuroticism reflected in responses to a children's personality inventory. *Brit. J. Educ. Psychol.*, 1962, *32*, 254–57.

Bradway, Katherine, and Thompson, Clare. Intelligence at adulthood: a twenty-five year follow-up. *J. Educ. Psychol.*, 1962, *53*, 1–14.

Brady, Dorothy. Equal pay for women workers. *Ann. Amer. Acad. Pol. Soc. Sci.*, 1947, *251* (3), 53–60.

Brim, O. G. Family structure and sex role learning by children. *Sociometry*, 1958, *21*, 1–16.

Britton, J. H. Influence of social class upon performance on the Draw-a-Man Test. *J. Educ. Psychol.*, 1954, *45*, 44–51.

Broderick, C., and Fowler, S. New patterns of relationships between the sexes among preadolescents. *Marr. Fam. Living*, 1961, *23*, 27–30.

Brooks, Rozanne. Woman's place is in the wrong. *Vital Speeches*, 1961, *28*, 151–54.

Brown, Daniel. Sex-role preference in young children. *Psychol. Monogr.*, 1956, *70*, No. 14 (Whole No. 421).

———. Masculinity-femininity development in children. *J. Consult. Psychol.*, 1957, *21*, 197–202.

———. Inversion and homosexuality. *Amer. J. Orthopsychiat.*, 1958, *28*, 424–29. (a)

———. Sex-role development in a changing culture. *Psychol. Bull.*, 1958, *55*, 232–42. (b)

———, and Tolor, A. Human figure drawings as indicators of sexual identification and inversion. *Percept. Mot. Skills*, 1957, *7*, 199–211.

Brown, Donald. Some educational patterns. *J. Soc. Issues*, 1956, *12* (4), 44–60.

———. Non-intellective qualities and the perception of the ideal student by the college faculty. *J. Educ. Sociol.*, 1960, *33*, 269–78.

Brown, F. G. Identifying college drop-outs with the Minnesota Counseling Inventory. *Personnel Guid. J.*, 1960, *39*, 280–82.

———. Predicted grade-point averages for Iowa State freshmen. (dittoed) Student Counseling Service, Iowa State University, 1962.

Brown, M. H., and Bryan, G. Elizabeth. Sex differences in intelligence. *J. Clin. Psychol.*, 1955, *11*, 303–4.

———, and Bryan, G. Elizabeth. Sex as a variable in intelligence test performance. *J. Educ. Psychol.*, 1957, *48*, 273–78.

Brown, Nora. Some educational influences on the choice of a science career by grammar school girls. *Brit. J. Educ. Psychol.*, 1953, *23*, 188–95.

Brunner, E., and Wayland, S. Education and marriage. *J. Educ. Sociol.*, 1958, *32*, 28–36.

Bruton, Margaret. Present-day thinking on the woman question. *Ann. Amer. Acad. Pol. Soc. Sci.*, 1947, *251* (3), 10–16.

Bryan, Alice, and Boring, E. G. Women in American psychology:

factors affecting their professional careers. *Amer. Psychologist,* 1947, *2,* 3–20.

Bunting, Mary. A huge waste: educated womenpower. *N.Y. Times Magazine,* May 7, 1961, pp. 23, 109, 112. (a)

———. The Radcliffe Institute for Independent Study. *Educ. Rec.,* 1961, *42,* 279–86. (b)

Burchinal, L., and Rossman, J. Relations among maternal employment indices and developmental characteristics of children. *Marr. Fam. Living,* 1961, *23,* 334–40.

Bureau of Labor Statistics. *Comparative Job Performance by Age: Office Workers.* Bull. No. 1273, Washington: U.S.G.P.O., 1960. (a)

———. *School and Early Employment Experience of Youth—A Report on Seven Communities,* 1952–1957. Bull. No. 1277, Washington: U.S.G.P.O., 1960. (b)

Burgemeister, Bessie. The permanence of interests of women college students. *Arch. Psychol., N.Y.,* 1940, No. 255.

Burton, R. Generality of honesty reconsidered. *Psychol. Rev.,* 1963, *70,* 481–99.

Butler, R. I., and Marcuse, F. L. Sex identification at different ages using the Draw-a-Person Test. *J. Proj. Tech.,* 1959, *23,* 299–302.

Butterworth, R., and Thompson, G. Factors related to age-grade trends and sex differences in children's preferences for comic books. *J. Genet. Psychol.,* 1951, *78,* 71–96.

Buxton, C. E., and Grant, D. A. Retroaction and gains in motor learning: II. Sex differences, and a further analysis of gains. *J. Exp. Psychol.,* 1939, *25,* 198–208.

Byers, L. M., and Mather, I. A. Adjustment of men and women student teachers. *Sch. Soc.,* 1950, *71,* 311–14.

Caffrey, J. Auding. *Rev. Educ. Res.,* 1955, *25,* 121–38.

Calderwood, D. Differences in the sex questions of adolescent boys and girls. *Marr. Fam. Living,* 1963, *25,* 492–95.

Cameron, J., Livson, N., and Bayley, Nancy. Infant vocalizations and their relationship to mature intelligence. *Science,* 1967, *157,* 331–33.

Caplow, T. *The Sociology of Work.* Minneapolis: Univ. of Minnesota Press, 1954.

———, and McGee, R. *The Academic Marketplace.* New York: Basic Books, 1958.

Carey, Gloria. Sex differences in problem-solving performance as a function of attitude differences. *J. Abnorm. Soc. Psychol.,* 1958, *56,* 256–60.

Carlson, E., and Carlson, Rae. Male and female subjects in personality research. *J. Abnorm. Soc. Psychol.,* 1960, *61,* 482–83.

Carmichael, O. The MA-3 in 1964: looking backward . . . looking forward. *Super. Stud.,* 1964, *6* (3), 21–26.

Carrier, N. A. Stress, personality, and performance on course examinations. Doctoral dissertation, Univ. of Michigan, 1956.

Carroll, Margaret. The working wife and her family's economic position. *Month. Lab. Rev.*, 1962, *85*, 366–74.

Carter, G. C. Are lady professors hard to please? *Sch. Soc.*, 1948, *68*, 13–15.

Carter, R. S. How invalid are marks assigned by teachers? *J. Educ. Psychol.*, 1952, *43*, 218–28.

Cass, James. While school keeps. *Sat. Rev.*, 1961, *44* (50), 52–53.

Cass, John, and Tiedeman, D. Vocational development and the election of a high school curriculum. *Personnel Guid. J.*, 1960, *38*, 538–45.

Cassidy, Rosalind, and Kozman, Hilda. *Counseling Girls in a Changing Society*. New York: McGraw-Hill, 1947.

Castenada, A., McCandless, B., and Palermo, D. The children's form of the Manifest Anxiety Scale. *Child Develpm.*, 1956, *27*, 317–26.

Cawley, Sister Anne Mary. A study of the vocational interest trends of secondary school and college women. *Genet. Psychol. Monogr.*, 1947, *35*, 185–247.

Centers, R., and Bugental, Daphne. Intrinsic and extrinsic job motivations among different segments of the working population. *J. Appl. Psychol.*, 1966, *50*, 193–97.

Charles, D. C., and Pritchard, Sally. Differential development of intelligence in the college years. *J. Genet. Psychol.*, 1959, *95*, 41–44.

Chervenik, Emily. What becomes of women college graduates? *Voc. Guid. Quart.*, 1955, *4*, 3–5.

————. Wisconsin co-ed graduates report. *Voc. Guid. Quart.*, 1956, *5*, 23–24.

Child, I. L. Children's preference for goals easy or difficult to obtain. *Psychol. Monogr.*, 1946, *60*, No. 4.

Chown, Sheila. Personality factors in the formation of occupational choice. *Brit. J. Educ. Psychol.*, 1959, *29*, 23–33.

Christensen, H. T. Lifetime family and occupational role projections of high school students. *Marr. Fam. Living*, 1961, *23*, 181–83.

————, and Swihart, Marilynn. Post-graduation role preferences of senior women in college. *Marr. Fam. Living*, 1956, *18*, 52–57.

Church, Ruth. Womanpower today and tomorrow. *Amer. J. Nurs.*, 1953, *53*, 446–47.

Cieutat, V. J. Sex differences and reinforcement in the conditioning and extinction of conversational behavior. *Psychol. Rep.*, 1962, *10*, 467–74.

Clark, E. T. Sex role preference in mentally retarded children. *Amer. J. Ment. Defic.*, 1963, *67*, 606–10.

Clark, J. Grade achievement of female college students in relation to non-intellective factors: MMPI items. *J. Soc. Psychol.*, 1953, *37*, 275–81.

————. The interpretation of the MMPI profiles of college students: mean scores for male and female groups. *J. Soc. Psychol.,* 1954, *40,* 319–21.

Clark, K. E. *America's Psychologists.* Washington: American Psychological Association, 1957.

Clark, W. H. Sex differences and motivation in the urge to destroy. *J. Soc. Psychol.,* 1952, *36,* 167–77.

Clark, W. W. Sex differences in mental abilities among students of high intelligence. *Calif. J. Educ. Res.,* 1954, *5,* 90–93.

——. Research findings on mental sex differences and their implications for education: an analysis of sex differences found in mental ability and achievement test results. Los Angeles: Calif. Test Bureau, 1958.

Cleveland Welfare Federation, The Occupational Planning Committee. *A Study of Older Women Clerical Workers in Cleveland.* Cleveland: Cleveland Welfare Federation, 1952.

Cline, V., Richards, J., and Abe, C. The validity of a battery of creativity tests in a high school sample. *Educ. Psychol. Measmt.,* 1962, *22,* 781–84.

——, Richards, J., and Needham, W. Creativity tests and achievement in high school science. *J. Appl. Psychol.,* 1963, *47,* 184–89.

Clover, V. T. Net income of employed wives with husband present. *Stud. in Econ. & Bus., Texas Tech. Coll.,* 1962, pp. 1–35.

Cole, C. C. *Encouraging Scientific Talent.* New York: College Entrance Examination Board, 1956.

College Entrance Examination Board. *Annual Report, 1949–1950.* New York: College Entrance Examination Board, 1950.

Conant, J. B. *The American High School Today.* New York: McGraw-Hill, 1959.

Conrad, F. A. Sex roles as factors in longevity. *Sociol. Soc. Res.,* 1962, *46,* 195–202.

Conyers, J. E. An exploratory study of employers' attitudes toward working mothers. *Sociol. Soc. Res.,* 1961, *45,* 145–56.

Cook, D., and Barre, Marguerite. The effect of specialized industrial norms on the use of the Minnesota Rate of Manipulation Test as a selective instrument in employment procedure. *J. Appl. Psychol.,* 1942, *26,* 785–92.

Cooper, Lillian. Predisposition toward parenthood: a comparison of male and female students. *Sociol. Soc. Res.,* 1957, *42,* 31–36.

Cooper, Sophia, and Garfinkle, S. *Population and Labor Force Projections for the United States, 1960 to 1975.* Washington: U.S.G.P.O., 1959.

Corso, J. F. Age and sex differences in pure tone threshholds. *J. Acoust. Soc. Amer.,* 1959, *31,* 498–507.

Coward, E. The development of number concepts in the pre-school child. Master's thesis, Univ. of Minnesota, 1940.

Crandall, V., and Rabson, Alice. Children's repetition choices in an intellectual achievement situation following success and failure. *J. Genet. Psychol.,* 1960, *97,* 161–68.

Crissey, W. J. E., and Daniel, W. J. Vocational interest factors in women. *J. Appl. Psychol.*, 1939, *23*, 488–94.

Cronin, Anne. *Report of the First Workshop, Oct.–Dec., 1962.* New York: Seven Colleges Vocational Workshops, 1963.

Crookes, T. G., and French, J. G. Intelligence and wastage of student mental nurses. *Occup. Psychol.*, 1961, *35*, 149–54.

Cutright, P. Students' decision to attend college. *J. Educ. Sociol.*, 1960, *33*, 292–99.

Dale, R. R. The happiness of pupils in co-educational and single-sex grammar schools: a comparative assessment. *Brit. J. Educ. Psychol.*, 1966, *36*, 39–47.

Damrin, Dora. Family size and sibling age, sex, and position as related to certain aspects of adjustment. *J. Soc. Psychol.*, 1949, *29*, 93–102.

Darley, F., and Winitz, H. Comparison of male and female kindergarten children on the WISC. *J. Genet. Psychol.*, 1961, *99*, 41–49.

Darley, J. G. Tested maladjustment related to clinically diagnosed maladjustment. *J. Appl. Psychol.*, 1937, *21*, 632–42.

———. *Clinical Aspects and Interpretation of the Strong Vocational Interest Blank.* New York: Psychological Corporation, 1941.

———. *Promise and Performance.* Berkeley: Univ. of Calif., Center for the Study of Higher Education, 1962.

———, and Hagenah, Theda. *Vocational Interest Measurement.* Minneapolis: Univ. of Minnesota Press, 1955.

David, H. Conference findings. In National Manpower Council, *Work in the Lives of Married Women.* New York: Columbia Univ. Press, 1958, pp. 199–207.

———. Work, women and children. In E. Ginzberg (ed.), *The Nation's Children.* New York: Columbia Univ. Press, 1960, pp. 180–98.

Davis, D., Hagan, Nellie, and Strouf, Judie. Occupational choice of twelve-year-olds. *Personnel Guid. J.*, 1962, *40*, 628–29.

Davis, F., and Olesen, Virginia. Initiation into a women's profession: identity problems in the status transition of coed to student nurse. *Sociometry*, 1963, *26*, 89–101.

Davis, J. A. *Great Aspirations.* Chicago: Aldine Publ. Co., 1964.

Davis, O. L., and Slobodian, June. Teacher behavior toward boys and girls during first grade reading instruction. *Amer. Educ. Res. J.*, 1967, *4*, 261–69.

DeLucia, Lenore. The toy preference test: a measure of sex-role identification. *Child Develpm.*, 1963, *34*, 107–17.

de Luget, Jacqueline. The contribution of home economics education to the position of women in the world today. *J. Home Econ.*, 1958, *50*, 625–28.

Dement, Alice. Higher education of the housewife: wanted or wasted? *J. Higher Educ.*, 1960, *31*, 28–32.

Denmark, Florence, and Guttentag, Marcia. The effect of college attendance on mature women: changes in self-concept and evaluation of student role. *J. Soc. Psychol.*, 1966, *69*, 155–58.

Dennis, L. (ed.). *Education and a Woman's Life.* Washington: American Council on Education, 1963.

Derthick, L. G. Guidance and the nation's need. *Personnel Guid. J.*, 1958, *37*, 107–13.

Diamond, S. The interpretation of interest profiles. *J. Appl. Psychol.*, 1948, *32*, 512–20.

———. Sex stereotypes and acceptance of sex role. *J. Psychol.*, 1955, *39*, 385–88.

Dietrich, Grace, and Hunnicutt, C. W. Art content preferred by primary-grade children. *Elem. Sch. J.*, 1948, *48*, 557–59.

Dinitz, S., Dynes, R., and Clarke, A. Preferences for male or female children: traditional or affectional? *Marr. Fam. Living*, 1954, *16*, 128–30.

Dixon, Marguerite. Adolescent girls tell about themselves. *Marr. Fam. Living*, 1958, *20*, 400–401.

Dobson, W. R., and Stone, D. R. College freshmen responses on the Minnesota Multiphasic Personality Inventory. *J. Educ. Res.*, 1951, *44*, 611–18.

Dolan, Eleanor. Educational goals for college women. *Assoc. Amer. Coll. Bull.*, 1953, *39*, 441–51.

———. Educated women: a mid-century evaluation. *Educ. Forum*, 1956, *20*, 219–28.

Donlon, Mary. Women's education today. *Educ. Rec.*, 1958, *39*, 246–52.

Doppelt, J. E., and Bennett, G. K. A longitudinal study of the Differential Aptitude Tests. *Educ. Psychol. Measmt.*, 1951, *11*, 228–37.

Dornbush, S., and Heer, D. The evaluation of work by females, 1940–1950. *Amer. J. Sociol.*, 1957, *63*, 27–29.

Doty, Carol, and Hoeflin, Ruth. A descriptive study of thirty-five unmarried graduate women. *J. Marr. Fam.*, 1964, *26*, 91–94.

Douglas, W. *Ministers' Wives.* New York: Harper, 1965.

Douvan, Elizabeth. Sex differences in adolescent character processes. *Merrill-Palmer Quart.*, 1960, *6*, 203–11.

———. Employment and the adolescent. In F. I. Nye and Lois Hoffman (eds.), *The Employed Mother in America.* Chicago: Rand McNally, 1963, pp. 142–64.

———, and Kaye, Carol. *Adolescent Girls.* Ann Arbor: Survey Research Center, Institute for Social Research, Univ. of Michigan, 1956.

———, and Kaye, Carol. Motivational factors in college entrance. In N. Sanford (ed.), *The American College.* New York: Wiley & Sons, 1962, pp. 199–224.

Drake, L. E. Differential sex responses to items of the MMPI. *J. Appl. Psychol.*, 1953, *37*, 46.

Dressel, P. L. Interests—stable or unstable. *J. Educ. Res.*, 1954, *48*, 95–102.

Drews, Elizabeth. What every Ablewoman should know. *J. Nat. Assoc. Women Deans Couns.*, 1961, *25*, 14–20.

Drinkwater, Barbara. Development of an attitude inventory to measure the attitude of high school girls toward physical education as a career for women. *Res. Quart. Amer. Assoc. Hlth. Phys. Educ. Recr.*, 1960, *31*, 575–80.

Droege, R., Crambert, A., and Henkin, J. Relationship between G.A.T.B. aptitude scores and age for adults. *Personnel Guid. J.*, 1963, *41*, 502–8.

Droppleman, L., and Schaefer, E. Boys' and girls' reports of maternal and paternal behavior. *J. Abnorm. Soc. Psychol.*, 1963, *67*, 648–54.

Duggan, Lucy. An experiment on immediate recall in secondary school children. *Brit. J. Psychol.*, 1950, *40*, 149–54.

Dunham, R., and Wright, Patricia. *Faculty and Other Professional Staff in Institutions of Higher Education, First Term 1961–62.* Washington: U.S.G.P.O., 1965.

Dunkleberger, C., and Tyler, Leona. Interest stability and personality traits. *J. Counsel. Psychol.*, 1961, *8*, 70–74.

Dunlap, K. Stammering: its nature, etiology, and therapy. *J. Comp. Psychol.*, 1944, *37*, 187–302.

Dunlop, Florence. Analysis of data obtained from ten years of intelligence testing in the Ottawa public schools. *Canad. J. Psychol.*, 1947, *1*, 87–91.

Dunn, Marie. Marriage role expectations of adolescents. *Marr. Fam. Living*, 1960, *22*, 99–104.

Dunsdon, M. I., and Fraser Roberts, J. A. A study of the performance of 2000 children on four vocabulary tests. *Brit. J. Stat. Psychol.*, 1955, *8*, 3–15.

———, and Fraser Roberts, J. A. A study of the performance of 2000 children on four vocabulary tests: II. Norms, with some observations on the relative variability of boys and girls. *Brit. J. Stat. Psychol.*, 1957, *10*, 1–16.

Dunteman, G. H. Discriminant analyses of the SVIB for female students in five college curricula. *J. Appl. Psychol.*, 1966, *50*, 509–15.

Durflinger, G. W. Academic and personality differences between women students who do complete the elementary teaching credential program and those who do not. *Educ. Psychol. Measmt.*, 1963, *23*, 775–83.

Durkin, Dolores. Sex differences in children's concepts of justice. *Child Develpm.*, 1960, *31*, 361–68.

Duvall, Elise. Conceptions of mother roles by five- and six-year-old children of working and non-working mothers. Doctoral dissertation, Florida State Univ., 1955.

Eagleson, O. W., and Bell, E. S. The values of Negro women college students. *J. Soc. Psychol.*, 1945, *22*, 149–54.

Eames, T. H. A study of the incidence of eye defects and sex among poor readers. *J. Educ. Res.*, 1939, *33*, 102–4.

Eckert, Ruth, and Stecklein, J. E. *Job Motivation and Satisfactions of College Teachers: A Study of Faculty Members in Minnesota Colleges.* Washington: U.S.G.P.O., 1961.

Edgerton, H. A. Technical aspects of the Fourth Annual Science Talent Search. *Educ. Psychol. Measmt.,* 1947, *7,* 3–21.

———, and Britt, S. Sex differences in the Science Talent Test. *Science,* 1944, *100,* 192–93.

Edmiston, R. W., and Starr, C. H. Youth's attitudes toward occupations. *Occupations,* 1948, *26,* 213–20.

Edwards, A. L. *Edwards Personal Preference Schedule, Manual.* (revised) New York: Psychological Corporation, 1959.

Edwards, T. B., and Wilson, A. B. The specialization of interests and academic achievement. *Harv. Educ. Rev.,* 1958, *28,* 183–96.

Eels, W. C. Women in the universities of the world. *Higher Education,* 1952, *9,* 61–65.

Ellis, Evelyn. Social psychological correlates of upward social mobility among unmarried career women. *Amer. Sociol. Rev.,* 1952, *17,* 558–63.

Ely, J. H., Kephart, N., and Tiffin, J. Ortho-rater norms and sex differences. *J. Appl. Psychol.,* 1950, *34,* 232–34.

Emmerich, W. Parental identification in young children. *Genet. Psychol. Monogr.,* 1959, *60,* 257–308. (a)

———. Young children's discriminations of parent and child roles. *Child Develpm.,* 1959, *30,* 403–19. (b)

———. Family role concepts of children ages six to ten. *Child Develpm.,* 1961, *32,* 609–24.

———. Variations in the parent role as a function of the parent's sex and the child's sex and age. *Merrill-Palmer Quart.,* 1962, *8,* 3–11.

Emmett, W. C. Evidence of a space factor at 11 and earlier. *Brit. J. Psychol., Statist. Sect.,* 1949, *2,* 3–16.

Empey, L. T. Role expectations of young women regarding marriage and a career. *Marr. Fam. Living,* 1958, *20,* 152–55.

Engle, E. T., and Shelesnyak, M. C. First menstruation and subsequent menstrual cycles of pubertal girls. *Hum. Biol.,* 1934, *6,* 431–53.

Engle, T. L. Achievement of pupils who have had double promotions in elementary school. *Elem. School J.,* 1935, *36,* 185–89.

Englehardt, Olga. The Minnesota Clerical Test: sex differences in norms for college groups. *J. Appl. Psychol.,* 1956, *34,* 412–14.

Enstrom, E. A. The extent of the use of the left hand in handwriting. *J. Educ. Res.,* 1962, *55,* 234–35.

Erb, E. D. Conformity and achievement in college. *Personnel Guid. J.,* 1961, *39,* 361–66.

Erickson, E. H. Sex differences in the play configurations of preadolescents. *Amer. J. Orthopsychiat.,* 1951, *21,* 667–92.

Erickson, Ethel, and Hansen, Hazel. *Maternity Protection of Employed Women.* Washington: U.S.G.P.O., 1952.

Espenschade, Anna. Motor performance in adolescence. *Monogr. Soc. Res. Child Develpm.*, 1940, *5,* No. 1.

Essig, M., and Morgan, D. H. Adjustment of adolescent daughters of employed women to family life. *J. Educ. Psychol.*, 1946, *37,* 219–33.

Everhart, R. W. Literature survey of growth and developmental factors in articulatory maturation. *J. Speech Hearing Disord.*, 1960, *25,* 59–69.

Eyde, Lorraine. *Work Values and Background Factors as Predictors of Women's Desire to Work.* Columbus: Bur. of Bus. Res., Ohio State Univ., 1962.

Eysenck, S. B. G. Social class, sex, and response to a five-part personality inventory. *Educ. Psychol. Measmt.*, 1960, *20,* 47–54.

Falk, L. L. Occupational satisfaction of female college graduates. *J. Marr. Fam.*, 1966, *28,* 177–85.

Fand, Alexandra. Sex role and self concept: a study of the feminine sex role as perceived by eighty-five college women for themselves, their ideal woman, the average woman and man's ideal woman. Doctoral dissertation, Cornell Univ., 1955.

Farber, S., and Wilson, R. (eds.). *The Potential of Women.* New York: McGraw-Hill, 1963.

Farnsworth, P. R. An historical, critical, and experimental study of the Seashore-Kwalwasser Test Battery. *Genet. Psychol. Monogr.*, 1931, *9,* 291–393.

Fauls, Lydia, and Smith, W. Sex-role learning of five-year-olds. *J. Genet. Psychol.*, 1956, *89,* 105–17.

Faust, Margaret. Developmental maturity as a determinant in prestige of adolescent girls. *Child Develpm.*, 1960, *31,* 173–84.

Fava, Sylvia. The status of women in professional sociology. *Amer. Sociol. Rev.*, 1960, *25,* 271–76.

Feld, Sheila. Feelings of adjustment. In F. I. Nye and Lois Hoffman (eds.), *The Employed Mother in America.* Chicago: Rand McNally, 1963, pp. 331–52.

Feldman, Frances. Supplementary income earned by married women. In National Manpower Council, *Work in the Lives of Married Women.* New York: Columbia Univ. Press, 1958, pp. 93–115.

Ferguson, L. W. Analysis of sex temperaments in terms of Thurstone-type attitude items. *J. Genet. Psychol.*, 1945, *66,* 233–38.

Ferguson, Lucy, and Maccoby, Eleanor. Interpersonal correlates of differential abilities. *Child Develpm.*, 1966, *37,* 549–71.

Fernberger, S. W. Persistence of stereotypes concerning sex differences. *J. Abnorm. Soc. Psychol.*, 1948, *43,* 97–101.

Ferrell, G. V. Comparative study of sex differences in school achievement of white and Negro children. *J. Educ. Res.*, 1949, *43,* 116–21.

Field, W. F. The effects on thematic apperception of certain experimentally aroused needs. Doctoral dissertation, Univ. of Maryland, 1951.

Fifer, G. Grade placement of secondary school pupils in relation to age and ability. *Calif. J. Educ. Res.*, 1952, *3*, 31–36.

Finch, F. H., and Odoroff, M. E. Sex differences in vocational interests. *J. Educ. Psychol.*, 1939, *30*, 151–56.

Fine, B. Women Engineers: Surely! Why not? *Cleveland Plain Dealer*, Aug. 19, 1962, p. 8–B.

Fisher, G. M. Sexual identification in mentally subnormal females. *Amer. J. Ment. Defic.*, 1961, *66*, 266–69.

———, Risley, T., and Silverstein, A. Sex differences in the performance of mental retardates on the Wechsler Adult Intelligence Scale. *J. Clin. Psychol.*, 1961, *17*, 170.

Fisher, J. K., and Waetjen, W. B. An investigation of the relationship between the separation by sex of eighth-grade boys and girls and English achievement and self-concept. *J. Educ. Res.*, 1966, *59*, 409–12.

Fisher, Rhoda. Preferences of different age and socio-economic groups in unstructured musical situations. *J. Soc. Psychol.*, 1951, *33*, 147–52.

Fisher, Sarah. *Relationships in Attitudes, Opinions, and Values Among Family Members.* Berkeley: Univ. of California Press, 1948.

Fitt, A. B., and Rogers, C. A. The sex factor in the Cattell Intelligence Tests, Scale III. *Brit. J. Psychol.*, 1950, *41*, 186–92.

Fjeld, Harriett. A comparison of major groups of college women on the Kuder Preference Record—Personal. *Educ. Psychol. Measmt.*, 1952, *12*, 664–68.

———, and Ames, Louise. Women psychologists: their work, training, and professional opportunities. *J. Soc. Psychol.*, 1950, *31*, 69–94.

Flanagan, J. C. The implications of recent research for the improvement of secondary education. *Amer. Educ. Res. J.*, 1964, *1*, 1–9.

———, et al. *The American High School Student.* Pittsburgh: Project Talent Office, Univ. of Pittsburgh, 1964.

Fleck, S., Lidz, T., and Cornelison, Alice. Comparison of parent-child relationships of male and female schizophrenic patients. *Arch. Gen. Psychiat.*, 1963, *8*, 1–7.

Fleming, C. M., Digaria, D., and Newth, H. Preferences and values among adolescent boys and girls. *Educ. Res.*, 1960, *2*, 221–24.

Flesher, Marie, and Pressey, S. L. War-time accelerates ten years after. *J. Educ. Psychol.*, 1955, *46*, 228–38.

Flood, W. E. Scientific interests of adults. *Nature, Lond.*, 1950, *166*, 592–93.

———, and Crossland, R. W. The origins of interests and motives for study of natural sciences and psychology among adult students in voluntary courses. *Brit. J. Educ. Psychol.*, 1948, *18*, 105–17.

Ford, C. F., and Tyler, Leona. A factor analysis of Terman and Miles' M-F Test. *J. Appl. Psychol.*, 1952, *36*, 251–53.

Ford, H. A. Supervision of women in industry. *Personnel J.*, 1951, *29*, 421–23.

Fort, Twila, and Porterfield, A. Some backgrounds and types of alcoholics among women. *J. Health Hum. Behav.*, 1961, *2*, 283–92.

Fox, W. H. The stability of measured interests. *J. Educ. Res.*, 1947, *41*, 305–10.

Franck, Kate, and Rosen, E. A projective test of M-F. *J. Consult. Psychol.*, 1949, *13*, 247–56.

Frank, L. K. The interpersonal and social aspects. In Irma Gross (ed.), *Potentialities of Women in the Middle Years*. East Lansing: Michigan State Univ. Press, 1956, pp. 105–26.

———, *et al.* Personality development in adolescent girls. *Monogr. Soc. Res. Child Develpm.*, 1951, *16*, No. 53.

Frank, Myrna, and Kiser, C. Changes in the social and demographic attributes of women in "Who's Who." *Milbank Mem. Fund Quart.*, 1965, *43*, 55–75.

Frankel, E. Characteristics of working and non-working mothers among intellectually gifted high and low achievers. *Personnel Guid. J.*, 1964, *42*, 776–80.

Fraser Roberts, J. A. On the difference between the sexes in dispersion of intelligence. *Brit. Med. J.*, 1945, *1*, 727–30.

———, Norman, R., and Griffiths, R. Studies on a child population. *Ann. Eugen.*, 1935, *6*, 319–38.

Freedman, M. B. The passage through college. *J. Soc. Issues*, 1956, *12* (4), 13–28.

———. Changes in six decades of some attitudes and values held by educated women. *J. Soc. Issues*, 1961, *17*, 19–28.

———. Studies of college alumni. In N. Sanford (ed.), *The American College*. New York: Wiley & Sons, 1962, pp. 847–86.

French, Elizabeth, and Lesser, G. Some characteristics of the achievement motive in women. *J. Abnorm. Soc. Psychol.*, 1964, *68*, 119–28.

French, J. W. The relationship of home and school experiences to scores on achievement tests. *J. Educ. Psychol.*, 1959, *50*, 75–82.

Friedan, Betty. *The Feminine Mystique*. New York: W. W. Norton, 1963.

Frumkin, R. M. The prestige and status of nursing and other women's occupations: a student nurse evaluation. *Ohio Nurses Rev.*, 1955, *30* (8), 14–16.

Fuchs, E., and Hammer, C. A survey of women's aptitudes for army jobs. *Personnel Psychol.*, 1963, *16*, 151–55.

Fuller, Frances. Influence of sex of counselor and of client on client expressions of feeling. *J. Counsel. Psychol.*, 1963, *10*, 34–40.

———. Preferences for male and female counselors. *Personnel Guid. J.*, 1964, *42*, 463–67.

———, and Batchelder, Mary. Opportunities for women at the administrative level. *Harv. Bus. Rev.*, 1953, *31*, 111–28.

Fund for the Advancement of Education. *Bridging the Gap Be-*

tween School and College. New York: Fund for the Advancement of Education, 1953.

Fund for the Advancement of Education. *They Went to College Early.* New York: Fund for the Advancement of Education, 1957.

Gadel, Marguerite. Productivity and satisfaction of full- and part-time female employees. *Personnel Psychol.*, 1953, *6*, 327–42.

Gaier, E., and Wambach, Helen. Self-evaluation of personality assets and liabilities of southern white and Negro students. *J. Soc. Psychol.*, 1960, *51*, 135–43.

Gainer, W. L. The ability of the WISC subtests to discriminate between boys and girls of average intelligence. *Calif. J. Educ. Res.*, 1962, *13*, 9–16.

Gaito, J. Sex differences in intelligence. *Psychol. Rep.*, 1959, *5*, 169–70.

Galler, Enid. Influence of social class on children's choices of occupations. *Elem. Sch. J.*, 1951, *51*, 439–45.

Gansl, I. Vocabulary: its measurement and growth. *Arch. Psychol.*, 1939, No. 236.

Gardner, D. B., Hawkes, G., and Burchinal, L. Noncontinuous mothering in infancy and development in later childhood. *Child Develpm.*, 1961, *32*, 225–34.

Garfield, S., Blek, L., and Melker, F. The influence of method of administration and sex differences on selected aspects of TAT stories. *J. Consult. Psychol.*, 1952, *16*, 140–44.

Garrett, W. S. Prediction of academic success in a school of nursing. *Personnel Guid. J.*, 1960, *38*, 500–503.

Garrison, K., and Scott, Mary. The relationship of selected personal characteristics to the needs of college students preparing to teach. *Educ. Psychol. Measmt.*, 1962, *22*, 753–58.

Gass, Gertrude. Counseling implications of woman's changing role. *Personnel Guid. J.*, 1959, *37*, 482–87.

Gates, A. I. Sex differences in reading ability. *Elem. Sch. J.*, 1961, *61*, 431–34.

Gesell, A., *et al. The First Five Years of Life.* New York: Harper, 1940.

Gettel, R. G. A plea for the uncommon woman. *Sch. Soc.*, 1958, *86*, 259–61.

Ghei, S. N. Needs of Indian and American college females. *J. Soc. Psychol.*, 1966, *69*, 3–11.

Gianopulos, A., and Mitchell, H. Marital disagreement in working wife marriages as a function of husband's attitude toward wife's employment. *Marr. Fam. Living*, 1957, *19*, 373–78.

Gibbons, D. C., and Griswold, M. Sex differences among juvenile court referrals. *Sociol. Soc. Res.*, 1957, *42*, 106–10.

Gilbert, G. M. Sex differences in musical aptitude and training. *J. Gen. Psychol.*, 1942, *26*, 19–33.

Ginzberg, E. Education and the role of women—a symposium. *NEA J.*, 1960, *49* (9), 48–53.

————. *The Development of Human Resources.* New York: Mc-Graw-Hill, 1966.

————, et al. *Occupational Choice.* New York: Columbia Univ. Press, 1951.

————, et al. *Life Styles of Educated Women.* New York: Columbia Univ. Press, 1966.

Glazener, Dorothy. Personal and professional activities of 1933–1952 graduates of Iowa State College, Division of Home Economics. Master's thesis, Iowa State Univ., 1955.

Gleason, G. T., and Klausmeier, H. The relationship between variability in physical growth and academic achievement among third- and fifth-grade children. *J. Educ. Res.,* 1958, *51,* 521–27.

Glenn, Hortense. Attitudes of women regarding gainful employment of married women. *J. Home Econ.,* 1959, *51,* 247–52.

Glick, P., and Carter, H. Marriage patterns and educational level. *Amer. Sociol. Rev.,* 1958, *23,* 294–300.

Glueck, S., and Glueck, Eleanor. Working mothers and delinquency. *Ment. Hyg., N.Y.,* 1957, *41,* 327–52.

Goodenough, Evelyn. Interest in persons as an aspect of sex difference in the early years. *Genet. Psychol. Monogr.,* 1957, *55,* 287–323.

Goolishian, H. A., and Foster, A. A note on sex differences on the Wechsler-Bellevue test. *J. Clin. Psychol.,* 1954, *10,* 289–99.

Gordon, Mary. A study in the applicability of the same minimum qualifying scores for technical schools to white males, WAF, and Negro males. *HRRC, Air Res. Develpm. Command, Techn. Rep.,* 1953, 53–54.

Goss, G., Farmer, F., and McFarlane, W. A comparison of dark adaptation (biophotometer) tests on French and English school children in a Quebec community. *Canad. Med. Assoc. J.,* 1941, *44,* 30–33.

Gough, H. G. Identifying psychological femininity. *Educ. Psychol. Measmt.,* 1952, *12,* 427–39.

————. *California Psychological Inventory, Manual.* Palo Alto: Consulting Psychologists Press, 1957.

————. A cross-cultural analysis of the CPI femininity scale. *J. Consult. Psychol.,* 1966, *30,* 136–41.

Gould, H. N., and Gould, M. R. Age of first menstruation in mothers and daughters. *J. Amer. Med. Assoc.,* 1932, *98,* 1349–52.

Gover, D. A. Socio-economic differential in the relationship between marital adjustment and wife's employment status. *Marr. Fam. Living,* 1963, *25,* 452–56.

Gray, H. Jung's psychological types in relation to occupation, race, body-build. *Stanford Med. Bull.,* 1946, *4,* 100–103.

————. Jung's psychological types in men and women. *Stanford Med. Bull.,* 1948, *6,* 29–36.

Gray, R., and Smith, T. Effect of employment on sex differences in attitudes toward the parental family. *Marr. Fam. Living,* 1960, *22,* 36–38.

Gray, Susan. The relation of individual variability to intelligence. *J. Educ. Psychol.*, 1944, *35*, 201–10.

————. A note on the values of southern college women, white and Negro. *J. Soc. Psychol.*, 1947, *25*, 239–41.

————. Masculinity-femininity in relation to anxiety and social acceptance. *Child Develpm.*, 1957, *28*, 203–14.

————, and Klaus, R. The assessment of parental identification. *Genet. Psychol. Monogr.*, 1956, *54*, 87–109.

Greulich, W., *et al.* A handbook of methods for the study of adolescent children. *Monogr. Soc. Res. Child Develpm.*, 1938, *3*, No. 2.

Grigg, C., and Middleton, R. Community of orientation and occupational aspirations of ninth grade students. *Soc. Forces*, 1960, *38*, 303–8.

Grobman, Hulda. Student performance in new high school biology program. *Science*, 1964, *143*, 265–66.

Gropper, G., and Fitzpatrick, R. *Who Goes to Graduate School?* Pittsburgh: American Institute for Research, 1959.

Gross, Irma (ed.). *Potentialities of Women in the Middle Years.* East Lansing: Michigan Univ. Press, 1956.

Guetzkow, H. An analysis of the operation of set in problem-solving behavior. *J. Gen. Psychol.*, 1951, *45*, 219–44.

Gugenheim, C. La formation des goûts professionnel; résultats d'une enquête effectuée dans un collège technique des jeunes filles. *Travail Hum.*, 1953, *16*, 241–52.

Guilford, J. P., and Martin, H. Age differences and sex differences in some introvertive and emotional traits. *J. Gen. Psychol.*, 1944, *31*, 219–29.

————, and Zimmerman, W. *The Guilford-Zimmerman Temperament Survey: Manual of Instructions and Interpretations.* Beverly Hills: Sheridan Supply Co., 1949.

Gunnell, Dorothy, and Nutting, Ruth. Prediction of achievement in schools of nursing. *Calif. J. Educ. Res.*, 1957, *8*, 184–91.

Gurin, Maizie, Nachman, Barbara, and Segal, S. The effect of the social context on the vocational counseling of college women. *J. Counsel. Psychol.*, 1963, *10*, 28–33.

Gurr, Muriel. A study of women executives and professional administrators. Doctoral dissertation, Northwestern Univ., 1956.

Habein, Margaret. Education and the role of women—a symposium. *NEA J.*, 1960, *49* (9), 48–53.

Hacker, Helen. Women as a minority group. *Soc. Forces*, 1951, *30*, 60–69.

Haggard, E. A. Socialization, personality, and academic achievement in gifted children. *Sch. Rev.*, 1957, *65*, 388–414.

Hahn, M. E. *Psychoevaluation: Adaptation, Distribution, Adjustment.* New York: McGraw-Hill, 1963.

Halfter, Irma. The comparative academic achievement of women. *Adult Educ.*, 1962, *12*, 106–15.

Haller, A. O., and Sewell, W. H. Farm residence and levels of educational and occupational aspiration. *Amer. J. Sociol.*, 1957, *62*, 407–12.

Halverson, H. M. The differential effects of nudity and clothing on muscle tonus in infancy. *J. Genet. Psychol.*, 1942, *61*, 55–67.

Hamburg, D. A., and Lunde, D. T. Sex hormones in the development of sex differences in human behavior. In Eleanor Maccoby (ed.), *The Development of Sex Differences.* Stanford, Calif.: Stanford Univ. Press, 1966, pp. 1–24.

Hamill, Katherine. Women as bosses. *Fortune,* 1956, *53* (6), 105–8, 214–20.

Hammond, W. H. An analysis of youth centre interests. *Brit. J. Educ. Psychol.*, 1945, *15*, 122–26.

Hampson, J. L. Determinants of psychosexual orientation. In F. A. Beach (ed.), *Sex and Behavior.* New York: Wiley & Sons, 1965, pp. 108–25.

———, and Hampson, Joan. The ontogenesis of sexual behavior in man. In W. C. Young (ed.), *Sex and Internal Secretions.* (2nd ed.) Vol. II. Baltimore: Williams & Wilkins, 1961, pp. 1401–32.

Hand, H. B. Working mothers and maladjusted children. *J. Educ. Sociol.*, 1957, *30*, 245–46.

Haney, R., Michael, W., and Gershon, A. Achievement, aptitude, and personality measures as predictors of success in nursing training. *Educ. Psychol. Measmt.*, 1962, *22*, 389–92.

Hansen, H. (ed.). *The World Almanac, 1963.* New York: World-Telegram and Sun, 1963.

Hardin, E., Reif, H., and Heneman, H. Stability of job preferences of department store employees. *J. Appl. Psychol.*, 1951, *35*, 256–59.

Hardyck, C. D. Sex differences in personality changes in age. *J. Gerontol.*, 1964, *19*, 78–82.

Harmon, Lenore. Women's working patterns related to their SVIB housewife and "own" occupational scores. *J. Counsel. Psychol.*, 1967, *14*, 299–301.

Harmon, L. R. High school ability patterns: a backward look from the doctorate. *Scientific Manpower Rep. No. 6.* Washington: Office of Scientific Personnel, Nat. Acad. Sci.–Nat. Res. Coun., 1965.

Harris, D. B. Sex differences in the life problems and interests of adolescents, 1935 and 1957. *Child Develpm.*, 1959, *30*, 453–59.

———, *et al.* The measurement of responsibility in children. *Child Develpm.*, 1954, *25*, 21–28.

———, and Tseng, Sing Chu. Children's attitudes toward peers and parents as revealed by sentence completions. *Child Develpm.*, 1957, *28*, 401–11.

Hartley, Ruth. Sex-role pressures and the socialization of the male child. *Psychol. Rep.*, 1959, *5*, 457–68.

———. Children's concepts of male and female roles. *Merrill-Palmer Quart.*, 1960, *6*, 83–91. (a)

Hartley, Ruth. Some implications of current sex-role patterns. *Merrill-Palmer Quart.*, 1960, *6*, 153–64. (b)

———. Current patterns in sex roles: children's perspectives. *J. Nat. Assoc. Women Deans & Couns.*, 1961, *25*, 3–13.

———. A developmental view of female sex-role definition and identification. *Merrill-Palmer Quart.*, 1964, *10*, 1–16.

———, Hardesty, F. and Gorfein, D. Children's preferences and expressions of sex preference. *Child Develpm.*, 1962, *33*, 221–27.

———, and Klein, A. Sex-role concepts among elementary school-age girls. *Marr. Fam. Living*, 1959, *21*, 59–64.

Hartshorne, H., and May, M. *Studies in Deceit.* New York: Macmillan, 1928.

———, May, M., and Maller, J. *Studies in Service and Self-Control.* New York: Macmillan, 1929.

Hartup, W. W. Some correlates of parental imitation in young children. *Child Develpm.*, 1962, *33*, 85–96.

———, and Zook, Elsie. Sex-role preferences in three- and four-year-old children. *J. Consult. Psychol.*, 1960, *24*, 420–26.

Hatch, Mary, and Hatch, D. L. Problems of married working women as presented by three popular working women's magazines. *Soc. Forces*, 1958, *37*, 148–53.

Hathaway, S. R., and McKinley, J. C. *Minnesota Multiphasic Personality Inventory, Manual.* New York: Psychological Corporation, 1951.

Hauser, P. M. More from the census of 1960. *Scient. American*, 1962, *207* (4), 30–37.

Havemann, E., and West, Patricia. *They Went to College.* New York: Harcourt, Brace, 1952.

Havens, P. S. Goals of women in higher education. *J. Amer. Assoc. Univ. Women*, 1955, *48*, 161–67.

Havighurst, R. J. Changing roles of women in the middle years. In Irma Gross (ed.), *Potentialities of Women in the Middle Years.* East Lansing: Michigan State Univ. Press, 1956, pp. 3–17.

———. *American Higher Education in the 1960's.* Columbus: Ohio State Univ. Press, 1960.

———, and Breese, Fay. Relation between ability and social status in a midwestern community: III. Primary mental abilities. *J. Educ. Psychol.*, 1947, *38*, 241–47.

Healy, Irene, and Borg, W. Personality characteristics of nursing school students and graduate nurses. *J. Appl. Psychol.*, 1951, *35*, 275–80.

———, and Borg, W. The vocational interests of nurses and nursing students. *J. Educ. Res.*, 1953, *46*, 347–52.

Hebb, D. O. Behavioral differences between male and female chimpanzees. *Bull. Canad. Psychol. Assoc.*, 1946, *6*, 56–58.

Heckel, R. V. The effects of fatherlessness on the preadolescent female. *Ment. Hyg., N.Y.*, 1963, *47*, 69–73.

Heer, D. M. Dominance and the working wife. *Soc. Forces,* 1958, *36,* 341–47.

———. Husband and wife perceptions of family power structure. *Marr. Fam. Living,* 1962, *24,* 65–67.

Heilbrun, A. B. Personality differences between adjusted and maladjusted college students. *J. Appl. Psychol.,* 1960, *44,* 341–46.

———. Male and female personality correlates of early termination in counseling. *J. Counsel. Psychol.,* 1961, *8,* 31–36.

———. Parental identification and college adjustment. *Psychol. Rep.,* 1962, *10,* 853–54. (a)

———. Psychological factors related to counseling readiness and implications for counselor behavior. *J. Counsel. Psychol.,* 1962, *9,* 353–58. (b)

———. Configural interpretation of the Edwards Personal Preference Schedule and the prediction of academic performance. *Personnel Guid. J.,* 1963, *42,* 264–68. (a)

———. Revision of the MMPI K correction procedure for improved detection of maladjustment in a normal college population. *J. Consult. Psychol.,* 1963, *27,* 161–65. (b)

Heilbrun, Carolyn. Educating female people. *Columbia Univ. Forum,* Spring 1962, pp. 33–37.

Heimann, R., and Schenck, Q. F. Relations of social class and sex differences to high school achievement. In J. Rothney, *Guidance Practices and Results.* New York: Harper, 1958, pp. 388–400.

Heinicke, C. M. Some effects of separating two-year-old children from their mothers—a comparative study. *Hum. Relat.,* 1956, *9,* 102–76.

Heist, P. The motivation of college women today: a closer look. *J. Amer. Assoc. Univ. Women,* 1962, *56,* 17–19.

———. The motivation of college women today: the cultural setting. *J. Amer. Assoc. Univ. Women,* 1963, *56,* 55–57.

———, et al. Personality and scholarship. *Science,* 1961, *133,* 362–67.

Helfrich, Margaret. The generalized role of the executive's wife. *Marr. Fam. Living,* 1961, *23,* 384–87.

Helmes, Winifred. Woman power and higher education. *J. Amer. Assoc. Univ. Women,* 1958, *51,* 203–6.

Helson, Ravenna. Childhood interest clusters related to creativity in women. *J. Consult. Psychol.,* 1965, *29,* 352–61.

———. Personality of women with imaginative and artistic interests: the role of masculinity, originality, and other characteristics in their creativity. *J. Person.,* 1966, *34,* 1–25.

Heron, A. The objective assessment of personality among female unskilled workers. *Educ. Psychol. Measmt.,* 1955, *15,* 117–26.

Herzberg, F., and Lepkin, M. A study of sex differences on the Primary Mental Abilities Test. *Educ. Psychol. Measmt.,* 1954, *14,* 687–89.

Heston, J. C. A comparison of four M-F scales. *Educ. Psychol. Measmt.*, 1948, *8*, 375–87.

Hetherington, Mavis, and Ross, L. Effect of sex of subject, sex of experimenter, and reinforcement condition on serial verbal learning, *J. Exp. Psychol.*, 1963, *65*, 572–75.

Hewer, Vivian, and Neubeck, G. Occupations of fathers and mothers of entering University of Minnesota freshmen, Fall, 1959. *Personnel Guid. J.*, 1962, *40*, 622–27.

———, and Neubeck, G. Attitudes of entering college freshmen toward the occupational motivations of married women. Student Counseling Bur. Bull. and Occup. Newsletter, Off. Dean of Students, Univ. of Minn., 1963, *16* (1), pp. 2–3.

———, and Neubeck, G. Attitudes of college students toward employment among married women. *Personnel Guid. J.*, 1964, *42*, 587–92. (a)

———, and Neubeck, G. *College Freshmen's Attitudes Toward Working Wives*. Res. Bull., Off. Dean of Students, Univ. of Minn., 1964, *6* (1), 21 pp. (b)

Hildreth, Gertrude. The social interests of young adolescents. *Child Develpm.*, 1945, *16*, 119–21.

Hill, A. H. Autobiographical correlates of achievement motivation in men and women. *Psychol. Rep.*, 1966, *18*, 811–17.

Hill, W. S. Women engineers in industry. In Jacquelyn Mattfeld and Carol Van Aken (eds.), *Women and the Scientific Professions*. Cambridge, Mass.: M.I.T. Press, 1965, pp. 195–200.

Himmelstein, P. Sex differences in shifting behavior in a level of aspiration experiment. *Psychol. Rep.*, 1956, *2*, 101–2.

Hinkle, L., *et al.* An examination of the relation between symptoms, disability, and serious illness, in two homogeneous groups of men and women. *Amer. J. Publ. Health*, 1960, *50*, 1327–36.

Hirsh, J. Suicide. *Ment. Hyg., N.Y.*, 1959, *43*, 516–25.

Hobart, C. W. The pregnant high school girl: an analysis and a proposal. *Personnel Guid. J.*, 1962, *40*, 786–90.

Hobson, J. R. Sex differences in primary mental abilities. *J. Educ. Res.*, 1947, *41*, 126–32.

Hodgkins, Jean. Influence of age on the speed of reaction and movement in females. *J. Gerontol.*, 1962, *17*, 385–89.

———. Reaction time and speed of movement in males and females of various ages. *Res. Quart. Amer. Assoc. Hlth. Phys. Educ. Recr.*, 1963, *34* (3), 335–43.

Hoffman, Lois. Effects of the employment of mothers on parental power relations and the division of household tasks. *Marr. Fam. Living*, 1960, *22*, 27–35.

———. Effects of maternal employment on the child. *Child Develpm.*, 1961, *32*, 187–97.

———. The decision to work. In F. I. Nye and Lois Hoffman (eds.), *The Employed Mother in America*. Chicago: Rand McNally, 1963, pp. 18–39. (a)

————. Effects on children: summary and discussion. *Ibid.*, 1963, pp. 190–212. (b)

Hoffman, L. R., and Maier, N. Sex differences, sex composition, and group problem solving. *J. Abnorm. Soc. Psychol.*, 1961, *63*, 453–56.

————, and Maier, N. Social factors influencing problem solving in women. *J. Person. Soc. Psychol.*, 1966, *4*, 382–90.

Holland, J. L. Student explanations of college choice and their relation to college popularity, college productivity, and sex differences. *Coll. & Univ.*, 1958, *33*, 313–20.

————. Determinants of college choice. *Coll. & Univ.*, 1959, *35*, 11–28.

Hollingworth, Leta. Differential action upon the sexes of forces which tend to segregate the feebleminded. *J. Abnorm. Psychol.*, 1922, *17*, 35–57.

————. *Children Above 180 IQ.* Yonkers-on-Hudson: World Book Co., 1942.

Honzik, Marjorie. Sex differences in the occurrence of materials in the play constructions of pre-adolescents. *Child Develpm.*, 1951, *22*, 15–36.

————. A sex difference in the age of onset of the parent-child resemblance in intelligence. *J. Educ. Psychol.*, 1963, *54*, 231–37.

Hood, A. B. Certain non-intellectual factors related to student attrition at Cornell University. Doctoral dissertation, Cornell Univ., 1957.

Hopwood, Kathryn. Expectations of university freshman women. *Personnel Guid. J.*, 1954, *32*, 464–69.

Hornaday, J., and Kuder, G. F. A study of male occupational interest scales applied to women. *Educ. Psychol. Measmt.*, 1961, *21*, 859–64.

Hornung, D. The faculty wife: a study in occupational aspirations. *J. Nat. Assoc. Deans of Women*, 1955, *18*, 167.

Horrocks, J. The adolescent. In L. Carmichael (ed.), *Manual of Child Psychology.* (2nd ed.) New York: Wiley & Sons, 1954, pp. 697–734.

Hottel, Althea. Perspectives for the education of women. *Educ. Rec.*, 1955, *36*, 112–19.

Howell, R. J. Sex differences and educational influences on a mental deterioration scale. *J. Gerontol.*, 1955, *10*, 190–93.

Hoyt, D., and Kennedy, C. Interest and personality correlates of career-motivated and homemaking-motivated college women. *J. Counsel. Psychol.*, 1958, *5*, 44–48.

Hubert, M. A. G., and Britton, J. H. Attitudes and practices of mothers rearing their children from birth to the age of two years. *J. Home Econ.*, 1957, *49*, 208–23.

Hughes, Mildred. Sex differences in reading achievement in the elementary grades. *Suppl. Educ. Monogr.*, 1953, No. 77, 102–6.

Hulin, C. Job satisfaction and turnover in a female clerical population. *J. Appl. Psychol.*, 1966, *50*, 280–85.

Hulin, C., and Smith, Patricia. Sex differences in job satisfaction. *J. Appl. Psychol.*, 1964, *48*, 88–92.

——, and Smith, Patricia. A linear model of job satisfaction. *J. Appl. Psychol.*, 1965, *49*, 209–16.

Hunter, E. C. Attitudes of college freshmen: 1934–1949. *J. Psychol.*, 1951, *31*, 281–96.

Iffert, R. E. Retention and withdrawal of college students. *Off. Educ. Bull.*, 1958 (1), pp. 22–24.

Impellizzeri, Irene. Nature and scope of the problem. In L. Miller (ed.), *Guidance for the Underachiever with Superior Ability.* Washington: U.S.G.P.O., 1961, pp. 1–14.

International Labour Office. Vocational guidance and training for women. *Inter. Lab. Rev.*, 1952, *66*, 56–76.

Irish, Lois. Needed: unique patterns for educating women. *Coll. Bd. Rev.*, 1962, *46*, 27–31.

Irvine, LaVerne. Sex differences and the relationships between certain personality variables. *Psychol. Rep.*, 1957, *3*, 595–97.

Isaacson, L., and Amos, Louise. Participation in part-time work by women college students. *Personnel Guid. J.*, 1957, *35*, 445–48.

Isaacson, R. Relation between N achievement, test anxiety, and curricular choices. *J. Abnorm. Soc. Psychol.*, 1964, *68*, 447–52.

Jackson, J. A survey of psychological, social, and environmental differences between advanced and retarded readers. *J. Genet. Psychol.*, 1944, *65*, 113–31.

Jackson, P. W., and Getzels, J. W. Psychological health and classroom functioning: a study of dissatisfaction with school among adolescents. *J. Educ. Psychol.*, 1959, *50*, 295–300.

——, and Guba, E. C. Need structure of in-service teachers: an occupational analysis. *Scholastic Rev.*, 1957, *65*, 176–92.

Jacobs, J. Aptitude and achievement measures in predicting high school academic success. *Personnel Guid. J.*, 1959, *37*, 334–41.

Jacobs, R. Stability of interests at the secondary school level. *Educ. Rec. Bull.*, 1949, No. 52, 83–87.

Jahnke, J., Crannell, C., and Morrissette, J. Sex differences and the MAS. *Educ. Psychol. Measmt.*, 1964, *24*, 309–12.

Jahoda, Marie, and Havel, Joan. Psychological problems of women in different social roles: a case history of problem formulation in research. *Educ. Rec.*, 1955, *36*, 325–35.

Janis, I., and Field, P. Sex differences and personality factors related to persuasibility. In C. Hovland and I. Janis (eds.), *Personality and Persuasibility.* New Haven: Yale Univ. Press, 1959, pp. 55–68.

Jenkins, M. D., and Randall, Constance. Differential characteristics of superior and unselected Negro college students. *J. Soc. Psychol.*, 1948, *27*, 187–202.

Johnson, Elizabeth. Sex differences and variability in the performance of retarded children on Raven, Binet, and Arthur Tests. *J. Clin. Psychol.*, 1952, *8*, 298–301.

Johnson, M. C., and Fenton, Anne. 1957 opening (Fall) college enrollment. *Higher Educ.*, 1958, *14*, 73–77.

Johnson, Miriam. Sex role learning in the nuclear family. *Child Develpm.*, 1963, *34*, 319–33.

Johnson, Winifred, and Terman, L. Some highlights in the literature of psychological sex differences published since 1920. *J. Psychol.*, 1940, *9*, 327–36.

Jones, H. E. The development of physical abilities. In N. Henry (ed.), Adolescence. *Yearb. Nat. Soc. Stud. Educ.*, 1944, *43*, Part I, pp. 100–122.

———. Sex differences in physical abilities. *Hum. Biol.*, 1947, *19*, 12–25. (a)

———. The sexual maturing of girls as related to growth in strength. *Res. Quart. Amer. Assoc. Hlth. Phys. Educ.*, 1947, *18*, 135–43. (b)

———. Motor performance and growth. *U. Calif. Publ. Child Develpm.*, 1949, *1*, No. 1.

———, and Seashore, R. The development of fine motor and mechanical abilities. In N. Henry (ed.), Adolescence. *Yearb. Nat. Soc. Stud. Educ.*, 1944, *43*, Part I, pp. 123–45.

Jones, Mary. A study of socialization patterns at the high school level. *J. Genet. Psychol.*, 1958, *93*, 87–111.

———. A comparison of the attitudes and interests of ninth-grade students over two decades. *J. Educ. Psychol.*, 1960, *51*, 175–86.

———, and Mussen, P. Self-conceptions, motivations, and interpersonal attitudes of early- and late-maturing girls. *Child Develpm.*, 1958, *29*, 491–501.

Jones, R. L., Gross, F., and Van Why, E. A longitudinal study of reading achievement in a group of adolescent institutionalized mentally retarded children. *Train. Sch. Bull.*, 1960, *57*, 41–47.

Jordan, A. M. Sex differences in mental traits. *High Sch. J.*, 1937, *20*, 254–61.

Josephina, C. A study of attitudes in the elementary grades. *J. Educ. Sociol.*, 1959, *33*, 56–60.

Jourard, S. M. Self-disclosure patterns in British and American college females. *J. Soc. Psychol.*, 1961, *54*, 315–20.

Jurgensen, C. E. Selected factors which influence job preferences. *J. Appl. Psychol.*, 1947, *31*, 553–64.

———. What do job applicants want? *Personnel*, 1949, *25*, 352–55.

Kaess, W. A., and Witryol, S. L. Memory for names and faces: a characteristic of social intelligence? *J. Appl. Psychol.*, 1955, *39*, 457–62.

Kagan, J. Child's symbolic conceptualization of parents. *Child Develpm.*, 1961, *32*, 625–36.

———, and Moss, H. The stability of passive and dependent behavior from childhood through adulthood. *Child Develpm.*, 1960, *31*, 577–91.

———, and Moss, H. *Birth to Maturity: A Study in Psychological Development*. New York: Wiley & Sons, 1962.

Kallen, D. J. Inner direction, other direction, and social integration setting. *Human Relat.*, 1963, *16*, 75–87.

Kaltenborn, H. S. Utilizing "older" women workers. In National Manpower Council, *Work in the Lives of Married Women*. New York: Columbia Univ. Press, 1958, pp. 57–73.

Kaplan, H., Kaplan, Helen, and Freedman, A. Residency training in psychiatry for physician mothers. *J. Amer. Med. Assoc.*, 1964, *189*, 11–14.

Karzon, Allaire. A tax revision proposal to encourage women into careers. In C. C. Cole, *Encouraging Scientific Talent*. New York: College Entrance Examination Board, 1956. Appendix A, pp. 198–208.

Katz, E. *Children's Preferences for Traditional and Modern Paintings*. New York: Bureau of Publications, Teachers College, 1944.

Kegan, Esther. Interests of women lawyers shown on the Kuder Preference Record. *Personnel Psychol.*, 1954, *7*, 449–507.

Keislar, E. Peer group ratings of high school pupils with high and low school marks. *J. Exp. Educ.*, 1955, *23*, 375–78.

Keller, M. Alcoholism: nature and extent of the problem. *Ann. Amer. Acad. Pol. Soc. Sci.*, 1958, *315*, 1–11.

Kelly, E. L. Consistency of adult personality. *Amer. Psychologist*, 1955, *10*, 659–81.

Kezur, E., Kapp, F., and Rosenbaum, M. Psychological factors in women with peptic ulcers. *Amer. J. Psychiat.*, 1951, *108*, 368–73.

Kiell, N., and Friedman, Bernice. Culture lag and housewifemanship: the role of the married female college graduate. *J. Educ. Sociol.*, 1957, *31*, 87–95.

Kimling-Erlenmeyer, L., and Jarvik, Lissy. Genetics and intelligence: a review. *Science*, 1963, *142*, 1477–79.

Kinsey, A. C., *et al. Sexual Behavior in the Human Female*. Philadelphia: W. B. Saunders, 1953.

Kirk, Barbara, Goodstein, L., and Cummings, R. The Strong Vocational Interest Blank and college nursing education. *Personnel Guid. J.*, 1961, *40*, 160–63.

Kiser, C., and Schachter, Nathalie. Demographic characteristics of women in "Who's Who." *Milbank Mem. Fund Quart.*, 1949, *27*, 392–433.

Kjerland, R. N. Age and sex differences in performance in motility and strength tests. *Proc. Iowa Acad. Sci.*, 1953, *60*, 519–22.

Klausmeier, H. J., Lehmann, I., and Beeman, A. Relationships among physical, mental, and achievement measures in children of low, average, and high intelligence. *Amer. J. Ment. Defic.*, 1959, *63*, 647–56.

———, and Wiersma, W. Relationship of sex, grade level, and locale to performance of high IQ students on divergent thinking tests. *J. Educ. Psychol.*, 1964, *55*, 114–19.

Klein, Viola. The stereotype of femininity. *J. Soc. Issues*, 1950, *6* (3), 3–12.

Kleist, M., Rittenhouse, C., and Farnsworth, P. Strong vocational interest scales for music teachers. *Occupations*, 1949, *28*, 100–101.

Klemer, R. Factors of personality and experience which differentiate single from married women. *Marr. Fam. Living*, 1954, *16*, 41–44.

Kligler, Deborah. The effects of the employment of married women on husband and wife roles. Doctoral dissertation, Univ. of Michigan, 1958.

Klopfer, W. G. Correlation of women's MF scores on the MMPI and Strong VIB. *J. Clin. Psychol.*, 1966, *22*, 216.

Kluckhohn, Florence. American women and American values. In L. Bryson (ed.), *Facing the Future's Risks*. New York: Harper, 1953, pp. 175–99.

Koch, Helen. The relation of "primary mental abilities" in five- and six-year-olds to sex of child and characteristics of his sibling. *Child Develpm.*, 1954, *25*, 209–23.

————. The relation of certain family constellation characteristics and the attitudes of children toward adults. *Child Develpm.*, 1955, *26*, 13–40.

Kohlberg, L., and Zigler, E. The impact of cognitive maturity on the development of sex role attitudes in the years 4 to 8. *Genet. Psychol. Monogr.*, 1967, *75*, 89–165.

Koile, E. A., and Bird, Dorothy. Preferences for counselor help on freshman problems. *J. Counsel. Psychol.*, 1956, *3*, 97–106.

Komarovsky, Mirra. Cultural contradictions and sex roles. *Amer. J. Sociol.*, 1946, *52*, 184–89.

————. *Women in the Modern World*. Boston: Little, Brown, 1953.

Kosa, J., and Coker, R. E. The female physician in public health: conflict and reconciliation of the sex and professional roles. *Sociol. Soc. Res.*, 1965, *49*, 294–305.

————, Rachiele, L., and Schommer, C. Psychological characteristics of ethnic groups in a college population. *J. Psychol.*, 1958, *46*, 265–75.

————, Rachiele, L., and Schommer, C. Marriage, career and religiousness among Catholic college girls. *Marr. Fam. Living*, 1962, *24*, 376–80.

————, and Schommer, C. O. Sex differences in the religious attitudes of Catholic college students. *Psych. Rep.*, 1962, *10*, 285–86.

Kossoris, M. D. Absenteeism and injury experience of older workers. *Month. Labor Rev.*, 1948, *67*, 16–19.

Kostick, M. M. A study of transfer: sex differences in the reasoning process. *J. Educ. Psychol.*, 1954, *45*, 449–58.

Krippner, S. The vocational preferences of high-achieving and low-achieving junior high school students. *Gifted Child Quart.*, 1961, *5*, 88–90.

Krippner, S. Sex, ability, and interest: a test of Tyler's hypothesis. *Gifted Child Quart.*, 1962, *6*, 105–10.

Krogman, W. The physical growth of children: an appraisal of studies 1950–1955. *Monogr. Soc. Res. Child Develpm.*, 1955, *20*, No. 1.

Kuaak, Nancy. A study of the characteristics of academically successful and unsuccessful freshman women who entered Northwestern University in the fall of 1954. Doctoral dissertation, Northwestern Univ., 1956.

Kuder, G. F. *Kuder Preference Record, Vocational–Form C.* Chicago: Science Research Associates, 1956.

———. *Kuder DD Occupational Interest Survey: General Manual.* Chicago: Science Research Associates, 1966.

Kuhlen, R. G. Adolescence. In C. Harris (ed.), *Encyclopedia of Educational Research.* (3rd ed.) New York: Macmillan, 1960, pp. 24–30.

———. Needs, perceived need satisfaction opportunities, and satisfaction with occupation. *J. Appl. Psychol.*, 1963, *47*, 56–64.

———, and Johnson, G. H. Change in goals with increasing adult age. *J. Consult. Psychol.*, 1952, *16*, 1–14.

Kuznets, G. M., and McNemar, Olga. Sex differences in intelligence-test scores. In G. Whipple (ed.), Intelligence: its nature and nurture. *Yearb. Nat. Soc. Stud. Educ.*, 1940, *39*, Part I, pp. 211–20.

Kyrk, Hazel. The economic role of women forty-five to sixty-five. In Irma Gross (ed.), *Potentialities of Women in the Middle Years.* East Lansing: Michigan State Univ. Press, 1956, pp. 127–41.

L'abate, L. Personality correlates of manifest anxiety in children. *J. Consult. Psychol.*, 1960, *24*, 342–48.

LaBrant, L. L. A study of certain language developments of children in grades four to twelve inclusive. *Genet. Psychol. Monogr.*, 1933, *14*, 387–491.

LaFarge, Phyllis. A warm-hearted guide to certain girls' schools. *Harper's*, 1963, *226* (1355), 73–79.

LaFollette, Isabel. Employment opportunities in the women's service exchange program of Madison, Wisconsin. In Irma Gross (ed.), *Potentialities of Women in the Middle Years.* East Lansing: Michigan State Univ. Press, 1956, pp. 159–67.

LaGrone, C. W. Sex and personality differences in relation to fantasy. *J. Consult. Psychol.*, 1963, *27*, 270–72.

Laime, Barbara, and Zytowski, D. Women's scores on the male and female forms of the SVIB. *Voc. Guid. Quart.*, 1963, *12*, 116–18.

Lajewski, H. C. *Child Care Arrangements of Fulltime Working Mothers.* U.S. Child Bur. Publ., No. 378. Washington: U.S.G.P.O., 1959.

Lally, Ann. Education and the role of women—a symposium. *NEA J.*, 1960, *49* (9), 48–53.

Landis, J. T., and Kidd, K. Attitudes and policies concerning marriages among high school students. *Marr. Fam. Living,* 1956, *18*, 128–36.

Landreth, Catherine. Four-year-olds' notions about sex-appropriateness of parental care and companionship activities. *Merrill-Palmer Quart.,* 1963, *9*, 175–82.

Lane, W. C. The lower-class girl in college: a study of Stanford freshman women. Doctoral dissertation, Stanford Univ., 1961.

Langhorne, M. C., and Secord, P. Variations in marital needs with age, sex, marital status, and regional location. *J. Soc. Psychol.,* 1955, *41*, 19–37.

Langwill, Katheryn. Taste perception and taste preferences of the consumer. *Food Tech.,* 1949, *3* (4), 136–39.

Lansky, L. M. The family structure also affects the model: sex-role identification in parents of preschool children. *Merrill-Palmer Quart.,* 1964, *10*, 39–50.

———, et al. Sex differences in aggression and its correlates in middle-class adolescents. *Child Develpm.,* 1961, *32*, 45–58.

———, and McKay, G. Sex role preferences of kindergarten boys and girls: some contradictory results. *Psychol. Rep.,* 1963, *13*, 415–21.

Laurence, Mary. Sex differences in the perception of men and women at four different ages. *J. Gerontol.,* 1964, *19*, 343–48.

Lauriat, Patience. Marriage and fertility patterns of college graduates. *Eugen. Quart.,* 1959, *6*, 171–79.

Layton, W. L. *Counseling Use of the Strong Vocational Interest Blank.* Minnesota Studies in Student Personnel Work, No. 8. Minneapolis: Univ. of Minnesota Press, 1958.

Lazowick, L. M. On the nature of identification. *J. Abnorm. Soc. Psychol.,* 1955, *51*, 175–83.

Leahy, Dorothy. Reading ability of college home economics students. *Calif. J. Educ. Res.,* 1959, *10*, 42–47.

Lee, Marilyn. Relationship of masculinity-femininity to tests of mechanical and clerical abilities. *J. Appl. Psychol.,* 1952, *36*, 377–80.

Lefkowitz, M. M. Some relationships between sex role preference of children and other parent and child variables. *Psychol. Rep.,* 1962, *10*, 43–53.

Lehman, H. C., and Witty, P. A. *The Psychology of Play Activities.* New York: Barnes, 1927.

———, and Witty, P. A. Sex differences in vocational attitudes. *J. Appl. Psychol.,* 1936, *20*, 576–85.

Lehman, I. J., Sinha, B., and Hartnett, R. Changes in attitudes and values associated with college attendance. *J. Educ. Psychol.,* 1966, *57*, 89–98.

Lentz, T. F. Sex differences in school marks with achievement test scores constant. *Sch. Soc.,* 1929, *29*, 65–68.

Leopold, Alice. Today's women college graduates. *Personnel Guid. J.,* 1959, *38*, 280–84.

Lesser, G., Davis, F., and Nahemow, Lucille. The identification of gifted elementary school children with exceptional scientific talent. *Educ. Psychol. Measmt.*, 1962, *22*, 349–64.

Lesser, G., Krawitz, Rhoda, and Packard, Rita. Experimental arousal of achievement motivation in adolescent girls. *J. Abnorm. Soc. Psychol.*, 1963, *66*, 59–66.

Levin, H., and Sears, R. R. Identification with parents as a determinant of doll play aggression. *Child Develpm.*, 1956, *27*, 135–53.

Levinson, B. M. A comparative study of the intelligence of Jewish pre-school boys and girls of orthodox parentage. *J. Genet. Psychol.*, 1957, *90*, 17–22.

Levy, D. M. Psychosomatic studies of some aspects of maternal behavior. *Psychosom. Med.*, 1942, *4*, 223–27.

Lewis, E. C. Counselors and girls. *J. Counsel. Psychol.*, 1965, *12*, 159–66.

———, Wolins, L., and Yelsma, Julie. The academic interests of college women: a factorial study. *Personnel Guid. J.*, 1967, *46*, 258–62.

Lewis, J. W. Utilizing the stepwise multiple regression procedure in selecting predictor variables by sex group. *Educ. Psychol. Measmt.*, 1962, *22*, 401–4.

Lewis, W. D. Sex distribution of intelligence among inferior and superior children. *J. Genet. Psychol.*, 1945, *67*, 67–75.

Liccione, J. V. The changing family relationships of adolescent girls. *J. Abnorm. Soc. Psychol.*, 1955, *51*, 421–26.

Likert, R., and Quasha, W. *The Revised Minnesota Paper Form Board Test, Manual.* New York: Psychological Corporation, 1948.

Lin, Yi-guang. Age and sex differences in the dimensionality of the self concept. Doctoral dissertation, Univ. of Michigan, 1962.

Lindzey, G., and Goldberg, M. Motivational differences between male and female as measured by the Thematic Apperception Test. *J. Person.*, 1953, *22*, 101–17.

Lingwood, Joan. Test performances of ATS recruits from certain civilian occupations. *Occup. Psychol.*, 1952, *26*, 35–46.

Linton, R. *Culture and Mental Disorders.* Springfield, Ill.: Charles C. Thomas, 1956.

Lipman, A. Educational preparation for the female role. *J. Educ. Sociol.*, 1959, *33*, 40–43.

Livingstone, Elizabeth. The recruitment of women supervisors. *Psychol. at Work*, 1951, *5*, 2–6.

———. Attitudes of women operatives to promotion. *Occup. Psychol.*, 1953, *27*, 191–99.

Livson, N., McNeill, D., and Thomas, Karla. Pooled estimates of parent-child correlations in stature from birth to maturity. *Science*, 1962, *138*, 818–20.

Lloyd-Jones, Esther. Progress report of pertinent research. In Irma Gross (ed.), *Potentialities of Women in the Middle Years.* East Lansing: Michigan State Univ. Press, 1956, pp. 19–29. (a)

————. Women today and their education. *Teachers Coll. Rec.*, 1956, *57*, 431–37. (b)

————. The Commission on the Education of Women. *Educ. Rec.*, 1957, *38*, 250–57.

————. Education for reentry in the labor force. In National Manpower Council, *Work in the Lives of Married Women.* New York: Columbia Univ. Press, 1958, pp. 27–40.

Lobaugh, D. Girls and grades: a significant factor in evaluation. *Sch. Sci. Math.*, 1947, *47*, 763–74.

Loch, W. E. Incidence and permanence of tonal dips in children. *Laryngoscope*, 1943, *53*, 347–56.

Locke, H., and Mackeprang, Muriel. Marital adjustment and the employed wife. *Amer. J. Sociol.*, 1949, *54*, 536–38.

Lough, Orpha. Women students in liberal arts, nursing, and teacher training curricula and the Minnesota Multiphasic Personality Inventory. *J. Appl. Psychol.*, 1947, *31*, 437–45.

Loutitt, C. M. Women: their roles and education. *J. Higher Educ.*, 1951, *22*, 202–8, 226.

Lowrie, S. H. Sex differences and age of initial dating. *Soc. Forces*, 1952, *30*, 456–61.

Lowther, F., and Downes, H. R. Women in medicine. *J. Amer. Med. Assoc.*, 1945, *129*, 512–14.

Lucito, L., and Gallagher, J. Intellectual patterns of highly gifted children on the WISC. *Peabody J. Educ.*, 1960, *38*, 131–36.

Ludeman, W. W. Declining female college attendance: causes and implications. *Educ. Forum*, 1961, *25*, 505–7.

Lund, F. H. Adolescent motivation: sex differences. *J. Genet. Psychol.*, 1944, *64*, 99–103.

————, Yeomans, E., and Geiges, E. Health indices in relation to age, sex, race, and socioeconomic status. *J. Soc. Psychol.*, 1946, *24*, 111–17.

Lyle, Mary. Graduates reflect on their education. *J. Home Econ.*, 1957, *49*, 9–12.

Lyness, P. E. Patterns in the mass communications tastes of the young audience. *J. Educ. Psychol.*, 1951, *42*, 449–67.

Lynn, D. B. A note on sex differences in the development of masculine and feminine identification. *Psychol. Rev.*, 1959, *66*, 126–35.

————. Sex differences in identification development. *Sociometry*, 1961, *24*, 372–83.

————. Sex-role and parental identification. *Child Develpm.*, 1962, *33*, 555–64.

————. The process of learning parental and sex-role identification. *J. Marr. Fam.*, 1966, *28*, 466–70.

————, and Sawrey, W. The effects of father-absence on Norwegian boys and girls. *J. Abnorm. Soc. Psychol.*, 1959, *59*, 258–62.

————, and Sawrey, W. Sex differences in the personality development of Norwegian children. *J. Genet. Psychol.*, 1962, *101*, 367–74.

MacBrayer, Caroline. Differences in perception of the opposite sex by males and females. *J. Soc. Psychol.*, 1960, *52*, 309–14.

McBride, Katherine. What is women's education? *Ann. Amer. Acad. Pol. Soc. Sci.*, 1947, *251* (3), 143–52.

McCall, J. R. *Sex Differences in Intelligence: A Comparative Factor Study.* Washington: Catholic Univ. of America Press, 1955.

McCarthy, Dorothea. The language development of the preschool child. *Univ. Minn. Inst. Child Welf. Monogr.*, 1930, 4.

————. Some possible explanations of sex differences in language development and disorders. *J. Psychol.*, 1953, *35*, 155–60.

————. Language development in children. In L. Carmichael (ed.), *Manual of Child Psychology*, (2nd ed.) New York: Wiley & Sons, 1954, pp. 492–630.

McClelland, D., *et al. The Achievement Motive.* New York: Appleton-Century-Crofts, 1953.

McConnell, R. R., and Heist, P. The diverse college student population. In N. Sanford (ed.), *The American College.* New York: Wiley & Sons, 1962, pp. 225–52.

McCord, Joan, McCord, W., and Thurber, Emily. Effects of maternal employment on lower-class boys. *J. Abnorm. Soc. Psychol.*, 1963, *67*, 177–82.

McCormack, R. L. Sex differences in the vocational interests of a professional group. Doctoral dissertation, Univ. of Minnesota, 1954.

McCurdy, H. G. Basal metabolism and academic performance in a sample of college women. *J. Educ. Psychol.*, 1947, *38*, 363–72.

McDonald, R., and Gynther, M. MMPI differences associated with sex, race, and class in two adolescent samples. *J. Consult. Psychol.*, 1963, *27*, 112–16.

McDowell, A., Brown, W., and McTee, A. Sex as a factor in spatial delayed-response performance by rhesus monkeys. *J. Comp. Physiol. Psychol.*, 1960, *53*, 429–32.

————, Brown, W., and McTee, A. Sex as a factor in delayed-response and reduced-cue discrimination learning by previously irradiated monkeys. *J. Genet. Psychol.*, 1962, *100*, 325–29.

MacFarlane, Catharine. Physiological changes and adjustments from the standpoint of a physician. In Irma Gross (ed.), *Potentialities of Women in the Middle Years.* East Lansing: Michigan State Univ. Press, 1956, pp. 49–58.

MacFarlane, Jean, Allen, Lucille, and Honzik, Marjorie. A developmental study of the behavior problems of normal children between twenty-one months and fourteen years. *Univ. Calif. Publ. Child Develpm.*, 1954, 2, 1–122.

McFate, M. Q., and Orr, F. G. Through adolescence with the Rorschach. *Rorschach Res. Exchg.*, 1949, *13*, 302–19.

McGregor, D., and Knickerbocker, I. Industrial relations and rational defense: a challenge to management. *Personnel*, 1941, *18*, 49–63.

McGuire, C. Sex role and community variability in test performance. *J. Educ. Psychol.,* 1961, *52,* 61–73.

McIntosh, Millicent. The education of women in the modern world. *Amer. Coun. Educ. Stud.,* 1949, *13* (35), 77–80.

McKee, J., and Sherriffs, A. The differential evaluation of males and females. *J. Person.,* 1957, *25,* 356–71.

———, and Sherriffs, A. Men's and women's beliefs, ideals, and self-concepts. *Amer. J. Sociol.,* 1959, *64,* 356–63.

McLeish, J. Sex differences in children's art judgment: a preliminary survey. *Leeds Inst. Educ. Res. Stud.,* 1951, No. 3, 70–83.

McNemar, Q. *The Revision of the Stanford-Binet Scale.* Boston: Houghton Mifflin, 1942.

Maccoby, Eleanor. Effects upon children of their mothers' outside employment. In National Manpower Council, *Work in the Lives of Married Women.* New York: Columbia Univ. Press, 1958, pp. 150–72.

———. The taking of adult roles in middle childhood. *J. Abnorm. Soc. Psychol.,* 1961, *63,* 493–503.

———. Sex differences in intellectual functioning. In Eleanor Maccoby (ed.). *The Development of Sex Differences.* Stanford, Calif.: Stanford Univ. Press, 1966, pp. 25–55. (b)

———. (ed.). *The Development of Sex Differences.* Stanford, Calif.: Stanford Univ. Press, 1966. (a)

Mace, D. R. The employed mother in the USSR. *Marr. Fam. Living,* 1961, *23,* 330–33.

Macmeeken, Agnes. *The Intelligence of a Representative Group of Scottish Children.* London: Univ. of London Press, 1939.

Maier, N. R., and Burke, R. J. Response availability as a factor in the problem-solving performance of males and females. *J. Person. Soc. Psychol.,* 1967, *5,* 304–10.

Maine, R. F., and Goodstein, L. D. Cross-validation of the Aaronson MF index with a college population. *Psychol. Rep.,* 1966, *19,* 1141–42.

Malcolm, D. D. Which interest inventory should I use? *J. Educ. Res.,* 1950, *44,* 91–98.

Malloy, J. An investigation of scholastic over- and under-achievement among female college freshmen. *J. Counsel. Psychol.,* 1954, *1,* 260–63.

Manis, M. Personal adjustment, assumed similarity to parents, and inferred parental-evaluations of the self. *J. Consult. Psychol.,* 1958, *22,* 481–85.

Manosevitz, M., and Lanyon, R. I. Fear survey schedule: a normative study. *Psychol. Rep.,* 1965, *17,* 699–703.

Marks, J. B. Interests, leadership and sociometric status among adolescents. *Sociometry,* 1954, *17,* 340–49.

———. Interests and leadership among adolescents. *J. Genet. Psychol.,* 1957, *91,* 163–72.

Marksberry, Mary Lee. Attitudes of college women toward selected roles in life. *Sch. Soc.,* 1952, *75,* 394–96.

Martin, W. E. Quantitative expression in young children. *Genet. Psychol. Monogr.*, 1951, *44*, 147–219.

Mason, W., Dressel, R., and Bain, R. Sex role and the career orientations of beginning teachers. *Harv. Educ. Rev.*, 1959, *29*, 370–83.

Matarazzo, Ruth, Matarazzo, J., and Saslow, G. The relationship between medical and psychiatric symptoms. *J. Abnorm. Soc. Psychol.*, 1961, *62*, 55–61.

Mattfeld, Jacquelyn, and Van Aken, Carol (eds.). *Women and the Scientific Professions.* Cambridge: M.I.T. Press, 1965.

Matthews, Esther. The marriage-career conflict in the career development of girls and young women. Doctoral dissertation, Harvard Univ., 1960.

———, and Tiedeman, D. Attitudes toward career and marriage and the development of life style in young women. *J. Counsel. Psychol.*, 1964, *11*, 375–84.

Maule, Frances. *Executive Careers for Women.* New York: Harper, 1961.

Maxham, H. K. A study of the viewpoints of women of different age groups. *J. Genet. Psychol.*, 1944, *64*, 311–15.

Maxwell, M., Lemere, F., and O'Hollaren, P. Changing characteristics of private-hospital alcoholic patients. *Quart. J. Stud. Alcohol*, 1958, *19*, 309–15.

Mead, Margaret. *Sex and Temperament in Three Primitive Societies.* New York: Morrow, 1939.

———. Towards mutual responsibility. *J. Soc. Issues*, 1950, *6* (3), 45–56.

———. Some theoretical considerations on the problem of mother-child separation. *Amer. J. Orthopsychiat.*, 1954, *24*, 471–83.

———. Cultural determinants of behavior. In W. C. Young (ed.), *Sex and Internal Secretions.* (2nd ed.) Vol. II. Baltimore: Williams & Wilkins, 1961, pp. 1433–79. (a)

———. Gender in the honors program. *Super. Stud.*, 1961, *4* (4), 2–6. (b)

———, and Kaplan, Frances. *American Women.* New York: Scribner's, 1965.

Mellone, M. A. A factorial study of picture tests for young children. *Brit. J. Psychol.*, 1944, *35*, 9–16.

Meltzer, H. Sex differences in children's attitudes to parents. *J. Genet. Psychol.*, 1943, *62*, 311–26.

Mendelsohn, G. A. Similarity of college counselor-counselee personality characteristics. Paper read at Amer. Personnel Guid. Assoc., Chicago, Apr., 1962.

Mendenhall, T. C. Women's education and the educated woman. *Sch. Soc.*, 1960, *88*, 436–39.

Meyer, Agnes. The middle-aged woman in contemporary society. In Irma Gross (ed.), *Potentialities of Women in the Middle Years.* East Lansing: Michigan State Univ. Press, 1956, pp. 145–58.

Meyer, W., and Bendig, A. W. A longitudinal study of the Primary Mental Abilities Test. *J. Educ. Psychol.,* 1961, *52,* 50–60.

Meyer, W. J., and Thompson, G. G. Sex differences in the distribution of teacher approval and disapproval among sixth-grade children. *J. Educ. Psychol.,* 1956, *47,* 385–96.

Michael, W., Zimmerman, W., and Guilford, J. An investigation of the nature of the spatial-relations and visualization factors in two high school samples. *Educ. Psychol. Measmt.,* 1951, *11,* 561–77.

Middletown, R., and Grigg, C. Rural-urban differences in aspirations. *Rural Sociol.,* 1959, *24,* 347–54.

Miele, J. A. Sex differences in intelligence: the relationship of sex to intelligence as measured by the Wechsler Adult Intelligence Scale and the Wechsler Intelligence Scale for Children. Doctoral dissertation, New York Univ., 1958.

Miles, Catherine. Expectations and achievements for women psychologists in middle life. Paper read at Amer. Psychol. Assoc., Philadelphia, Aug., 1963.

Milisen, R., and Johnson, W. A comparative study of stutterers, former stutterers, and normal speakers whose handedness has been changed. *Arch. Speech,* 1936, *1,* 59–86.

Miller, J. L. L. Occupational choice and the educational system. *J. Educ. Sociol.,* 1960, *34,* 117–26.

Mills, C. A. Geographic and time variations in body growth and age at menarche. *Hum. Biol.,* 1937, *9,* 43–56.

Milner, Esther. Effects of sex role and social status on the early adolescent personality. *Genet. Psychol. Monogr.,* 1949, *40,* 231–325.

Milton, G. A. The effects of sex-role identification upon problem-solving skill. *J. Abnorm. Soc. Psychol.,* 1957, *55,* 208–12.

————. Sex differences in problem solving as a function of role appropriateness of the problem content. *Psychol. Rep.,* 1959, *5,* 705–8.

Minuchin, Patricia. Sex-role concepts and sex typing in childhood as a function of school and home environments. *Child Develpm.,* 1965, *36,* 1033–48.

Mitchell, Blythe. The Metropolitan Readiness Tests as predictors of first-grade achievement. *Educ. Psychol. Measmt.,* 1962, *22,* 765–72.

Mitchell, E. D. Interest profiles of university women. *Voc. Guid. Quart.,* 1957, *6,* 85–89.

Mitchell, J. P. Coming problems in the labor force. In National Manpower Council, *Work in the Lives of Married Women.* New York: Columbia Univ. Press, 1958, pp. 16–23.

Mitchell, Mildred. Status of women in the American Psychological Association. *Amer. Psychologist,* 1951, *6,* 193–201.

Mohr, Jennie. Home-making problems of working women. *Smith Coll. Stud. Soc. Wk.,* 1948, *19* (1), 27–62.

Mollenkopf, W. G. The effectiveness of an easier "male" mechanical test for use with women. *USN Bur. Nav. Pers. Tech. Bull.,* 1956, No. 56–6, ii.

Money, J. Sex hormones and other variables in human eroticism. In W. C. Young (ed.), *Sex and Internal Secretions.* (2nd ed.) Vol. II. Baltimore: Williams & Wilkins, 1961, pp. 1383–1400.

Montagu, A. *The Natural Superiority of Women.* New York: Macmillan, 1953.

Montague, Anita. A factorial analysis of the "basic" interest patterns of two hundred women college students in various curricular groups. Doctoral dissertation, Temple Univ., 1960.

Moore, Bernice. Education and the role of women—a symposium. *NEA J.,* 1960, *49* (9), 48–53.

————, and Holtzman, W. What Texas knows about youth. *Nat. Parent-Teacher,* 1958, *53* (1), 22–24.

Moore, Joan. Patterns of women's participation in voluntary associations. *Amer. J. Sociol.,* 1961, *66,* 592–98.

Moore, T. Language and intelligence: a longitudinal study of the first eight years. *Hum. Develpm.,* 1967, *10,* 88–106.

More, D. M. Developmental concordance and discordance during puberty and early adolescence. *Monogr. Soc. Res. Child Develpm.,* 1955, *18* (Whole No. 1).

Morgan, A. B. Sex differences in adults on a test of logical reasoning. *Psych. Rep.,* 1956, *2,* 227–30.

Morgan, Donna. Perception of role conflicts and self concepts among career and noncareer college educated women. Doctoral dissertation, Columbia Univ., 1962.

Moss, H. and Kagan, J. Maternal influences on early I.Q. scores. *Psychol. Rep.,* 1958, *4,* 655–61.

————, and Kagan, J. Stability of achievement and recognition seeking behaviors from early childhood through adulthood. *J. Abnorm. Soc. Psychol.,* 1961, *62,* 504–13.

Moss, J. J., and Gingles, Ruby. The relationship of personality to the incidence of early marriage. *Marr. Fam. Living,* 1959, *21,* 373–77.

Mueller, Kate. Problems in counseling women. In E. G. Williamson (ed.), *Trends in Student Personnel Work.* Minneapolis: Univ. of Minnesota Press, 1949, pp. 356–70.

————. *Educating Women for a Changing World.* Minneapolis: Univ. of Minnesota Press, 1954. (a)

————. Sex differences in campus regulations. *Personnel Guid. J.,* 1954, *32,* 528–32. (b)

————, and Mueller, J. Socio-economic background of women students at Indiana University. *Educ. Psychol. Measmt.,* 1949, *9,* 321–29.

Muller, L., and Muller, Ouida. Dividends on human investment. In L. Muller and Ouida Muller (eds.), *New Horizons for College Women.* Washington: Public Affairs Press, 1960, pp. 101–13.

Mulvey, Mary. Psychological and sociological factors in prediction of career patterns of women. *Genet. Psychol. Monogr.*, 1963, *68*, 309–86.

Murphy, F. Women and the scientific revolution. *J. Amer. Assoc. Univ. Women*, 1959, *53*, 19–22.

Mussen, P., and Martin, W. Childhood and preadolescence. In C. Harris (ed.), *Encyclopedia of Educational Research*. (3rd ed.) New York: Macmillan, 1960, pp. 194–99.

Myrdal, Alva, and Klein, Viola. *Women's Two Roles: Home and Work*. London: Routledge & Kegan Paul, Ltd., 1956.

Nadelhoffer, Luella. Gynecological problems—their effect on the working woman. *Amer. J. Publ. Health*, 1960, *50*, 1337–41.

Nadler, E., and Morrow, W. Authoritarianism attitudes toward women, and their correlates. *J. Soc. Psychol.*, 1959, *49*, 113–23.

Nance, R. D. Masculinity and femininity in prospective teachers. *J. Educ. Res.*, 1949, *42*, 658–66.

National Education Association. Interesting facts and figures on American education. *NEA Res. Bull.*, 1963, *41*, 3–9. (a)
———. Principals of small high schools. *Ibid.*, 1963, *41*, 15–18. (b)
———. Teachers in public schools. *Ibid.*, 1963, *41*, 23–26. (c)
———. Need for college teachers grows. *Ibid.*, 1963, *41*, 108–15. (d)
———. Graduates and dropouts in the labor force. *Ibid.*, 1963, *41*, 120–21. (e)
———. Census of all teachers. *Ibid.*, 1964, *42*, 67–74. (a)
———. Principals: their schools, staff, age, sex, degrees, and experience. *Ibid.*, 1964, *42*, 89–92. (b)
———. School statistics, 1964–65. *Ibid.*, 1965, *43*, 3–8.
———. Estimates of school statistics, 1966–67. *Ibid.*, 1967, *45*, 3–11.

National Manpower Council. *Womanpower*. New York: Columbia Univ. Press, 1957.
———. *Work in the Lives of Married Women*. New York: Columbia Univ. Press, 1958.

National Science Foundation. Summary characteristics of scientists reporting to the National Registry of Scientific and Technical Personnel, 1960. *Scient. Manpower Bull.*, No. 17, 1962.
———. Summary of American science manpower, 1962. *Scient. Manpower Bull.*, No. 20, 1964.

Naylor, J., and Vincent, N. Predicting female absenteeism. *Personnel Psychol.*, 1959, *12*, 81–84.

Nemir, Rosa Lee. Women physicians assess emotional health of the family. *J. Amer. Med. Women's Assoc.*, 1958, *13*, 132–33.

Neugarten, Bernice. Kansas City study of adult life. In Irma Gross (ed.), *Potentialities of Women in the Middle Years*. East Lansing: Michigan State Univ. Press, 1956, pp. 35–45.

Neuman, Rebecca. When will the educational needs of women be met? Some questions for the counselor. *J. Counsel. Psychol.*, 1963, *10*, 378–83.

Newcomer, Mabel. *A Century of Higher Education for American Women*. New York: Harper, 1959.

Nichols, R. C. Subtle, obvious, and stereotype measures of masculinity-femininity. *Educ. Psychol. Measmt.*, 1962, *22*, 449–61.
———. Career decisions of very able students. *Science*, 1964, *144*, 1315–19.
———, and Astin, A. W. Progress of the Merit scholar: an eight-year follow-up. *Personnel Guid. J.*, 1966, *44*, 673–81.
Nolan, Francena. Effects on rural children. In F. I. Nye and Lois Hoffman (eds.), *The Employed Mother in America*. Chicago: Rand McNally, 1963, pp. 122–24. (a)
———. Rural employment and husbands and wives. *Ibid.*, 1963, pp. 241–50. (b)
Norman, R. D. Concealment of age among psychologists: evidence for a popular stereotype. *J. Soc. Psychol.*, 1949, *30*, 127–35.
———. Sex differences and other aspects of young superior adult performance on the Wechsler-Bellevue. *J. Consult. Psychol.*, 1953, *17*, 411–18.
Norris, L. W. How to educate a woman. *Sat. Rev.*, 1954, *37* (48), 9–10, 38–40.
Northby, A. S. Sex differences in high-school scholarship. *Sch. Soc.*, 1958, *86*, 63–64.
Norton, J. L. Patterns of vocational interest development and actual job choice. *J. Genet. Psychol.*, 1953, *82*, 235–62.
Nye, F. I. *Family Relationships and Delinquent Behavior*. New York: Wiley & Sons, 1958.
———. Employment status of mothers and adjustment of adolescent children. *Marr. Fam. Living*, 1959, *21*, 240–44. (a)
———. Employment status of mothers and marital conflict, permanence, and happiness. *Soc. Probl.*, 1959, *6*, 260–67. (b)
———. Maternal employment and marital interaction: some contingent conditions. *Social Forces*, 1961, *40*, 113–19.
———. Personal satisfaction. In F. I. Nye and Lois Hoffman (eds.), *The Employed Mother in America*. Chicago: Rand McNally, 1963, pp. 320–30. (a)
———. Adjustment to children. *Ibid.*, 1963, pp. 353–62. (b)
———. Recreation and community. *Ibid.*, 1963, pp. 363–71. (c)
———. Adjustment of the mother: summary and a frame of reference. *Ibid.*, 1963, pp. 384–99. (d)
———, and Hoffman, Lois. The socio-cultural setting. *Ibid.*, 1963, pp. 3–17. (b)
———, and Hoffman, Lois (eds.). *The Employed Mother in America*. Chicago: Rand McNally, 1963. (a)
———, Perry, J., and Ogles, R. Anxiety and anti-social behavior in preschool children. *Ibid.*, pp. 82–94.
Obst, Frances. A study of selected psychometric characteristics of home economics and non-home economics women at the University of California, Los Angeles. *Calif. J. Educ. Res.*, 1959, *10*, 180–84.
Oettinger, Katherine. Maternal employment and children. In Na-

tional Manpower Council, *Work in the Lives of Married Women.* New York: Columbia Univ. Press, 1958, pp. 133–49.

Ohio State Employment Service Testing Staff. A General Aptitude Test Battery study with high-school seniors. *Educ. Psychol. Measmt.,* 1949, *9,* 281–89.

Olivier, S. Influence de la mixité. *BINOP,* 1958, *14,* Numéro Spécial, 123–29.

O'Neil, Patricia, and Madaus, G. F. Differences in interest patterns between graduates of diploma and basic collegiate programs in nursing. *J. Counsel. Psychol.,* 1966, *13,* 300–305.

Osborne, R. T., and Sanders, Wilma. Variations in Graduate Record Examination performance by age and sex. *J. Gerontol.,* 1954, *9,* 179–85.

Overall, J. E. A masculinity-femininity scale for the Kuder Preference Record. *J. Gen. Psychol.,* 1963, *69,* 209–16.

Paivio, A., and Lambert, W. Measures and correlates of audience anxiety ("stage fright"). *J. Person.,* 1959, *27,* 1–17.

Palmore, E. B. Differences in the retirement patterns of men and women. *Gerontologist,* 1965, *5,* 4–8.

Palubinskas, Alice. Personality changes in college women during four years of college experience. *Proc. Iowa Acad. Sci.,* 1952, *59,* 389–91.

Parker, Aileen. Career and marriage orientation in the vocational development of college women. *J. Appl. Psychol.,* 1966, *50,* 232–35.

Parrish, J. B. Professional womanpower as a national resource. *Quart. Rev. Econ. Bus.,* 1961, *1* (1), 54–63.

———. Women in top level teaching and research. *J. Amer. Assoc. Univ. Women,* 1962, *55,* 99–107.

———. Employment of women chemists in industrial laboratories. *Science,* 1965, *148,* 657–58.

Parsley, K., and Powell, M. Achievement gains or losses during the academic year and over the summer vacation period: a study of trends in achievement by sex and grade level among students of average intelligence. *Genet. Psychol. Monogr.,* 1962, *66,* 285–342.

———, et al. Are there really sex differences in achievement? *J. Educ. Res.,* 1963, *57,* 210–12.

Parsons, T. Age and sex in the social structure of the United States. In C. Kluckhohn, H. Murray, and D. Schneider (eds.), *Personality in Nature, Society, and Culture.* New York: Knopf, 1953, pp. 363–75.

———. The American family: its relations to personality and to the social structure. In T. Parsons and R. Bales, *Family, Socialization and Interaction Process.* Glencoe, Ill.: Free Press, 1955, pp. 3–33.

———, and Bales, R. *Family, Socialization and Interaction Process.* Glencoe, Ill.: Free Press, 1955.

Patel, A. S., and Gordon, J. E. Some personal and situational determinants of yielding to influence. *J. Abnorm. Soc. Psychol.*, 1960, *61*, 411–18.

Paterson, D. G. *et al. Minnesota Mechanical Ability Tests.* Minneapolis: Univ. of Minnesota Press, 1930.

Patterson, Alicia. Address to the Radcliffe Alumnae Association, Cambridge, Mass., October 18, 1961.

Pauley, F. R. Sex differences and legal school entrance age. *J. Educ. Res.*, 1951, *45*, 1–9.

Pavlos, A. J. Sex differences among rural Negro children on the Wechsler Intelligence Scale for Children. *Proc. W. Va. Acad. Sci.*, 1961, *33*, 109–14.

Payne, R. Adolescents' attitudes toward the working wife. *Marr. Fam. Living*, 1956, *18*, 345–48.

Pearce, C. A. Employment status of older workers. *Indus. Bull. N.Y. St. Dept. Labor*, 1949, *28*, 34–40.

Penny, R. Age and sex differences in motivational orientation to the communicative act. *Child Develpm.*, 1958, *29*, 163–71.

Perkins, H. V. Factors influencing change in children's self-concepts. *Child Develpm.*, 1958, *29*, 221–30.

Perrone, P. A. Values and occupational preferences of junior high school girls. *Personnel Guid. J.*, 1965, *44*, 253–57.

Perry, J. B. The mother substitutes of employed mothers: an exploratory inquiry. *Marr. Fam. Living*, 1961, *23*, 362–67.

Peterson, E. T. The impact of maternal employment on the mother-daughter relationship. *Marr. Fam. Living*, 1961, *23*, 355–61.

Phillips, B. N. Sex, social class, and anxiety as sources of variation in school achievement. *J. Educ. Psychol.*, 1962, *55*, 316–22.

Pierce, J. V. The educational motivation patterns of superior students who do and do not achieve in high school. (mimeo.) Univ. of Chicago, 1959.

————. Sex differences in achievement motivation. (mimeo.) Univ. of Chicago, 1961.

————, and Bowman, P. H. *The Educational Motivations of Superior Students Who Do and Do Not Achieve in High School.* U.S. Off. Educ. Proj. No. 208, Coop. Res. Monogr. No. 2. Washington: U.S.G.P.O., 1960.

Pinckney, G. A. Relative strengths of impulse, ego, and superego in female college students. *Percept. Motor Skills*, 1963, *17*, 340.

Pintler, Margaret, Phillips, Ruth, and Sears, R. Sex differences in the projective doll play of preschool children. *J. Psychol.*, 1946, *21*, 73–80.

Plant, W. T. Sex, intelligence, and sorority or fraternity membership and changes in ethnocentrism over a two-year period. *J. Genet. Psychol.*, 1958, *93*, 53–57.

Poffenberger, T., and Norton, D. Sex differences in achievement motive in mathematics as related to cultural change. *J. Genet. Psychol.*, 1963, *103*, 341–50.

Pohlman, E., and Robinson, F. P. Client reactions to some aspects of the counseling situation. *Personnel Guid. J.,* 1960, *38,* 546–51.

Portenier, L. G. Mechanical aptitudes of university women. *J. Appl. Psychol.,* 1945, *29,* 477–82.

Powell, Kathryn. Maternal employment in relation to family life. *Marr. Fam. Living,* 1961, *23,* 350–55.

———. Personalities of children and child-raising attitudes of mothers. In F. I. Nye and Lois Hoffman (eds.), *The Employed Mother in America.* Chicago: Rand McNally, 1963, pp. 125–32. (a)

———. Family variables. *Ibid.,* 1963, pp. 231–40. (b)

Powell, M. Age and sex differences in degree of conflict within certain areas of psychological adjustment. *Psychol. Monogr.,* 1955, *69,* No. 387.

President's Commission on the Status of Women. *American Women.* Washington: U.S.G.P.O., 1963.

Preston, R. C. Reading achievement of German and American children. *Sch. Soc.,* 1962, *90,* 350–54.

Pronko, N. H., *et al.* An experiment in pursuit of "color-blindness." *J. Genet. Psychol.,* 1949, *74,* 125–42.

Rabban, M. Sex-role identification in young children in two diverse social groups. *Genet. Psychol. Monogr.,* 1950, *42,* 81–158.

Raboch, J., and Nedoma, K. Sex chromatin and sexual behavior. *Psychosom. Med.,* 1958, *20,* 55–59.

Radcliffe Committee on Graduate Education for Women. *Graduate Education for Women.* Cambridge: Harvard Univ. Press, 1956.

Ramsey, C., and Nelson, L. Change in values and attitudes toward the family. *Amer. Sociol. Rev.,* 1956, *21,* 605–9.

Raushenbush, Esther. Unfinished business: continuing education for women. *Educ. Rec.,* 1961, *42,* 261–69.

———. Second chance: new education for women. *Harper's,* 1962, *225* (1349), 147–52.

Reed, M. R. The masculinity-femininity dimension in normal and psychotic subjects. *J. Abnorm. Soc. Psychol.,* 1957, *55,* 289–94.

Reese, H. W. Sociometric choices of the same and opposite sex in late childhood. *Merrill-Palmer Quart.,* 1962, *8,* 173–74.

———. Attitudes toward the opposite sex in late childhood. *Merrill-Palmer Quart.,* 1966, *12,* 157–63.

Reid, Margaret. The economic contribution of homemakers. *Ann. Amer. Acad. Pol. Soc. Sci.,* 1947, *251* (3), 61–69.

Remmers, H. H., and Gage, N. L. The abilities and interests of pharmacy freshmen. *Amer. J. Pharm. Educ.,* 1948, *12,* 1–65.

Renier, E. La privation de la présence au retour de l'école. *Enfance,* 1957, No. 4, 491–504.

Reymert, M. L., and Rotman, M. Auditory changes in children from ages ten to eighteen. *J. Genet. Psychol.,* 1946, *68,* 181–87.

Reynolds, E., and Wines, Janet. Individual differences in physical changes associated with adolescence in girls. *Amer. J. Dis. Children*, 1948, *75*, 329–50.

Rezler, Agnes. Characteristics of high school girls choosing traditional or pioneer vocations. *Personnel Guid. J.*, 1967, *45*, 659–65.

Rhinehart, J. Sex differences in dispersion at the high school and college levels. *Psychol. Monogr.*, 1947, *6*, No. 282.

Rice, B. F. The lady's not for learning. *Sat. Rev.*, 1961, *44* (28), 57.

Riesman, D. Women . . . their orbits and their education. *J. Amer. Assoc. Univ. Women*, 1958, *51*, 77–81.

Rigg, M. G. The relative variability of boys and girls. *J. Genet. Psychol.*, 1940, *56*, 211–14.

Rimland, B., and Steinemann, J. Development and standardization of Women's Mechanical Test, Form 6W. *USN Bur. Naval Personnel Tech. Bull.*, 1958, No. 58–14.

Roberts, Eunice. Concerning curricula for women. *Personnel Guid. J.*, 1953, *32*, 165–67.

Roberts, Helen. Factors affecting the academic underachievement of bright high-school students. *J. Educ. Res.*, 1962, *56*, 175–83.

Roe, Anne. *Psychology of Occupations*. New York: Wiley & Sons, 1956.

——. What to look for in a career. In L. Muller and Ouida Muller (eds.), *New Horizons for College Women*. Washington: Public Affairs Press, 1960, pp. 66–78.

——. Women in science. *Personnel Guid. J.*, 1966, *44*, 784–87.

Rogers, C. R. *On Becoming a Person*. Boston: Houghton Mifflin, 1961.

——, and Dymond, Rosalind (eds.). *Psychotherapy and Personality Change*. Chicago: Univ. of Chicago Press, 1954.

Rogers, Dorothy. *The Psychology of Adolescence*. New York: Appleton-Century-Crofts, 1962.

Rollins, Mabel. Monetary contributions of wives to family income in 1920 and 1960. *Marr. Fam. Living*, 1963, *25*, 226–27.

Romney, A. K. Variations in household structure as determinants of sex-typed behavior. In F. A. Beach (ed.), *Sex and Behavior*. New York: Wiley & Sons, 1965, pp. 208–20.

Rose, A. M. The adequacy of women's expectations for adult roles. *Soc. Forces*, 1951, *30*, 69–77.

——. Reference groups of rural high school youth. *Child Develpm.*, 1956, *27*, 351–63.

Rose, Caroline. American women in the home and family. *Amer. Rev.*, 1961, *2*, 33–43.

Rosenberg, B. G., and Sutton-Smith, B. The measurement of masculinity and femininity in children. *Child Develpm.*, 1959, *30*, 373–80.

——, and Sutton-Smith, B. A revised conception of masculine-feminine differences in play activities. *J. Genet. Psychol.*, 1960, *96*, 165–70.

————, and Sutton-Smith, B. The relationship of ordinal position and sibling sex status to cognitive abilities. *Psychonomic Science*, 1964, *1*, 81–82. (a)

————, and Sutton-Smith, B. Ordinal position and sex-role identification. *Genet. Psychol. Monogr.*, 1964, *70*, 297–328. (b)

Rosenberg, N. Stability and maturation of Kuder interest patterns during high school. *Educ. Psychol. Measmt.*, 1953, *13*, 449–58.

Rosenzweig, S., and Fleming, Edith. Apperceptive norms for the Thematic Apperception Test: II. An empirical investigation. *J. Person.*, 1949, *17*, 483–503.

Roshko, B. Jobs that women don't get. *N.Y. Times Mag.*, March 17, 1957, pp. 26, 47–49.

Ross, Dorothy. The story of the top one per cent of the women at Michigan State University. (mimeo.) Counseling Center, Michigan State Univ., 1963.

Rossi, Alice. Women in science: why so few? *Science*, 1965, *148*, 1196–1202. (a)

————. Barriers to the career choice of engineering, medicine, or science among American women. In Jacquelyn Mattfeld and Carol Van Aken (eds.), *Women and the Scientific Professions*. Cambridge, Mass.: M.I.T. Press, 1965, pp. 51–127. (b)

Rossman, J. An investigation of maternal employment among college women—a twenty-five year follow-up. Doctoral dissertation, Univ. of Minnesota, 1963.

————, and Campbell, D. Why college-trained mothers work. *Personnel Guid. J.*, 1965, *43*, 986–92.

Rothbart, Mary, and Maccoby, Eleanor. Parents' differential reactions to sons and daughters. *J. Person. Soc. Psychol.*, 1966, *4*, 237–43.

Rothe, Mary, and Mewark, Christine. Homemakers in voluntary community activities. *Marr. Fam. Living*, 1958, *20*, 175–78.

Rothney, J. *Guidance Practices and Results*. New York: Harper, 1958.

Rouman, J. School children's problems as related to parental factors. *J. Educ. Res.*, 1956, *50*, 105–12.

Roy, P. Maternal employment and adolescent roles: rural-urban differentials. *Marr. Fam. Living*, 1961, *23*, 340–49.

Rundquist, E. A. Sex, intelligence, and school marks. *Sch. Soc.*, 1941, *53*, 452–56.

Russell, D. G., and Sarason, I. G. Test anxiety, sex, and experimental conditions in relation to anagram solution. *J. Person. Soc. Psychol.*, 1965, *1*, 493–96.

St. John, C. Opinion of parents on certain behaviors of women teachers and other employed women. *Ontario J. Educ. Res.*, 1965, *8*, 23–33.

Salley, Ruth, and Weintraub, Ruth. Women college graduates report on employment. *J. Educ. Res.*, 1949, *42*, 376–80.

Samuels, Fra. Sex differences in reading achievement. *J. Educ. Res.*, 1943, *36*, 594–603.

Sanders, Marion. A proposition for women. *Harper's*, 1960, *221* (1324), 41–48.

Sanford, N. Developmental status of the freshmen. In N. Sanford (ed.), *The American College*. New York: Wiley & Sons, 1962, pp. 253–82.

————, *et al.* Personality development through the college years. *J. Soc. Issues*, 1956, *12*, No. 4.

Sapir, Selma. Sex differences in perceptual motor development. *Percep. Motor Skills*, 1966, *22*, 987–92.

Sarason, S., *et al.* Rorschach behavior and performance of high and low anxious children. *Child Develpm.*, 1958, *29*, 277–85. (a)

————, *et al.* Classroom observations of high and low anxious children. *Child Develpm.*, 1958, *29*, 287–95. (b)

————, and Gladwin, T. Psychological and cultural problems in mental subnormality: a review of research. *Genet. Psychol. Monogr.*, 1958, *57*, 3–290.

Sarnoff, I., *et al.* A cross-cultural study of anxiety among American and English school children. *J. Educ. Psychol.*, 1958, *49*, 129–36.

Scandrette, Onas. Differential need patterns of women elementary and secondary level student teachers. *J. Educ. Res.*, 1962, *55*, 376–79.

Schachter, M. Le facteur "sexe" et le test de Rorschach. *Acta Neurol. Psychiat. Belg.*, 1950, *50*, 157–58.

Scheinfeld, A. *Men and Women*. New York: Harcourt, Brace, 1943.

Schenet, N. G. An analysis of absenteeism in one war plant. *J. Appl. Psychol.*, 1945, *29*, 27–39.

Schiller, B. Verbal, numerical, and spatial abilities of young children. *Arch. Psychol.*, 1934, No. 161, 67.

Schletzer, Vera. What do women do with advanced degrees? Paper read at Amer. Psychol. Assoc., Philadelphia, Aug., 1963.

Schneider, Lynn. The relationship between identification with mother and home or career orientation in women. Doctoral dissertation, Columbia Univ., 1962.

Schneidler, Gwendden, and Paterson, D. G. Sex differences in clerical aptitude. *J. Educ. Psychol.*, 1942, *33*, 303–9.

Schoeppe, Aileen. Sex differences in adolescent socialization. *J. Soc. Psychol.*, 1953, *38*, 175–85.

————, Haggard, E., and Havighurst, R. Some factors affecting sixteen-year-olds' success in five developmental tasks. *J. Abnorm. Soc. Psychol.*, 1953, *48*, 42–52.

Schuell, Hildred. Sex differences in relation to stuttering: Part I. *J. Speech Disord.*, 1946, *11*, 277–98.

————. Sex differences in stuttering: Part II. *J. Speech Disord.*, 1947, *12*, 23–38.

Schulman, Mary, and Havighurst, R. J. Relations between ability and social status in a midwestern community. IV: Size of vocabulary. *J. Educ. Psychol.*, 1947, *38*, 437–42.

Schutz, R. E. Patterns of personal problems of adolescent girls. *J. Educ. Psychol.*, 1958, *49*, 1–5.

———, and Baker, R. A comparison of the factor structure of the Kuder Occupational, Form D, for males and females. *Educ. Psychol. Measmt.*, 1962, *22*, 485–92.

Science Research Associates. *Purdue Pegboard Profile Sheet.* Chicago: Science Res. Assoc., 1948.

Scottish Council for Research in Education. *The Trend of Scottish Intelligence.* London: Univ. of London Press, 1949.

———. *Social Implications of the 1947 Scottish Mental Survey.* London: Univ. of London Press, 1953.

Scully, J. Colour vision testing in school children. *Med. Offr.*, 1947, *77*, 207–8.

Sears, Pauline. Doll play aggression in normal young children. *Psychol. Monogr.*, 1951, *65*, No. 6 (Whole No. 323).

Sears, R. R. Relation of early socialization experience to aggression in middle childhood. *J. Abnorm. Soc. Psychol.*, 1961, *63*, 466–92.

———. Development of gender role. In F. A. Beach (ed.), *Sex and Behavior.* New York: Wiley & Sons, 1965, pp. 133–59.

———, Maccoby, Eleanor, and Levin, H. *Patterns of Child Rearing.* Evanston, Ill.: Row, Peterson, 1957.

———, Pintler, Margaret, and Sears, Pauline. Effect of father separation on preschool children's doll play aggression. *Child Develpm.*, 1946, *17*, 219–43.

———, et al. Some child-rearing antecedents of aggression and dependency in young children. *Genet. Psychol. Monogr.*, 1953, *47*, 135–234.

Seashore, H. G. Women are more predictable than men. *J. Counsel. Psychol.*, 1962, *9*, 261–70.

———, Wesman, A., and Doppelt, J. The standardization of the Wechsler Intelligence Scale for Children. *J. Consult. Psychol.*, 1950, *14*, 99–110.

Seder, Margaret. Vocational interests of professional women: Part I. *J. Appl. Psychol.*, 1940, *24*, 130–43. (a)

———. Vocational interests of professional women: Part II. *J. Appl. Psychol.*, 1940, *24*, 265–72. (b)

Senders, Virginia. The Minnesota plan for women's continuing education: a progress report. *Educ. Rec.*, 1961, *42*, 270–78.

———. New directions in education of college women. Paper read at Amer. Personnel Guid. Assoc., Chicago, Apr., 1962.

Seward, Georgene. Cultural conflict and the feminine role: an experimental study. *J. Soc. Psychol.*, 1945, *22*, 177–94.

Sexton, Patricia. Speaking for the working-class wife. *Harper's*, 1962, *225* (1349), 129–33.

Shaffer, R. H. Kuder interest patterns of university business school seniors. *J. Appl. Psychol.*, 1949, *33*, 489–93.

Shapiro, D., and Tagiuri, R. Sex differences in inferring personality traits. *J. Psychol.*, 1959, *47*, 127–36.

Sharp, L. J. Employment status of mothers and some aspects of mental illness. *Amer. Sociol. Rev.*, 1960, *25*, 714–17.

———, and Nye, F. I. Maternal mental health. In F. I. Nye and Lois Hoffman (eds.), *The Employed Mother in America*. Chicago: Rand McNally, 1963, pp. 309–19.

Shaw, D. J. Sexual bias in the WAIS. *J. Consult. Psychol.*, 1965, *29*, 590–91.

Shaw, M. C. Definition and identification of academic underachievers. In L. Miller (ed.), *Guidance for the Underachiever with Superior Ability*. Washington: U.S.G.P.O., 1961, pp. 15–30.

———, and Dutton, B. The use of the Parent Attitude Research Inventory with the parents of bright academic underachievers. *J. Educ. Psychol.*, 1962, *53*, 203–8.

———, Edson, K., and Bell, H. The self-concept of bright underachieving high school students as revealed by an adjective check list. *Personnel Guid. J.*, 1960, *39*, 193–96.

———, and McCuen, J. The onset of academic underachievement in bright children. *J. Educ. Psychol.*, 1960, *51*, 103–9.

Shepler, B. A comparison of M-F measures. *J. Consult. Psychol.*, 1951, *15*, 484–86.

Sherman, A. W., Jr. Emancipation status of college students. *J. Genet. Psychol.*, 1946, *68*, 171–80.

———. Personality factors in the psychological weaning of college women. *J. Person.*, 1957, *25*, 451–64.

Sherman, M. H. Psychotherapy with adolescent girls in a court clinic. *J. Genet. Psychol.*, 1958, *92*, 3–9.

Sherriffs, A. C., and Jarrett, R. F. Sex differences in attitudes about sex differences. *J. Psychol.*, 1953, *35*, 161–68.

———, and McKee, J. Qualitative aspects of beliefs about men and women. *J. Person.*, 1957, *25*, 451–64.

Shock, N. The effect of menarche on basal physiological functions in girls. *Amer. J. Physiol.*, 1943, *139*, 288–91.

———. Physiological changes in adolescence. In N. Henry (ed.), Adolescence. *Yearb. Nat. Soc. Stud. Educ.*, 1944, *43*, Part I, pp. 56–79.

———. Some physiological aspects of adolescence. *Texas Rep. Biol. Med.*, 1946, *4*, 289–310.

Shorr, J. E. The development of a test to measure the intensity of values. *J. Educ. Psychol.*, 1953, *44*, 266–74.

Shuttleworth, F. K. Sexual maturation and the physical growth of girls age six to nineteen. *Monogr. Soc. Res. Child Develpm.*, 1937, *2*, No. 5.

———. The physical and mental growth of girls and boys age six to nineteen in relation to age at maximum growth. *Monogr. Soc. Res. Child Develpm.*, 1939, *4*, No. 3.

———. The adolescent period: a graphic atlas. *Monogr. Soc. Res. Child Develpm.*, 1949, *14*, No. 1. (a)

———. The adolescent period: a pictorial atlas. *Monogr. Soc. Res. Child Develpm.*, 1949, *14*, No. 2. (b)

Siegel, Alberta, and Curtis, Elizabeth. Familial correlates of orientation toward future employment among college women. *J. Educ. Psychol.*, 1963, *54*, 33–37.

————, and Haas, Miriam. The working mother: a review of research. *Child Develpm.*, 1963, *34*, 513–42.

————, *et al.* Dependence and independence in the children of working mothers. *Child Develpm.*, 1959, *30*, 533–46.

Silverstein, A. B., and Fisher, G. Reanalysis of sex differences in the standardization data of the Wechsler Adult Intelligence Scale. *Psychol. Rep.*, 1960, *7*, 405–6.

Silverstein, B., *et al.* The relative intelligibility of male and female talkers. *J. Educ. Psychol.*, 1953, *44*, 418–28.

Simpson, R., and Simpson, Ida. Occupational choice among career-oriented college women. *Marr. Fam. Living*, 1961, *23*, 377–83.

Singer, S. L., and Stefflre, B. The relationship of job values and desires to vocational aspirations of adolescents. *J. Appl. Psychol.*, 1954, *38*, 419–22. (a)

————, and Stefflre, B. Sex differences in job values and desires. *Personnel Guid. J.*, 1954, *32*, 483–84. (b)

Sinick, D. Two anxiety scales correlated and examined for sex differences. *J. Clin. Psychol.*, 1956, *12*, 394–95.

Skager, R., and Weinberg, C. Relationships between selected social factors and extent of high school counseling. *Personnel Guid. J.*, 1967, *45*, 901–6.

Sklarew, B. H. The relationship of early separation from parents to differences in adjustment in adolescent boys and girls. *Psychiatry*, 1959, *22*, 399–405.

Slovic, P. Risk-taking in children: age and sex differences. *Child Develpm.*, 1966, *37*, 169–76.

Smith, Constance. New directions in education for college women. Paper read at Amer. Personnel Guid. Assoc., Chicago, Apr., 1962.

Smith, T., and Nash, P. Differences in interest patterns according to high school major sequences. *Calif. J. Educ. Res.*, 1958, *9*, 179–85.

Smith, M. W. Evidence of potentialities of older workers in a manufacturing company. *Personnel Psychol.*, 1952, *5*, 11–18.

Smith, S. Women are people. In L. Muller and Ouida Muller (eds.), *New Horizons for College Women*. Washington: Public Affairs Press, 1960, pp. 23–32.

Smuts, R. W. *Women and Work in America*. New York: Columbia Univ. Press, 1959.

Sobol, Marion. Commitment to work. In F. I. Nye and Lois Hoffman (eds.), *The Employed Mother in America*. Chicago: Rand McNally, 1963, pp. 40–63.

Society of Women Engineers. *Profile of a Woman Engineer*. New York: Society of Women Engineers, 1963.

Sommer, R. Sex differences in the retention of quantitative information. *J. Educ. Psychol.*, 1958, *49*, 187–92.

Sopchak, A. L. Parental "identification" and "tendency toward disorders" as measured by the Minnesota Multiphasic Personality Inventory. *J. Abnorm. Soc. Psychol.,* 1952, *47,* 159–65.

Sorenson, A. G., and Morris, Irma. Attitudes and beliefs as sources of vocational preference. *J. Educ. Res.,* 1962, *56,* 20–27.

Spiro, Evelyn. Patterns of women's work and occupational health and safety. *Amer. J. Publ. Health,* 1960, *50,* 1318–26.

Stalnaker, J. M. Sex differences in ability to write. *Sch. Soc.,* 1941, *54,* 532–35.

———. Research in the National Merit Scholarship Program. *J. Counsel. Psychol.,* 1961, *8,* 268–71.

Stanton, Jeannette. Parttime employment for the older worker. *J. Appl. Psychol.,* 1951, *35,* 418–21.

Steel, M., Balinsky, B., and Lang, H. A study on the use of a work sample. *J. Appl. Psychol.,* 1945, *29,* 14–21.

Steiner, I. D. Sex differences in the resolution of A-B-X conflicts. *J. Person.,* 1960, *28,* 118–28.

Steinmann, Anne. Lack of communication between men and women. *Marr. Fam. Living,* 1958, *20,* 350–52.

———. The vocational roles of older married women. *J. Soc. Psychol.,* 1961, *54,* 93–101.

———, Levi, J., and Fox, D. Self-concept of college women compared with their concept of ideal woman and men's ideal woman. *J. Counsel. Psychol.,* 1964, *11,* 370–74.

Stephens College Board on Occupations. *Occupational Planning for College Women.* (rev. ed.) Columbia, M.: Stephens College, 1950.

Stephenson, C. M. The married female school teacher: a continued study. *Marr. Fam. Living,* 1960, *22,* 69–70.

Stewart, L. H. Interest patterns of a group of high-ability, high-achieving students. *J. Counsel. Psychol.,* 1959, *6,* 132–39.

Stivers, E. N. Motivation for college of high school boys and girls. Doctoral dissertation, Univ. of Chicago, 1958.

———. Motivation for college in high school girls. *Sch. Rev.,* 1959, *67,* 320–34.

Stoddard, G. D. *On the Education of Women.* New York: Macmillan, 1950.

Stolz, H., and Stolz, Lois. Adolescent problems related to somatic variations. In N. Henry (ed.), Adolescence. *Yearb. Nat. Soc. Stud. Educ.,* 1944, *43,* Part I, pp. 80–99.

Stolz, Lois. Effects of maternal employment on children: evidence from research. *Child Develpm.,* 1960, *31,* 749–82.

———, et al. *Father Relations of War-Born Children.* Stanford, Calif.: Stanford Univ. Press, 1954.

Stone, C. P., and Barker, R. G. Aspects of personality and intelligence in postmenarcheal and premenarcheal girls of the same chronological ages. *J. Comp. Psychol.,* 1937, *23,* 439–55.

———, and Barker, R. G. The attitudes and interests of premenarcheal and postmenarcheal girls. *J. Genet. Psychol.*, 1939, *54*, 27–71.

Stone, F. Beth, and Vinton, N. R. MMPI differences between emotionally disturbed and delinquent adolescent girls. *J. Clin. Psychol.*, 1963, *19*, 227–30.

Stone, L., Kennedy, C., and Danskin, D. Factors related to students' selection of Kansas State University and to selection of curriculum. Studies in Student Personnel Work, Res. Rep. No. 24. Kansas State Univ., Student Counseling Center, 1963.

Stott, M. B. Some differences between boys and girls in vocational guidance. *Occup. Psychol., Lond.*, 1945, *19*, 121–31.

Strange, F. B., and Palmer, J. O. A note on sex differences on the Wechsler-Bellevue Tests. *J. Clin. Psychol.*, 1953, *9*, 85–87.

Stright, I. L. Some factors affecting college success. *J. Educ. Psychol.*, 1947, *38*, 232–40.

Strong, E. K. *Vocational Interests of Men and Women.* Stanford, Calif.: Stanford Univ. Press, 1943.

———. *Vocational Interests 18 Years After College.* Minneapolis: Univ. of Minnesota Press, 1955.

———, et al. *The 1966 Revision of the Strong Vocational Interest Blank for Men.* Stanford, Calif.: Stanford Univ. Press, 1966.

Stroud, J. B., and Lindquist, E. F. Sex differences in achievement in the elementary and secondary schools. *J. Educ. Psychol.*, 1942, *33*, 357–67.

Stuart, I. R., et al. The question of constitutional influence on perceptual style. *Percept. Motor Skills*, 1965, *20*, 419–20.

Summerskill, J. Dropouts from college. In N. Sanford (ed.), *The American College.* New York: Wiley & Sons, 1962, pp. 627–57.

———, and Darling, C. D. Sex differences in adjustment to college. *J. Educ. Psychol.*, 1955, *46*, 355–61.

Sumner, F. C., and Johnson, E. Sex differences in levels of aspiration and in self-estimates of performance in a classroom situation. *J. Psychol.*, 1949, *27*, 483–90.

Super, D. E. *The Psychology of Careers.* New York: Harper, 1957.

———, and Crites, J. *Appraising Vocational Fitness.* (rev. ed.) New York: Harper, 1962.

———, and Dunlap, J. Interest in work and play. In D. Fryer and E. Henry (eds.), *Handbook of Applied Psychology*, Vol. I. New York: Rinehart, 1950, pp. 100–108.

Sussman, M. B. Needed research on the employed mother. *Marr. Fam. Living*, 1961, *23*, 368–73.

Sutherland, M. B. Coeducation and school attainment. *Brit. J. Educ. Psychol.*, 1961, *31*, 158–69.

Sutton-Smith, B., Roberts, J., and Rosenberg, B. Sibling associations and role involvement. *Merrill-Palmer Quart.*, 1964, *10*, 25–38.

Swanson, E. O., and Berdie, R. F. The relation of the Minnesota college state-wide program test scores to first year grade point averages in Minnesota colleges and a survey of scholastic aptitude in Minnesota colleges. *Res. Bull., Off. Dean Stud.,* Univ. of Minnesota, 1961, *3,* No. 1.

Sweeney, E. J. Sex differences in problem solving. *Stanford Univ. Dept. Psychol. Tech. Rep.,* 1953, No. 1.

Swinehart, J. W. Socio-economic level, status aspiration, and maternal role. *Amer. Sociol. Rev.,* 1963, *28,* 391–99.

Symonds, P. M. Changes in sex differences in problems and interests of adolescents with increasing age. *J. Genet. Psychol.,* 1937, *50,* 83–89.

Sysiharju, Anna-Liisa. *Equality, Home, and Work.* Helsinki, Finland: Mikkelissa, 1960.

Tagatz, G. E. Grouping by sex at the first and second grade level. *J. Educ. Res.,* 1966, *59,* 415–18.

Talland, G. A. Sex differences in self assessment. *J. Soc. Psychol.,* 1958, *48,* 25–35.

Tasch, Ruth. Interpersonal perceptions of fathers and mothers. *J. Genet. Psychol.,* 1955, *87,* 59–65.

Taschuk, W. A. An analysis of the self-concept of grade nine students. *Alberta J. Educ. Res.,* 1957, *3,* 94–103.

Taylor, H. Education and the role of women—a symposium. *NEA J.,* 1960, *49* (9), 48–53.

Teahan, J. Parental attitudes and college success. *J. Educ. Psychol.,* 1963, *54,* 104–9.

Teegarden, Lorene. Manipulative performance of young adult applicants at a public employment office—Part II. *J. Appl. Psychol.,* 1942, *26,* 754–69.

Templin, Mildred. General information of kindergarten children: a comparison with the Probst study after 26 years. *Child Develpm.,* 1958, *29,* 87–96.

Terman, L. M. *Mental and Physical Traits of a Thousand Gifted Children.* Stanford, Calif.: Stanford Univ. Press, 1925.

———, and Merrill, Maud. *Measuring Intelligence.* Boston: Houghton Mifflin, 1937.

———, and Miles, Catherine. *Sex and Personality: Studies in Masculinity and Femininity.* New York: McGraw-Hill, 1936.

———, and Oden, Melita. *The Gifted Child Grows Up.* Stanford, Calif.: Stanford Univ. Press, 1947.

———, and Oden, Melita. *The Gifted Group at Mid-Life.* Stanford, Calif.: Stanford Univ. Press, 1959.

———, and Tyler, Leona. Psychological sex differences. In L. Carmichael (ed.), *Manual of Child Psychology.* New York: Wiley & Sons, 1954, pp. 1064–1114.

Tharpe, R. G. Psychological patterning in marriage. *Psychol. Bull.,* 1963, *60,* 97–117.

Thiede, W. B. Some characteristics of juniors enrolled in selected curricula at the University of Wisconsin. *J. Exp. Educ.,* 1950, *19,* 1–62.

Thistlethwaite, D. L. *Recruitment and Retention of Talented College Students.* Nashville, Tenn.: Vanderbilt Univ., 1963.

Thomas, J. L. Catholic college spinsters? *Soc. Order,* 1952, *2,* 357–62.

Thompson, Clara. Towards a psychology of women. *Pastoral Psychol.,* 1953, *4* (34), 29–38.

Thorndike, R. L., and Gallup, G. H. Verbal intelligence of the American adult. *J. Gen. Psychol.,* 1944, *30,* 75–85.

————, and Henry, F. Differences in reading interests related to differences in sex and intelligence level. *Elem. Sch. J.,* 1940, *40,* 751–63.

Thorpe, L., Clark, W., and Tiegs, E. *Manual, California Test of Personality.* Los Angeles: Calif. Test Bureau, 1953.

Thumin, F. J., and Wittenberg, Angela. Personality as related to age and mental ability in female job applicants. *J. Gerontol.,* 1965, *20,* 105–7.

Todd, F. J., Terrell, G., and Frank, C. Differences between normal and underachievers of superior ability. *J. Appl. Psychol.,* 1962, *46,* 183–90.

Tomasson, R. F. The Swedes do it better. *Harper's,* 1962, *225* (1349), 178–80.

Torpey, W. G. The role of women in professional engineering. *J. Engin. Educ.,* 1962, *52,* 656–58.

Torrance, E. P. Factors affecting creative thinking in children: an interim research report. *Merrill-Palmer Quart.,* 1961, *7,* 171–80.

————. Changing reactions of preadolescent girls to tasks requiring creative scientific thinking. *J. Genet. Psychol.,* 1963, *102,* 217–23.

Tozer, A. H. D., and Larwood, H. J. C. An analysis of intelligence test scores of students in a university department of education. *Brit. J. Psychol.,* 1953, *44,* 347–58.

Travis, R. C. Balancing skill as a measure of recovery from rotation. *Amer. J. Psychol.,* 1945, *58,* 361–78.

Traxler, A. E., and Spaulding, Geraldine. Sex differences in achievement of independent school pupils as measured by Stanford Achievement Test, Form K. *Educ. Rec. Bull.,* 1954, *63,* 69–80.

————, and Vecchione, N. Scores of seniors in six secondary schools on the Allport-Vernon-Lindzey Study of Values. *Educ. Rec. Bull.,* 1959, *74,* 75–89.

Triggs, Frances. A further comparison of interest measurement by the Kuder Preference Record and the Strong Vocational Interest Blank for Women. *J. Educ. Res.,* 1944, *38,* 193–200.

————. The measured interests of nurses: a second report. *J. Educ. Res.,* 1948, *42,* 113–21.

Trilling, Diana. Female-ism: new and insidious. *Mademoiselle,* 1960, *51* (2), 97–99.

Trumbull, R. A study of relationships between factors of personality and intelligence. *J. Soc. Psychol.,* 1953, *38,* 161–73.

Tuckman, J. A comparison of norms for the Minnesota Rate of Manipulation Test. *J. Appl. Psychol.,* 1944, *28,* 121–28.

————. Ranking of women's occupations according to social status, earnings, and working conditions. *Occupations,* 1950, *28,* 290–94.

Tuckman, J., and Connon, Helen. Attempted suicide in adolescents. *Amer. J. Psychiat.,* 1962, *119,* 228–32.

Tuddenham, R. D. Studies in reputation: III. Correlates of popularity among elementary-school children. *J. Educ. Psychol.,* 1951, *42,* 257–76.

———. Studies in reputation: I. Sex and grade differences in school children's evaluations of their peers. *Psychol. Monogr.,* 1952, *66,* No. 1.

———. The influence of a distorted group norm upon individual judgment. *J. Psychol.,* 1958, *46,* 227–41.

———. The influence of a distorted group norm upon judgments of adults and children. *J. Psychol.,* 1961, *52,* 231–39.

———, and Snyder, Margaret. Physical growth of California boys and girls from birth to eighteen years. *Univ. of California Publ. Child Develpm.,* 1954, *1,* No. 2.

Turner, J. Science for the misses. *Science,* 1959, *129,* 749.

Tyler, F. T. Individual and sex differences. In C. Harris (ed.), *Encyclopedia of Educational Research.* (3rd ed.) New York: Macmillan, 1960, pp. 680–88.

———, and Michaelis, J. U. K scores applied to MMPI scales for college women. *Educ. Psychol. Measmt.,* 1953, *13,* 459–66.

Tyler, Leona. The measured interests of adolescent girls. *J. Educ. Psychol.,* 1941, *32,* 561–72.

———. Relationships between Strong Vocational Interest scores and other attitude and personality factors. *J. Appl. Psychol.,* 1945, *29,* 58–67.

———. The relationship of interests to abilities and reputation among first-grade children. *Educ. Psychol. Measmt.,* 1951, *11,* 255–64.

———. The development of "vocational interests": I. The organization of likes and dislikes in ten-year-old children. *J. Genet. Psychol.,* 1955, *86,* 33–44.

———. A comparison of the interests of English and American school children. *J. Genet. Psychol.,* 1956, *88,* 175–81.

———. Research on instruments used by counselors in vocational guidance. *J. Counsel. Psychol.,* 1962, *9,* 99–105.

———. The antecedents of two varieties of vocational interests. *Genet. Psychol. Monogr.,* 1964, *70,* 177–227.

Uhr, L. Sex as a determinant of driving skills: women drivers! *J. Appl. Psychol.,* 1959, *43,* 35.

U.S. Bureau of the Census. *Statistical Abstract of the United States, 1966,* 87th ed. Washington: U.S.G.P.O., 1966.

U.S. Office of Education. Retention and withdrawal of college students. *U.S. Off. Educ. Bull.,* 1957, No. 1. (a)

———. Retention in high schools in large cities. *U.S. Off. Educ. Bull.,* 1957, No. 15. (b)

U.S. Public Health Service. *Vital Statistics of the United States, 1960.* Vol. I. Washington: U.S.G.P.O., 1961. (a)

——. *Ibid.,* Vol. II. 1961. (b)

Vacher, Carole. The self concept of underachieving freshmen and upperclass women college students. *J. Coll. Stud. Personnel,* 1963, *5,* 28–31, 44.

Valien, P., and Horton, C. Some demographic characteristics of outstanding Negro women. *J. Negro Educ.,* 1954, *23,* 406–20.

Vane, Julia, and Eisen, Virginia. Wechsler-Bellevue performance of delinquent and non-delinquent girls. *J. Consult. Psychol.,* 1954, *18,* 221–25.

Vener, A. M., and Snyder, C. A. The preschool child's awareness of adult sex roles. *Sociometry,* 1966, *29,* 159–68.

Verniaud, W. M. Occupational differences in the Minnesota Multiphasic Personality Inventory. *J. Appl. Psychol.,* 1946, *30,* 604–13.

Vernon, P. E. *Intelligence and Attainment Tests.* London: Univ. of London Press, 1960.

Veroff, J. A. A projective measure of the achievement motivation of adolescent males and females. Honors thesis, Wesleyan Univ., 1950.

——, *et al.* The use of thematic apperception to assess motivation in a nationwide interview study. *Psychol. Monogr.,* 1960, *74* (12), 1–32.

——, Wilcox, S., and Atkinson, J. The achievement motive in high school and college age women. *J. Abnorm. Soc. Psychol.,* 1953, *48,* 108–19.

Vetter, Louise, and Lewis, E. C. Some correlates of homemaking vs. career preference among college home economics students. *Personnel Guid. J.,* 1964, *42,* 593–98.

Vollmer, H. M., and Kinney, J. A. Supervising women is different. *Personnel J.,* 1955, *34,* 260–62.

von Mering, Faye. Professional and non-professional women as mothers. *J. Soc. Psychol.,* 1955, *42,* 21–34.

Votaw, D. F., and Moses, Peggy Lou. Analysis of abilities of student groups in Southwest Texas State Teachers College seeking the profession of teaching. *J. Educ. Res.,* 1956, *49,* 681–88.

Wade, L. A human relations approach to sickness and absenteeism and other employee problems. *AMA Archives,* 1955 (Dec.), pp. 592–608.

Wagman, M. Sex and age differences in occupational values. *Personnel Guid. J.,* 1965, *44,* 258–62.

Wallin, P. Cultural contradictions and sex roles: a repeat study. *Amer. Sociol. Rev.,* 1950, *15,* 288–93.

——. Sex differences in attitudes toward in-laws. *Amer. J. Sociol.,* 1954, *59,* 466–69.

Walt, Dorothy. The motivation for women to work in high-level professional positions. Doctoral dissertation, American Univ., 1962.

Walter, L. M., and Marzolf, S. S. The relation of sex, age, and school achievement to levels of aspiration. *J. Educ. Psychol.,* 1951, *42,* 285–92.

Walters, J., and Ojemann, R. H. A study of the components of adolescent attitudes concerning the role of women. *J. Soc. Psychol.,* 1952, *35,* 101–10.

Warner, W. L., and Abegglen, J. Successful wives of successful executives. *Harv. Bus. Rev.,* 1956, *34* (2), 64–70.

Warren, J., and Heist, P. Personality attributes of gifted college students. *Science,* 1960, *132,* 330–37.

Warren, Phyllis Ann. Vocational interests and the occupational adjustment of college women. *J. Counsel. Psychol.,* 1959, *6,* 140–47.

Watley, D., and Martin, H. T. Prediction of academic success in a college of business administration. *Personnel Guid. J.,* 1962, *41,* 147–54.

Wattenberg, W. W., and Saunders, F. Sex differences among juvenile offenders. *Sociol. Soc. Res.,* 1954, *39,* 24–31.

Webb, A. P. Sex-role preferences and adjustment in early adolescents. *Child Develpm.,* 1963, *34,* 609–18.

Webber, V. L., and Leahy, D. M. Home economics majors compared with other majors in education on the A.C.E. test. *Calif. J. Educ. Res.,* 1958, *9,* 74–79, 85.

Webster, H. Some quantitative results. *J. Soc. Issues,* 1956, *12* (4), 29–43.

Wechsler, D. *The Measurement and Appraisal of Adult Intelligence.* Baltimore: Williams & Wilkins, 1958.

Weider, A., and Noller, P. Objective studies of children's drawings of human figures: I. Sex awareness and socio-economic level. *J. Clin. Psychol.,* 1950, *6,* 319–25.

———, and Noller, P. Objective studies of children's drawings of figures: II. Sex, age, and intelligence. *J. Clin. Psychol.,* 1953, *9,* 20–23.

Weil, Mildred. An analysis of the factors influencing married women's actual or planned work participation. *Amer. Sociol. Rev.,* 1961, *26,* 91–96.

Weinberg, J. R. The effects of degree and personalization of failure on performance. *J. Person.,* 1960, *28,* 266–78.

Weingarten, Violet. *The Mother Who Works Outside the Home.* New York: Child Study Assoc. of America, 1961.

Weinstein, Beatrice, *et al.* The adjustment of children in a suburban community who were accelerated in elementary school. *J. Sch. Psychol.,* 1966, *5,* 60–63.

Weinstein, E., and Geisel, P. An analysis of sex differences in adjustment. *Child Develpm.,* 1960, *31,* 721–28.

Weintraub, S. Sex differences in reading achievement. *Reading Teacher,* 1966, *20,* 155–65.

Weisgarber, C. A. The predictive value of the Minnesota Multiphasic Personality Inventory with student nurses. *J. Soc. Psychol.*, 1951, *33*, 3–11.

Weiss, R. S., and Samuelson, Nancy. Social roles of American women: their contribution to a sense of usefulness and importance. *Marr. Fam. Living*, 1958, *20*, 358–66.

Weitz, H., Clarke, Mary, and Jones, Ora. The relationship between choice of a major field of study and academic preparation and performance. *Educ. Psychol. Measmt.*, 1955, *15*, 23–38.

———, and Colver, R. The relationship between the educational goals and the academic performance of women, a confirmation. *Educ. Psychol. Measmt.*, 1959, *19*, 373–80.

Wells, Jean. Labor turnover of women factory workers, 1950–55. *Monthly Labor Rev.*, 1955, *78*, 889–94.

Wells, W., Hilton, Sylvia, and Liebman, N. Tension during a small personal crisis. *J. Soc. Psychol.*, 1959, *50*, 269–76.

Werts, C. E. Sex differences in college attendance. *Nat. Merit Scholar. Corp. Res. Rep.*, 1966, 2 (6).

Wesman, A. G. Separation of sex groups in test reporting. *J. Educ. Psychol.*, 1949, *40*, 223–29.

White, Becky. The relationship of self concept and parental identification to women's vocational interests. *J. Counsel. Psychol.*, 1959, *6*, 202–6.

White, K. Social background variables related to career commitment of women teachers. *Personnel Guid. J.*, 1967, *45*, 648–52.

White, L., Jr. *Educating Our Daughters.* New York: Harper, 1950.

———. The changing context of women's education. *Marr. Fam. Living*, 1955, *17*, 291–95.

White, Martha (ed.). *The Next Step: A Guide to Part Time Opportunities in Greater Boston for the Educated Woman.* Cambridge, Mass.: Radcliffe Institute for Independent Study, 1964.

Wightwick, M. I. Vocational interest patterns. *Teach. Coll. Contr. Educ.*, 1945, No. 900.

Wilcox, S. A projective measure of the achievement motivation of college women. Honors thesis, Univ. of Michigan, 1951.

Williams, A. R. The magazine reading of secondary school children. *Brit. J. Educ. Psychol.*, 1951, *21*, 186–98.

Williams, Josephine. Patients and prejudice: lay attitudes toward women physicians. *Amer. J. Sociol.*, 1946, *51*, 283–87.

———. The woman physician's dilemma. *J. Soc. Issues*, 1950, *6* (3), 38–44.

Williamson, E. G. *et al. A Study of Participation in College Activities.* Minneapolis: Univ. of Minnesota Press, 1954.

Wilson, F. T. Sex differences in beginning reading in a progressive school. *J. Educ. Res.*, 1939, *32*, 570–82.

Wilson, Pauline. College women who express futility. *Teach. Coll. Contr. Educ.*, 1950, No. 956.

Winch, R. F. Courtship in college women. *Amer. J. Sociol.*, 1949, *55*, 269–78.

Winkler, J. B. Age trends and sex differences in the wishes, identifications, activities and fears of children. *Child Develpm.*, 1949, *20*, 191–200.

Witkin, H. A. Sex differences in perception. *Trans. N.Y. Acad. Sci.*, 1949, *12*, 22–26.

———, et al. *Personality Through Perception.* New York: Harper, 1954.

———, et al. *Psychological Differentiation.* New York: Wiley & Sons, 1962.

Wolfbein, S. *Employment and Unemployment in the United States.* Chicago: Science Research Associates, 1964.

Wolfle, D. *America's Resources of Specialized Talent.* New York: Harper, 1954.

———. Diversity of talent. *Amer. Psychologist,* 1960, *15*, 535–45.

———. Women in science and engineering. *Science,* 1964, *145*, 1389.

Women's Bureau. *Women Workers and Their Dependents.* Bull. No. 239. Women's Bureau, U.S. Dept. of Labor, Washington: U.S.G.P.O., 1952.

———. *Medical Technologists and Laboratory Technicians.* Medical Series Bull. No. 203–4. G.P.O., 1954.

———. *Bibliography on Employment Problems of Older Women.* G.P.O., 1956. (a)

———. *Employment After College: Report on Women Graduates, Class of 1955.* G.P.O., 1956. (b)

———. *Employment Opportunities for Women Mathematicians and Statisticians.* Bull. No. 262. G.P.O., 1956. (c)

———. *Employment of Older Women—An Annotated Bibliography.* G.P.O., 1957.

———. *Employment Opportunities for Women in Legal Work.* Bull. No. 265. G.P.O., 1958.

———. *Careers for Women in the Physical Sciences.* Bull. No. 270. G.P.O., 1959. (a)

———. *Careers for Women in Retailing.* Bull. No. 271. G.P.O., 1959. (b)

———. *Part-time Employment of Women.* Bull. No. 273. G.P.O., 1960.

———. *Careers for Women in the Biological Sciences.* Bull. No. 278. G.P.O., 1961. (a)

———. *Careers for Women as Life Underwriters.* Bull. No. 279. G.P.O., 1961. (b)

———. *Careers for Women as Technicians.* Bull. No. 282. G.P.O., 1961. (c)

———. *State Hour Laws for Women.* Bull. No. 277. G.P.O., 1961. (d)

———. *Fifteen Years After College—A Study of Alumnae, Class of 1945.* Bull. No. 283. G.P.O., 1962.

———. *1962 Handbook on Women Workers.* Bull. No. 285. G.P.O., 1963.

——. *1965 Handbook on Women Workers*. Bull. No. 290. G.P.O., 1966. (a)

——. *Continuing Education Programs for Women*. Pamphlet No. 10. G.P.O., 1966. (b)

——. *College Women Seven Years After Graduation*. Bull. No. 292. G.P.O., 1966. (c)

Woodrow Wilson Foundation. *Report on Activities, 1957–1961*. Princeton, N.J.: Woodrow Wilson Foundation, 1961.

Wright, B., and Tuska, Shirley. Interpersonal origins of women's plans to teach. Paper read at Amer. Psychol. Assoc., Los Angeles, Sept., 1964.

Wright, J. C. "My daughter a scientist!" *Clearing House*, 1958, *33*, 142–45.

Wylie, Ruth. The performance of girls and women on the Grove modification of the Kent-Shakow Formboard Series. *J. Psychol.*, 1948, *25*, 99–103.

Yarrow, Marian. Maternal employment and child rearing. *Children*, 1961, *8*, 223–28.

——, et al. Child-rearing in families of working and nonworking mothers. *Sociometry*, 1962, *25*, 122–40.

Yates, Dorothy. The mentally superior girl and marriage. *Nervous Child*, 1944, *4*, 70–77.

Yellin, D. I'm married to a working mother. *Harper's*, 1956, *213* (1274), 34–37.

Zander, A., and Van Egmond, E. Relationship of intelligence and social power to the interpersonal behavior of children. *J. Educ. Psychol.*, 1958, *49*, 257–68.

Zapf, R. M. Relationship between belief in superstitions and other factors. *J. Educ. Res.*, 1945, *38*, 561–79.

Zapoleon, Marguerite. The working girl. *Personnel Guid. J.*, 1953, *32*, 68–71.

——. *The College Girl Looks Ahead*. New York: Harper, 1956.

——. The myth of marriage. In L. Muller and Ouida Muller (eds.), *New Horizons for College Women*. Washington: Public Affairs Press, 1960, pp. 79–87.

——. *Occupational Planning for Women*. New York: Harper, 1961.

Zeaman, Jean. Some of the personality attributes related to achievement in college: a comparison of men and women students. Doctoral dissertation, Michigan State Univ., 1956.

Zeligs, Rose. Children's attitudes toward annoyances. *J. Genet. Psychol.*, 1962, *101*, 255–66.

Zissis, Cecelia. The relationship of selected variables to the career-marriage plans of university freshman women. Doctoral dissertation, Univ. of Michigan, 1962.

Zuk, G. H. Sex-appropriate behavior in adolescence. *J. Genet. Psychol.*, 1958, *93*, 15–32.

Index

---

* Appendix pages appear in italics.

DATE DUE

APR 2 8 '70			
F			
MAY 3 '71			
MAY 7 '75			
DEC 1 0 '75			
AP 17 79			
MY 2 79			
JE 18 '81			
SEP 29 '87			
GAYLORD			PRINTED IN U.S.A.